MICROSOFT® CERTIFIED APPLICATION DEVELOPER
& MICROSOFT® CERTIFIED SOLUTION DEVELOPER

MCAD/MCSD XML Web Services and Server Components Development with Visual Basic® .NET™ Study Guide

(Exam 70-310)

MICROSOFT® CERTIFIED APPLICATION DEVELOPER
& MICROSOFT® CERTIFIED SOLUTION DEVELOPER

MCAD/MCSD XML Web Services and Server Components Development with Visual Basic® .NET™ Study Guide

(Exam 70-310)

"Microsoft is a registered trademark of Microsoft Corporation in the United States and other countries. McGraw-Hill/Osborne is an independent entity from Microsoft Corporation, and not affiliated with Microsoft Corporation in any manner. This publication may be used in assisting students prepare for a Microsoft Certified Professional Exam. Neither Microsoft Corporation nor McGraw-Hill/Osborne warrants that use of this publication will ensure passing the relevant exam."

Kenneth S. Lind

McGraw-Hill Osborne

New York Chicago San Francisco Lisbon London Madrid
Mexico City Milan New Delhi San Juan Seoul Singapore Sydney Toronto

The McGraw-Hill Companies

McGraw-Hill/Osborne
2600 Tenth Street
Berkeley, California 94710
U.S.A.

To arrange bulk purchase discounts for sales promotions, premiums, or fund-raisers, please contact **McGraw-Hill**/Osborne at the above address. For information on translations or book distributors outside the U.S.A., please see the International Contact Information page immediately following the index of this book.

**MCAD/MCSD XML Web Services and Server Components Development
with Visual Basic® .NET™ Study Guide (Exam 70-310)**

Copyright © 2003 by The McGraw-Hill Companies. All rights reserved. Printed in the United States of America. Except as permitted under the Copyright Act of 1976, no part of this publication may be reproduced or distributed in any form or by any means, or stored in a database or retrieval system, without the prior written permission of publisher, with the exception that the program listings may be entered, stored, and executed in a computer system, but they may not be reproduced for publication.

1234567890 DOC DOC 0198765432

Book p/n 0-07-222654-4 and CD p/n 0-07-222655-2
parts of
ISBN 0-07-222653-6

Publisher	**Acquisitions Coordinator**	**Computer Designers**
Brandon A. Nordin	Jessica Wilson	Lucie Ericksen
		Jim Kussow
Vice President &	**Technical Editor**	John Patrus
Associate Publisher	Marj Rempel	
Scott Rogers		**Illustrators**
	Copy Editor	Lyssa Wald
Acquisitions Editor	Robert Campbell	Michael Mueller
Nancy Maragioglio		Melinda Moore Lytle
	Proofreader	
Senior Project Editor	Linda Medoff	**Series Design**
Betsy Manini		Roberta Steele
	Indexer	
	Valerie Perry	

This book was composed with Corel VENTURA™ Publisher.

Information has been obtained by **McGraw-Hill**/Osborne from sources believed to be reliable. However, because of the possibility of human or mechanical error by our sources, **McGraw-Hill**/Osborne, or others, **McGraw-Hill**/Osborne does not guarantee the accuracy, adequacy, or completeness of any information and is not responsible for any errors or omissions or the results obtained from the use of such information.

I dedicate this book to my long-suffering wife
Dorette, who has been a "computer widow" almost
since the day we got married. Dorette, thank you
for your unwavering support in my professional
endeavors. You know as well as I do that the future
for us will be one of glorious freedom from the
shackles of normal life. I would like to take this
opportunity to ask for your hand again,
25 years later.

—Kenneth S. Lind

Author

Kenneth S. Lind, MCSD, MCAD, MCSE+I, MCSE, MCP+SB, MCT, and CTT+, is an independent training consultant and author working out of Toronto, Ontario. Kenneth has over 20 years experience in software development and has developed applications using C, FORTRAN, C++, Java, VB, C#, and assembler. Kenneth left his native Sweden after receiving an engineering degree in Telecommunication, a move he never regretted. Kenneth has specialized in object-oriented (OO) development and its use in Java and C++. His most recent project has been co-authorship of a certification study guide for C# .NET published by McGraw-Hill/Osborne. Kenneth can be reached at KennethSLind@Hotmail.com.

Technical Editor

Marj Rempel (MCSD, MCSE, MCT, CTT+, JCP, A+, CCNA) is a computer professor for Durham College. Since attending the University of Waterloo in the dark ages of computer processing, over 25 years ago, Marj has been involved in software development for mainframe computers and—for the past 15 years—in the PC arena using C, Java, Visual Basic, and Visual C# .NET. After spending three years teaching software development in the corporate field, she recently accepted her current position as a professor and specializes in teaching computer-related subjects. Marj is the co-author of a certification study guide for C# .NET.

LearnKey

LearnKey provides self-paced learning content and multimedia delivery solutions to enhance personal skills and business productivity. LearnKey claims the largest library of rich streaming-media training content that engages learners in dynamic media-rich instruction complete with video clips, audio, full motion graphics, and animated illustrations. LearnKey can be found on the Web at www.LearnKey.com.

CONTENTS AT A GLANCE

CONTENTS

Τhis book was written to assist you in preparing for and passing the Developing XML Web Services and Server Components with Microsoft Visual Basic .NET and the Microsoft .NET Framework Exam 70-310. The text and exercises were created to help familiarize you with the topics you will be tested on during the actual exam.

In This Book

While this book is designed to be a focused exam preparation tool, you will also find discussion of the theory and methodologies behind working with the .NET Framework. The hands-on exercises were designed to give you additional experience with the .NET Framework while reinforcing understanding of the concepts.

In Every Chapter

The Study Guide series contains a number of chapter elements that were designed to help you identify important items, to reinforce key points, and to offer expert tips for taking the exam. Each chapter contains the following:

- **Certification Objectives** Each chapter begins with a listing of the exam objectives that will be covered in the chapter.

- **Exam Watch** These are tips I have designed to help you focus your studies on areas that will be important for the exam.

- **Practice Exercises** Hands-on experience is a key factor to success on exam day, and these practice exercises are designed to help you reinforce your skills. It's important that you work through these exercises rather than simply reading them, so that you increase your exposure to and familiarity with the .NET Framework.

- **On the Job** Designed to let you benefit from my experience, this element provides insights into the practical application of the theories presented in the text.

■ **Scenarios & Solutions**   This element introduces you to common real-life situations that you may encounter on the job and provides you with a quick solution.

SCENARIO & SOLUTION

What should I do when I upgrade if I have variables declared within blocks of code (such as If, Do loops, Select)?	The Upgrade Wizard will move the variable declarations to the procedure level. You should review the use of these variables to make sure the functionality is still correct.
What should I do if my code has arrays that begin with a lower bound of anything other than 0?	You should go through all of the code to make sure it will continue to work when arrays have a lower bound of 0. You can either make necessary changes to your Visual Basic 6.0 code, or you can first run the Upgrade Wizard and then make changes to the .NET code. The Upgrade Wizard will insert comments in spots where there is the potential for a problem.
What should I do if my application uses DAO or RDO to bind controls to a database?	You should upgrade the data access to ADO if you want the Upgrade Wizard to automatically change the means of data binding to ADO.NET.

■ **The Certification Summary**   This is a general review of the material that was presented in the chapter. These summaries provide a quick-review option prior to taking the exam.

 ■ **The Two-Minute Drill**   At the end of every chapter, you will find a listing of the key objective points from the chapter. These are great as a final review study tool.

Q&A ■ **The Self Test**   Our self-assessment section presents questions similar to those you'll find on the actual exam; it is designed to help you identify those areas in which you may need additional study. Complete answers with explanations are located at the end of each chapter.

author's
note   *Please be aware that the questions and answers at the end of some chapters do not match the order of those found in the corresponding chapters on the CD-ROM.*

On the CD-ROM

This book includes a CD-ROM with simulation assessment and training software. Be sure to look through the software—it includes more than one hour of interactive instructional video training, and also a self-assessment test engine containing practice test questions that are found *only* on the CD-ROM.

The CD-ROM with this book also contains the code for many of the exercises so that it's not necessary for you to recreate the code from scratch. The Glossary for the book also appears there. These features can be accessed only through the CD-ROM.

PDF versions of the chapters from the book are also available on the CD-ROM. Please be aware, though, that the questions and answers at the end of some chapters in the printed book do not match the order of those in corresponding chapters on the CD-ROM.

For more information about the CD-ROM, please see Appendix A.

ACKNOWLEDGMENTS

I would like to thank the very supportive and hard-working staff at McGraw-Hill/Osborne for working with me as a team to make this book a reality. Thanks go to Betsy Manini for understanding my formatting problems, Marj Remple for her technical insights, Robert Campbell for turning my Swinglish into English, and Jessica Wilson for keeping us in control. I would also like to thank Nancy Maragioglio, who provided the management needed to bring this book to fruition.

Finally, I would like to thank my wife Dorette, my daughter Inga, and my son Anders, for their support and for not calling the Men in White when I mumbled incoherently about Visual Basic .NET and XML in a never-ending sequence of days and nights.

—*Kenneth S. Lind*

Welcome to MCAD/MCSD XML Web Services and Server Components Development with Visual Basic .NET Study Guide (Exam 70-310). The author has written this book to help prepare you for the Developing XML Web Services and Server Components with Microsoft Visual Basic .NET and the Microsoft .NET Framework certification exam. Whether you're preparing for your MCSD or getting started with your MCAD, this book will guide you through the key points of each of the exam objectives.

MCAD vs. MCSD

How do you know whether to pursue MCAD or MCSD? Consider your career plan—while the MCAD is a less comprehensive certification than the MCSD, it may reflect your actual interests and skills better than the MCSD. You may decide to start with the MCAD and then add exams until you reach the MCSD level as your career changes.

According to Microsoft, candidates for the MCAD certification credential are professionals who use Microsoft technologies to develop and maintain department-level applications, components, Web or desktop clients, or back-end data services or who work in teams developing enterprise applications.

Candidates for the MCSD certification, on the other hand, are lead developers who design and develop leading-edge enterprise solutions with Microsoft development tools, technologies, platforms, and the Microsoft .NET Framework.

MCSD certification encompasses the skill set of the MCAD certification, and MCAD can be considered an interim step toward MCSD certification.

MCSD Certification Requirements

Achieving the MCSD certification requires passing four core exams and one elective exam. The core exams are listed in the following boxed text.

MCSD CORE EXAMS
Solution Architecture Exam (Required) Exam 70-300: Analyzing Requirements and Defining .NET Solution Architectures
Web Application Development Exams (One Required) Exam 70-305: Developing and Implementing Web Applications with Microsoft Visual Basic .NET and Microsoft Visual Studio .NET Or Exam 70-315: Developing and Implementing Web Applications with Microsoft Visual C# .NET and Microsoft Visual Studio .NET
Windows Application Development Exams (One Required) Exam 70-306: Developing and Implementing Windows-Based Applications with Microsoft Visual Basic .NET and Microsoft Visual Studio .NET Or Exam 70-316: Developing and Implementing Windows-Based Applications with Microsoft Visual C# .NET and Microsoft Visual Studio .NET
Web Services and Server Components Exams (One Required) Exam 70-310: Developing XML Web Services and Server Components with Microsoft Visual Basic .NET and the Microsoft .NET Framework Or Exam 70-320: Developing XML Web Services and Server Components with Microsoft Visual C# and the Microsoft .NET Framework

In addition to the core exams, you must pass one of the following elective exams:

- **Exam 70-229:** Designing and Implementing Databases with Microsoft SQL Server 2000, Enterprise Edition

- **Exam 70-230:** Designing and Implementing Solutions with Microsoft BizTalk Server 2000 Enterprise Edition

- **Exam 70-234:** Designing and Implementing Solutions with Microsoft Commerce Server 2000

MCAD Certification Requirements

Microsoft's MCAD requires only three core exams and one elective, and it permits the use of some exams as either core or elective credit.

MCAD CORE EXAMS

Web or Windows Application Development Exams (One Required)

Exam 70-305: Developing and Implementing Web Applications with Microsoft Visual Basic .NET and Microsoft Visual Studio .NET

Or

Exam 70-315: Developing and Implementing Web Applications with Microsoft Visual C# .NET and Microsoft Visual Studio .NET

Or

Exam 70-306: Developing and Implementing Windows-Based Applications with Microsoft Visual Basic .NET and Microsoft Visual Studio .NET

Or

Exam 70-316: Developing and Implementing Windows-Based Applications with Microsoft Visual C# .NET and Microsoft Visual Studio .NET

Web Services and Server Components Exams (One Required)

Exam 70-310: Developing XML Web Services and Server Components with Microsoft Visual Basic .NET and the Microsoft .NET Framework

Or

Exam 70-320: Developing XML Web Services and Server Components with Microsoft Visual C# and the Microsoft .NET Framework

In addition to the core exams, you must pass one of the following elective exams:

- **Exam 70-229:** Designing and Implementing Databases with Microsoft SQL Server 2000, Enterprise Edition

- **Exam 70-230:** Designing and Implementing Solutions with Microsoft BizTalk Server 2000 Enterprise Edition

- **Exam 70-234:** Designing and Implementing Solutions with Microsoft Commerce Server 2000

Furthermore, the following examinations may be used for elective credit if they have not been used toward core exam credit:

- **Exam 70-305:** Developing and Implementing Web Applications with Microsoft Visual Basic .NET and Microsoft Visual Studio .NET

- **Exam 70-306:** Developing and Implementing Windows-Based Applications with Microsoft Visual Basic .NET and Microsoft Visual Studio .NET

- **Exam 70-310:** Developing XML Web Services and Server Components with Microsoft Visual Basic .NET and the Microsoft .NET Framework

- **Exam 70-315:** Developing and Implementing Web Applications with Microsoft Visual C# .NET and Microsoft Visual Studio .NET

- **Exam 70-316:** Developing and Implementing Windows-Based Applications with Microsoft Visual C# .NET and Microsoft Visual Studio .NET

- **Exam 70-320:** Developing XML Web Services and Server Components with Microsoft Visual C# and the Microsoft .NET Framework

exam
ⓦatch

For the latest information on available exams, visit www.microsoft.com/ traincert. Exams are subject to change without notice, so be sure to check this site frequently as you prepare for your exam.

Exam Credit

When you pass Exam 70-310, you immediately achieve the status of Microsoft Certified Professional (MCP) and earn credit toward either the MCAD or MCSD certification:

- **Core credit** toward MCSD (Microsoft Certified Solutions Developer) certification.

- **Core credit** toward MCAD (Microsoft Certified Application Developer) certification.

Skills Being Measured

You can view the complete set of skills being measured at the MCSD web site at www.microsoft.com/traincert/mcp/mcsd/requirements.asp. According to Microsoft, the following is a quick summary of what you'll be faced with on the exam.

Creating and Managing Microsoft Windows® Services, Serviced Components, .NET Remoting Objects, and XML Web Services

- Create and manipulate a Windows service.

- Write code that is executed when a Windows service is started or stopped.

- Create and consume a serviced component.

- Implement a serviced component.

- Create interfaces that are visible to COM.

- Create a strongly named assembly.

- Register the component in the global assembly cache.

- Manage the component by using the Component Services tool.

- Create and consume a .NET Remoting object.

  - Implement server-activated components.

  - Implement client-activated components.

  - Select a channel protocol and a formatter. Channel protocols include TCP and HTTP. Formatters include SOAP and binary.

  - Create client configuration files and server configuration files.

  - Implement an asynchronous method.

  - Create the listener service.

  - Instantiate and invoke a .NET Remoting object.

- Create and consume an XML web service.

  - Control characteristics of Web methods by using attributes.

  - Create and use SOAP extensions.

  - Create asynchronous Web methods.

  - Control XML wire format for an XML web service.

  - Instantiate and invoke an XML web service.

- Implement security for a Windows service, a serviced component, a .NET Remoting object, and an XML web service.

- Access unmanaged code from a Windows service, a serviced component, a .NET Remoting object, and an XML web service.

Consuming and Manipulating Data

- Access and manipulate data from a Microsoft SQL Server™ database by creating and using ad hoc queries and stored procedures.

- Create and manipulate DataSets.

  - Manipulate a DataSet schema.

- Manipulate DataSet relationships.
- Create a strongly typed DataSet.
- Access and manipulate XML data.
  - Access an XML file by using the Document Object Model (DOM) and an XmlReader.
  - Transform DataSet data into XML data.
  - Use XPath to query XML data.
  - Generate and use an XSD schema.
  - Write a SQL statement that retrieves XML data from a SQL Server database.
  - Update a SQL Server database by using XML.
  - Validate an XML document.

Testing and Debugging

- Create a unit test plan.
- Implement tracing.
  - Configure and use trace listeners and trace switches.
  - Display trace output.
- Instrument and debug a Windows service, a serviced component, a .NET Remoting object, and an XML web service.
  - Configure the debugging environment.
  - Create and apply debugging code to components and applications.
  - Provide multicultural test data to components and applications.
  - Execute tests.
- Use interactive debugging.
- Log test results.
  - Resolve errors and rework code.
  - Control debugging in the Web.config file.
  - Use SOAP extensions for debugging.

Deploying Windows Services, Serviced Components, .NET Remoting Objects, and XML Web Services

- Plan the deployment of and deploy a Windows service, a serviced component, a .NET Remoting object, and an XML web service.

- Create a setup program that installs a Windows service, a serviced component, a .NET Remoting object, and an XML web service.

  - Register components and assemblies.

- Publish an XML web service.

  - Enable static discovery.

- Publish XML web service definitions in the UDDI.

- Configure client computers and servers to use a Windows service, a serviced component, a .NET Remoting object, and an XML web service.

- Implement versioning.

- Plan, configure, and deploy side-by-side deployments and applications.

- Configure security for a Windows service, a serviced component, a .NET Remoting object, and an XML web service.

  - Configure authentication type. Authentication types include Windows authentication, Microsoft .NET Passport, custom authentication, and none.

  - Configure and control authorization. Authorization methods include file-based authorization and URL-based authorization.

  - Configure and implement identity management.

Performance-Based vs. Knowledge-Based Questions

The exam questions fall into two broad categories, knowledge-based and performance-based. Knowledge-based questions are designed to test your knowledge of specific facts. Performance-based questions are designed to measure your ability to perform on the job by presenting examples of situations and scenarios that a developer might encounter in the real world.

- **Free response items** Traditional multiple-choice items, these questions are designed to test your basic knowledge of facts.

- **Case study-based items** Designed to simulate what situations developers actually encounter on the job, these questions test your ability to analyze information and make decisions.

You should take advantage of the sample questions available for download from the Exam and Testing Procedures Web page at www.microsoft.com/traincert/ mcpexams/faq/procedures.asp.

Signing Up

To schedule your exam, call any Sylvan Prometric or VUE center. Online registration is also available through the Register for an Exam Web page at www.microsoft.com/traincert/mcpexams/register. This site gives you information about the registration process and locations of testing centers near you.

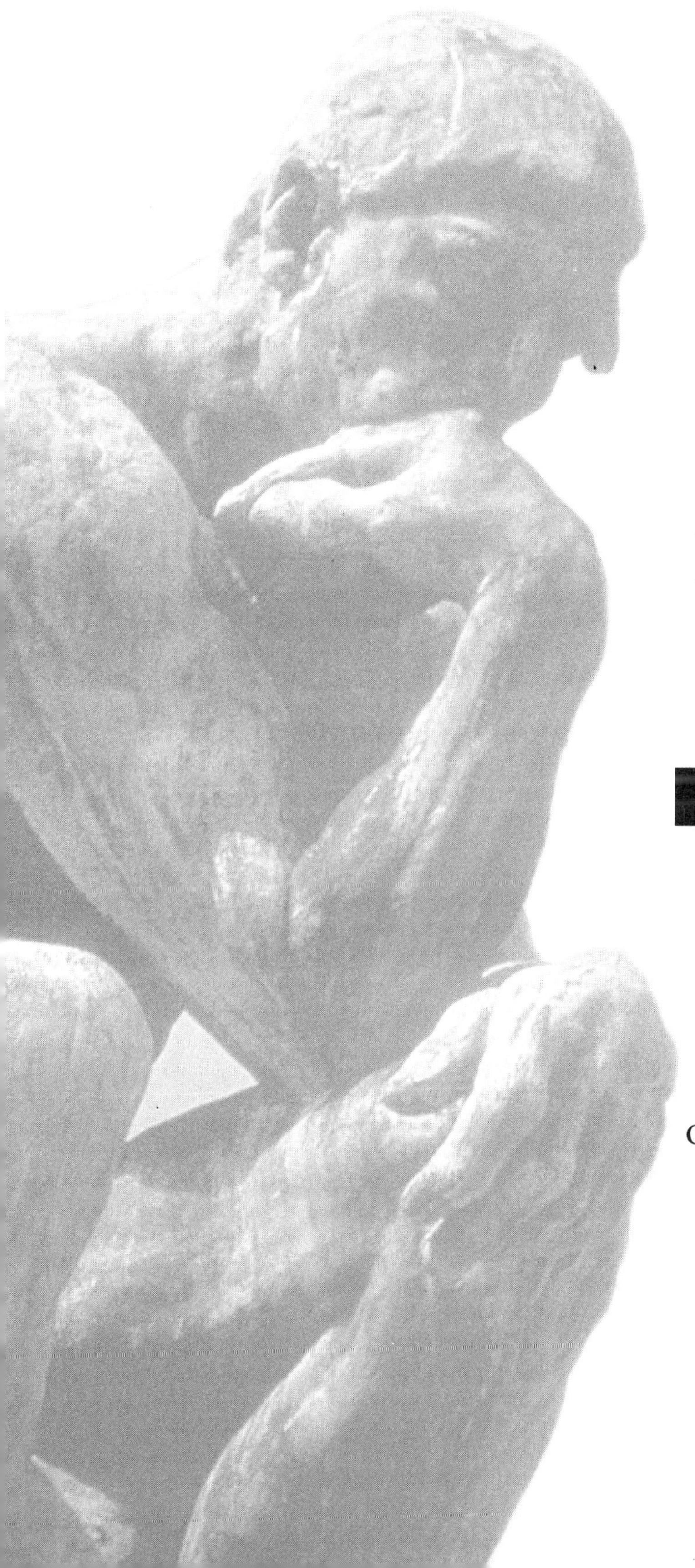

MCAD/MCSD

MICROSOFT® CERTIFIED APPLICATION DEVELOPER
& MICROSOFT® CERTIFIED SOLUTION DEVELOPER

1

Introduction to XML Services

CERTIFICATION OBJECTIVES

- 1.01 Overview of .NET
- 1.02 Visual Basic .NET
- 1.03 Implementation in Visual Basic .NET
- 1.04 .NET Assemblies
- 1.05 .NET Component Models
- ✓ Two-Minute Drill
- Q&A Self Test

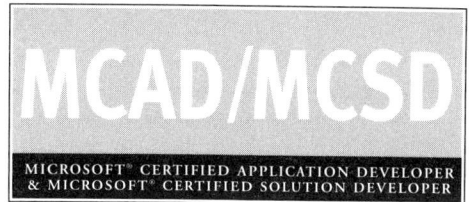

I n this the first chapter of the *MCAD/MCSD XML Web Services and Server Components Development with Visual Basic .NET Study Guide (Exam 70-310)*, I will present the background of the .NET Framework and the different languages and products that make up the Framework.

You will specifically learn about the .NET Framework and how the Common Language Runtime (CLR) and the Common Type System (CTS) work together. The computer language the 70-310 exam uses is Visual Basic .NET, and you will also get a refresher in how to use it.

When Microsoft released the .NET platform, the world of computing changed for all computer professionals, even though the term .NET means different things to different professionals. Network administrators think of .NET as the new servers including the new .NET Server Operating System, while for us developers it means the .NET Framework and the new Visual Studio .NET. In both cases, Microsoft has significantly altered the way we'll work. The XML Web Services is one big part of that change.

So without further ado, let's start preparing for the XML exam!

CERTIFICATION OBJECTIVE 1.01

Overview of .NET

Traditional development for the Windows platform has involved the use of different computer language products that were monolithic in nature—they were complete solutions in themselves. One of the problems with this type of development language is that the language also becomes the development environment, and interoperability between applications developed in different computer languages is very hard to achieve without additional services such as Microsoft Transaction Server (MTS) or the COM+ service.

Microsoft has addressed the issues surrounding the existing development languages and the inherent problems of those environments by developing the .NET Framework. The key to .NET is not the language—the key is the framework that the application is using. In the following sections, you will learn about the .NET Framework.

.NET Framework

The .NET Framework will have an effect on virtually every computer system, if Microsoft's investment pays off. The major goal of the .NET Framework is to make this environment available on all computers. To that end, .NET

- Is platform independent
- Provides a common runtime environment
- Uses common data types

To implement a system that meets these goals, Microsoft's engineers designed a new type of computer platform that encapsulates (hides) the hardware and the operating system from the developer. These parts make up the .NET Framework:

- Common Language Runtime (CLR)
- Common Language Specification (CLS)
- Microsoft Intermediate Language (MSIL)
- Base Class Library (BCL)

Figure 1-1 depicts the architecture of the .NET Framework.

The most important feature of the .NET Framework, and from a developer's point of view the most exciting one, is the Common Language Runtime (CLR)—the CLR is the software platform that our applications are written to run on. Another way to look at the CLR is to say that the CLR implements the Common Type System (CTS). The following sections will delve deeper into these parts of the .NET Framework.

Common Language Runtime

The Common Language Runtime is the platform under which our code will run, and the language of the CLR is Microsoft Intermediate Language, which is the language our application will be compiled to. The reason you compile to an intermediate language is to avoid the hardware and operating system dependencies that traditional environments give us. The CLR in turn will compile the MSIL into the native language of the hardware platform. Figure 1-2 shows the major parts of the CLR.

Think of the CLR as the operating system and the hardware platform in one—this design makes it possible for us to write applications that can run on any

FIGURE 1-1   The .NET Framework

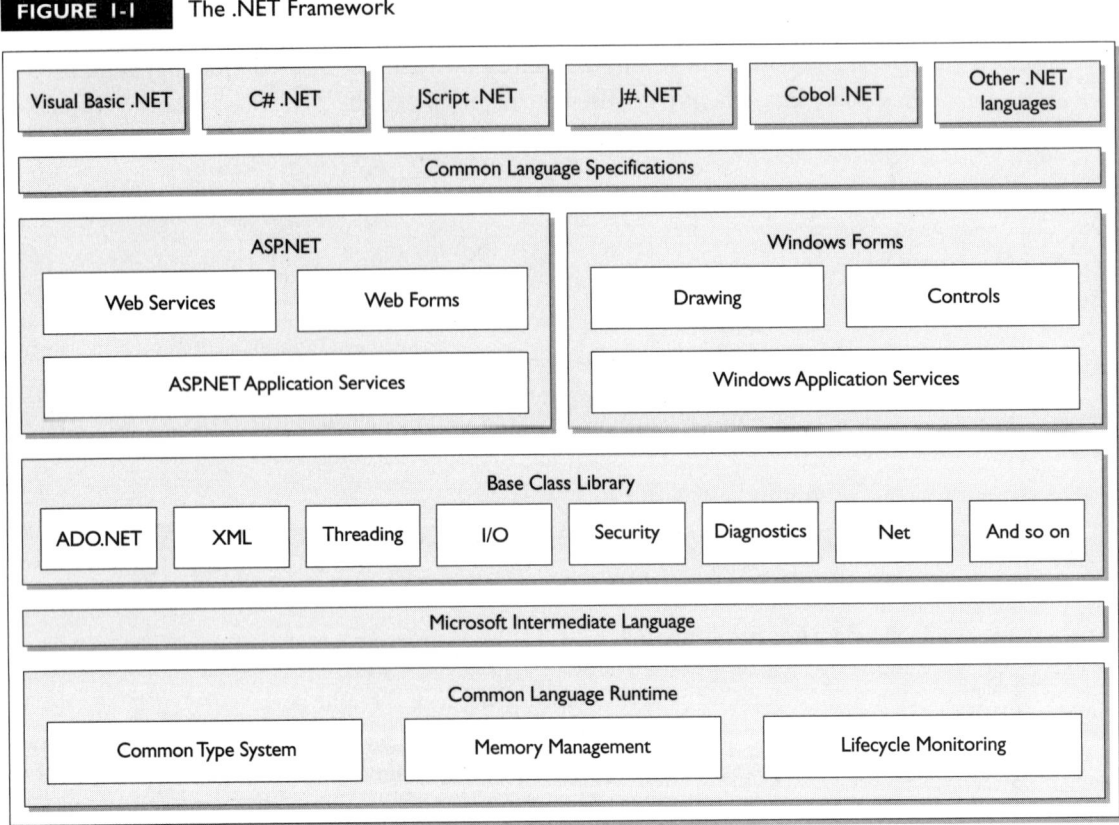

computer that implements the .NET Framework. As you see in Figure 1-2, the CLR contains the Common Type System (CTS). CTS provides the definitions of all data types that are used in any .NET application. The reason for defining the data types as part of the runtime environment is to standardize all the data types. In other words, if I use an integer in one programming language, it will be the same size and behave the same way when accessed from another computer language. Table 1-1 lists some of the data types defined in the CTS and the Visual Basic .NET equivalents. The CTS data types are implemented in the System namespace, resulting in names of the form System.Int32.

The data types are actually classes that encapsulate the primitive data type. This allows you access to functionality through the data type—for example, to convert the data to a string representation (ToString). All of this functionality is defined in the CTS and implemented in the CLR, giving all .NET languages the same data

| FIGURE 1-2 | The Common Language Runtime |

| TABLE 1-1 | The Visual Basic .NET Data Types Related to the CTS |

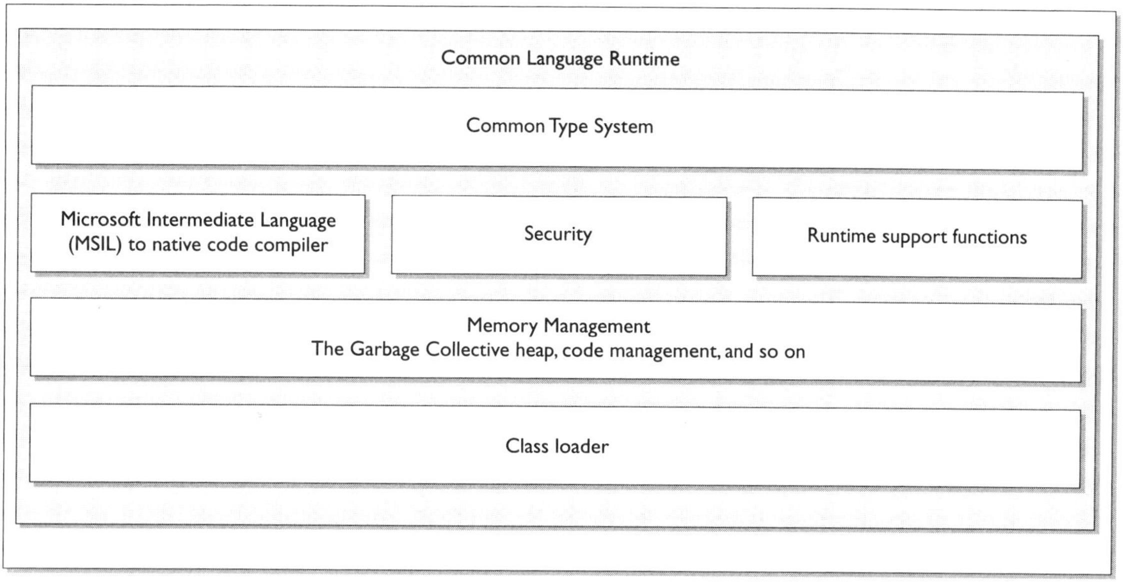

Visual Basic .NET Data Type	CLR Data Type	Description
Sbyte	System.Sbyte	8-bit signed integer
Short	System.Int16	16-bit signed integer
Integer	System.Int32	32-bit signed integer
Long	System.Int64	64-bit signed integer
Byte	System.Byte	8-bit unsigned integer
UInt16	System.UInt16	16-bit unsigned integer
UInt32	System.UInt32	32-bit unsigned integer
UInt64	System.UInt64	64-bit unsigned integer
Single	System.Single	Single-precision floating point value
Double	System.Double	Double-precision floating point value
Char	System.Char	Unicode character
Decimal	System.Decimal	Exact decimal with 28 significant digits
Boolean	System.Boolean	Boolean value

types. The CLR is the implementation of the Common Language Specification described in the next section.

Common Language Specification

The overriding rules for how the .NET Framework defines data types, accesses methods, and controls the visibility of everything are just a few of the items specified by the CTS. The CTS actually specifies what the language rules are that the Visual Basic .NET compiler's output must comply with. The CTS rules are part of the code security rules that ensure that you do not try to execute code that potentially can harm the computer. The Visual Basic .NET compiler produces as its output Intermediate Language (IL) code that is the language of the CLR as specified by the CTS. If you shake your head at these acronyms the way I do, hold out a little bit more and we will be done with the theory.

The Intermediate Language code is actually the code that is produced by all of the .NET language compilers. This common language that is used at runtime makes it possible to mix and match components written in any of the .NET languages.

e x a m
ⓦ a t c h
Microsoft Intermediate Language (MSIL) is the current name for the language of the CLR, but do not be surprised to see it referred to as IL.

There are dissassemblers and assemblers that allow you to work with the IL code should you be so inclined; personally, I feel that working with the assembly-level code is a step backward.

To sum up, the .NET Framework is based on a language specification (CTS) that is implemented as a runtime environment (CLR) that also provides common data types (CTS). When you installed the .NET Framework, you installed an environment for which you can write software; however, although the .NET Framework contains the language compilers, it provides no help for going much further than building console (command-line) applications.

The part of the .NET Framework that gives us the ability to build complex applications right out of the gate is the Base Class Library, which contains the classes used to build Windows Forms, among other things.

Base Class Library

The .NET Framework is totally object oriented, as is the Base Class Library. This library of classes that is used to build the complex applications you have become familiar with is built upon a hierarchy that uses a "dotted" notation to keep the different parts of the application separated. For example, to refer to the Int32 class in the System namespace, you would write System.Int32. The namespace can be thought of as an alias for a longer name.

The Base Class Library (BCL) is what gives the .NET Framework its power and its look and feel. When you need to build a Windows Form, you start by inheriting from the System.Windows.Forms.Form class. This is the class that provides the basic behavior we expect a Form to have. This ability to draw on a library of common classes is very powerful.

The BCL is very big—I could fill a book just on the classes in the BCL and all the members (properties, methods, and events) of those classes. Fortunately, you do not have to memorize all those classes; generally the exam will not test you on your ability to remember minutiae of the common classes. I will point out the few exceptions to this rule as you reach them in the following chapters. The documentation for the BCL is in the Microsoft Developer Network Library (MSDN) that was delivered with Visual Studio .NET, or you can view the library online at http://msdn.microsoft.com.

The BCL provides the base classes that are used to build most of the applications you will work with, although a couple of "packages" are added to the BCL to add specific high-level support for a particular technology or architecture. Two such "packages" are ADO.NET for databases and ASP.NET for web development. The following sections will look closer at these "packages."

ADO.NET

The latest version of the ActiveX Data Objects (ADO) from Microsoft is the ADO.NET that is supplied with the .NET Framework. The database support provided through ADO.NET enables, among other things, the use of disconnected recordsets that allow you to store the client's data locally with no connection to the database while the client works on the data. Later, when you need to update the database with the changes that occurred on the client, you send those updates back to the database. The disconnected recordset is but one of the many different technologies that have come of age in the ADO.NET package.

exam
ⓦatch

The exam will use code to connect to databases and use the data from databases in a large number of its questions, even though a given question is not related to the database. This type of question is designed to make sure you know how to use the technology (ADO.NET) and are able to answer the question without being led astray by the complexity of the code presented.

Due to this focus on database connectivity and data manipulation through ADO.NET, I will devote all of Chapter 6 to the topic. Another package that is added into the .NET Framework helps us write Web applications—that package, ASP.NET, is presented in the next section.

ASP.NET

Microsoft presented the first version of Active Server Pages (ASP) as part of Internet Information Services (IIS) version 3, which was released early in the product life cycle of Windows NT Server 4. The current version of IIS is version 5, which was released with Windows 2000—ASP.NET is the version of ASP that works together with IIS 5 and the .NET Framework.

Any Web-based application operates like this: The client sends a request to the web server using the Hypertext Transfer Protocol (HTTP). The request is for a file with the ASP.NET file extension—.aspx. When IIS receives the request for the file with the .aspx extension, IIS redirects the request to the ASP.DLL component that will execute the .aspx file and return Hypertext Markup Language (HTML) code to the client. Figure 1-3 shows this process.

The processing that takes place in the ASP.NET program uses the object model of ASP.NET to gain access to the request from the client (Request Object), process the request, and build the package that will be returned to the client (Response Object). The ASP.NET objects also help with the data storage between calls from the client (Session Object) and the web application as a whole (Application Object). The building of a Web application is a topic for a different exam.

The preceding discussion has been a whirlwind tour of the .NET Framework and its technologies. The coverage is by no stretch of the imagination exhaustive and should be used only as a reminder of what the .NET Framework is all about.

The next section is a review of the Visual Basic .NET language.

FIGURE 1-3 How an ASP.NET request is handled

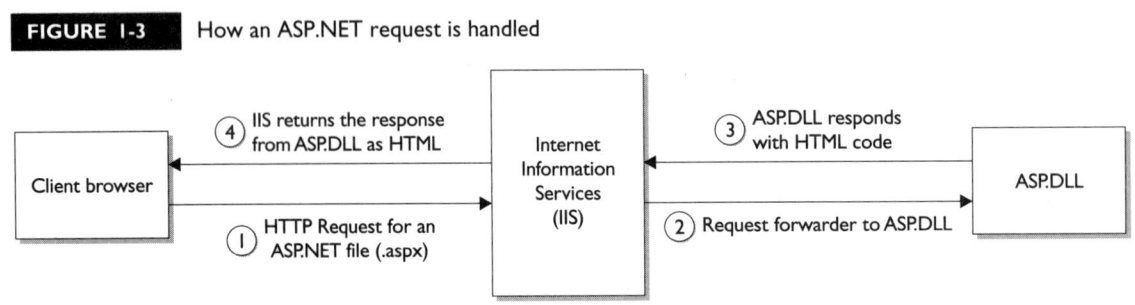

CERTIFICATION OBJECTIVE 1.02

Visual Basic .NET

With the release of the .NET Framework, Microsoft included four languages that are the core languages that will be supported. They are Visual Basic .NET, Visual C++ .NET, Visual C# .NET, and JScript .NET. One additional language has been announced to replace the current J++ language: Visual J# .NET. These languages have one thing in common: they all produce IL code that will be run against the CLR. This book focuses on the Visual Basic .NET language.

If you are a VB 6 developer, you will find that the language syntax in Visual Basic .NET is fairly familiar. The capabilities of the language have, however, been greatly enhanced over the preceding version. Some of the capabilities that have been added to Visual Basic .NET are

- Full object-oriented (OO) capabilities
    - True inheritance
    - Method overloading
    - Operator overloading
    - Parameterized constructors
    - Shared members
- Structured exception (error) handling
- Threading models

The basis for these capabilities is the .NET Framework and specifically the Common Language Specification. The addition of the full object-oriented support has moved Visual Basic into a new realm where you can build more than just Windows forms.

In previous versions of the Visual Basic language, we had the capability to build object-oriented components such as COM components by using the class file. The model, unfortunately, did not include the OO concept of inheritance, where you can create increasingly more specialized classes built on more general classes.

In this section, you will have a look at some of the new capabilities as a quick introduction to Visual Basic .NET. The basics of writing code in the Visual Basic

.NET language are not within the scope of this book. For you to learn the language, I recommend *Visual Basic .NET: A Beginner's Guide* by Jeffrey Kent, (Osborne/McGraw-Hill, 2002).

Object-Oriented Visual Basic .NET

Because the .NET Framework and the .NET languages are fully object-oriented (OO) implementations, it is advantageous to use the OO model when building applications using Visual Basic .NET. This section is a refresher for the OO terminology and what makes up the OO world.

OO is based on the real world, where you see and use objects; for example, you can see a car and you can use a car; you can agree that a car is an object. The car itself is constructed of multiple objects (wheels, seats, engine, transmission, and so on), in what you call composition—one object is built from other objects.

When you use OO, you implement the project in a different fashion than when you build a procedural application. There are a number of project management solutions for an OO project; Microsoft calls their project model the Microsoft Solutions Framework (MSF). The purpose of the Object-Oriented Analysis and Design (OOAD) process is to take a physical, real-world set of objects that represents the problem (in the problem domain), break it down into the smallest component steps, and in the end reassemble the components into an object model that describes the real-world problem domain in such a fashion that it can be implemented in a software application.

Some of the techniques used in OOAD to build object models follow.

Inheritance   In considering the car object, you can conclude that the car was itself composed of multiple objects. But if you take a step back and look at the car as a whole, you can see that the car looks very much the same as most other vehicles on the road—the differences lie in the number of objects that compose the vehicle, as well as the shape and color of the objects. When you look at objects that are related in such a way, call the relationship an *inheritance*—the car inherits from the more general vehicle.

A basic OO technique is to be able to create objects based on other objects, and it is a technique you have wanted to have in Visual Basic for a long time. The inheritance can be phrased using the *is a* term, for example, a car *is a* vehicle. See the discussion of the implementation of inheritance later in this section.

Containment   In *containment,* the sum of all the objects makes up the whole. One way to look at it is to say that you have an object model in which an object contains other objects; For example, think of the car: the car as an object is made up of many other objects, wheels, engine, transmission, and so on. Containment is described using the wording *has a*; for example, a car *has an* engine.

Polymorphism   Another very powerful practice is the ability to write code at design time without knowing what the object will be at run time. What makes this technique work is that you can build models of objects that are related as siblings to each other.

Polymorphism uses late binding to be able to determine the object at run time.

Overloading   *Overloading* is a technique that allows you to create methods with the same name that can take different parameter types. It is the data type of the parameter (or parameters) that determines the signature of the method; for example, `GetHelp(topic as String)` and `GetHelp(topicID as Integer)` are two overloaded methods with different signatures.

Overriding   *Overriding* is a technique in which one object (the child) inherits from another object (the base). The base object has a method defined that performs some operation, and the child wants to further enhance the method to perform the task specifically for itself. By defining the same method (the signature must be the same) in the child object as in the base, you override the base method.

Continuing our earlier vehicle example, you can say that the vehicle object (the parent) defines a method you call `Start(speed as Integer)` that sends messages to the engine to start and accelerate to the speed requested. In the car object (the child), you need to handle the transmission and the brakes in a special manner, so you define a method that has the same signature (`Start(speed as Integer)`) to perform those extra steps.

In the next section, you will look at how to implement some of these techniques using Visual Basic .NET.

CERTIFICATION OBJECTIVE 1.03

Implementation in Visual Basic .NET

Before I delve into the implementation of some of the new features in Visual Basic .NET, I must define what a class is and what an object is, and how they are related. In thinking of classes and objects, I usually consider that an object is the physical implementation of the class. The class is the code we write that describes how the object will behave after we have created a "physical" object in memory—also known as *instantiating* the object.

In the following section, you will look at inheritance by writing the code for a couple of classes.

Inheritance

To give an example of inheritance in Visual Basic .NET, you will continue your vehicle example. The first thing you will do is define a vehicle class that is the "blueprint" for the vehicle; the class definition will look like this code segment:

```
' Define the Vehicle class
Public Class Vehicle
    ' Declare the Speed and Fuel properties plus the accessors
    Private m_Speed As Integer
    Private m_Fuel As Decimal
    Public Property Speed() As Integer
        Get
            Return m_Speed
        End Get
        Set
            m_Speed = Value
        End Set
    End Property
    Public Property Fuel() As Decimal
        Get
            Return m_Fuel
        End Get
        Set
            m_Fuel = Value
        End Set
    End Property
' By marking the following methods as Overridable we make it
' possible to override them in any child class
    Public Overridable Sub Starter(FinalSpeed As Integer)
        ' no implementation, we do not know how to start the generic vehicle
    End Sub
    Public Overridable Sub Stopper()
        ' no implementation, we do not know how to stop the generic vehicle
    End Sub
End Class
```

In designing this class, you made some assumptions: the vehicle can have a speed and hold some fuel. Otherwise, the class does not do too much. To reuse the vehicle class when you create the car class, you include a second line in the class declaration that specifies the inheritance, as can be seen in the following code segment:

```
' Declare the Car class as a child class of the Vehicle class
Public Class Car
    Inherits Vehicle
' The only thing we need to perform in this declaration is the implementation
' of the Starter() and Stopper() methods. They are going to override
' the same methods that we declared in the parent class.
' The keyword Overrides specifies that we truly want to override
' the original methods
    Public Overrides Sub Starter(FinalSpeed As Integer)
       StartEngine()
      ReleaseParkingBrake()
      Accelerate(FinalSpeed)
    End Sub
    Public Overrides Sub Stopper()
       Break()
      ApplyParkingBrake()
      StopEngine()
    End Sub
End Class
```

Now we have a generic car, and if we want to create a specialization of this car, we can inherit from the car class and customize the methods that are needed. In the next code segment, you can see a sports car class being declared:

```
' Declare the SportsCar class based on the Car class
Public Class SportsCar
    Inherits Car
    Public Overrides Sub Starter(FinalSpeed As Integer)
       StartEngine()
       ReleaseParkingBrake()
       AccelerateFast(FinalSpeed)
    End Sub
End Class
```

The sports car has only one extra bit of functionality—it can accelerate fast. This was an example of how classes can inherit from other classes that have inherited from yet other classes. A class diagram seen in Figure 1-4 illustrates the preceding example.

Once you have related your objects with inheritance, you can start looking at ways to make the same method call handle many different situations by using overloading. The next section details method overloading.

Overloading

There are times when you really want to have the same method name accept many different parameter data types, and this is where overloading comes in. *Overloading* is the technique that allows you to have multiple methods with the same name but

FIGURE 1-4

The class diagram
for the vehicle
example

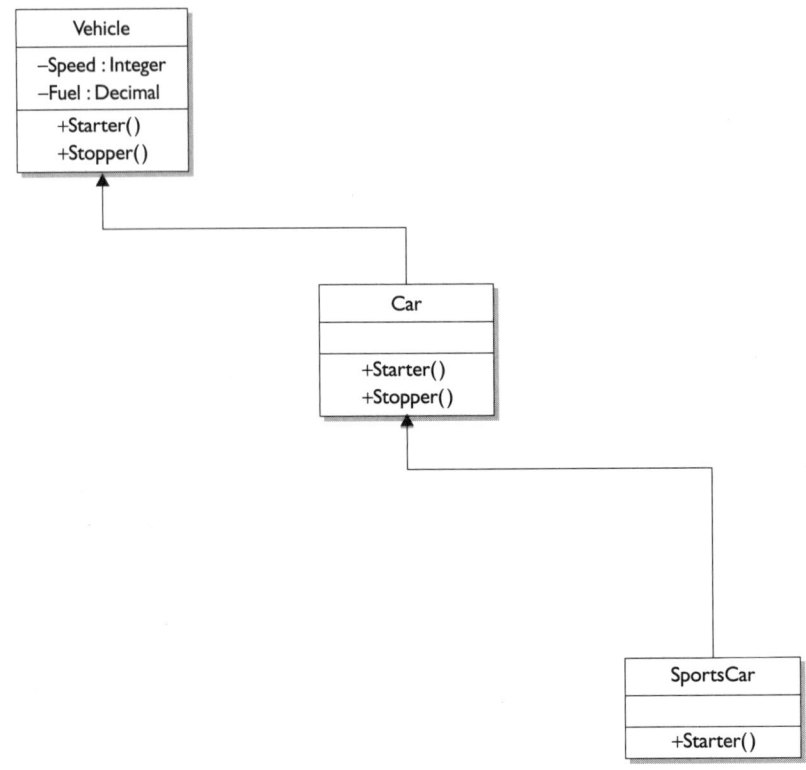

taking different parameters, giving you the ability to select the method according to what data you pass it. Say, for example, you have the following function declaration:

```
Public Function SearchRecord(RecordID As Integer) As DataSet
    strSQL As String
    strSQL = "SELECT * FROM EMPLOYEES WHERE RECID = " + RecordID
    ' Open the database and search it
    ' Return the DataSet ds
. . .
    Return ds
End Function
```

Now suppose you need to search for records by first name. The natural way would be to declare a new function to perform that task using the following signature declaration:

```
Public Function SearchRecord(FirstName As String) As DataSet
```

That is all it takes to overload a function. Let us look at an example that uses overloading.

The following code segment defines a class that has six overloaded
SearchRecord() functions with different signatures; Sub Main() is the
entry point of the program:

```
Module Test
Public Class TestClass

    Sub SearchRecord()
        System.Console.WriteLine("SearchRecord()")
    End Sub

    Sub SearchRecord(o As Object)
        System.Console.WriteLine("SearchRecord(Object)")
    End Sub

    Sub SearchRecord(ByVal Value As Integer)
        System.Console.WriteLine("SearchRecord(Integer)")
    End Sub

    Sub SearchRecord(a As Integer, b As Integer)
        System.Console.WriteLine("SearchRecord(Integer, Integer)")
    End Sub

    Sub SearchRecord(values() As Integer)
        System.Console.WriteLine("SearchRecord(Integer[])")
    End Sub

    Sub SearchRecord(s As String, d As Double)
        System.Console.WriteLine("SearchRecord(String, Double)")
    End Sub
End Class

    Sub Main()
        Dim tsc As TestClass
        tsc = new TestClass()
        tsc.SearchRecord()
        tsc.SearchRecord(42)
        tsc.SearchRecord(CType(42, Object))
        tsc.SearchRecord(42, 12)
        tsc.SearchRecord(New Integer() {1, 42, 12})
        tsc.SearchRecord("The String", 3.1415)
    End Sub
End Module
```

This code is a complete command-line program that can be compiled and
executed from a command window. To be able to use the compiler from a command
window, you will need to start the command window with all the environment

settings for the Visual Studio .NET—this command prompt is opened by choosing Start | Programs | Microsoft Visual Studio .NET | Visual Studio .NET Tools | Visual Studio .NET Command Prompt.

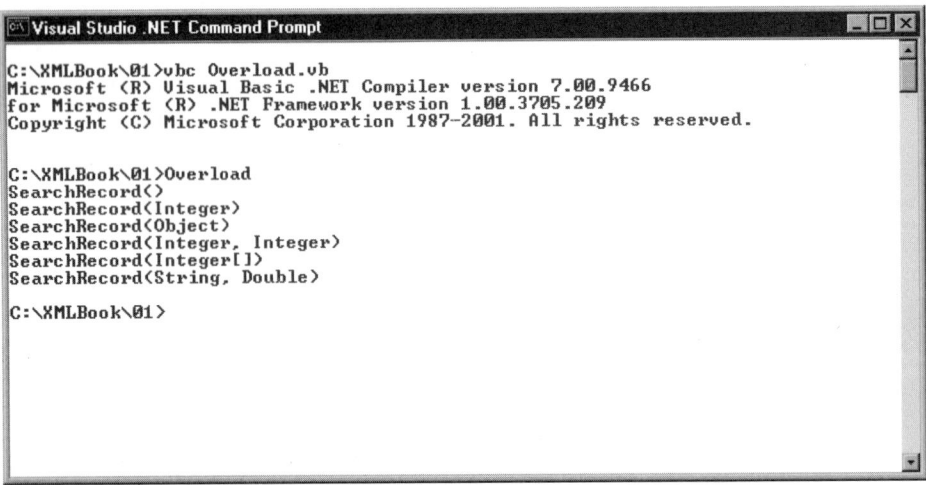

on the Job

I make a shortcut on the desktop of the Visual Studio .NET Command Prompt menu item.

Once you are in the command window, you can copy the Overload.vb file from the Chapter 1 folder of the CD-ROM that accompanies this book. That file contains the preceding code, or you can type the code using your favorite editor. In order to compile the program, you need to use the vbc.exe Visual Basic .NET compiler using the following command-line command:

```
C:\XMLBook\01>vbc Overload.vb
```

Now you can run the program by typing its name at the command prompt; the different overloaded methods are called according to the signature of each method, Figure 1-5 shows the output of the program.

exam Watch

Make sure you are familiar with overloading; code samples using this technique may appear in the exam.

Another new feature of Visual Basic .NET is error handling through the Try/Catch/Finally structure, as you will see in the next section.

FIGURE 1-5   The output of the overload example

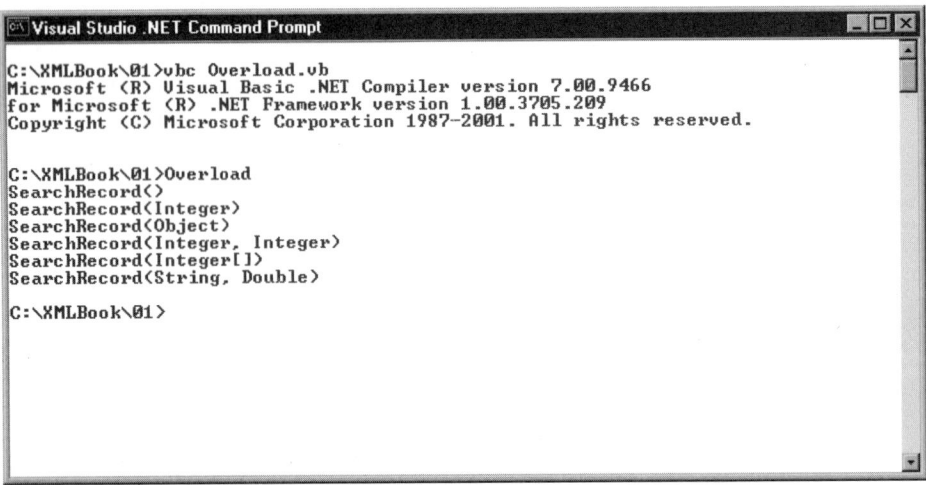

```
C:\XMLBook\01>vbc Overload.vb
Microsoft (R) Visual Basic .NET Compiler version 7.00.9466
for Microsoft (R) .NET Framework version 1.00.3705.209
Copyright (C) Microsoft Corporation 1987-2001. All rights reserved.


C:\XMLBook\01>Overload
SearchRecord()
SearchRecord(Integer)
SearchRecord(Object)
SearchRecord(Integer, Integer)
SearchRecord(Integer[])
SearchRecord(String, Double)

C:\XMLBook\01>
```

Exception Handling

One of the real issues in software development is that you can only code solutions for errors you can expect—you do that by validating data that is sent to methods to make sure the data meets the design requirements of the application. The problem is that any number of errors can happen that you never had a chance to anticipate; for example, the server that holds the file the client wants to open just experienced a network outage—how does our application react to that outage, and how do you code to ensure that the error won't crash the client application?

Addressing these unanticipated errors falls in the realm of exception handling. If you used to program in VB 6, you will have the error-handling technique down pat by now. You declare an error handler, then you try to solve the error to be able to continue the program, or else you fail the program gracefully so that the client has a chance to get some information about the error.

What is new in Visual Basic .NET (and all the .NET languages) is that the language now implements C++-style exception handling. The exception handling is broken up in guard blocks that contain code that will execute or not depending on what error phase execution is in.

The first guard block is the `Try` block. Code in the `Try` block will execute as long as there is no error condition.

The second guard block is the `Catch` block. The code in the `Catch` block will execute if there is an error resulting in an exception and the `Catch` block has been declared to handle that exception.

The last type is the `Finally` block. The code in the `Finally` block is guaranteed to execute—after the completion of either the `Try` block or any `Catch` block. The following code segment shows the `Try/Catch/Finally/`structure.

```
Try
    ' This is the start of a structured exception handler.
    ' Place executable statements that may generate
    ' an exception in this block.
Catch [optional filters]
    ' The code in this block will run if any statement in
    ' the Try block fails and the filter on the Catch statement is true.
[Additional Catch blocks]
Finally
    ' This code always runs immediately before
    ' the Try statement exits.
End Try
    ' Ends a structured exception handler.
```

The filter statement on the `Catch` block is optional; if there is no filter, that `Catch` block will be executed for all errors. Let's look at some examples of the use of the `Try/Catch/Finally` blocks.

In the first example, you will try to divide by zero. Because you know that you are not allowed to do that, you will catch the division by zero and continue with some additional divisions. The source file for this example (ZeroDiv.vb) is on the CD-ROM in the Chapter 1 folder.

```
Module Zero
Public Class Maths
    Public Function Div(a As Integer, b As Integer) As Integer
    ' perform integer division
      Try
         Return a \ b
      Catch
         System.Console.Writeline("An error occurred")
      Finally
         System.Console.Writeline("Finally was called")
      End Try
    End Function
End Class

    Sub Main(ByVal Argh() As String)
       Dim zd As Maths
       zd = new Maths()

       System.Console.WriteLine("{0} divided by {1} equals {2}",
                       Argh(0), Argh(1), zd.Div(Argh(0),Argh(1)))
    End Sub

End Module
```

As you can see in Figure 1-6, the error is caught, but the `Finally` block is always executed as well. To compile the program, you use the following command:

```
vbc ZeroDiv.vb
```

The first version caught every error and ignored it. Now you will look at a final version that will return a value of –1 for a division by zero error; to do that, you need to catch the right exception. The exception you need to catch is `System.DivideByZeroException`. In the following code segment, you can see the addition of the filter condition to the `Catch` statement. The reason the exception is called `e` is that by convention you want a very short variable name, and *e* is a good mnemonic for an exception. You then print the exception text and set the value to be returned to –1:

```
Module Zero
Public Class Maths
    Public Function Div(a As Integer, b As Integer) As Integer
```

```vb
' perform integer division
  Dim i As Integer
  Try
    Return a \ b
  Catch e As System.DivideByZeroException
    System.Console.Writeline(e.ToString())
    ' Define the return data to indicate the error
    i = -1
  Finally
    System.Console.Writeline("Finally was called")
  End Try
  ' return the data
  Return i
End Function

End Class

Sub Main(ByVal Argh() As String)
  Dim zd As Maths
  zd = new Maths()

  System.Console.WriteLine("{0} divided by {1} equals {2}",
                      Argh(0), Argh(1), zd.Div(Argh(0),Argh(1)))
End Sub

End Module
```

The output from the ZeroDivF program can be seen in Figure 1-7.

FIGURE 1-6   The output from the first version of exception handling

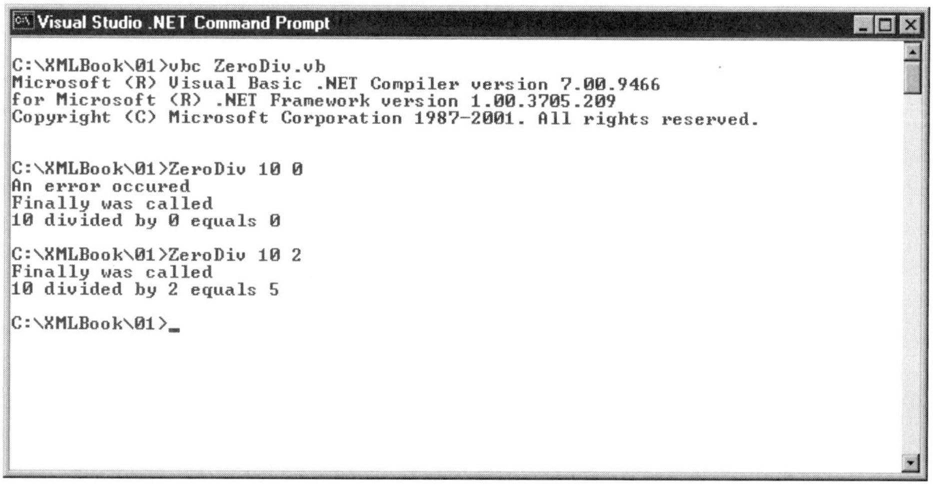

FIGURE 1-7   The output from the ZeroDivF program

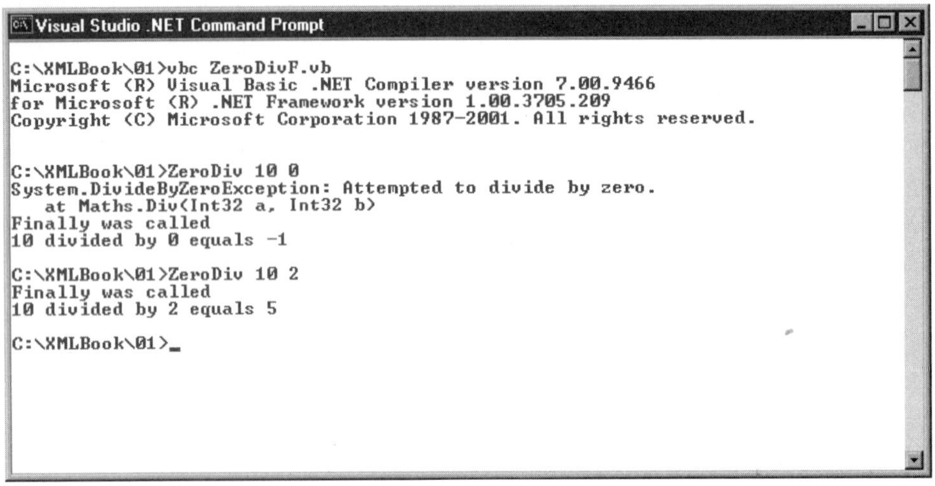

```
Visual Studio .NET Command Prompt                                    _ □ ✕

C:\XMLBook\01>vbc ZeroDivF.vb
Microsoft (R) Visual Basic .NET Compiler version 7.00.9466
for Microsoft (R) .NET Framework version 1.00.3705.209
Copyright (C) Microsoft Corporation 1987-2001. All rights reserved.


C:\XMLBook\01>ZeroDiv 10 0
System.DivideByZeroException: Attempted to divide by zero.
   at Maths.Div(Int32 a, Int32 b)
Finally was called
10 divided by 0 equals -1

C:\XMLBook\01>ZeroDiv 10 2
Finally was called
10 divided by 2 equals 5

C:\XMLBook\01>_
```

e x a m
ⓦa t c h   *Exception handling and the fact that the `Finally` block always executes make their way into many of the code samples used in the exam.*

CERTIFICATION OBJECTIVE 1.04

.NET Assemblies

In the Microsoft development world before the .NET Framework, there was a problem that faced developers and administrators alike: the DLL Hell. This term describes the situation that can and does occur when you develop component-based applications. Most applications are divided between multiple physical files: an executable (.exe file) plus multiple dynamic-link library (DLL) files. In order for an application to make use of the components, the DLLs must register themselves in the computer's Registry. If one DLL alters another's registration, you have a broken reference; if the physical file is overwritten, you have a broken reference.

One possible solution for these problems is to store all of an application's files in a private folder, and that usually works. However, if the component you need is in a system library (part of the operating system), there could be other issues: if the DLL is replaced when the operating system is updated, you have a potential version problem, and there is no mechanism in the Registry to support multiple versions, nor to request a specific version.

The solution to this dilemma is to stop using the computer's central Registry, to let all files carry information about themselves as part of the file, including version information, and to separate an application's local components from the system's global components. This is what was done with assemblies in the .NET Framework.

Microsoft has defined the assembly and its role in .NET in the following terms: In the .NET Framework, an assembly is the physical unit that can be executed, deployed, versioned, and secured. All .NET Framework applications contain one or more assemblies.

Assembly Versions

The .NET Framework assists you by providing a number of features to ensure proper versioning between components in an application:

- The .NET infrastructure enforces versioning rules so that an application that needs version 1.1.1.1 will not end up getting version 1.0.0.0.

- The versioning rules can be specified across the assemblies that are part of the application.

- Shared assemblies are signed with a strong name (which includes a public key, a simple name, a version, and a culture). Assemblies that are not shared do not require strong names.

- The .NET Framework permits different versions of the same assembly to execute at the same time.

The versioning is maintained in the assembly. In addition, the signatures of all public methods and metadata for the assembly are stored in the manifest (the manifest is the fingerprint of the assembly). The versioning rules that can be applied for an application allow the developer and the administrator to specify what version of an assembly should be used.

Assembly Deployment

The assembly is the unit of deployment for a .NET application. Assemblies can be deployed using three different methods: the Microsoft Installer (MSI) deployment, a CAB (cabinet archive) file, or the XCOPY deployment. The XCOPY deployment is very interesting because all you need to do is use the system command **xcopy** to copy the assembly into the application directory—the assembly holds all the information about itself in the manifest. For more information on the deployment of XML Web Service applications and assemblies, see Chapter 9.

The XCOPY deployment will work only when you deploy to a private assembly that is stored together with the application. For shared assemblies that are available to all applications on the computer, you need to register the assembly with the GAC (Global Assembly Cache). The registration of the assembly with the GAC results in a uniquely named folder being created and the assembly files being copied into that folder. The GAC is then updated with the name and version of the folder.

Uninstalling a private assembly is as easy as deleting the assembly, but uninstalling a shared assembly requires that the assembly be uninstalled from the GAC.

The assembly contains MSIL code (from the compilation of your code), resources, and the manifest (which is data that describes the assembly). Every assembly must have a manifest, which can be a separate file in the assembly or contained in one of the modules. The manifest defines the following, among other things:

- The name and version number of the assembly
- A list of other assemblies this assembly depends on. This list contains the names and version numbers of the assemblies.
- Types that are exposed by the assembly. This is a public interface that the assembly exposes.
- The security permissions that the assembly requires.

Figure 1-8 shows the relationship between the assembly and the content of the assembly.

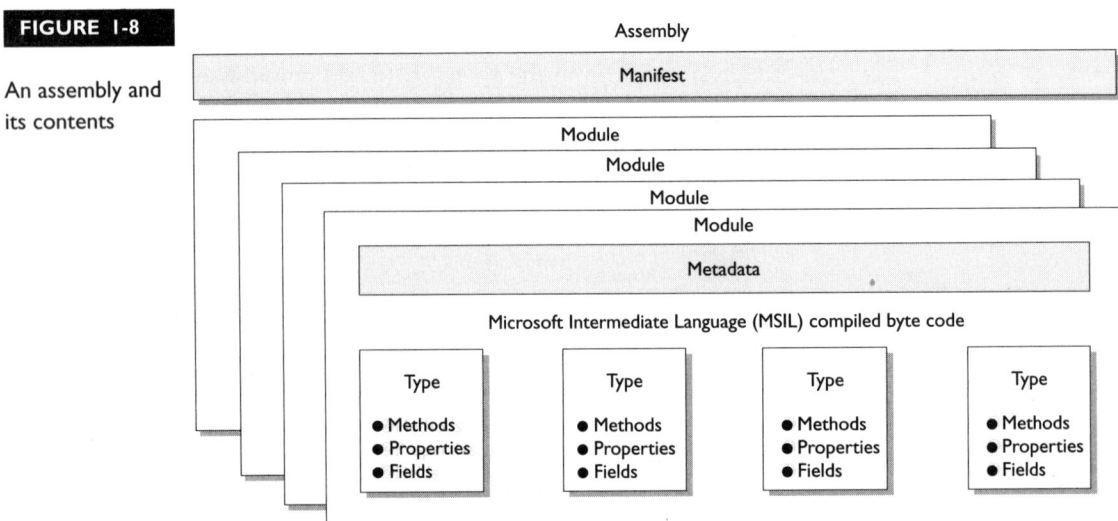

FIGURE 1-8

An assembly and its contents

The assembly is the file that is stored on the disk; as part of that file, the metadata defines all the aspects of the assembly. The manifest is the part of the metadata that defines the assembly and its properties. The assembly can be stored as either a `.dll` (dynamic link library) or an `.exe` (Portable Executable—PE) file. The PE file contains metadata, as do all assemblies; so when you compile your application to an .exe file, you create an assembly.

CERTIFICATION OBJECTIVE 1.05

.NET Component Models

With the creation of the .NET Framework and the move away from the Registry-based metadata storage that was used in the COM and DCOM environments, there are new component models available for us when you build distributed environments. The 70-310 Developing XML Web Services and Server Components with Microsoft Visual Basic .NET and the Visual Studio .NET Framework exam is centered around the design and implementation of the four component models that are part of the .NET Framework. The models are

- **Windows Services** This topic deals with how to write and implement services that will run when the operating system starts, rather than when a user starts the program. The Windows Services are the topic of Chapter 2.

- **Windows-Serviced Components** Here you interact with the COM+ world that continues to be the distributed environment most common in the Microsoft Windows environment. In Chapter 3, you will see how to create .NET assemblies that are callable from any COM component, as well as how to call COM components from our Visual Basic .NET applications.

- **.NET Remoting Objects** This is a very interesting subject—you will build .NET components that are called remotely using a large variety of communications protocols and data packet formatters. Some of the technology you will meet in Chapter 4 deals with the SOAP protocol. The Remoting objects also need to work in an asynchronous manner so that the caller can continue to work while the called object performs the task.

- **XML Web Services** XML Web Services, the component model that this exam is named from, will be covered in Chapter 5. We'll also explore how they can be used to build a truly distributed environment where software components are made available through the web servers using standard communications and web protocols.

That ends our whirlwind tour of the .NET Framework and Visual Basic .NET. The next chapter will focus on the Windows Services and how you can build and secure them.

FROM THE CLASSROOM

It has been my experience that when I teach Object-Oriented Analysis and Design to programmers, there is always this feeling of disbelief when they learn that they are going to design an application without writing any code, and that they will actually not use any computers in the class; but by the end of day three; everyone is very comfortable with the concept that you model the solution to a business problem using real-world objects that you have validated against the real problem domain.

Building any application without performing an OOAD session will impact the lifespan of the application, as the maintenance usually becomes so laborious that the application is rewritten, making the application more expensive in the long run.

Using OOAD to build the object model before any coding takes place is imperative if you want to be able to easily maintain and grow the application.

The implementation of an object model becomes a mechanical task when the model is optimized—and in reality, the computer language has very little impact, as long as it is object oriented like Visual Basic .NET.

SCENARIO & SOLUTION

How do I override methods?	To declare overridden methods, the signature must be the same for the two methods and the original must be declared with the Overridable keyword, while the overridden method must be marked with the Overrides keyword.
How do I install an assembly that is shared between many applications on the computer?	Assemblies must be installed in the Global Assembly Cache (GAC) to be shareable.
How do I provide for error handling in my Visual Basic .NET program?	The error handling technique used in the .NET languages is the Try/Catch/Finally construction, where the code between Try and Catch is executed, and if an exception (Error) occurs, execution is transferred to the appropriate Catch block that matches the exception. If there is an optional Finally block, the code in that block will always be executed.

How do I declare that one class is derived from another class?	Inheritance means that one class is derived from a base class; to declare that derivation, the child class declaration uses the Inherits keyword as in this code segment:
	
	`Public Class Child`
	`    Inherits BaseClass`

How do I overload methods?	Overloaded methods are methods with the same name but with a different signature (list of parameters); to declare the overloaded method, you need to declare the method with a different number of parameters, or different data-type parameters.

CERTIFICATION SUMMARY

Although this chapter has no direct exam-related information, you will find that the information here is used in almost every question in the exam. You will see questions that give you the class definition of some class, including exception handling and other new techniques. A question will be focused on one item in the code, but if you are not familiar with the Visual Basic .NET language, this exam will be very hard.

The things to remember are related to the object-oriented aspects of Visual Basic .NET and how to implement an OO design. Unfortunately, I cannot create a book with all the needed information on the language, so you will need to build your experience in programming with the language—this book will give you the knowledge about the .NET Framework that the exam is all about.

✓ TWO-MINUTE DRILL

❏ Visual Basic .NET data types are aliases for the data types defined in the Common Type System.

❏ Inheritance is when the relationship between two objects *is a.*

❏ Containment is the relationship that is expressed as *has a.*

❏ The signature of a method is based on the name of the method and the number and data types of the parameters. The return data type is not part of the signature.

❏ Overloading is when the same method name is redefined using a different signature (different parameter data types).

❏ Overriding is when the same method with the identical signature is redefined.

❏ Polymorphism is late binding, when you do not know the object until run time.

❏ The `Finally` block will always execute in a `Try/Catch/Finally` structure.

❏ All compiler output is packaged in assemblies.

❏ The assembly contains the manifest, which describes the assembly including the version of the assembly.

❏ The executable file (`.exe`) is stared in the Portable Executable (PE) format that is an assembly.

❏ Local copies of assemblies are not shareable.

❏ Sharable assemblies are stored in the Global Assembly Cache (GAC).

SELF TEST

1. You are developing an XML Web Service that will provide stock quotes to a large number of users located over all continents. You have found that the connection to your database that holds the data fails from time to time, resulting in some clients' connections hanging and in forcing the client to restart the connection.

   You write the following code segment to connect to the database to solve the problem:

   ```
   Public Sub DBCon(ConStr As String)
    ' Connect to the database
    Try
    ' Perform the connection here
    ...
    Catch e As DivideByZeroException
    ' Clean up from the connection failure and inform the client
    System.Console.Writeline("There was a problem connecting to the Database")
    End Try
    ...
   End Sub
   ```

   After you implement this change, your clients still report that their connections hang when there is a problem with the database connection. You must solve the problem in the most efficient manner. What will your approach be?

   A. Add a `Finally` block after the `Catch` statement to ensure the connection does not hang.

   B. Remove the match condition from the `Catch` statement.

   C. Add a second `Catch` statement as follows:

   ```
   Catch e As DbExceptions
   ```

   D. Rewrite the error handler by using the ON ERROR GOTO syntax.

2. You are developing a class model consisting of two classes—`Base` and `Child`. The class `Base` is declared as follows:

   ```
   Public Class Base
   Private x As Integer
    Public Overridable Function WhatX() As Integer
    Return X
    End Function
   End Class
   ```

   The code for the `Child` class is as follows:

   ```
   Public Class Child
    Inherits Base
    Public Overrides Function WhatX() As Integer
   ```

```
Return X * 3.14159
End Function
End Class
```

What is the result when you try to compile and run your classes?

A. Error at compile time "error BC30390: 'Base.x' is not accessible in this context because it is 'Private'."

B. Error at run time, the variable X is not visible from the WhatX function in the `Child` class.

C. Error at compile time, the syntax for the overridden function is wrong.

D. Success, no errors.

3. You are experimenting with the exception handling in Visual Basic .NET. As part of your learning experience, you analyze the following code that a coworker gave to you:

```
Public Sub TryTest(x As Integer, y As Integer)
  Try
  System.Console.Writeline(x\y)
  Catch e as System.DivideByZeroException
  System.Console.Writeline("You can not divide by zero, sorry")
  Finally
  System.Console.Writeline("Try again")
  End Try
End Sub
```

You test the `TryTest()` method by executing the following two calls to it:

```
TryTest(336, 8)
TryTest(336, 0)
```

What will the resulting output be?

A. 42
    You cannot divide by zero, sorry.

B. Try again.
    You cannot divide by zero, sorry.
    Try again.

C. 42
    Try again.
    Try again.

D. 42
    Try again.
    You cannot divide by zero, sorry.
    Try again.

4. You are a Visual Basic .NET developer that delivered version 1.0 of an assembly to be deployed by the software maintenance group. The assembly was successfully deployed to the GAC of the four servers that required the assembly. It is now three weeks later, and you have found that you need to deploy a new version 2.0 of the assembly. This must be done without affecting the current applications that can work only with the current version 1.0 that is installed in the GAC. How would you deploy the assembly?

A. Copy the assembly to the /bin directory of all the applications.

B. Deploy in the GAC.

C. Deploy in the GAC and change the Registry to reflect the two versions.

D. Deploy in the GAC using an alias for the version 2.0 assembly.

5. You are a Visual Basic .NET Developer, and your manager has just returned from a conference where she learned about the .NET Framework. Now your manager has asked you to further explain what MSIL is, and what it is used for. How will you explain MSIL?

A. The MSIL is the language of the Common Language Runtime—it is the language that the .NET compilers produce as their output. Because MSIL is portable, you can have platform-independent applications.

B. The MSIL is the assembly language the assemblies are written in. Because MSIL is tied directly to the Intel Pentium platform, it can be optimized for use on all Windows computers.

C. The MSIL is the internal language that defines the Common Type System. Because MSIL is portable, the CTS is a platform-independent system.

D. The MSIL is the language used to define resources such as forms; it is used only inside of Visual Studio .NET.

6. You are a Visual Basic .NET developer, and you are working on a database application that needs to access data that is stored in both Microsoft SQL Server databases and DB/2 databases. You need to select the best technology to connect to these databases. What technology can be used to perform the connections from a Visual Basic .NET application? Select all that apply:

A. VBSql

B. ADO

C. ADO.NET

D. ASP.NET

7. You are a Visual Basic .NET developer, and your current task is to develop a class that will encapsulate a string. The string can be created by calling the `MakeString()` method. You need to create a version of the `MakeString()` method that will take an Integer, a Double, a String, or a Boolean as the parameter. Which of the following signatures will build that solution? Select all that apply; each answer makes up a part of the total answer:

A. `Public Overridable MakeString(x As Integer)`
   `Public Overrides MakeString(x As Double)`

B. `Public Shared MakeString(x As String)`
   `Public Shared MakeString(x As Boolean)`

C. `Public MakeString(x As String)`
   `Public MakeString(x As Boolean)`

D. `Public Shared MakeString(x As Integer)`
   `Public Shared MakeString(x As Double)`

E. `Public MakeString(x As Integer)`
   `Public MakeString(x As Double)`

F. `Public Overrides MakeString(x As String)`
   `Public Overrides MakeString(x As Boolean)`

8. You are reviewing the design plan for an application. You notice that the designer suggests using polymorphism to be able to solve one of the challenges in the application. You want to use a different word to describe polymorphism. Select the correct term:

   A. Late binding

   B. Early binding

   C. Data binding

   D. Parameter binding

9. You are a Visual Basic .NET developer, and you have developed the exception-handling routine for the `TryTest()` method, as can be seen in the following code segment:

```
Public Sub TryTest(x As Integer, y As Integer)
 Try
 System.Console.Writeline(x\y)
 Catch
 System.Console.Writeline("You have an error")
 Catch e as System.DivideByZeroException
 System.Console.Writeline("You can not divide by zero, sorry")
 Finally
 System.Console.Writeline("Try again")
 End Try
End Sub
```

You issue the following call to test the error handling:

```
TryTest(42, 0)
```

What is the output from the call? Select all that apply; each answer makes up a part of the final answer:

A. 42

B. You cannot divide by zero, sorry

C. Try again

D. You have an error

10. True or False? Shared assemblies must be signed with a strong name.

A. True

B. False

SELF TEST ANSWERS

1. ☑   **B.** The match statement is used to specify what type of exception the `Catch` block will be responsible for. In the sample code, the `Catch` statement matches the `DivideByZero Exception`. The `DivideByZeroException` is not related with the database connection. The most efficient way to solve the problem is to remove the filter, thus making the `Catch` statement match all exceptions.

    ☒   **A, C, and D.** Answer **A** is incorrect because the `Finally` block will always be executed and would not be the right place to determine the outcome of the connection attempt. Answer **C** is incorrect because, although the catch match was set to the connection exception that might be raised, there is no indication that `DbException` is that exception; actually, there is no such exception. Answer **D** is incorrect because that would be a very inefficient way of solving the problem, plus the ON ERROR GOTO syntax is legacy VB 6 syntax.

2. ☑   **A.** Because the variable `Base.X` is scoped to be Private, the compiler will report the error.

    ☒   **B, C, and D.** Answer **B** is incorrect because the classes will not compile as written. Answer **C** is incorrect because the syntax for the overridden function is correct. Answer **D** is incorrect because there is a problem at compile time.

3. ☑   **D.** The first call to `TryTest` will result in the correct answer, 42, followed by the `Finally` block printing "Try again." The second call to `TryTest` results in the `Catch` block being executed followed by the `Finally` block.

    ☒   **A, B, and C.** Answer **A** is incorrect, because the `Finally` block will execute for each call to `TryTest`. Answer **B** is incorrect because the first call prints out the result 42. **C** is incorrect because the attempted division by zero will throw an exception that the `Catch` block will handle.

4. ☑   **B.** Because the assembly contains its own manifest that contain the version information, as do all modules in the assembly, there can be many versions of the same assembly in the GAC at the same time. The applications that need a specific version can request that version from the GAC.

    ☒   **A, C, and D. A** is incorrect, because copying the assembly to the /bin directory of all the applications will in effect make that assembly the one that the applications will try to work with, resulting in problems for the applications that require version 1.0, which is in the GAC. Answer **C** is incorrect, since there is no need to update the Registry, and even so the assemblies have their own metadata storage. Answer **D** is incorrect because there is no alias for assemblies in the GAC.

5. ☑ **A.** The MSIL (Microsoft Intermediate Language) is the language of the Common Language Runtime—it is the language that all .NET compilers produce; and because MSIL is used only by the CLR, it is one of the reasons you can build platform-independent applications.

   ☒ **B, C,** and **D.** Answer **B** is incorrect because the MSIL is not the assembly language of the assemblies, it is the language of the CLR, and MSIL is not related to the Intel platform. Answer **C** is incorrect because the CTS is described in the CLR and not by MSIL, and the CTS does not make the system platform independent. Answer **C** is incorrect because the MSIL is not the language used to define resources.

6. ☑ **C.** The current version of the Microsoft ActiveX Data Objects (ADO.NET) is the technology that is used in the .NET environment to connect to all data sources.

   ☒ **A, B,** and **D.** Answer **A** is incorrect because VBSql was an older technology used in earlier Visual Basic versions. Answer **B** is incorrect because ADO is the connectivity that would be used in VB 6 applications. Answer **D** is incorrect because ASP.NET is the package for building Web applications.

7. ☑ **C** and **E.** The answer to the question is overloading; to overload methods, the signature must be different, the parameter lists must have different numbers of parameters, and the data types must be different.

   ☒ **A, B, D,** and **F.** Answers **A** and **F** are incorrect because overriding replaces one method with another, but the signature must be the same. Answers **B** and **D** are incorrect because a Shared method is static to the class, and that will not solve the problem.

8. ☑ **A.** Late binding is the implementation of polymorphism. Late binding the application will resolve the data type of the object at run time.

   ☒ **B, C,** and **D.** Answer **B** is incorrect because with early binding the data type is known at design time and cannot change after. Answer **C** is incorrect because data binding refers to one of the technologies used in Rapid Application Development (RAD). Answer **D** is also incorrect because parameter binding does not exist.

9. ☑ **C** and **D.** Because the first `Catch` statement will catch all exceptions, **D** will be printed followed by the output **C** from the `Finally` statement.

   ☒ **A** and **B.** Answer **A** is incorrect because the division by zero will not return a calculated value. Answer **B** is also incorrect because the `Catch` block that has the match for the `DivideByZeroException` will never be reached.

10. ☑ **A.** This statement is true. For security reasons, every shared assembly must be signed with a strong name.

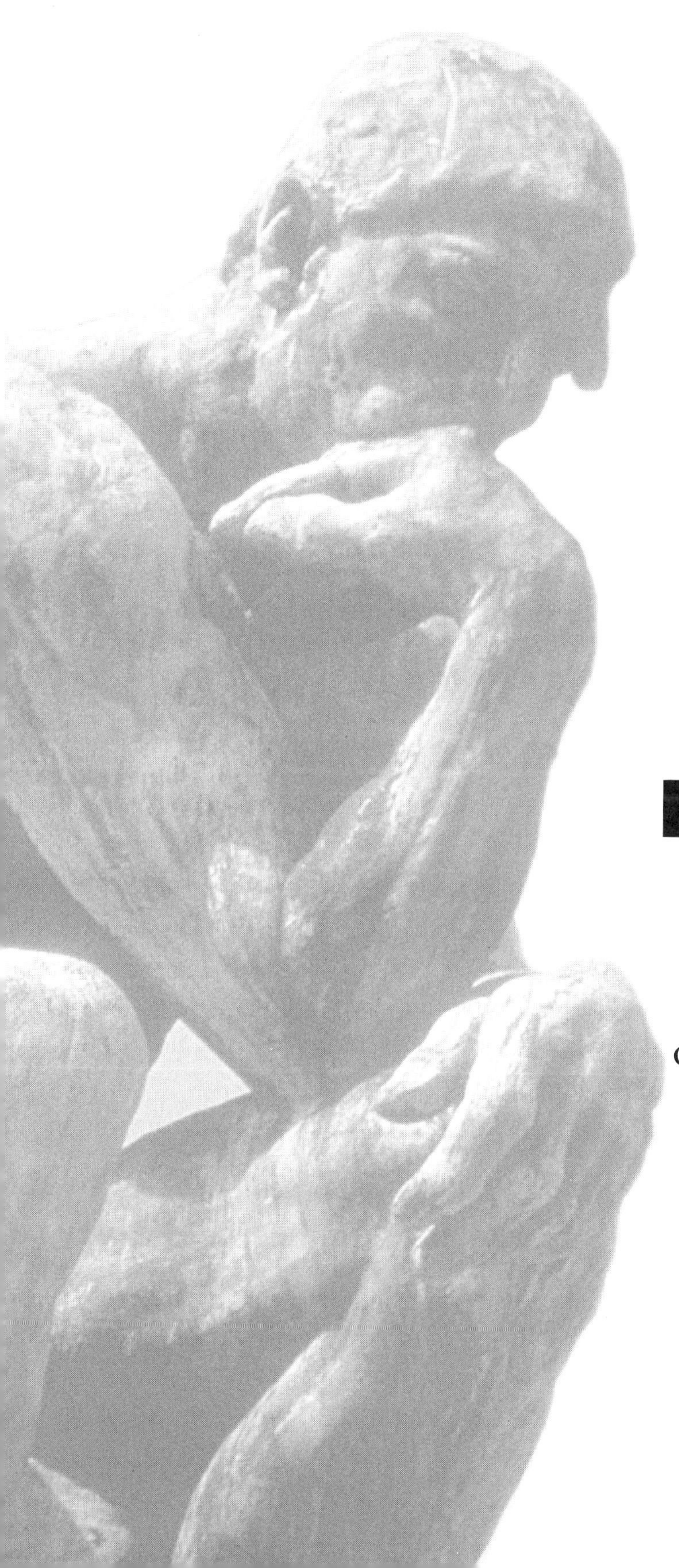

MCAD/MCSD

MICROSOFT® CERTIFIED APPLICATION DEVELOPER & MICROSOFT® CERTIFIED SOLUTION DEVELOPER

2

Developing a Windows Service

CERTIFICATION OBJECTIVES

2.01	Windows Services Technology
2.02	Develop a Windows Service
2.03	Windows Services Architecture
✓	Two-Minute Drill
Q&A	Self Test

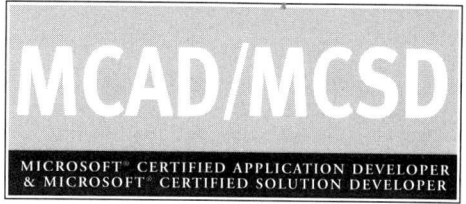

In this chapter, you will learn about the Windows Services, previously known as NT Services. A Windows service is any application that needs to execute for long periods of time in its own session on a server. A Windows service starts without any intervention from a user when the server's operating system boots, and it can authenticate using either the local SYSTEM account or a domain user's account; in this way, the Windows service can use the security context that best fits its purpose. The Windows Services also include software applications that have no interaction with the screen on the server where they are executed, such as an e-mail service or a web service.

Note that at this time, support for Windows developing Services is available only in the Enterprise Edition. Support is not available in the Standard Edition of Visual Studio .NET. The examples in this chapter are written using the Enterprise Edition of Visual Studio .NET.

Windows Services Technology

The Windows Services technology is one of the important building blocks that you will use when building applications that must always run on the server, and that perform services for many users. Examples of Windows services are applications such as Internet Information Services (IIS), the Tardis clock service, and Microsoft Simple Mail Transport Protocol (SMTP). These services all run in the background, perform services for potentially many users or systems, and have no user interface. Windows services are managed through management applications that are specifically written to interact with them, or you can use the Services application that is available from the operating system.

I have used the term "server" to refer to the computer where a Windows service is running, but that is not the whole story. The Windows NT and Windows 2000 families of operating systems, as well as Windows XP Professional, all can run Windows Services. However, Windows 9x, Windows Me, and Windows XP Home edition do not have the ability to run the Windows Services as part of the operating system. In these operating systems, a Windows service is executed as a user process that requires a user to be logged on to the computer.

e x a m
ⓦ a t c h

Windows services are used to extend the operating system; they are similar to daemons in Unix.

Take a look at the Services application and what you can control in the services running on a server. If you are running Windows 2000 or Windows XP Professional, you access the Services application from the Run | Programs | Administrative Tools menu. If the Administrative Tools menu is missing in your Windows 2000 or XP Professional operating system, you will need to make it available by selecting Run | Settings | Task Bar & Start Menu.

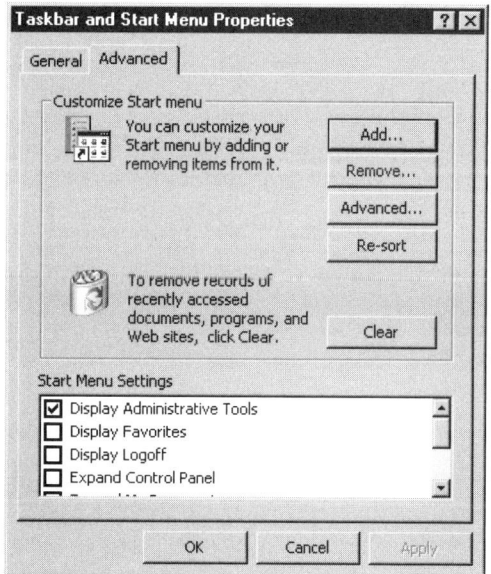

After you select Services in the Administrative Tools menu (shown in the following illustration), you will see a list of services that are installed on your server along with the current status of each service (shown in Figure 2-1),

FIGURE 2-1 The Services application

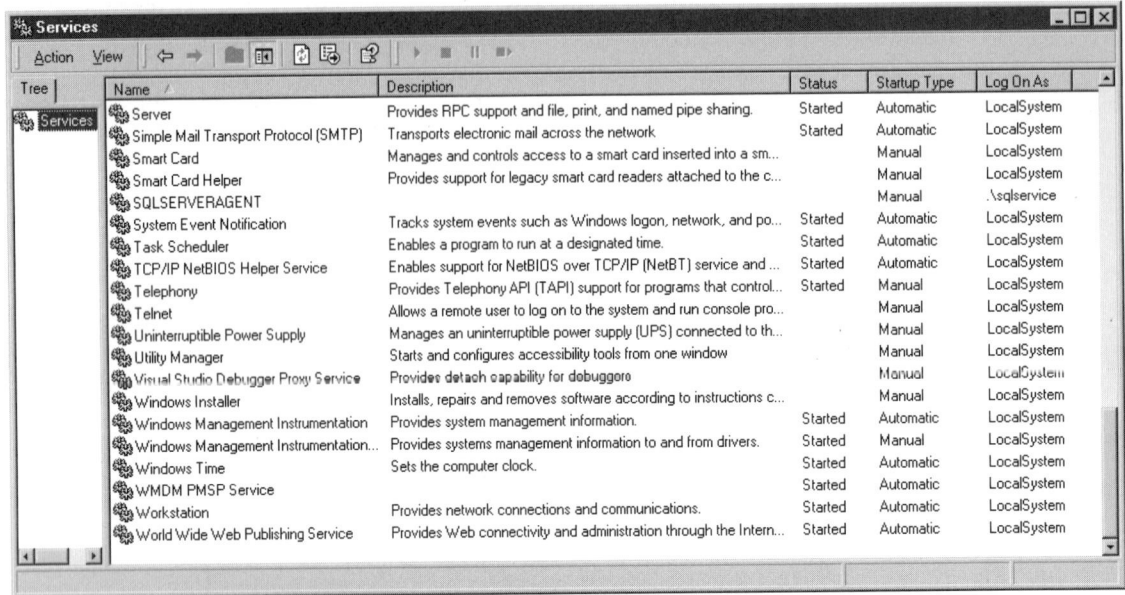

indicating whether it is stopped, paused, running, or disabled. You can also see (from the startup type) if the service will automatically start with the operating system, or if it must be manually started.

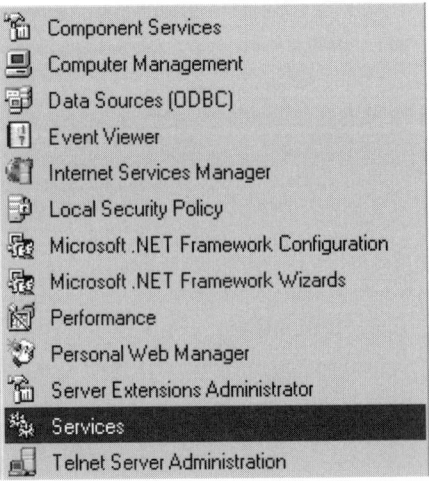

The listing of Windows Services is all-inclusive, meaning that all the known information about each service is displayed in the Services application. Further, the

Description field is sometimes very long and contains the long form of the service's name. In order to control the properties of a Windows service, you double-click the service in the Services application. Here, you can see the properties of the World Wide Web Publishing service, which is the name of the web server part of IIS:

As you can see, the properties that can be set on the General tab include the display name of the service as well as the description. You can also set the `startup` property to inform the operating system what type of startup you wish to have. The options are

- **Automatic** The service will be started as part of the operating system's boot sequence.
- **Manual** The service is enabled and will be started by the administrator (or by another service that requires it) when needed.
- **Disabled** The service will never be started unless the `startup` property is changed.

on the Job *Set a service to Disabled if you want to be sure that it never starts automatically, but set it to Manual if you want the service to start if another service depends on it.*

In the Service Status area, you will see the current state of the service as well as the controls to Start, Pause, Stop, or Resume the service. The Start Parameters field is used to pass parameters to the service when it starts.

The Log On pane defines the account that will be used by the service to establish a security context. This service is not started when a user logs in to the server; rather, the service must authenticate to the server in order to get access to resources like memory, the processor, and the network. The default security account is the local SYSTEM account, which is the highest-permission account on any Windows server. Using the SYSTEM account is a very good idea as long as the service does not have to access resources over the network. Because the SYSTEM account has such powerful permissions, it is limited to the local system only, meaning that a service cannot access any remote resources using it. If the service requires access to remote resources, you should use a domain user's account to start the service. You can also associate the service with a specific hardware profile if specific settings are needed for the service.

exam
ⓌatcH

If the Windows service needs to access remote resources, you need to associate it with a user account because the SYSTEM account cannot be used to access remote resources.

The Recovery pane gives you control over what action to take if the service fails. The settings are for the first and second failures as well as any subsequent failures.

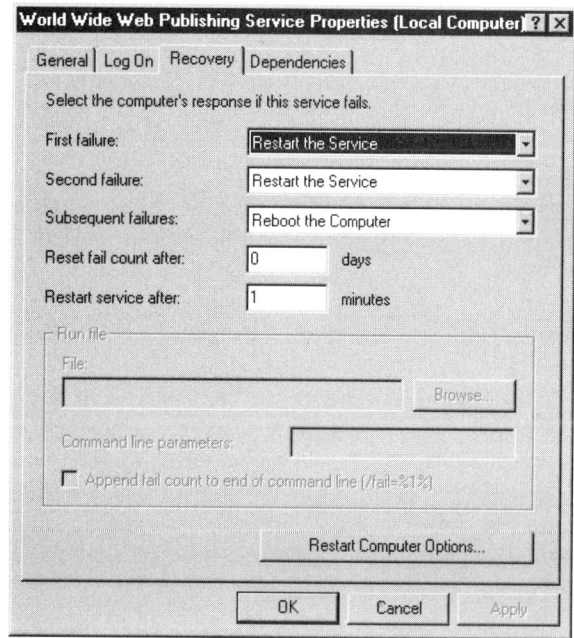

The Dependencies pane enables you to view the services that depend on your services as well as the services your service depends on. The system checks dependencies to make sure your service doesn't start unless some other service has started first.

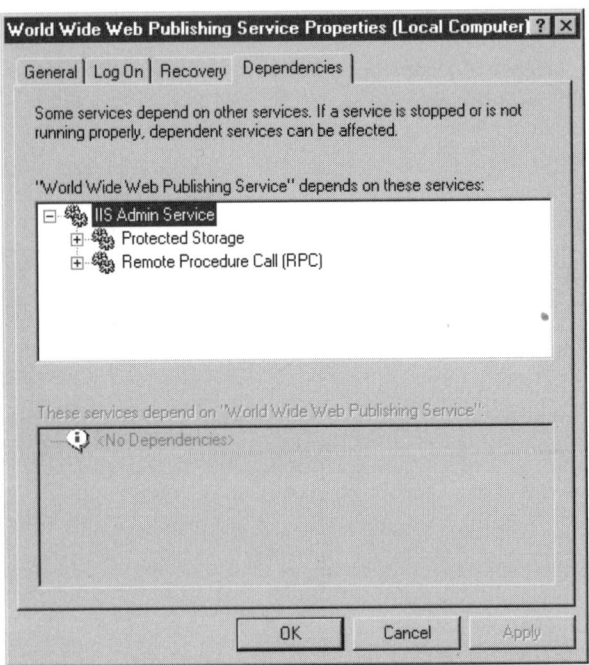

FROM THE CLASSROOM

When you start building Windows services, the first question that usually pops up is this: What can you use service for? The answer is actually simple—anything!

Okay, I hear you, that is an unfair answer, but it is true. Some of the most exciting aspects of the Windows operating system have been implemented as Windows services. For example, IIS is implemented as a service, as is Microsoft SQL Server and Microsoft Exchange Server. These are large and powerful applications, but they are implemented as services so that they can act together with the operating system, with no user intervention at all.

I usually recommend to my students that they begin by building services that perform some small but interesting service for them. The following are some Windows services that have been built in just a week's time: a time server that synchronizes the computer with a Network Time Protocol (NTP) server, a card deck service that returns a random card, a simple web server...the list goes on.

Use the information in this chapter to build software that moves you and your projects forward.

The majority of these settings are controlled through the installation process. I will spend more time on this topic later in this chapter.

Now that you have seen the Services application, proceed to build a small service to look at the mechanics of building and installing a service.

CERTIFICATION OBJECTIVE 2.02

Developing a Windows Service

In this section, you are going to build a Windows service that logs messages in the event log as its only function. We'll set this limitation for now so that you can look at the different aspects of the service. In order to build a Windows service, you will need to have a minimum of the Professional Edition of Visual Basic .NET (the Standard Edition does not support Windows Services development).

EXERCISE 2-1

The Windows Service Skeleton

1. Create a new project in Visual Studio .NET. Make it a Visual Basic .NET project and select Windows Service from the Template list as shown here. Give the project the name **ServiceOne** and save it to the C:\VB directory.

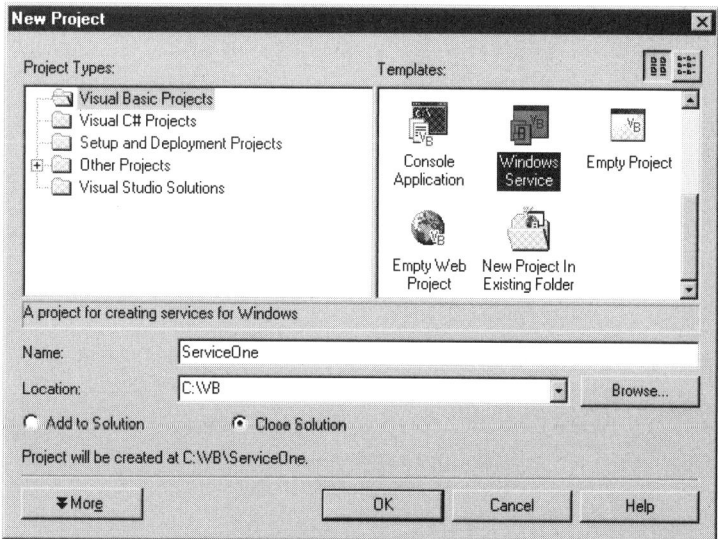

2. Once the project is created, you should change the name of the Windows service to the name you have decided on, in our case, ServiceOne. To change the name, select the service in the Property Explorer and change the (name) and `ServiceName` properties as shown here:

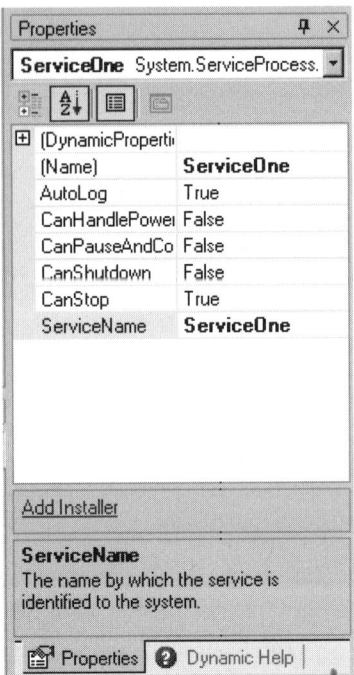

3. Right-click the project in the Solution Explorer and select Properties in the context menu. In the Project Properties dialog, change the Startup Object to ServiceOne and click OK. This step tells the compiler what class contains the startup code; if you don't change this property, the project will not compile but will report a missing `Sub Main()`.

4. Click "click here to switch to code view" in Design view to open the code module.

> To add components to your class, drag them from the Server Explorer or Toolbox and use the Properties window to set their properties. To create methods and events for your class, click here to switch to code view.

Note that as you changed the name of the Windows service, Visual Studio .NET adjusted the names in the source code.

5. The code that was created by the Windows Service Wizard is shown in the following code listing:

```
Imports System.ServiceProcess

Public Class ServiceOne
    Inherits System.ServiceProcess.ServiceBase

#Region " Component Designer generated code "

    Public Sub New()
        MyBase.New()
        ' This call is required by the Component Designer.
        InitializeComponent()
        ' Add any initialization after the InitializeComponent() call
    End Sub

    'UserService overrides dispose to clean up the component list.
    Protected Overloads Overrides Sub Dispose(ByVal disposing As Boolean)
        If disposing Then
            If Not (components Is Nothing) Then
                components.Dispose()
            End If
        End If
        MyBase.Dispose(disposing)
    End Sub

    ' The main entry point for the process
    <MTAThread()> _
    Shared Sub Main()
        Dim ServicesToRun() As System.ServiceProcess.ServiceBase

        ' More than one NT Service may run within the same process. To add
        ' another service to this process, change the following line to
        ' create a second service object. For example,
        '
        '   ServicesToRun = New System.ServiceProcess.ServiceBase () _
        '   {New Service1, New MySecondUserService}
        '
        ServicesToRun = New System.ServiceProcess.ServiceBase()
                    {
                        New ServiceOne()
                    }
        System.ServiceProcess.ServiceBase.Run(ServicesToRun)
    End Sub

    'Required by the Component Designer
    Private components As System.ComponentModel.IContainer

    ' NOTE: The following procedure is required by the Component Designer
    ' It can be modified using the Component Designer.
    ' Do not modity it using the code editor.
    <System.Diagnostics.DebuggerStepThrough()> _
```

```
       Private Sub InitializeComponent()
        '
        'ServiceOne
        '
        Me.ServiceName = "ServiceOne"
    End Sub
#End Region

       Protected Overrides Sub OnStart(ByVal args() As String)
          ' Add code here to start your service. This method should set things
          ' in motion so your service can do its work.
       End Sub

       Protected Overrides Sub OnStop()
          ' Add code here to perform any tear-down necessary to stop
          ' your service.
       End Sub

    End Class
```

The bolded text in the preceding listing is the one area that needs to be modified after the service is constructed by Visual Studio .NET. You will need to make sure that the object that is instantiated is the class you are building—the Visual Studio .NET editor does not correctly update the name when you change the name of the class.

on the job

Visual Studio .NET does not change the class name that is instantiated in the `Main()` *method.*

You are going to give this service some low-level functionality that will record events in an event log. The Windows service has predefined events that you want to write code for: service start, stop, and pause, among others. We'll discuss events in greater detail later in the chapter. For now, notice that these events are points in the life of the Windows service, and the Windows service code that is generated by Visual Studio .NET includes the handlers for two of those three events: `OnStart()` and `OnStop()`. You will write code in these event handlers so that you can see how the service operates.

6. The first thing you must do before you can start writing information into the event log is to make sure that there is an event log and to connect to it. To do this, switch to the Design view of the Windows service and open up the Toolbox, then select the Components tab in the Toolbox. Drag and drop the EventLog component on to the Windows Service Design window, where it will be called EventLog1. The result is shown next.

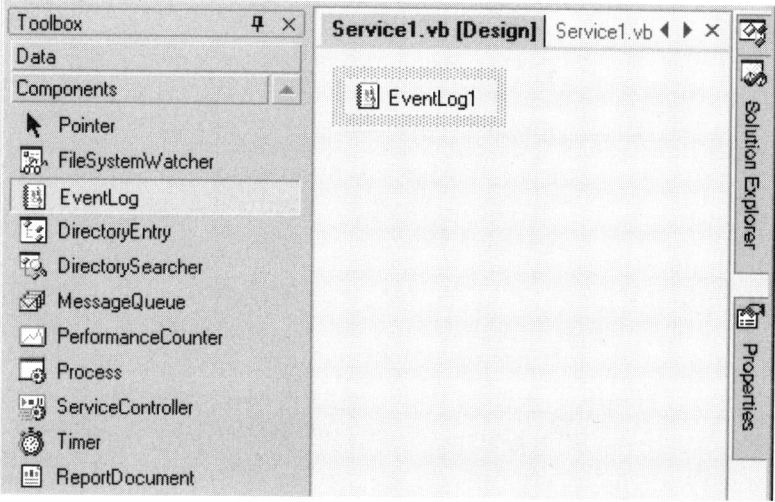

7. The logical place to add code that will control the use of the event log you added to the project is in the constructor of the Windows service class; this way, the event log is configured for use as soon as the service starts. The following code segment shows how to open an event log:

```
Public Sub New()
    MyBase.New()
    ' This call is required by the Component Designer.
    InitializeComponent()
    ' Add any initialization after the InitializeComponent() call
    ' Test if the event log exists; if not, create it
    If (Not System.Diagnostics.EventLog.SourceExists_
    ("ServiceOne")) Then_
        EventLog.CreateEventSource("ServiceOne", "ServiceOneLog")
    End If
    ' Set the source and log properties for the event log
    EventLog1.Source = "ServiceOne"
    EventLog1.Log = "ServiceOneLog"
End Sub
```

The event log is exposed to our Windows service through the System.Diagnostics namespace. By verifying that the event log exists and creating it if it does not, you are guaranteed that, when you associate the EventLog1 component that was added to the service with our event log, the log will be there.

8. Now you will add code to the `OnStart()` event handler to write an event to the event log. The following code segment shows how to do this:

```
Protected Overrides Sub OnStart(ByVal args() As String)
' Add code here to start your service. This method should set things
' in motion so your service can do its
work.    EventLog1.WriteEntry("ServiceOne is starting")
End Sub
```

9. Add the following to the `OnStop()` method:

```
    Protected Overrides Sub OnStop()
        ' Add code here to perform any tear-down
        ' necessary to stop your service.
EventLog1.WriteEntry("ServiceOne is stopping")    End Sub
```

10. Build the Windows service to make sure it compiles by selecting Build Solution from the Build menu. The Windows service cannot be run directly from Visual Studio .NET but needs to be registered in the Windows Registry and started by the Service Manager. If you try to run it directly, the message shown here is the result:

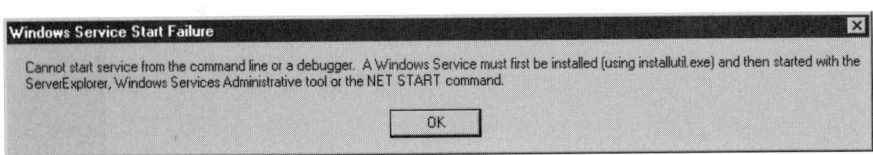

The solution is to include an Installer project with the Windows service project.

11. To add the Installer: switch to the Design view, right-click the background, and select Add Installer from the context menu as shown next:

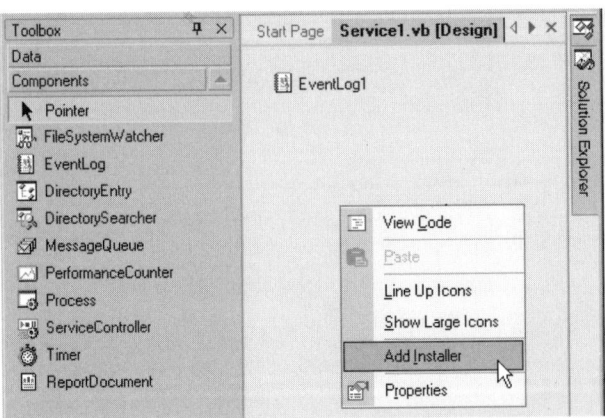

The result is shown in the following illustration, where you can see the Design view of the new ProjectInstaller.vb file. You will notice that there are two instances of the ProjectInstaller class: first the ServiceInstaller1 that will install our Windows service and then the ServiceProcessInstaller1 that is used to install the Windows service's associated process.

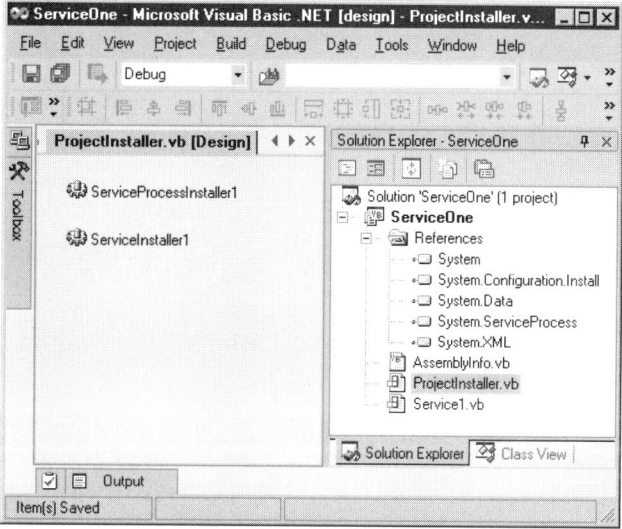

12. Change the name of the ServiceInstaller1 component to **ServiceOneInstaller**.

13. Verify that the StartType property is set to Automatic.

14. Right-click the ServiceOne project in the Solution Explorer and click Properties in the context menu.

15. Verify that ServiceOne is selected as the startup object on the General screen.

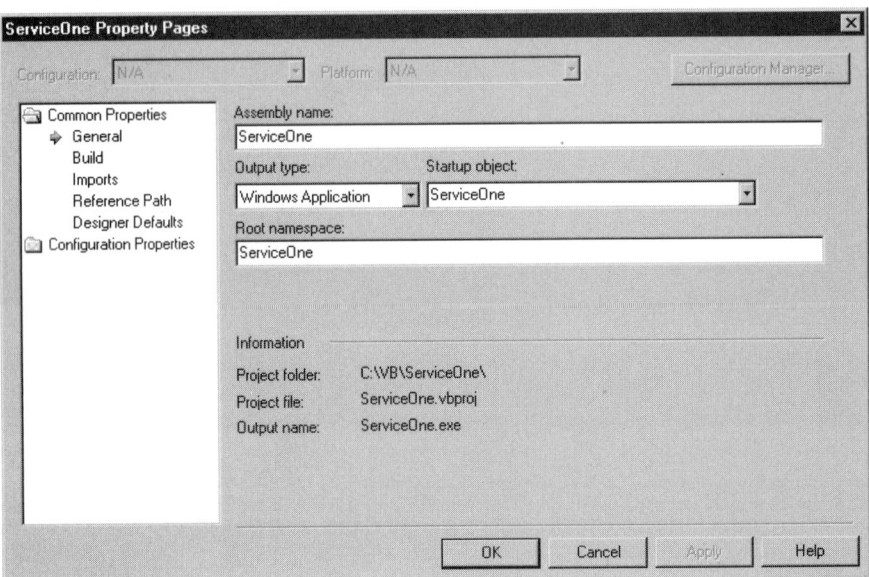

16. Build the project. Now you have the Windows service built to the point that it is ready to be installed. The installation on a server is performed by creating a Setup project. This Setup project will register the Windows service with the Windows Registry to make it runnable.

17. To do this, you will add a Setup and Deployment project to the solution by selecting Add Project | New Project from the File menu.

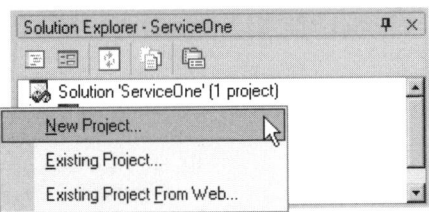

18. In the Add New Project dialog, select Setup And Deployment Projects from the Project Types list, and select Setup Project from the Templates list.

19. Name the Project **ServiceOneSetup**. Click OK.

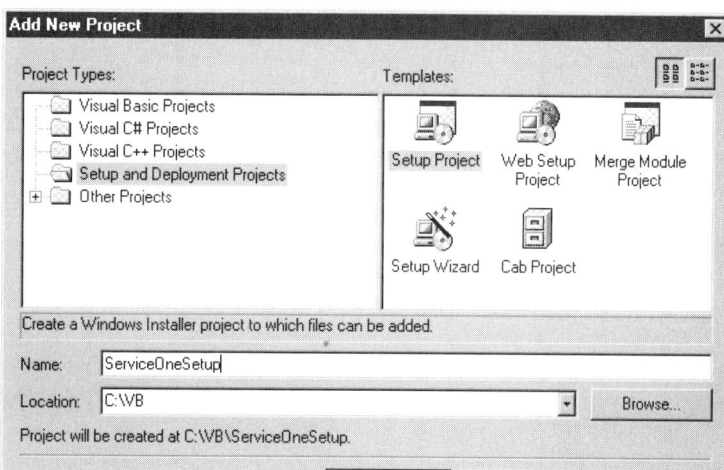

The resulting solution is shown next:

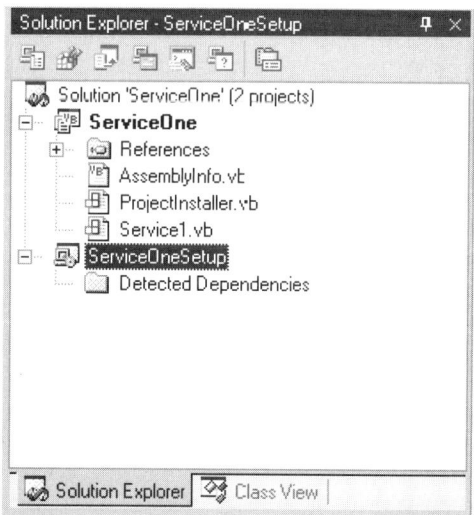

20. Right-click the ServiceOneSetup project and select Add | Project Output from the context menu. This step will provide the information for the installation process.

21. The Add Project Output Group dialog box is displayed. Verify that the ServiceOne Windows service is selected in the Project control and that Primary Output is selected. Click OK.

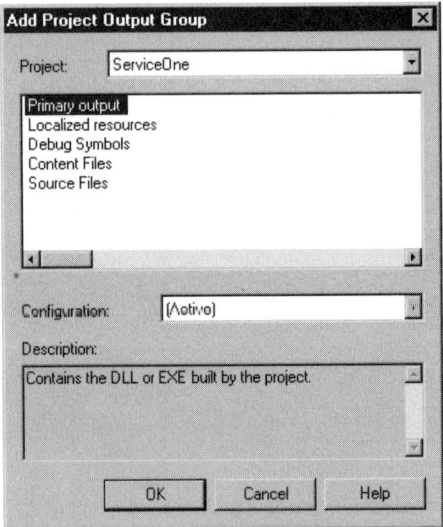

22. Now you need to add the directions that will install the Windows service. Right-click the ServiceOneSetup project in the Solution Explorer and select View | Custom Actions from the context menu as shown here:

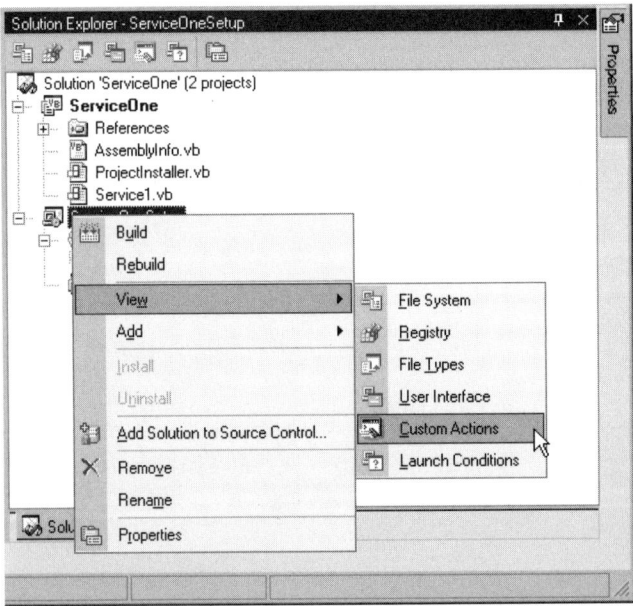

23. The Custom Actions editor is displayed.

24. Right-click Custom Actions in the Custom Action editor. Select Add Custom Action... from the context menu to open the dialog to select the items in the project.

25. Select and double-click the Applications Folder in the Look In: combo control.

26. Select Primary Output From ServiceOne (Active). Click OK.

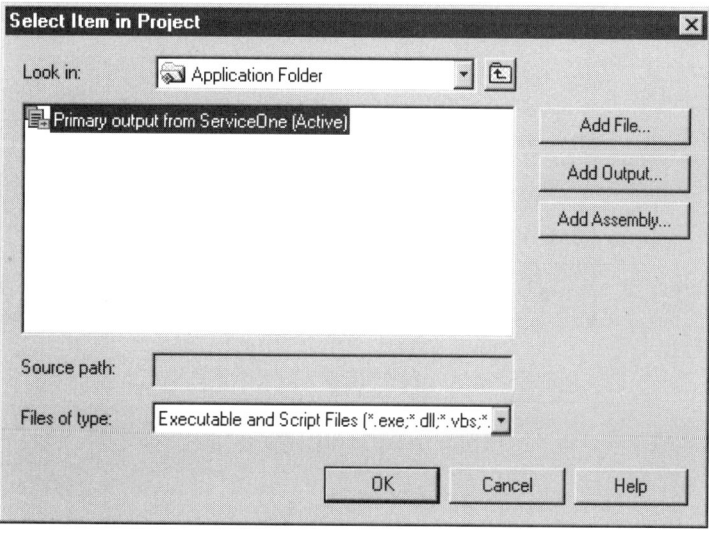

27. The output is now added to the four nodes of the Custom Actions editor.

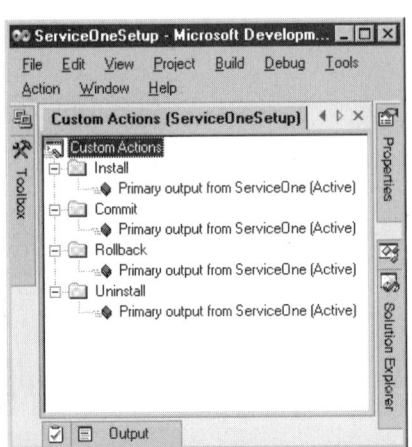

28. Build the solution by right-clicking the ServiceOneSetup project in the Solution Explorer and clicking Build in the context menu, and then exit from Visual Studio .NET. The next steps are performed outside of the development environment from the Windows user interface.

29. Open My Computer from the Desktop and navigate to the C:\VB\ ServiceOneSetup\Debug\ServiceOneSetup.msi file. Launch the ServiceOneSetup.msi program by double-clicking the file. The Installation Wizard starts.

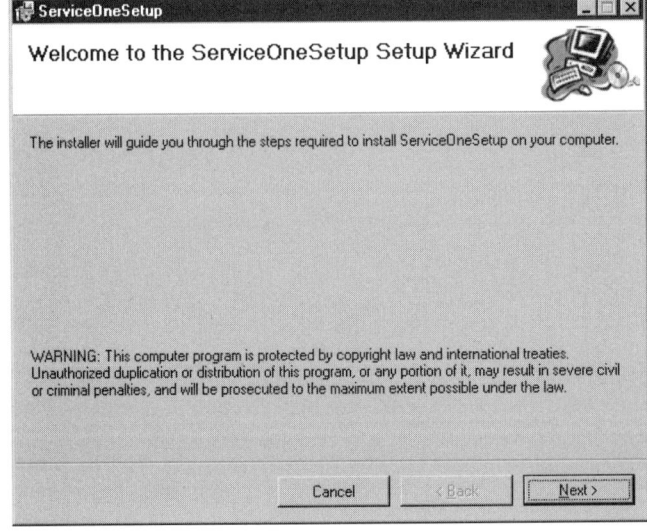

30. As you navigate through the Installation Wizard, you will need to verify or provide information. In the second screen, you should make the service available to all users and verify the installation location. Click Next.

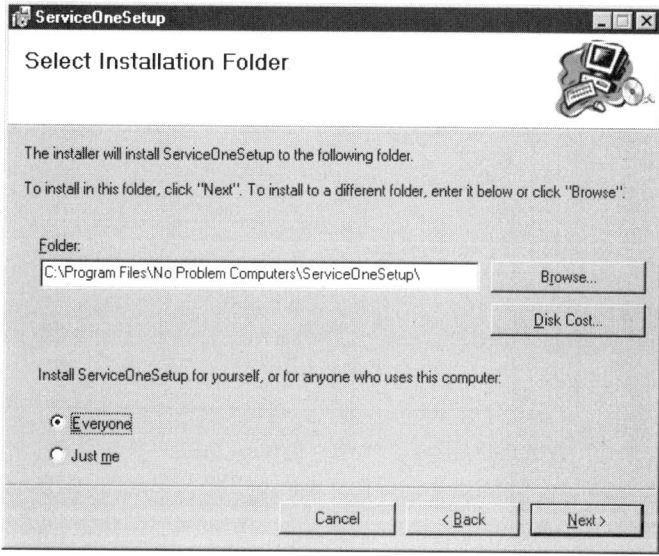

31. Click Next to start the installation.

32. As the service installs, you will be asked for security information. The account you provide must have permission to run as a service on the server; you might have to ask the Network Administrator to help you set up the service account, or see Appendix E for instructions on how to create accounts in Windows 2000.

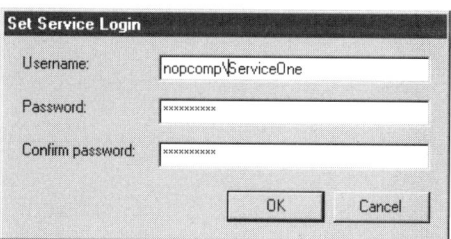

Once you have entered the security account for the Windows service, the installation will complete.

You will now look at the service you have built, and what the output is so far. When the service is installed, it will not start automatically; the automatic start happens only when the computer is rebooted. To view and modify the state of the Windows service, you will have to open the Services application.

33. Start the Services application from the Start | Settings | Control Panel | Administrative Tools | Services shortcut. The result is shown next:

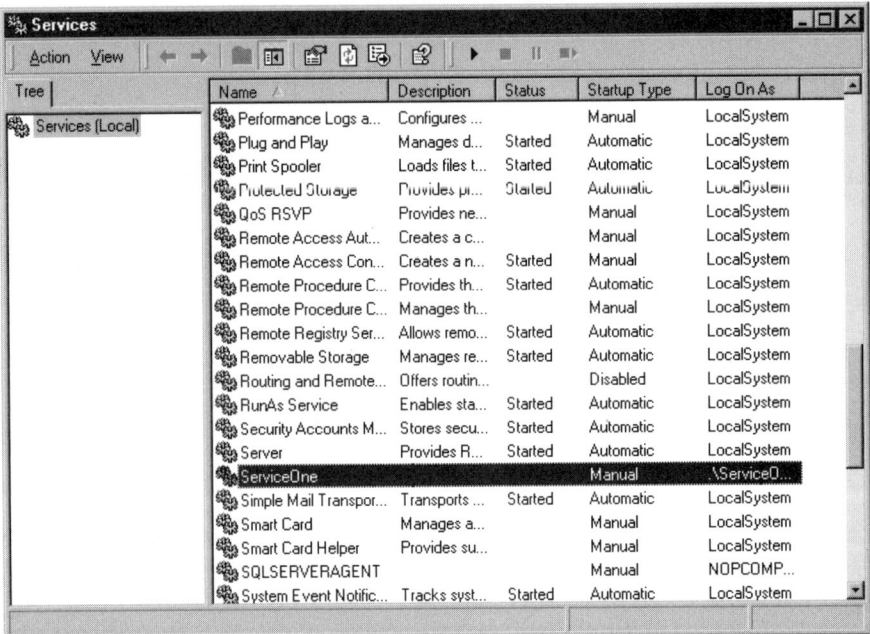

34. Locate the Windows service (ServiceOne) and double-click the name to open the ServiceOne Properties dialog box.

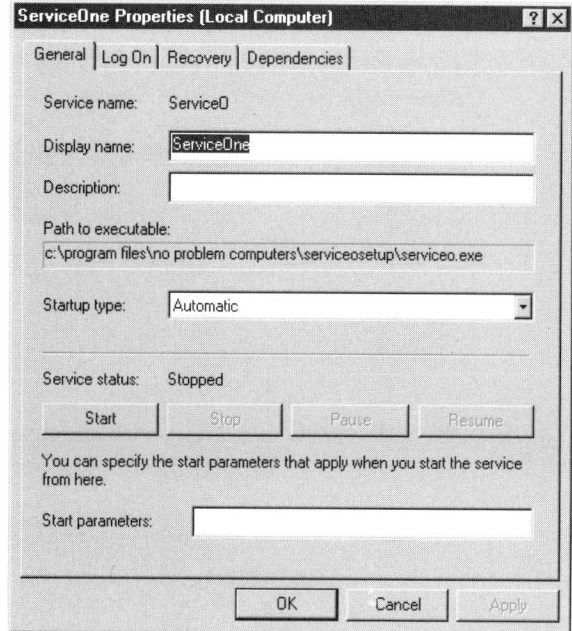

35. The current state of the Windows service is stopped. To start the service control, click Start.

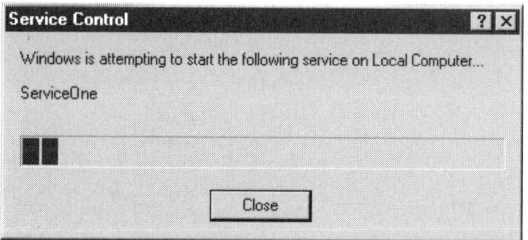

36. After the service has started, you can locate the information in the event log by opening the event log from Start | Settings | Control Panel | Administrative Tools | Event Viewer.

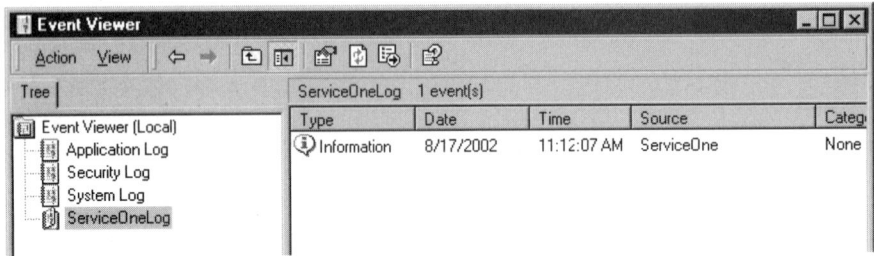

37. Select the ServiceOneLog in the left pane, and double-click the event in the right pane to see the event information.

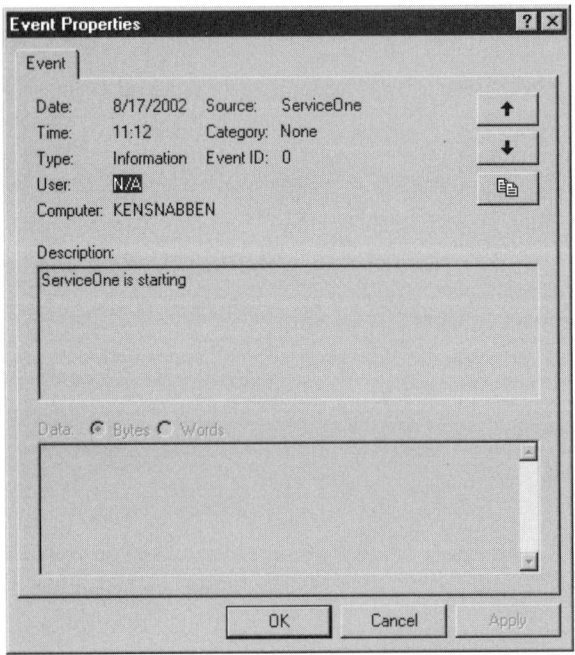

38. Stop the service using the Services application. After the service stops, go back to the Event Viewer and locate the event that was logged when the service was

stopped. The event should appear as shown next. You may have to refresh the view in the Event Viewer to see new information—right-click the event log name (ServieceOneLog) and select Refresh from the Context menu.

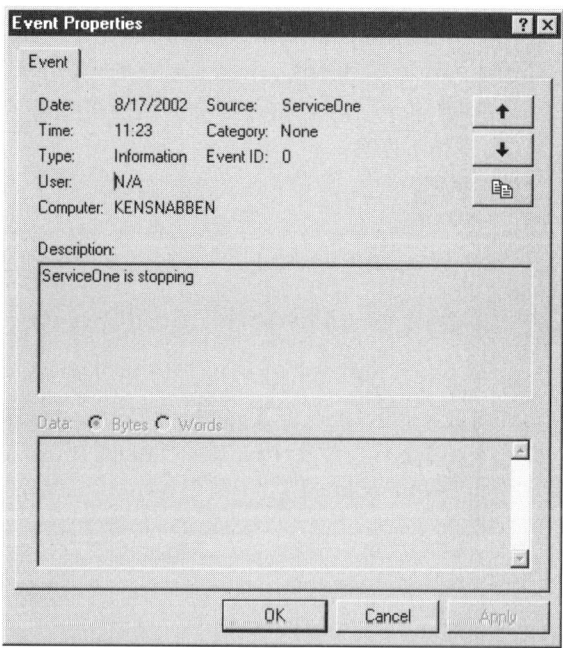

The Windows service you have built so far does not perform anything really useful except log information when it starts and stops. Next you will expand the service by adding functionality to the service to log the `Pause` and `Continue` events.

The `Pause` event is used by Windows services to perform a logical suspension of the service, and it is up to you, the designer, to determine what a logical pause is. For example, if you are building an e-mail service, the pause might be useful because it could be interpreted as meaning to stop accepting new e-mail but send everything that is in the output queue.

The `Continue` event is the logical step that will move the Windows service from being paused to running again.

on the Job

The Pause-Continue functionality is implemented using overridden methods from the ServiceBase class; the implementation is unique for each service. For example, the Login service in the Windows environment will continue to provide login functionality while paused, but it will not perform any replication of security information. On the other hand, the Internet Information Services, when paused, will not accept any new connections, although it will allow already-connected sessions to complete.

EXERCISE 2-2

Implementing the Pause Event

1. Start Visual Studio .NET and open the preceding project, ServiceOne.

2. Open the code module for the ServiceOne Windows service.

3. Use the Class and Method combo controls in the code editor to select (Overrides) in the Class Name control and OnPause() in the Method Name control.

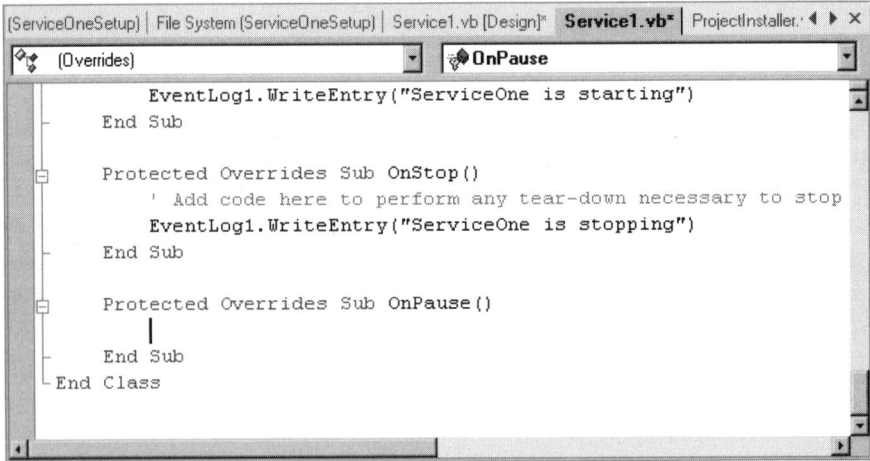

4. You will now be located in the OnPause() method. Add the following code to write information to the event log that the service is paused:

```
EventLog1.WriteEntry("ServiceOne is pausing")
```

5. Use the same technique as in steps 3 and 4 to add the `OnContinue()` method with code to write information in the event log that the service continued.

   ```
   EventLog1.WriteEntry("ServiceOne is continuing")
   ```

6. To enable the use of the Pause and Continue functionality, you will need to change a property in the Windows service. This is done by setting the CanPauseAndContinue property to True.

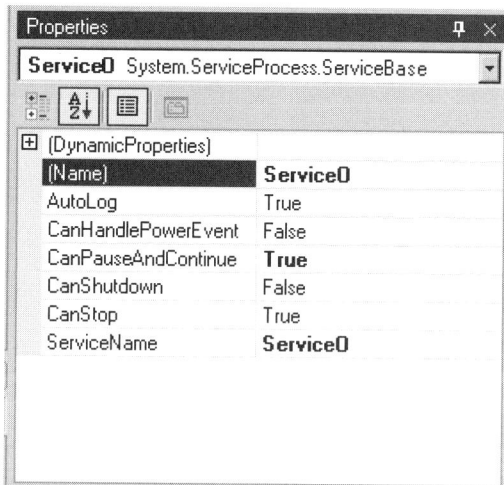

7. Compile the solution; exit Visual Studio .NET.

8. In order to install a new version of the service, you will need to uninstall the current version. Open the Add/Remove Programs application in the control panel, select the Windows service, and remove it from the server as shown next. You must reboot your server at this point, even though you are not prompted to do so. The service is only marked for removal when you run the Add/Remove Program application and is actually removed when the system reboots.

exam
ⓦatch

In order to be able to reinstall a Windows service, the old version must be uninstalled first. This way, the Registry is maintained without corruption.

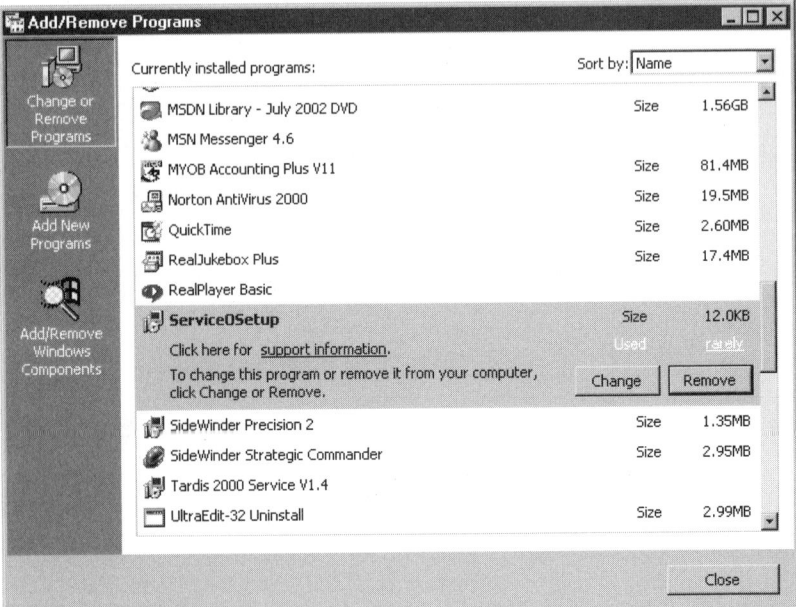

9. Install the application again.

10. Test the functionality you added by pausing and continuing the service. View the events in the Event Viewer. The next illustration shows the Pause event, and the illustration following it shows the Continue event.

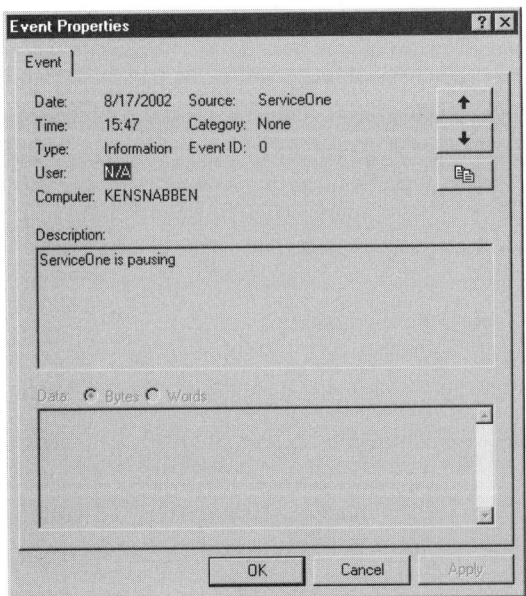

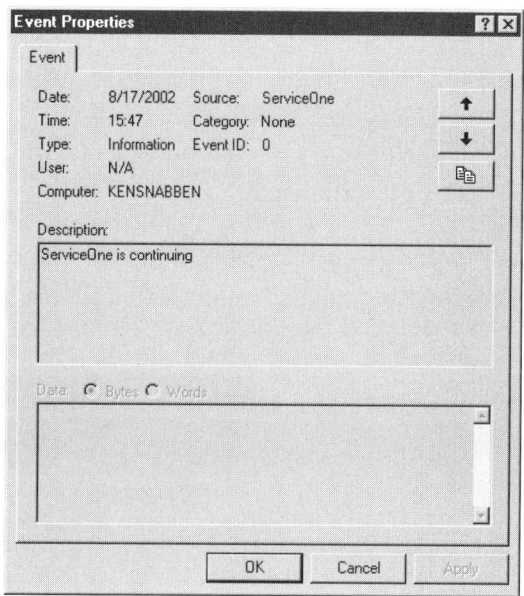

The program you have developed in this exercise is a very good example of the skeleton of a Windows service. It records the events in the event log, and the only thing missing now is some functionality. In the next exercise, you will write a service that will ping a remote host and report on the availability of the host by writing information in the event log.

EXERCISE 2-3

The Network Testing Service

This exercise builds on the knowledge you gained in Exercises 2-1 and 2-2. Here, you will add the functionality to the skeleton code that will make the Windows service perform a ping to a remote host using a configurable delay. The exercise makes use of a timer and the socket classes from the .NET Framework.

1. Create a new Visual Basic .NET project, and make sure it is based on the Windows Service template. The project should be named PingService and placed in the C:\VB folder. Follow the steps from Exercise 2-1 to rename the service to **PingService** and build the Windows service.

2. Configure the PingService Windows service to use the event log. Use **PingService** as the service name and **PingServiceLog** as the log name.

3. Configure the `OnStart()`, `OnStop()`, `OnPause()`, and `OnContinue()` methods to write information into the event log.

4. Add the Installer.

5. Add the Setup and Deployment project to the solution.

6. Configure the Project Output for the Setup project. The resulting Solution Explorer window should look like this:

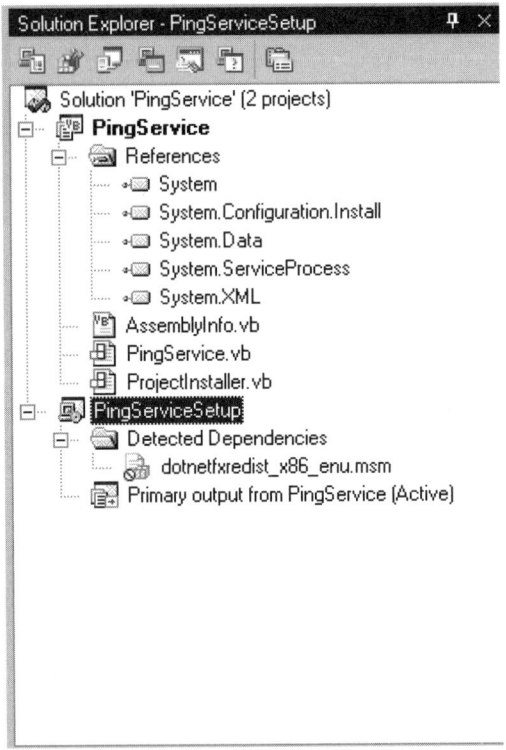

7. Build and test the PingService Windows service. Once the skeleton service is created, you can start adding functionality to the PingService—you will add a timer that will trigger the service to ping the remote host, as well as the socket to perform the ping on.

8. Add a Timer object to the PingService design view by dragging the Timer from the Toolbox. Rename the Timer from Timer1 to PingTimer.

9. Change the `Interval` property for the PingTimer from the default of 100 ms to 3600000 ms (60 min).

10. Verify that the `Enabled` property of PingTimer is False.

11. Declare two attributes for the PingService class: PingInterval as an Integer with a default value of 180000, and PingAddress as a String with a default value of "`www.osborne.com`".

```
Public Class PingService
    Inherits System.ServiceProcess.ServiceBase
    Dim PingInterval As Integer = 180000            ' 3 minutes interval
    Dim PingAddress As String = "www.osborne.com"  ' host to ping
...
```

12. Add code in the `OnStart()` method to configure and start the PingTimer.

```
Protected Overrides Sub OnStart(ByVal args() As String)
    ' Add code here to start your service. This method should set things
    ' in motion so your service can do its work.
    EventLog1.WriteEntry("ServiceOne is starting")
    PingTimer.Interval = PingInterval
    PingTimer.Enabled = True
End Sub
```

13. Implement the Elapsed event handler for the PingTimer: Select PingTimer in the Class Name combo control in the code editor, and then select Elapsed in the Method Name combo control. The Elapsed event handler will be executed when the timer has waited the number of milliseconds specified in the `Interval` property. The following code instantiates an object from the Pinger class and calls the `Ping()` method on the object. If the `Ping()` method returns a negative value, it means the host could not be contacted; you will then write a message in the event log.

```
Private Sub PingTimer_Elapsed(ByVal sender As Object, ByVal e As
System.Timers.ElapsedEventArgs) Handles PingTimer.Elapsed
    Dim pi As Pinger = New Pinger()
    If pi.Ping(PingAddress) < 1 Then
        EventLog1.WriteEntry(PingAddress & " does not respond.")
    End If
End Sub
```

14. Implement the Pinger class, adding the `Ping()` method as shown in the following code segment:

```
Class Pinger
    Dim s As Socket = New
            Socket(System.Net.Sockets.AddressFamily.InterNetwork,
            SocketType.Dgram, ProtocolType.Udp)
    Try
        Dim ipHostInfo As System.Net.IPHostEntry = System.Net.Dns.Resolve(addr)
```

```
      Dim ipe As New IPEndPoint(ipHostInfo.AddressList(0), 8)
      s.Connect(ipe)
   Catch
      Return -1
   End Try
   Return 1
End Class
```

In the preceding code segment, the `Ping()` method returns –1 if there is a problem resolving the address or connecting to the remote host.

15. Build and install the PingService.

16. Start the service.

17. Monitor the events in the event log.

18. Remove the network connection to your server to simulate a failed host. View the resulting event in the event log as shown next:

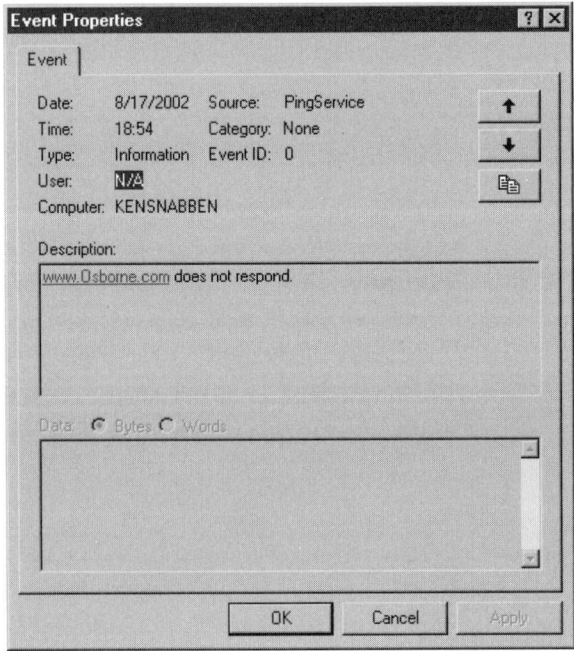

Now that you have looked at how to build and control the life of a Windows service, you will investigate the architecture of the services.

CERTIFICATION OBJECTIVE 2.03

Windows Services Architecture

The Windows services that you built in the preceding section follow the same architecture as all Windows services regardless of the language they are built in. Table 2-1 enumerates the three parts of all service architectures.

What makes the Windows service fairly easy to build is that the class that implements the service program inherits from the System.ServiceProcess.ServiceBase class. The ServiceBase class provides the necessary communication structures for our Windows service to be able to communicate with the Windows Service Controller.

TABLE 2-1   The Components of the Windows Service Architecture

Architectural Component	Description	Inherits from System.ServiceProcess.
Service program	The actual program that performs the work of the Windows service, this is what you developed in Exercise 2-3. The service program defines what actions to take when the Windows service is started, stopped, paused, or continued.	ServiceBase
Service control program	The service control program is in most cases the Services application from Application Tools. This is the component that controls the state of the Windows service; it can send messages to the service to start, stop, pause, or continue.	ServiceController
Service configuration program	This is the program that installs the Windows service; in our example, this is the Setup and Deployment project. Windows services must have their information added to the Windows Registry in order for the service to run without the intervention of the user.

A traditional .NET deployment using the XCOPY method does not work; instead, there must be an installation program that enables control of how the Windows service is installed. | ServiceProcessInstaller |

exam
ⓦatch

The three parts of the Windows service architecture are implemented using inheritance from the three base classes—ServiceBase, ServiceController, and ServiceProcessInstaller.

The `System.ServiceProcess` namespace includes the classes needed to implement the three components of the Windows Service Architecture as can be shown in Table 2-1. In addition to the `ServiceBase` class that is implemented to produce the service program, there is the `ServiceController` class that is implemented to build the service controller program that sends messages to the service, as well as the `ServiceProcessInstaller` class that is implemented together with the `ServiceInstaller` class to create the installation program.

Windows Service Configuration

A Windows service that is installed is configured through the Windows Registry. The Windows Registry, or the Registry for short, is a hierarchical database that is entirely stored in the memory of the server. The Registry is made up of areas that traditionally are called *hives.* The hive you are interested in is the HKEY_LOCAL_MACHINE, which is used by Windows to store information on items that are general to the computer and have no relationship to a specific user. To start the Registry editor, you will need to open the Run dialog from the Start | Run menu, type in **regedt32**, and click OK to start the editor.

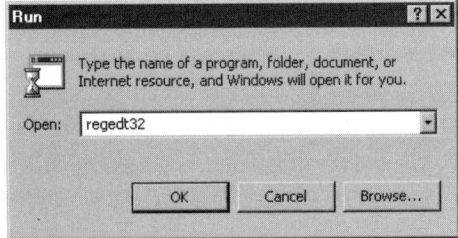

When the editor opens, locate

HKEY_LOCAL_MACHINE\System\CurrentControlSet\Services

by navigating through the editor as shown here:

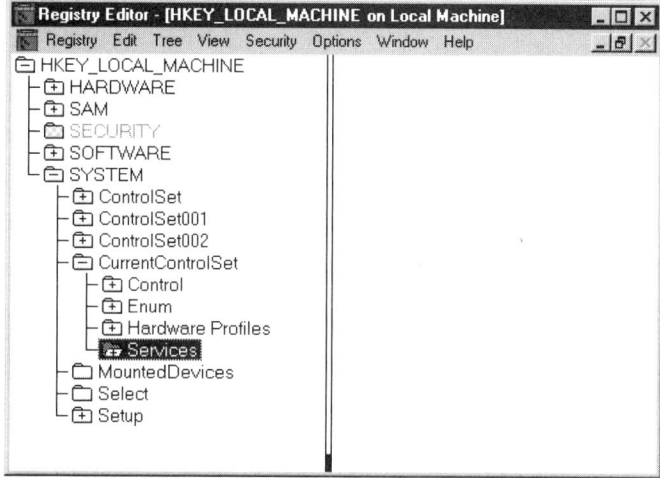

Expand the Services key and locate the PingService key as shown next:

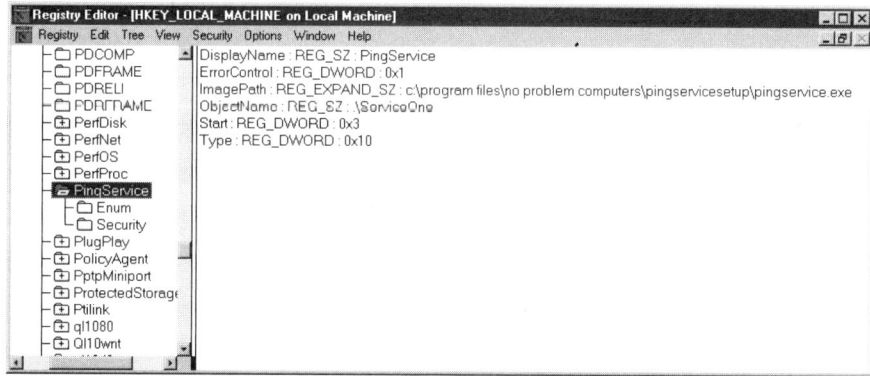

Through this key, you can configure the Windows service and set, among other things, the `startup` property (Disabled, Manual, or Automatic) and how the service handles errors.

exam
ⓦatch

The Registry key where Windows services store their properties is HKEY_LOCAL_MACHINE\System\CurrentControlSet\Services.

I need to warn you that modifying the Registry without full information on what the modification will do is very dangerous. You must be very careful with the Registry; read up on the values and settings in the MSDN library and Microsoft TechNet.

Most of the settings that can be set through the Registry can also be set through the Services application; indeed it is recommended to use the Services application for all configurations, rather than working directly in the Registry for the reasons just stated.

Windows Service Control

You have seen that the Services application that you use to configure a Windows service can also be used to control the state of the Windows service. There are additional service control programs that can be used to perform the same types of actions on Windows services. The net.exe utility has been part of virtually all Microsoft operating systems that have a network component. Using the net.exe command-line utility, you can enumerate the currently running services (**net start**), start a service (**net start pingservice**) or stop a service (**net stop pingservice**), as can be seen in the following segment:

```
C:\>net start
These Windows 2000 services are started:

    Alerter
    Application Management
    Automatic Updates
    Background Intelligent Transfer Service
    COM+ Event System
...
    Simple Mail Transport Protocol (SMTP)
    System Event Notification
    Tardis time service
    Task Scheduler
    TCP/IP NetBIOS Helper Service
    Telephony
    Windows Management Instrumentation
    Windows Management Instrumentation Driver Extensions
    Windows Time
    WMDM PMSP Service
    Workstation
    World Wide Web Publishing Service

The command completed successfully.
```

```
C:\>net start pingservice
The PingService service is starting.
The PingService service was started successfully.

C:\>net stop pingservice

The PingService service was stopped successfully.

C:\>
```

Next you will build our own Windows service controller for the PingService you built in Exercise 2-3 by using the ServiceController class.

EXERCISE 2-4

The Service Controller

1. Open the PingService in Visual Studio .NET.

2. Add an instance of a ServiceController component from the Toolbox.

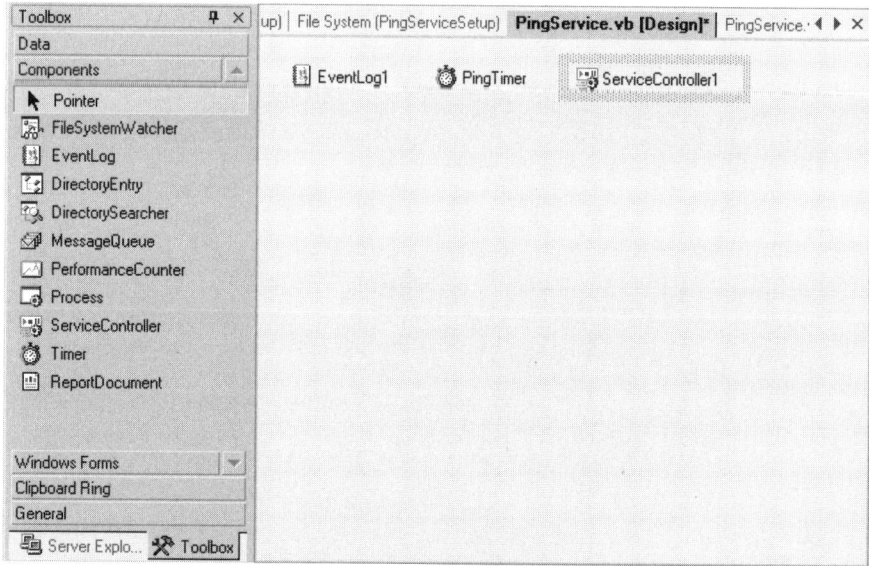

3. Build and install the service. The next part of this exercise is to build a Windows Form to control the PingService.

4. Start a new Visual Basic .NET project, and select a Windows Application template. Name the project **PingControl** and place it in the C:\VB folder.

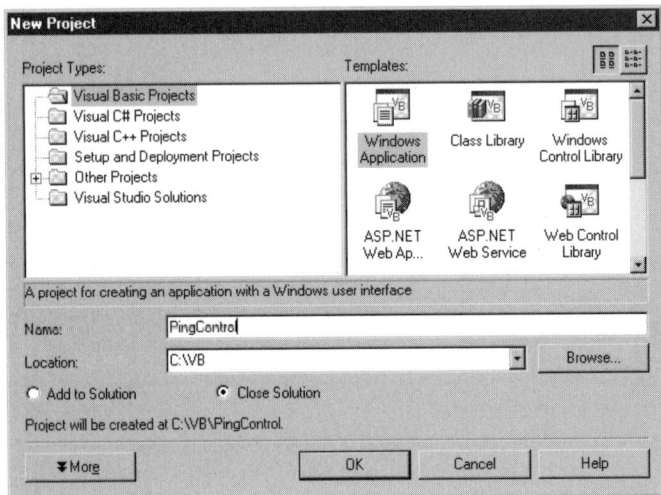

5. When the project is created, set a reference to the System.ServiceProcess.dll library. You can do this by right-clicking References in the Solution Explorer and then clicking Add Reference in the context menu. Locate and select System.ServiceProcess.dll in the Add Reference dialog. Click Select followed by OK to add the reference to your project.

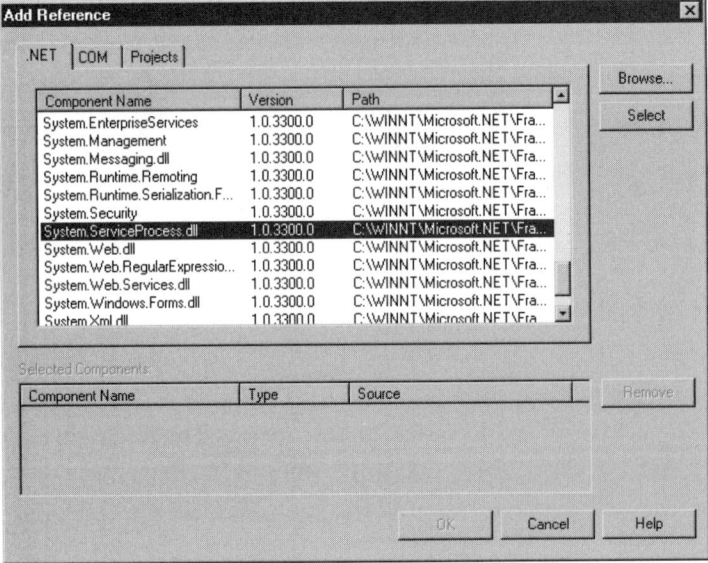

6. Add two Button controls to the Form.

7. Change the name of the first Button control to **btnStartService** and the Text property to **Start**.

8. Change the name of the second Button control to **btnStopService** and the Text property to **Stop**.

9. Add an Import statement to the beginning of the source file to import the System.ServiceProcess namespace.

e x a m
ⓦatch

The ServiceController class has a number of methods that you can use to control the Windows service, among them Start() and Stop() to control the state of the service and ExecuteCommand() to send commands and parameters to the service.

10. Implement the click event handler for the Start button as follows:

```
Private Sub btnStartService_Click(ByVal sender As System.Object,
                               ByVal e As System.EventArgs)
                               Handles btnStartService.Click
    ' create a new ServiceController object
    ' that is connected to the PingService Windows service
    Dim sc As ServiceController = New ServiceController("PingService")
    ' call the Start() method of the ServiceController
    cc.Start()
    ' the next call is blocking, it waits until the service is running
    sc.WaitForStatus(ServiceControllerStatus.Running)

    ' verify that the service is running
    Dim st As ServiceControllerStatus = sc.Status
    If st = ServiceControllerStatus.Running Then
       MessageBox.Show("The PingService is running")
    End If
End Sub
```

11. Implement the click event handler for the Stop button as follows:

```
Private Sub btnStopService_Click(ByVal sender As System.Object,
                              ByVal e As System.EventArgs)
                              Handles btnStartService.Click
    ' create a new ServiceController object
    ' that is connected to the PingService Windows service
    Dim sc As ServiceController = New ServiceController("PingService")
    ' call the Start() method of the ServiceController
    sc.Stop()
    ' the next call is blocking, it waits until the service is running
    sc.WaitForStatus(ServiceControllerStatus.Stopped)

    ' verify that the service is running
    Dim st As ServiceControllerStatus = sc.Status
```

```
       If st = ServiceControllerStatus.Stopped Then
           MessageBox.Show("The PingService is stopped")
       End If
   End Sub
```

12. Build and run the application. After you click Start, you should see this MessageBox.

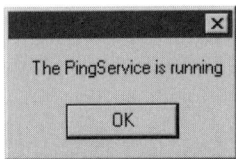

13. Click Stop and the MessageBox shown next should be the result.

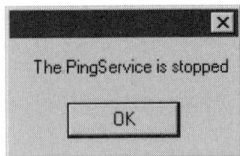

That takes us to the end of the Windows Services portion of this book. Be sure to check out some of the common scenarios and solutions in the sidebar I have provided.

SCENARIO & SOLUTION

How do I modify how the Windows service starts?	The start behavior of a Windows service is controlled through the Start key in the Registry key for the service. You can modify the value in this key through the Services application in the Administrative Tools folder in the control panel or through the Registry editor.
	The values that can be assigned to the start property are Automatic, Manual, and Disabled; or if you modify the Registry directly, you need to use 0x1 for Manual, 0x2 for Automatic, and 0x4 for Disabled.
What is the service account?	The service account is the security account the service will use to authenticate to the Windows operating system. You can configure two different types of accounts that will be used by the service.
	The SYSTEM account has unlimited control on the server but cannot be used to access resources located outside the local server.
	A user account is used when the service must access resources remotely. The permissions that the service has are determined by the permissions for the user account.

SCENARIO & SOLUTION

How do I implement pause and continue for a Windows service?	The pause and continue behavior of a Windows service are implemented by first setting the CanPauseAndContinue property for the service to True. Once you have done this, you will need to override OnPause() and OnContinue() from the ServiceBase class to provide the behavior of the service.
Where do I write the code that will perform the actions of the Windows service?	The usual way to design the Windows service is to develop a class that defines the service. You instantiate the object from this class in the OnStart() method and clean up the object in the OnStop() method. Think in an object-oriented way.
Why do I have to override the OnPause() and OnContinue() methods?	The pause and continue functionality for a Windows service is defined in the ServiceBase class that all Windows services inherit from. The implementation of the base class provides the communication between the Windows service and the service controller; if you choose to override these two methods, you only have to implement the service's behavior rather than all communication with the service controller.
How do I install a Windows service?	Windows services must be installed using a program that can insert the proper information into the Windows Registry. Without that information, the Windows service will not start. To create the installation program, you add a Setup and Deployment project to your Windows service solution.
Why do I have to uninstall a Windows service before reinstalling it?	Because the Windows service uses the Registry to maintain properties, the Registry must be cleaned up before you can install another copy of the same service.
Why do the Windows services use the Registry?	This is a very valid question. You have learned that the .NET Framework uses XML manifests in all assemblies that replace the Windows Registry, but that is not true for Windows services. The operating system must know where the service is located and how to start it, and the only place current versions of Windows operating systems can read properties is in the Registry.
Do I have to build my own service controller?	No, the Services application in Administrative Tools performs the majority of control and configuration tasks most services need. The only time you need to build your own service controller is when your Windows service requires extensive customization after installation.

CERTIFICATION SUMMARY

In this chapter, I explored building and controlling a Windows service. The Windows service will be tested in the exam as frequently as any other of the components that make up the XML Web Services. Be prepared for code listings where you will have to determine what the result is when the service starts or pauses.

Remember the three programs that make up the service architecture—service, controller, and installation program—and the classes that support those programs (ServiceBase, ServiceController, ServiceProcessInstaller).

TWO-MINUTE DRILL

Creating and Manipulating a Windows Service

❏ Set CanPauseAndContinue to True when you need to implement OnPause() and OnContinue().

❏ Set the startup property to Automatic if the Windows service must start with the operating system.

❏ Set the startup property to Disabled to make the service unavailable.

❏ Set the startup property to Manual if your Windows service should start only if another service is started (or if you want to control when it starts). You also must set the dependencies between the two services.

❏ Always look at the Main() method of the service after you have renamed it from Service1. Visual Studio .NET does not update the instantiation of the service.

❏ Implement use of the event log to communicate to the administrator when the Windows service changes state.

❏ Add a Setup and Deployment project to create the installation application.

❏ When you build your own Windows service controller, you need to add a reference to the System.ServiceProcess.dll library.

Writing Code That Is Executed When a Windows Service Is Started or Stopped

❏ Implement the OnStart() method to control how the Windows service starts.

❏ Implement the OnStop() method to control how the Windows service stops.

❏ Create the functionality for a Windows service in a class that is instantiated in the OnStart() method.

---

*Please be aware that the questions and answers at the end of this chapter for the Two-Minute Drill, the Self Test Questions, and the Self Test Answers may *not* match the order of those found in the corresponding chapter on the CD-ROM.

SELF TEST

Creating and Manipulating a Windows Service

1. You are developing a Windows service that will be installed on multiple servers in your company. This Windows service is going to be used to log network statistics to a central database server. Because of occasional network problems that will send large numbers of error reports to the database server, it has been decided that the Windows service must be able to suspend its reporting and then later resume. You need to implement this Windows service. How will you implement the Windows service? Select all answers that apply.

   A. Set `CanSuspendAndResume` to True.

   B. Override `Resume()`.

   C. Override `OnPause()`.

   D. Set `CanPauseAndContinue` to True.

   E. Override `Suspend()`.

   F. Override `OnContinue()`.

2. You are developing a Windows service that will send e-mail through an e-mail server that requires the sender to authenticate before e-mail is accepted. You built your Windows service and installed it with default settings. Now the users of the Windows service report that no e-mail is sent by the Windows service. You must make the Windows service work. What is the most efficient solution that will make the Windows service send e-mail?

   A. Override the `OnMail()` method.

   B. Change the Installer to register the e-mail server.

   C. Rewrite the send e-mail method.

   D. Change the Service account to a user account.

3. You are designing a Windows service. After generating the project in Visual Studio .NET, you rename the source file to STwo.vb, and the service itself to STwo. When you build the Windows service, you receive an error message that Service1 cannot be found. How will you modify the Windows service so that you can successfully build it?

   A. Modify the `Main()` method to instantiate the `STwo` class rather than the `Service1` class.

   B. Change the `Service1` class declaration in the STwo.vb file to **STwo**.

   C. Change the `Name` property of the STwo.vb file to **STwo**.

   D. Change the namespace for the project to **STwo**.

4. Which class does a Windows service always inherit from?

   A. `System.ServiceProcess.ServiceBase`

   B. `System.Service.ServiceBase`

   C. `System.Process.ServiceBase`

   D. `System.ServiceBase`

5. You are developing a Windows service, and now you need to add the Installer to the service. Where will you find the link to Add Installer?

   A. Under the Build menu

   B. Under the Project menu

   C. In the Properties window

   D. In the Toolbox

6. You are developing a Windows service, and you need to locate the information for the installed service in the Registry. Which Registry key is correct?

   A. HKEY_LOCAL_MACHINE\CurrentControlSet\Services

   B. HKEY_LOCAL_MACHINE\System\CurrentControlSet\Services

   C. HKEY_LOCAL_MACHINE\Services

   D. HKEY_LOCAL_MACHINE\System\Services

7. Before you distribute a Windows service named PingPong, you need to identify the program to run in order to start the installation. What is the name of the installation program?

   A. Setup.exe

   B. PingPong.exe

   C. ServiceInstaller.exe

   D. xcopy.exe

8. You are developing a Windows service and need to develop an application that will give you control of the service. What must you do to be able to control a Windows service from an application?

   A. Add a reference to the System.ServiceControl.dll library.

   B. Import the `System.ServiceController` namespace.

   C. Add a reference to the System.ServiceController.dll library.

   D. Import the `System.ServiceProcess` namespace.

9. True or False? A Windows service will fail to install if it does not include code to write to the event log?

    A. True

    B. False

Writing Code That is Executed When a Windows Service is Started or Stopped

10. You are developing a Windows service. You need to send a command to the service that will be used to store three parameters for the service. What method will you use to call on the service to send it a command?

    A. `OnParameters()`

    B. `ExecuteCommand()`

    C. You need to update the Registry, then call `OnStop()` and `OnStart()`

    D. `ServiceControler.Recycle()`

SELF TEST ANSWERS

Creating and Manipulating a Windows Service

1. ☑ **C, D,** and **F.** In order to implement suspend, and resume behavior, you need to override the OnPause() and OnContinue() methods. The CanPauseAndContinue property must also be set to True.

☒ **A, B,** and **E.** Answer **A** is incorrect because the CanSuspendAndResume property does not exist. Answer **B** and **E** are incorrect because those methods do not exist.

2. ☑ **D.** The default service account is the SYSTEM account, but this account cannot connect to remote resources, such as e-mail servers, across the network.

☒ **A, B,** and **C.** Answer **A** is incorrect because there is no OnMail() method to override. Answer **B** is incorrect because the Installer program cannot register a remote application. Answer **C** is incorrect because rewriting the method is not very efficient, and the problem will still exist; the SYSTEM account cannot be used with remote resources.

3. ☑ **A.** The Visual Studio .NET forgets to change the class that is instantiated in the Main() method; it needs to be manually changed.

☒ **B, C,** and **D.** Answer **B** is incorrect because Visual Basic .NET already performed that task. **C** is incorrect because the file is already renamed. Answer **D** is incorrect because the namespace is already renamed by Visual Studio .NET.

4. ☑ **A.** The base class that all Windows services inherit from is System.ServiceProcess.ServiceBase.

☒ **B, C,** and **D.** These are incorrect, since those classes do not exist.

5. ☑ **C.** The link can be found in the bottom of the Properties window.

☒ **A, B,** and **D.** These answers are incorrect because the link is available only in the Properties window.

6. ☑ **B.** The correct key is located in the HKEY_LOCAL_MACHINE hive under System\CurrentControlSet\Services.

☒ **A, C,** and **D.** These answers are incorrect because **B** is correct.

7. ☑ **A.** When the Setup and Deployment project is built, the result is an .msi file that has the name of the project and a setup.exe file, either of which can be used to start the installation.

☒ **B, C,** and **D.** These answers, although enticing names, are all wrong. PingPong.exe is probably the service itself, ServiceInstaller.exe is made up, and xcopy.exe will not update the Registry.

8. ☑ **C.** You need to add a reference to the System.ServiceController.dll library in order to have access to the Windows services installed on a server.

    ☒ **A, B, and D.** Answer **A** is incorrect because the library is named System.ServiceController.dll. Answer **B**, because there is no such namespace. Answer **D** is also incorrect. There is no such namespace.

9. ☑ **B.** This statement is false. There is no need for a Windows service to write to the event log. It has become a standard that Windows services logs state changes in the event log, but it is not enforced.

Writing Code That Is Executed When a Windows Service Is Started or Stopped

10. ☑ **B.** The correct answer is the `ExecuteCommand()` method of the `ServiceController` class.

    ☒ **A, C, and D.** Answer **A** is incorrect because there is no such method. Answer **C** is also incorrect. Although this looks enticing, it will not work as written. Answer **D** is incorrect; there is no such method.

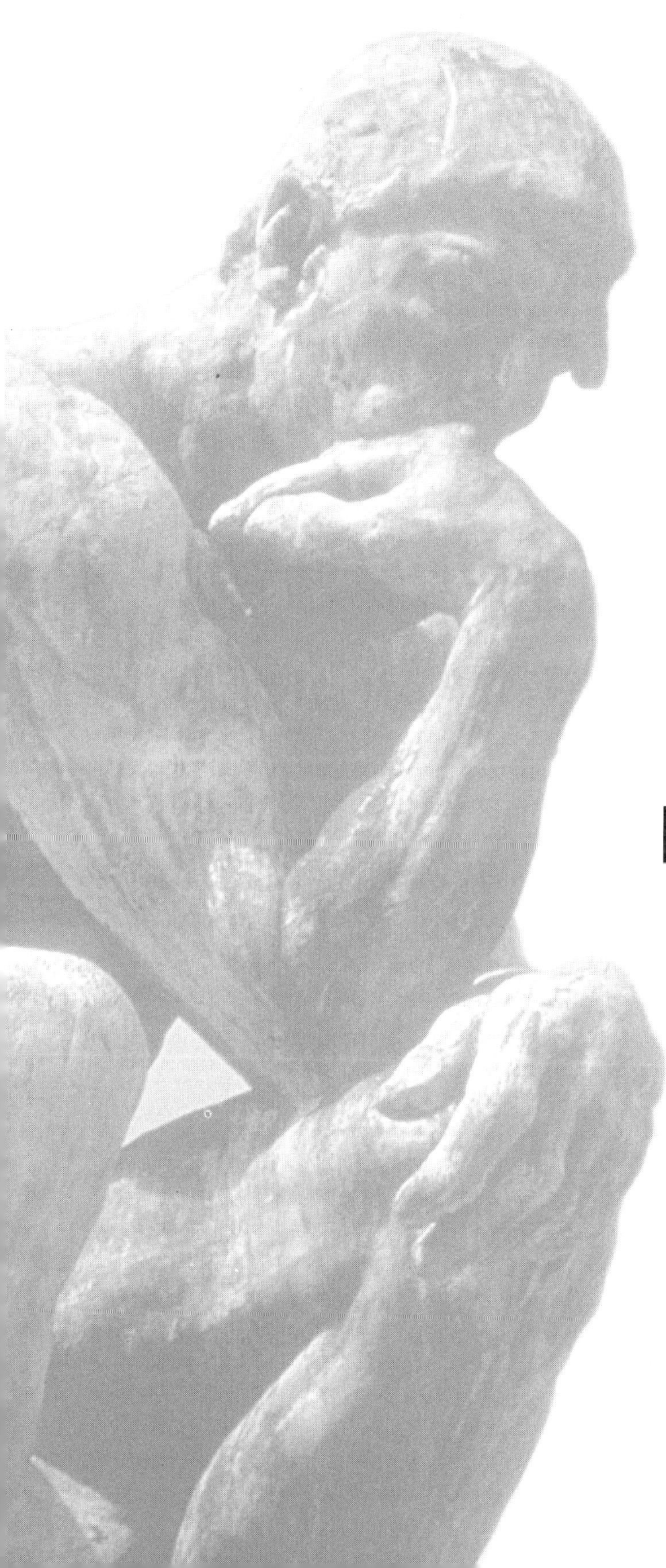

MCAD/MCSD

MICROSOFT® CERTIFIED APPLICATION DEVELOPER
& MICROSOFT® CERTIFIED SOLUTION DEVELOPER

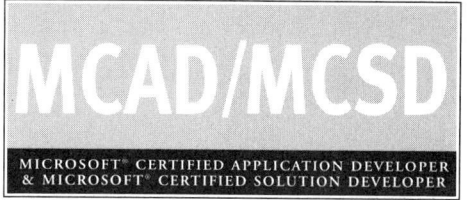

3

Creating and Managing Microsoft Windows–Serviced Components

CERTIFICATION OBJECTIVES

Y ou may suppose that now that you have the .NET Framework and assemblies that don't need to be registered in the Registry, you have finally moved beyond the COM components. Nothing can be further from the truth; there are millions of COM components in production, and a large number of applications use MTS and Component Services. So, what are you to do? Throw away all the COM components and rewrite them in Visual Basic .NET? I don't think so! You need to find a way that will allow the two environments to coexist, and that is where *serviced components* come in.

A serviced component is a .NET component that has been configured to work in the Component Services environments of Windows 2000 and in later iterations. This chapter will explore the world of Component Services, which includes COM and serviced components.

Component Services

The Component Services environment of Windows 2000 or later versions provides the services of an *object resource broker (ORB)*. The ORB allows clients to make requests to Component Services for a component, which is hosted by Component Services on behalf of the client; thus, the client's method calls and data are marshaled by Component Services.

In order to be able to install a .NET component in Component Services, you need to have a reference to the System.EnterpriseServices.dll library and import the System.EnterpriseServices namespace. This namespace provides the main classes, interfaces, and attributes for communicating with Component Services. The System .EnterpriseServices namespace gives us the ContextUtil class that is used in order for an object to participate in transactions and interact with the security information relating to the object. The ServicedComponent class is what gives the .NET component the ability to be hosted in Component Services. All .NET component classes that are to be hosted within Component Services must inherit from this class.

There are also numerous attributes, classes, and method attributes defined in the namespace; for example, the Transaction attribute, AutoComplete attribute, and ConstructionEnabled attribute are contained in the System.EnterpriseServices namespace.

Transactions

A *transaction* is defined as a group of operations that either completes as a whole *(commits)* or returns all operations to the state prior to the transaction *(rolls back)* if it fails to complete. Transactions are described as an all-or-nothing workflow.

Components in the Component Services environment have the ability to participate in transactions by voting on the outcome of the operations. The voting is performed by the code of the component calling methods that signify successful completion or failure of the process the component performs. When a component is instantiated in Component Services, the component's participation in transactions can be found in the Transaction attribute. The following list describes the possible values for the Transaction attribute:

- **Disabled**   The class will not use transactions and will ignore any transactions from the parent object.
- **NotSupported**   The class will not be instantiated within the context of a transaction.
- **Required**   The class requires a transaction. If no transaction exists, one will be created.
- **RequiresNew**   The class will always create a new transaction regardless of whether one already exists.
- **Supported**   The class will participate in an existing transaction but will not create a new one if one is not present.

exam
ⓦatch

The <Transaction()> attribute must be set to Required, RequiresNew, or Supported for the component to be able to vote on the transaction outcome.

The following code segment shows how to use the Transaction attribute:

```
Imports System.EnterpriseServices
<Transaction(TransactionOption.Required)> Public Class Savings
      Inherits ServicedComponent

   Public Function GetBalance() as Decimal
      ' Get balance code
   End Function
End Class
```

The class needs a means of voting on the outcome of the transaction. This is done by using methods of the ContextUtil object. The following methods are used to vote on the transaction:

- **SetAbort()**   Vote for failure of the transaction. If any part of the transaction calls SetAbort() and votes for a failure, the object is destroyed at the return of the method call.

- **SetComplete()**   Vote for success of the transaction. In this instance, the object is destroyed at the return of the method call.

- **EnableCommit()**   Vote for success of the transaction. The object will not be destroyed after the method call, allowing us to keep state across method calls.

- **DisableCommit()**   Vote for the unsuccessful completion of the transaction. The object will not be destroyed after the return of the method call.

exam
Ⓦatch

The object is deactivated if you call SetComplete() or SetAbort(). If you need to keep state (maintain an active object) between calls to the object, use EnableCommit() or DisableCommit() instead.

The following code sample shows how to use the transaction methods:

```
Public Sub Debit(ByVal id As Long, ByVal amount As Decimal)
    Try
        ' Update the account
        . . .
        ' Signal success by calling SetComplete()
        ContextUtil.SetComplete()
    Catch e As Exception
        ' Signal failure by calling SetAbort()
        ContextUtil.SetAbort()
        ' Pass the exception to the caller
        Throw e
    End Try
End Sub
```

This code segment can be rewritten by using the AutoComplete attribute of the method as in this code segment:

```
<AutoComplete()>Public Sub Debit(ByVal id As Long, ByVal amount As Decimal)
    ' Update the account
    . . .
End Sub
```

The AutoComplete attribute makes it possible for us to write code that will signal success if the method returns normally and failure if an exception is thrown.

Object Pooling

Object pooling allows a preset number of objects to be created in advance. This way, the objects are ready for the client when called for. When a client requests an object, it is taken from the pool of available objects, and when the client request is finished, the object is returned to the pool.

The object pool will improve the performance for objects that require large amounts of processing time to create and bind to resources during creation of the object.

To enable object pooling, you use the ObjectPooling attribute—this attribute has two parameters that control the initial size of the pool as well as the maximum size.

- **MinPoolSize**   Controls the initial size of the pool.
- **MaxPoolSize**   Sets the maximum number of objects that can be created in the pool. If the number of objects in the pool has reached the MaxPoolSize value and additional requests for objects are received, the requests will be queued until objects are made available.

on the job   *Always set a MaxPoolSize if you enable pooling. That way, the server will not be affected by a client application that keeps requesting more objects.*

The return of objects to the object pool is controlled by the `CanBePooled()` method. If your object supports object pooling and can safely be returned to the pool, return True; if not, return False.

The following code segment illustrates the use of the ObjectPooling attribute:

```
<ObjectPooling(Enabled:=True,MinPoolSize:=3,MaxPoolSize:=42)> _
   Public Class Savings
       Inherits ServicedComponent

   Public Function GetBalance() As Decimal
   ...
   End Function

   Protected Overrides Function CanBePooled() As Boolean
       Return True
   End Function
End Class
```

Set the size of the pool to meet the expected number of concurrent accesses to the object.

Constructor Strings

One issue with the Component Services environment is that there is no possibility to take advantage of custom constructors—only the default constructor of the class will be executed. That means that you cannot take advantage of the ability to pass values to the constructor to initialize the instance. To solve this problem, the Construct() method provided in the ServicedComponent class gives us the ability to pick up a string from the Component Service environment that is used during the construction phase.

The ConstructionEnabled attribute indicates that the class is using the construction string from the Component Services environment. By overriding the Construct() method, the class can be customized during instantiation. The following code listing shows how to implement the Construct() method:

```
<ConstructionEnabled(True)> Public Class Savings
    Inherits ServicedComponent

    Private strX As String

    Protected Overrides Sub Construct(ByVal s As String)
        ' This method is called by the Component Service after the
        ' constructor.
        strX = s
    End Sub
End Class
```

Figure 3-1 shows how the string is entered in the Component properties dialog from Component Services console.

There are additional methods that can be overridden from the ServicedComponent class; these include Activate() and Deactivate(). The Activate() method will be called as the object is used from the pool, and the Deactivate() method is called every time the object is returned to the pool.

on the
Ⓙo b

Use the Deactivate() method to clean up any changes to initialized members that might have taken place during the use of the object.

FIGURE 3-1

Setting the
construction
string

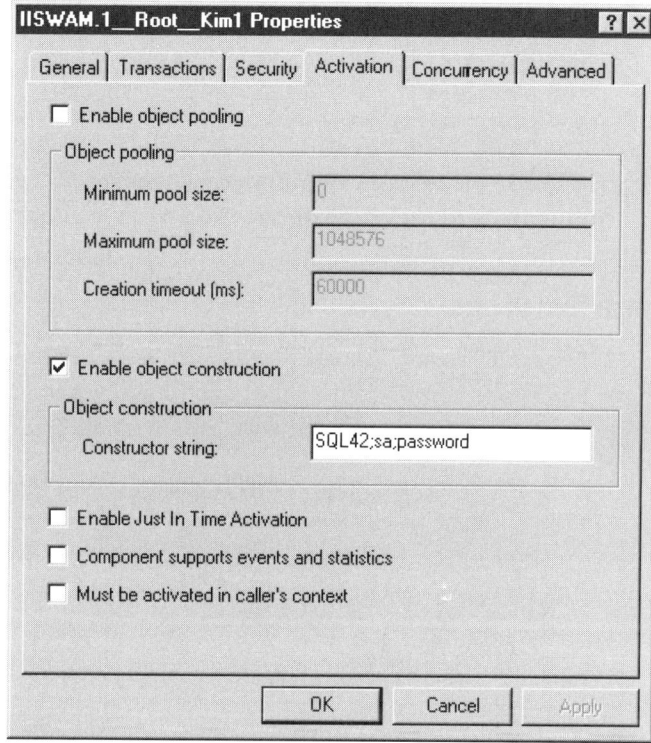

There has always been an issue with how to give components in an application
access to common data, and the Component Services solution is to use the Shared
Property Manager (SPM). The following code gives an example of how to create and
use a shared property:

```
Friend Function GetSharedProperty() As SharedProperty
    Dim bFlag As Boolean
    Dim strValue As String
    Dim spm As New SharedPropertyGroupManager()
    Dim spg As SharedPropertyGroup
    Dim sp As SharedProperty

    'create a group called "Messages"
    spg = spm.CreatePropertyGroup("Messages", PropertyLockMode.SetGet, _
            PropertyReleaseMode.Process, bFlag)
    'create a property called "History" for storing the event history
    sp = spg.CreateProperty("History", bFlag)
```

```
        If bFlag = False Then      'if nothing exists, set default value
            sp.Value = ""
        End If
        Return sp                  'return the shared property object
    End Function
```

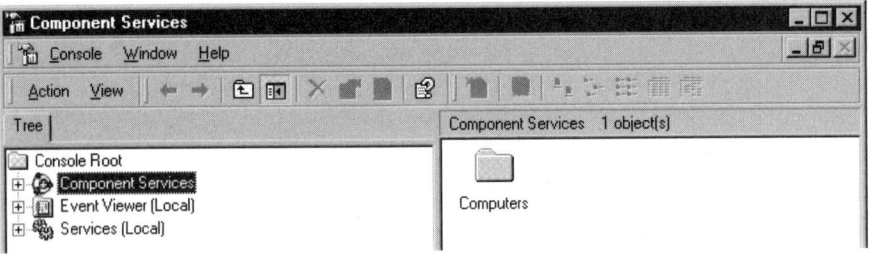

e x a m
ⓦ a t c h   *Use the Shared Property Manager whenever there is a need for serviced components in the same application to share data.*

Component Services

Component Services is managed through the Components Services console from the Administrative Tools folder (Start | Settings | Control Panel | Administrative Tools | Component Services). The console is shown next.

The console is also used to read and manage the event log, as well as the services running on a computer. By expanding Components Services in the left panel, you will see a Computers folder that lists the computers this console can manage. Expand Computers, My Computer, and then COM+ Applications to see the installed component applications.

Each application contains the components that make up that particular application. To view these components, expand System Application and then Components, as shown in Figure 3-2.

If a component is in use, the icon in the right panel will rotate to indicate that the component is running.

You can right-click any of the objects to display a context menu that includes, among other things, a menu to the properties of the object. It is through this properties dialog that you can modify the settings for the component.

Assembly Configuration

In order to support the installation of a .NET assembly into Component Services, four entries must be made in a file that is stored as part of the Visual Basic .NET

FIGURE 3-2

The components
in the system
application

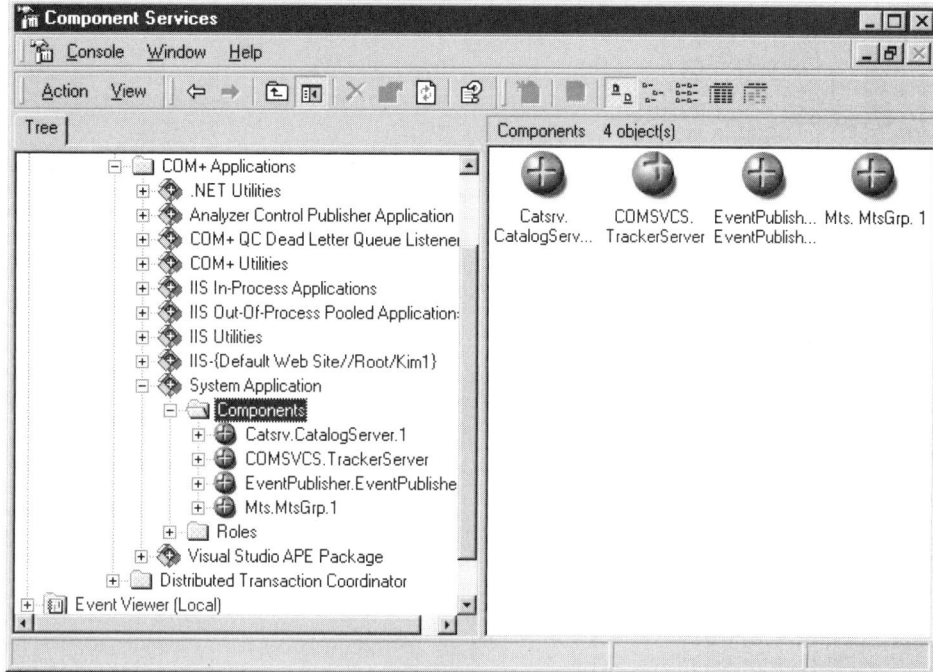

project for the component. The AssemblyInfo.vb file contains settings that affect the metadata of the assembly, and the following four entries must be used in order to support a .NET assembly:

- **ApplicationName** This attribute is used to specify the application that the component will be installed in.

- **Description** Sets the description of the Component Services application.

- **ApplicationActivation** Specifies whether the Component Services application is implemented as a library or server application. A library application will work only with clients on the local computer. When the client requests the object, it will execute outside of Component Services. The server activation manages the execution of the component in Component Services.

- **AssemblyKeyFile** Set this attribute to the file that contains the strong-name key pair generated by the sn.exe utility.

The following is a sample of how to set these attributes in the AssemblyInfo.vb file:

```
<Assembly: ApplicationName("Masiw Components")>
<Assembly: Description("VB .NET Vineyard Components")>
```

```
<Assembly: ApplicationActivation(ActivationOption.Server)>
<Assembly: AssemblyKeyFile("KeyFile.snk")>
```

exam
Watch

Without the strong-name key, the assembly will not install in Component Services.

Once the assembly is built, it must be registered—yes, you heard right, you need to register the assembly in the Registry. The Component Services environment is still the old COM environment, so you must comply with its rules by entering the relevant information in the Registry to make our component available. To that end, the .NET Framework ships with a utility—Regsvcs.exe—that eases registration. To register an application, use the following syntax:

```
Regsvcs.exe myApplication.dll
```

The result is that the components in the *myApplication*.dll library are registered in the Registry and installed in Component Services. Regsvcs.exe verifies that there is no entry for the components in the Registry before performing the registration, and if there is a preexisting entry, the existing entry will be deleted. This ensures that you have only current information in the Registry.

on the
Job

The Windows Registry is very much a part of Component Services, but through the use of Regsvcs.exe, you do not have to directly edit the Registry. To be on the safe side when updating components, I usually delete the application in the Component Services console before reinstalling,

When all the components in the assembly are registered in Component Services, you can optionally defer the registration until the first time a client application requests a component that inherits from ServiceComponent. This is called *automatic registration*.

Now that you have covered the theory of serviced components, it is time to start building and using them.

Building a Serviced Component

You will build a serviced component that highlights the use of the object pool.

EXERCISE 3-1

Building the Serviced Component

1. Create a new Visual Basic .NET project based on a Class Library template. Name the project **PoolComponent**:

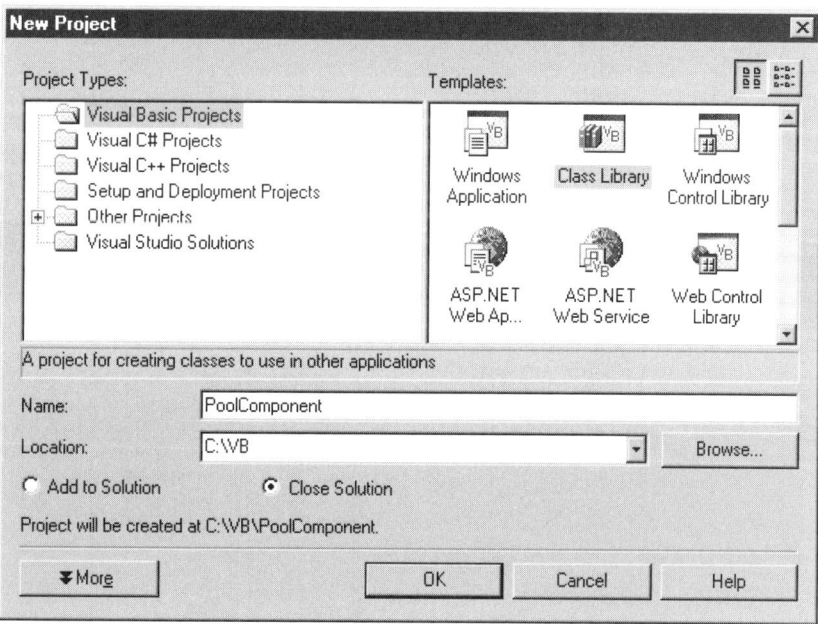

2. After the project is created, delete the Class1.vb file.

3. Add a new Class file, naming it **Pool.vb**.

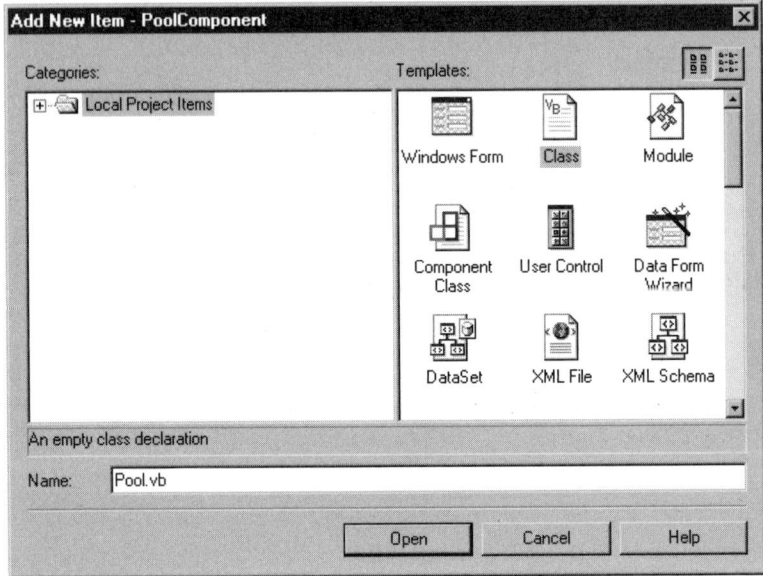

4. Add a new Class file, naming it **NPool.vb**.

5. Add a new Class file, naming it **Util.vb**. The Solution Explorer should resemble this image after the Class files are created:

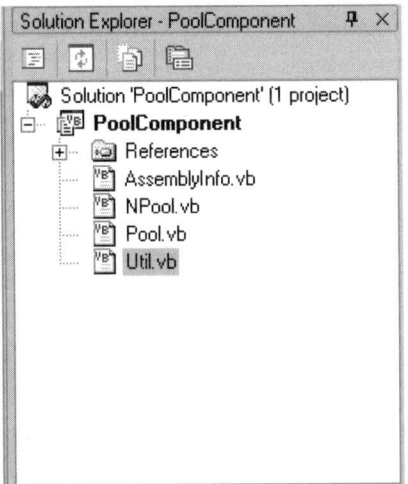

Next, you will implement the utilities in the Util.vb source file. This is where you keep the common shared properties methods.

6. Set a reference to the System.EnterpriseServices.dll library—on the Project menu, select Add Reference...; on the .NET tab, select System.EnterpriseServices and click Select; and then click OK.

7. Open the Util.vb source file.

8. Import the following namespaces: System.EnterpriseServices and System .Runtime.InteropServices. These namespaces give us support for Component Services as well as COM interfaces.

9. Define the Utils class as follows:

```
Imports System.EnterpriseServices
Imports System.Runtime.InteropServices
<ClassInterface(ClassInterfaceType.AutoDual)> _
  Public Class Utils
     Inherits ServicedComponent
    ...
End Class
```

The attribute declares the class to have a dual COM interface so that the component can be used by clients built with Visual Basic 6.0 or VBScript.

10. In the Util class, define a method named `GetHistory()`, as shown in this code segment:

```
'use the shared property manager to retrieve current event history
Public Function GetHistory() As String
    Dim strValue As String
    Dim sp As SharedProperty = GetSharedProperty()
    strValue = sp.Value
    sp.Value = ""   'clear report string
    Return strValue
End Function
```

The `GetSharedProperty()` method is defined further down in this exercise; it returns a reference to the shared property for this component.

11. Declare a module named **modUtil**, and place it after the class definition for the Utils class.

12. In the modUtil module, declare a function named `GetSharedProperty()` that returns a SharedProperty. Mark the function as a friend. The code should look this way:

```
Module modUtil
  Friend Function GetSharedProperty() As SharedProperty
    Dim bFlag As Boolean
    Dim spm As New SharedPropertyGroupManager()
    Dim spg As SharedPropertyGroup, sp As SharedProperty

    spg = spm.CreatePropertyGroup("Messages", PropertyLockMode.SetGet, _
            PropertyReleaseMode.Process, bFlag)
    sp = spg.CreateProperty("History", bFlag)

    If bFlag = False Then
      sp.Value = ""
    End If
    Return sp
  End Function
End Module
```

The `GetSharedProperty()` method will return a reference to the same shared property for every call. This way, you have a means of sharing this property between multiple instances of the same class.

Next you will implement the `Pool` class:

13. Open the Pool.vb file in the editor.

14. Import the System.EnterpriseServices and System.Runtime.InteropServices namespaces.

15. Define the Pool class as follows:

```
<Transaction(TransactionOption.Required), _
 ClassInterfaceAttribute(ClassInterfaceType.AutoDual), _
 ObjectPooling(Enabled:=True, MinPoolSize:=5, MaxPoolSize:=42), _
 ConstructionEnabled(True)> _
 Public Class Pool
    Inherits ServicedComponent

End Class
```

The attributes define this class to require transactions, to support a dual COM interface, to have pooling enabled with a minimum number of objects set to 5 and the maximum to 42, and to have the constructor string enabled.

16. Declare a private string variable in the Pool class, naming the variable **strX**.

17. Declare a private sub method AddToSharedProperty(ByVal strY As String) to the Pool class. Add code to the method as follows:

```
Private Sub AddToSharedProperty(ByVal strY As String)
  'get the "History" shared property
  Dim sp As SharedProperty = GetSharedProperty()
  sp.Value = sp.Value.ToString & "Pool-" & strY & "(" & strX & ")" & vbCrLf
End Sub
```

This method gets a reference to the shared property and appends the parameter to that property.

18. Declare a default constructor, and call the AddToSharedProperty() method with a string to indicate that the constructor executed.

```
Public Sub New()
    AddToSharedProperty("Constructor")
End Sub
```

19. Declare a Construct() method. It should be protected and overridden from the ServicedComponent base class. Assign the parameter to the strX variable, and call the AddToSharedProperty() method to indicate that Construct() executed.

```
Protected Overrides Sub Construct(ByVal s As String)
    strX = s
    AddToSharedProperty("Contruct")
End Sub
```

20. Declare a protected overridden CanBePooled() method. Call the AddToSharedProperty() method to indicate you were called and return True.

```
Protected Overrides Function CanBePooled() As Boolean
    AddToSharedProperty("CanBePooled")
    Return True
End Function
```

21. Declare a public function CtoF(ByVal c As Decimal) As Decimal that returns the temperature in Fahrenheit given that c is in Celsius. Mark the function to be AutoComplete. Call `AddToSharedProperty()` to indicate the method was called.

```
<AutoComplete()> Public Function CtoF(ByVal c As Decimal) As Decimal
    Return (c * 9 / 5) + 32
    AddToSharedProperty("CtoF")
End Function
```

22. Declare a public function FtoC(ByVal f As Decimal) As Decimal that returns the temperature in Celsius given that f is in Fahrenheit. Mark the function to be `AutoComplete`. Call `AddToSharedProperty()` to indicate the method was called.

```
<AutoComplete()> Public Function FtoC(ByVal f As Decimal) As Decimal
    Return (f - 32) * 5 / 9
    AddToSharedProperty("FtoC")
End Function
```

23. Implement the `Activate()` and `Deactivate()` overridden methods, calling `AddToSharedProperty()` in each method to indicate you were there.

```
Protected Overrides Sub Activate()
    AddToSharedProperty("Activate")
End Sub
Protected Overrides Sub Deactivate()
    AddToSharedProperty("DeActivate")
End Sub
```

Next you will implement the NPool class. To perform this action, you will copy methods from the Pool class, as the functions will be the same except for the pooling behavior.

24. Open the NPool.vb source file in the editor.

25. Import the System.EnterpriseServices and System.Runtime.InteropServices namespaces.

26. Define the NPool class to require transactions, support the dual COM interface, support Construction strings, and not support object pooling.

```
<Transaction(TransactionOption.Required), _
ClassInterfaceAttribute(ClassInterfaceType.AutoDual), _
ObjectPooling(Enabled:=False), ConstructionEnabled(True)> _
```

```
Public Class NPool
    Inherits ServicedComponent
...
End Class
```

27. Declare a private string variable in the NPool class; name the variable **strX**.

28. Copy the following methods from the Pool class to the NPool class: `Activate()`, `Deactivate()`, `CtoF()`, `FtoC()`, `New()`, `AddToSharedProperty()`, and `Construct()`.

29. Change the `AddToSharedProperty()` method to identify the NPool class.

```
Private Sub AddToSharedProperty(ByVal strY As String)
    'get the "History" shared property
    Dim sp As SharedProperty = GetSharedProperty()
    sp.Value = sp.Value.ToString & "No Pool-" & strY _
        & "(" & strX & ")" & vbCrLf
End Sub
```

30. Save and build the component, resolving any build errors.

In order for us to be able to register the component, you will need to create a strong-name key file and add it to the assembly.

EXERCISE 3-2

Create a Strong-Name Key

1. Open the PoolComponent project.

2. Start a Visual Studio .NET Command Prompt. Click Start | Programs | Microsoft Visual Studio .NET | Visual Studio .NET Tools | Visual Studio .NET Command Prompt.

3. Change directory to the location of the PoolComponent project (C:\VB\PoolComponent).

4. Use the strong-name utility (sn.exe) to generate the strong-name key for the component.

```
C:\>cd \VB\PoolComponent
C:\VB\PoolComponent>sn -k PoolComponent.snk

Microsoft (R) .NET Framework Strong Name Utility  Version 1.0.3705.0
```

```
Copyright (C) Microsoft Corporation 1998-2001. All rights reserved.

Key pair written to PoolComponent.snk
C:\VB\PoolComponent>
```

5. Switch back to Visual Studio .NET.

6. Open the AssemblyInfo.vb file in the editor.

7. Import the System.EnterpriseService namespace.

8. Add the following assembly attributes:

```
<Assembly: ApplicationActivation(ActivationOption.Server)>
<Assembly: ApplicationName("Pool Component")>
<Assembly: Description("Study Guide serviced component exercise")>
<Assembly: AssemblyKeyFile("PoolComponent.snk")>
```

9. Save the project.

10. On the Build menu, click the Build Solution.

11. Close Visual Studio .NET.

    After building the serviced component, you need to register it to make it available in Component Services.

12. Return to the Visual Studio .NET command prompt, or open a new one.

13. Navigate to the directory where the PoolComponent.dll component is located (C:\VB\PoolComponent\bin).

14. Execute the Regsvcs.exe command to register the component.

```
C:\VB\PoolComponent\bin>Regsvcs.exe PoolComponent.dll
Microsoft (R) .NET Framework Services Installation Utility Version 1.0.3705.0
Copyright (C) Microsoft Corporation 1998-2001. All rights reserved.

Installed Assembly:
        Assembly: C:\VB\PoolComponent\bin\PoolComponent.dll
        Application: Pool Component
        TypeLib: c:\vb\poolcomponent\bin\PoolComponent.tlb

C:\VB\PoolComponent\bin>
```

To verify that the component was successfully installed as a serviced component, open the Component Service console, drill down to the COM+ applications, and locate the Pool component, shown here.

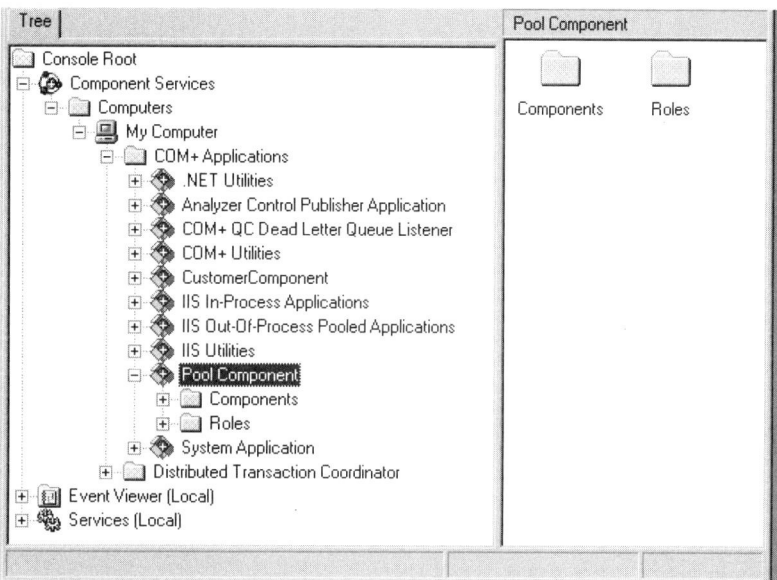

15. To configure the Pool component, open the properties for the PoolComponent
.Pool component and select the Activation tab. Enable the constructor string
to be "Pooled:" as shown here:

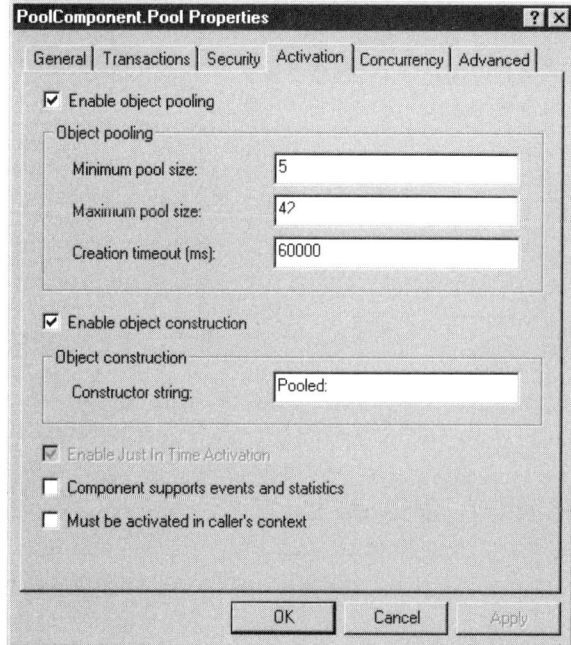

16. Configure the PoolComponent.NPool component, enabling the constructor string to be "Non-pooled:"

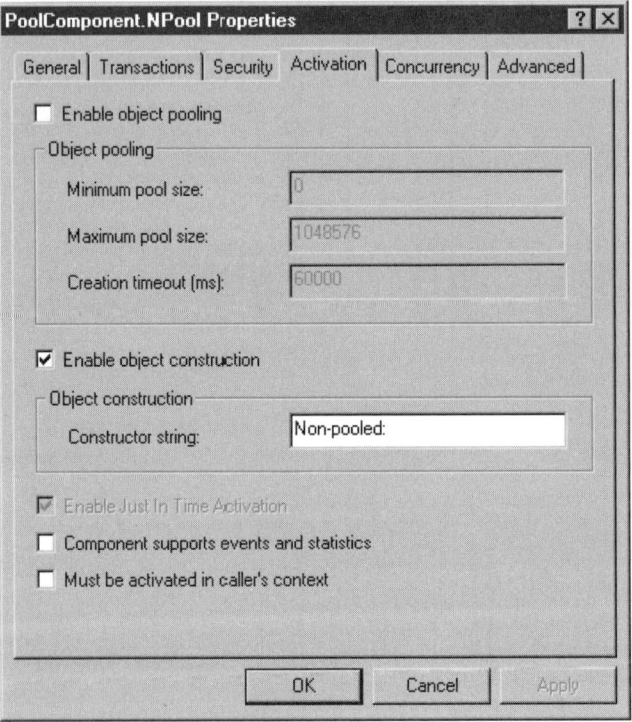

17. Close the Component Services console.

That is the last step in building and configuring the serviced component; the next task is to use or consume the component.

FROM THE CLASSROOM

The enterprise environment that has been the leader in the Microsoft world for the last five to six years started out as Microsoft Transaction Server (MTS). This addition to the Windows NT operating system, together with the release of Visual Basic 6, made it possible for us as Visual Basic developers to build functioning enterprise applications. MTS was the object resource broker that made a business tier possible.

FROM THE CLASSROOM

With Windows 2000, the resource broker was renamed Component Services to announce that it had changed significantly; at the same time, the component object model (COM) that was used in the MTS environment changed to COM+.

Today large numbers of applications are operating in the distributed environment, and it is imperative that the .NET components work seamlessly with the existing environment. That is what the System.EnterpriseServices namespace and library provides to us.

One of the major benefits of the distributed environment with a resource broker that handles the instantiation of the class and the invocation of the methods is that the object is part of a transaction and is thus able to extend the transaction space from the database environment to include the software components that perform the data manipulations.

Each object has the ability to vote on the outcome of the entire transaction that it is one part of; it does so by calling methods on the ContextUtil class. This class represents the environment the object is currently executing in.

Another feature of the Component Services environment is that objects are made available to the client just-in-time —the object is recycled between method calls. The client signals that the object is no longer needed by calling the `SetComplete()` or `SetAbort()` method, which also votes on the transaction. This feature has a problematic side—state—as there is no way of storing data in the object between calls (it is destroyed). This poses a bit of a conundrum; programmers work around the issue of state either by clever coding or by using the Shared Property Manager (SPM). The SPM is an object provided by Component Services that allows objects in the same application to store and read shared data that is stored by Component Services.

Even though there will be literature advocating .NET Remoting in preference to Component Services, Component Services will be around for quite some time, and thus warrants study.

CERTIFICATION OBJECTIVE 3.03

Consuming a Serviced Component

You are going to consume the Pool component in a Windows application that will convert temperatures and display how the component behaves when pooled and not pooled.

In order for the client application to be able to consume the serviced component, there must be a reference set to the serviced component. This reference reads in the manifest (type library) of the serviced component. The namespace of the serviced component must also be imported to make the classes and methods available.

Support for Component Services comes from the System.EnterpriseServices.dll library—this library must be referenced in the project as well.

Once the references and namespaces are set, the code to use a class in a serviced component follows the same pattern as when you use a class from any assembly. As an example, the following code segment uses the `Pool` class from our earlier exercises:

```
Dim obj As Pool
obj = New Pool()
lblFahrenheit.Text = obj.CtoF(CType(txtCelsius.Text, Decimal))
```

In the following exercise, you will build an application that highlights the pooling of objects and the methods that are called by Component Services in order to manage the serviced components.

EXERCISE 3-3

Building the Consumer Application

You are going to build a Windows form that has a couple of Textbox controls for data display and input, as well as two Button controls to call the Pool and NPool conversion routines.

1. Create a new Visual Basic .NET project based on the Windows Application Template, naming the project **WinPool**.

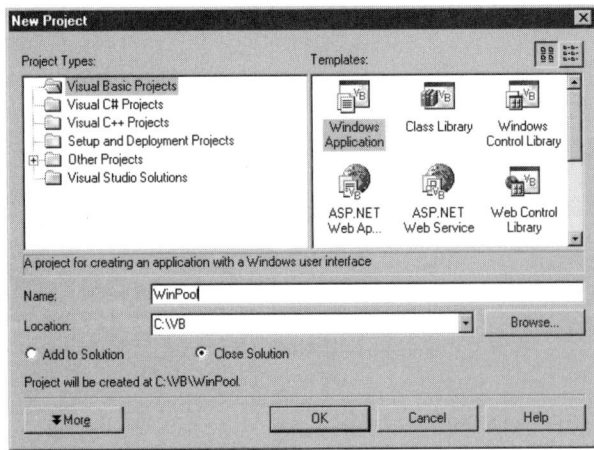

2. Rename the form to **frmPoolTest**.

3. Set the `Text` property of the form to "Pool Component".

4. Add a reference to the PoolComponent serviced component by browsing for the PoolComponent.dll.

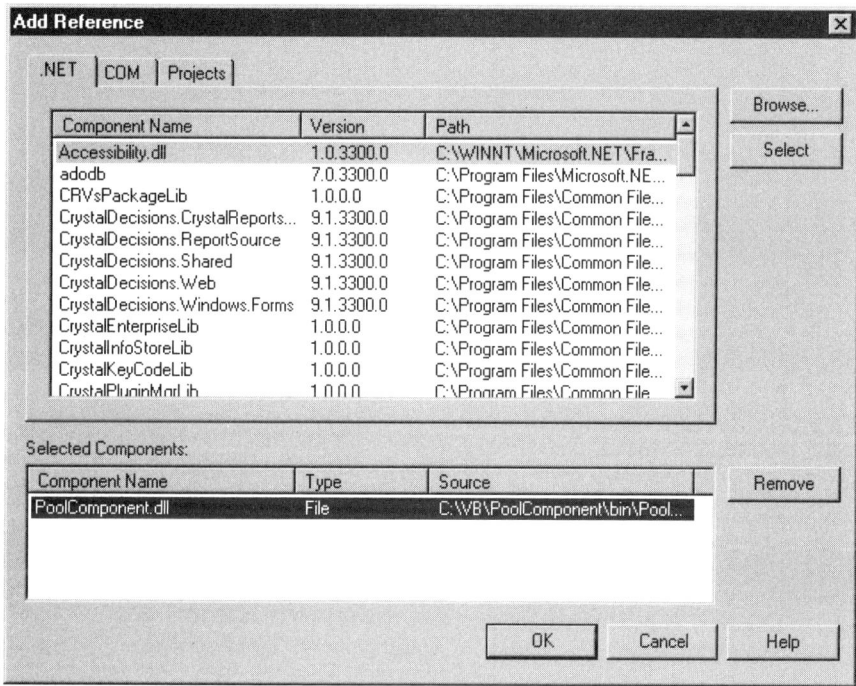

5. Add a reference to the System.EnterpriseServices.dll.

6. Add a statement to the frmPoolComponent to import the PoolComponent namespace.

7. Add a TextBox to the form, set the MultiLine property to True, add a vertical scrollbar, and name the TextBox **txtStatus**.

8. Add a TextBox to the form, setting the name of the control to **txtCelsius**.

9. Add a Label to the form, setting the name to **lblFahrenheit**.

10. Add a Button to the form, setting the name to **btnCtoF**, and change the Text property to "C->F".

11. Add a TextBox to the form, setting the name of the control to **txtFahrenheit**.

12. Add a Label to the form, setting the name to **lblCelsius**.

13. Add a Button to the form, setting the name to **btnFtoC**, and change the Text property to "F->C".

14. Add a CheckBox control to the form, naming the control **chkPooled**.

15. Change the Text property of the chkPool control to "Pooled".

The layout of the form is shown next.

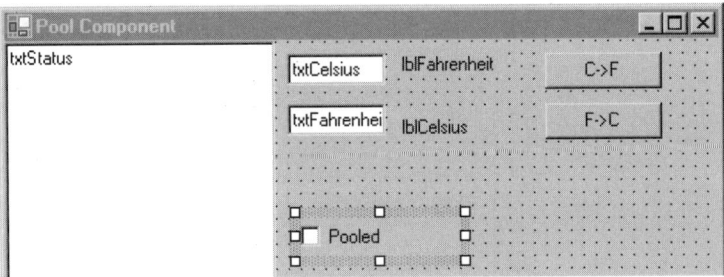

16. Implement a private method named UpdateStatus() that instantiates the Utils class and calls the GetReport() method. Concatenate the returned string from GetReport() with the content of the txtStatus control, and end by setting the reference to the Utils object to nothing, as in this code segment:

```
Private Sub UpdateStatus()
    'display the event status
    Dim r As New Utils()
    txtStatus.Text += r.GetReport() + vbCrLf
    r = Nothing
End Sub
```

17. Implement the click event for the btnCtoF button to check the chkPool control and call the methods on the Pool class if selected; otherwise, call the NPool methods. Call the UpdateStatus() method after each interaction with the Pool or NPool classes to update the txtStatus control. Start the event handler by clearing the txtStatus control.

Create multiple objects of the class and call the conversion method to convert the number in txtCelsius to degrees Fahrenheit in lblFahrenheit.

The purpose of this event handler is to create a number of objects and call the methods to see the interaction between the serviced component and the client application.

The code is shown in this code segment:

```
Private Sub btnCtoF_Click(ByVal sender As System.Object, _
        ByVal e As System.EventArgs) Handles btnCtoF.Click
    txtStatus.Text = ""
    If chkPool.Checked Then
        Dim obj As Pool
        obj = New Pool()
        UpdateStatus()
        lblFahrenheit.Text = obj.CtoF(CType(txtCelsius.Text, Decimal))
        UpdateStatus()
        lblFahrenheit.Text = obj.CtoF(CType(txtCelsius.Text, Decimal))
        UpdateStatus()
        Dim a As New Pool()
        Dim b As New Pool()
        Dim c As New Pool()
        Dim d As New Pool()
        UpdateStatus()
        lblFahrenheit.Text = a.CtoF(CType(txtCelsius.Text, Decimal))
        UpdateStatus()
        lblFahrenheit.Text = b.CtoF(CType(txtCelsius.Text, Decimal))
        UpdateStatus()
        lblFahrenheit.Text = c.CtoF(CType(txtCelsius.Text, Decimal))
        UpdateStatus()
        lblFahrenheit.Text = d.CtoF(CType(txtCelsius.Text, Decimal))
        UpdateStatus()
    Else
        Dim obj As NPool
        obj = New NPool()
        UpdateStatus()
        lblFahrenheit.Text = obj.CtoF(CType(txtCelsius.Text, Decimal))
        UpdateStatus()
        lblFahrenheit.Text = obj.CtoF(CType(txtCelsius.Text, Decimal))
        UpdateStatus()
        Dim a As New NPool()
        Dim b As New NPool()
        Dim c As New NPool()
        Dim d As New NPool()
        UpdateStatus()
        lblFahrenheit.Text = a.CtoF(CType(txtCelsius.Text, Decimal))
        UpdateStatus()
        lblFahrenheit.Text = b.CtoF(CType(txtCelsius.Text, Decimal))
        UpdateStatus()
        lblFahrenheit.Text = c.CtoF(CType(txtCelsius.Text, Decimal))
        UpdateStatus()
```

```
        lblFahrenheit.Text = d.CtoF(CType(txtCelsius.Text, Decimal))
        UpdateStatus()
    End If
End Sub
```

18. Implement the click event for the btnFtoC button to check the chkPool control and call the methods on the Pool class if selected; otherwise, call the NPool methods. Call the `UpdateStatus()` method after each interaction with the Pool or NPool class to update the txtStatus control. Start the event handler by clearing the txtStatus control.

19. Create multiple objects of the class and call the conversion method to convert the number in txtFahrenheit to degrees Celsius in lblCelsius. The purpose of this event handler is to create a number of objects and call the methods to see the interaction between the serviced component and the client application.

    The code is shown in this code segment:

```
Private Sub btnFtoC_Click(ByVal sender As System.Object, _
        ByVal e As System.EventArgs) Handles btnFtoC.Click
    txtStatus.Text = ""     If chkPool.Checked Then
        Dim obj As Pool
        obj = New Pool()
        UpdateStatus()
        lblCelsius.Text = obj.FtoC(CType(txtFahrenheit.Text, Decimal))
        UpdateStatus()
        lblCelsius.Text = obj.FtoC(CType(txtFahrenheit.Text, Decimal))
        UpdateStatus()
        Dim a As New Pool()
        Dim b As New Pool()
        Dim c As New Pool()
        Dim d As New Pool()
        UpdateStatus()
        lblCelsius.Text = a.FtoC(CType(txtFahrenheit.Text, Decimal))
        UpdateStatus()
        lblCelsius.Text = b.FtoC(CType(txtFahrenheit.Text, Decimal))
        UpdateStatus()
        lblCelsius.Text = c.FtoC(CType(txtFahrenheit.Text, Decimal))
        UpdateStatus()
        lblCelsius.Text = d.FtoC(CType(txtFahrenheit.Text, Decimal))
        UpdateStatus()
```

```
        Else
            Dim obj As NPool
            obj = New NPool()
            UpdateStatus()
            lblCelsius.Text = obj.FtoC(CType(txtFahrenheit.Text, Decimal))
            UpdateStatus()
            lblCelsius.Text = obj.FtoC(CType(txtFahrenheit.Text, Decimal))
            UpdateStatus()
            Dim a As New NPool()
            Dim b As New NPool()
            Dim c As New NPool()
            Dim d As New NPool()
            UpdateStatus()
            lblCelsius.Text = a.FtoC(CType(txtFahrenheit.Text, Decimal))
            UpdateStatus()
            lblCelsius.Text = b.FtoC(CType(txtFahrenheit.Text, Decimal))
            UpdateStatus()
            lblCelsius.Text = c.FtoC(CType(txtFahrenheit.Text, Decimal))
            UpdateStatus()
            lblCelsius.Text = d.FtoC(CType(txtFahrenheit.Text, Decimal))
            UpdateStatus()
        End If
    End Sub
```

20. Locate the constructor for the form; include code to clear the txtStatus, txtFahrenheit, txtCelisus, lblFahrenheit, and lblCelsius controls.

```
Public Sub New()
    MyBase.New()
    'This call is required by the Windows Form Designer.
    InitializeComponent()

    'Add any initialization after the InitializeComponent() call
    txtStatus.Text = ""
    txtFahrenheit.Text = ""
    txtCelsius.Text = ""
    lblFahrenheit.Text = ""
    lblCelsius.Text = ""
End Sub
```

21. Save and build the WinPool project.

22. Run the WinPool project. Enter **32** as the value in the txtCelsius control, make sure the chkPool control is cleared, and click C->F. The result is shown next.

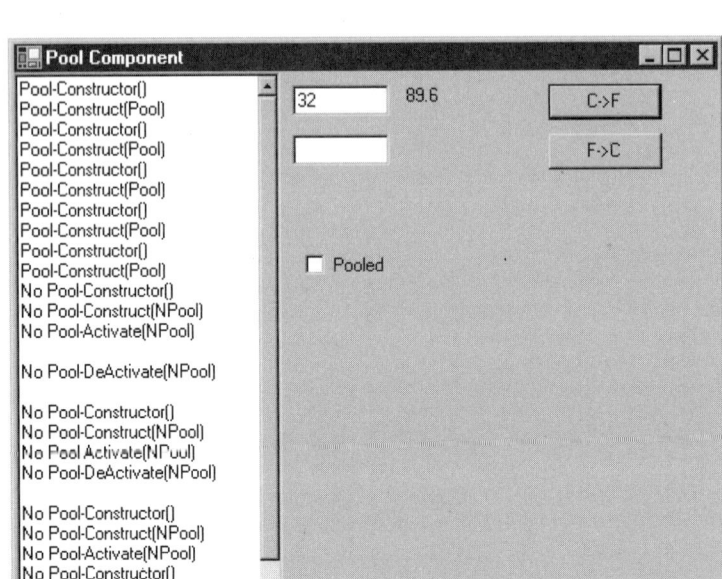

The status information tells the story of how the serviced component operates in Component Services. Note the five instances of the `Pool` object that are instantiated first—this is because you set the MinPoolSize parameter to five when you built the control. Notice also that the `Construct()` method is called, because the Construction String value has been set, Pool-Construct(Pool).

```
Pool-Constructor()
Pool-Construct(Pool)
...
No Pool-Constructor()
No Pool-Construct(NPool)
No Pool-Activate(NPool)
No Pool-DeActivate(NPool)
...
```

For every NPool object constructed, there is a call to the constructor followed with a call to the `Construct()` method. The `Activate()`–`Deactivate()`

methods are called when the CtoF() method is called. After the call, the object is destroyed.

23. Run the WinPool application with the same settings as in step 21, except in this instance, check the Pooled check box. The result is found in Figure 3-3.

Because the five objects for the pool were already created in the preceding step, you only use the object in this step.

```
Pool-Activate(Pool)
Pool-DeActivate(Pool)
Pool-CanBePooled(Pool)
. . .
```

Note that for every use of a Pool object, there is a call to Activate followed by a call to Deactivate when the object is no longer needed. The CanBePooled() method is called to make sure the object can be returned to the pool.

FIGURE 3-3

The WinPool application using the Pool class

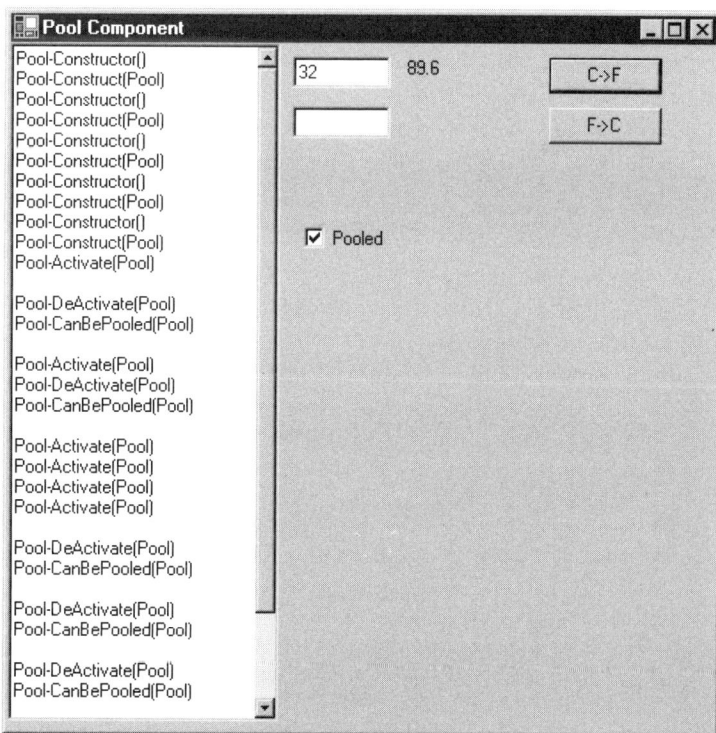

exam
ⓦatch

The overridden `CanBePooled()` method should return True if it is safe to return the object to the pool.

SCENARIO & SOLUTION

How do I declare a class to be part of a serviced component?	In order to mark a class as being a serviced component, you need to derive the class from the `System.ServicedComponent` class. A number of attributes control the behavior of the class, but there are no required attributes that must be used with the class declaration that makes the class a part of the serviced component.

How do I program transactions?	The first step is to mark the class with the <Transaction> attribute and set the transaction value. Possible values are:
	    Disabled—ignore transactions.
	    NotSupported—no support for transactions.
	    Required—transactions are required, will join an existing transaction, or if there is no existing one, will create a new transaction.
	    RequiresNew—transactions are required, and it must be a new transaction.
	    Supported—will participate if there is a transaction.
	Once the transaction support is defined, you need to vote on the transaction outcome by calling the `SetComplete()` method to vote for success or the `SetAbort()` method to vote for failure. They are member methods of the ContextUtil class.

Do I always have to vote on the transaction programmatically?	No, you can mark a method using the <AutoComplete()> attribute; this way, a normal completion of the method votes for success and any exception votes for failure of the transaction.
How do I pass a string to the class when the class is being instantiated?	Mark the class with the <ConstructionEnabled(True)> attribute, and override the `Construct(s As String)` method to receive the string from Component Services during instantiation of the object.
What is object pooling?	Object pooling is the feature of Component Services that allows a class to have multiple object instances that are kept for future use of a client. The impact on the performance of the system is dramatic if the instantiation of the object is lengthy.
What is the strong name?	The strong name consists of an assembly's identity strengthened by a public key and a digital signature generated over the assembly. Assemblies with the same strong name are expected to be identical. The strong name is used to ensure that the assembly has not been compromised, and to identify the assembly when installed.

SCENARIO & SOLUTION

What is AutoDual?	Using AutoDual requests that the compiler build a dual COM interface as well as providing a type library for use by legacy components. Microsoft discourages the use of AutoDual because of the reliance on the old component registration and the inherent problems with the old system.
Why do I have to register the serviced component?	Component Services relies on the Windows Registry for information on the serviced components; in order for our Visual Basic .NET assembly to be used by Component Services, it must be registered.
Why do I have to set a reference in the client to the serviced component?	You need to set the reference to provide the assembly manifest to Visual Studio .NET so that it can verify the type information.

CERTIFICATION SUMMARY

In this chapter, you explored serviced components and the environment where these components reside. In earlier versions of the Windows NT operating system, this environment was called Microsoft Transaction Server—the name was changed when Windows 2000 was released to Component Services.

The focus of the exam is the same focus I have used in this chapter—how to build a serviced component using Visual Basic .NET. One of the more important issues is the use of attributes to control the behavior of classes and methods. The exam tests your knowledge of how to declare a class that will be assembled into a serviced component.

The assembly of multiple classes into a serviced component requires a strong-name key file generated by sn.exe and that the assembly manifest reference that strong-name key file. The content of the manifest is controlled by the AssemblyInfo.vb file that is part of the project.

To consume a serviced component, you need to set a reference to the serviced component, as well as to the System.EnterpriseServices.dll library; by importing the namespace of the serviced component, you are ready to treat the classes as if they were local to your project.

✓ TWO-MINUTE DRILL

Building a Serviced Component

❏ It is the System.EnterpriseServices namespace that contains all the support for serviced components.

❏ Component Services gives components the ability to be transactional, i.e., to vote on the outcome of a transaction.

❏ Transactions are an all-or-nothing workflow.

❏ Use the ContextUtil class to call `SetComplete()` to indicate success, or `SetAbort()` to indicate failure.

❏ Component Services can use object pooling; set the MinPoolSize and MaxPoolSize attributes to configure pooling.

❏ If an object is marked to be pooled, the `CanBePooled()` method will be called after each deactivation of the object.

❏ Set the ConstructionEnabled attribute to True and override the `Construct()` method to implement Construction Strings.

❏ Manage the serviced components by using the Component Services console.

❏ Create a strong-name key file using the sn.exe utility.

❏ Configure the serviced components assembly by adding four attributes to the AssemblyInfo.vb file.

❏ Register the serviced component with Component Services using the Regsvcs.exe utility.

Consuming a Serviced Component

❏ Set a reference to the serviced component in the client.

❏ Import the serviced component namespace in the client.

❏ Set a reference to the System.EnterpriseServices.dll library in the client application.

❏ The lifetime of the serviced component is controlled by Component Services.

---

*Please be aware that the questions and answers at the end of this chapter for the Two-Minute Drill, the Self Test Questions, and the Self Test Answers may *not* match the order of those found in the corresponding chapter on the CD-ROM.

SELF TEST

Building a Serviced Component

1. You have been given the source code for a class a developer at your company has worked on. The class is shown in the following code segment:

```
<Transaction(TransactionOption.Required), _
 ClassInterfaceAttribute(ClassInterfaceType.AutoDual), _
 ObjectPooling(Enabled:=True, MinPoolSize:=5, MaxPoolSize:=42), _
 ConstructionEnabled(True)>_
 Public Class MyClass
    Inherits ServicedComponent
  Public Sub MySub()
    Try
      UpdateDatabase()
      ContextUtilSetComplete()
    Catch e As Exception
      ContextUtil.SetAbort()
      Throw e
    End Try
  End Sub
End Class
```

How will you rewrite the MyClass class to avoid the `SetComplete()` and `SetAbort()` calls?

A. Will you use this code?

```
<Transaction(TransactionOption.Required), _
 ClassInterfaceAttribute(ClassInterfaceType.AutoDual), _
 ObjectPooling(Enabled:=True, MinPoolSize:=5, MaxPoolSize:=42), _
 ConstructionEnabled(True)>_
    Public Class MyClass
    Inherits ServicedComponent
   <AutoComplete(True)> Public Sub MySub()
       UpdateDatabase()
   End Sub
End Class
```

B. Will you use this code?

```
<Transaction(TransactionOption.Required), _
 ClassInterfaceAttribute(ClassInterfaceType.AutoDual), _
 ObjectPooling(Enabled:=True, MinPoolSize:=5, MaxPoolSize:=42), _
 ConstructionEnabled(True)>_
```

```
      Public Class MyClass
        Inherits ServicedComponent
     <AutoComplete(True)> Public Sub MySub()
          UpdateDatabase()
      End Sub
    End Class
```

C. Will you use this code?

```
<ClassInterfaceAttribute(ClassInterfaceType.AutoDual), _
 ObjectPooling(Enabled:=True, MinPoolSize:=5, MaxPoolSize:=42), _
 ConstructionEnabled(True)>_
   Public Class MyClass
     Inherits ServicedComponent
   <AutoComplete(True)> Public Sub MySub()
        UpdateDatabase()
   End Sub
 End Class
```

D. Or, will you use this code?

```
<ClassInterfaceAttribute(ClassInterfaceType.AutoDual), _
 ObjectPooling(Enabled:=True, MinPoolSize:=5, MaxPoolSize:=42), _
 ConstructionEnabled(True)>_
   Public Class MyClass
     Inherits ServicedComponent
   <AutoComplete(True)> Public Sub MySub()
        UpdateDatabase()
   End Sub
 End Class
```

2. You are developing a serviced component that will retrieve a dataset from a database and return it to the client. As part of the instantiation of the object, you need to pass a string that represents the connection string for the database. Which two answers are correct? Select two correct answers. Each answer makes up part of the solution.

   A. Add the <ConstructorEnabled(True)> attribute to the class declaration.

   B. Add the <ConstructionEnabled(True)> attribute to the class declaration.

   C. Implement the method with the signature Protected Overridden Construct(ByVal s As String).

   D. Implement the method with the signature Protected Overrides Construct(ByVal s As String).

3. You need to have a number of components in a Component Services application use the same connection string to a database. The string is built during execution and cannot be built using construction strings. What is the best solution for this application?

A. Define a Public variable in the Application object, and program all components to use this variable.

B. Use a Shared Property Manager and program all components to use this Shared Property Manager.

C. Store the connection string in the Registry, and program all components to use this value from the Registry.

D. Develop a Windows service that is used to store the connection string, and program all components to use this value from the service.

4. From what class is `Deactivate()` derived?

A. `System.EnterpriseServices`

B. `System.ServiceComponent`

C. `System.MarshalByRefObject`

D. `System.EnterpriseServices.ServicedComponent`

5. You are developing a serviced component. You now need to create an assembly that can be installed in Component Services. What steps do you need to perform? Select all right answers.

A. Create an AssemblyKeyFile using the sn.exe utility.

B. Create an AssemblyKeyFile using the assemblykey.exe utility.

C. Create a strong ApplicationName using the sn.exe utility.

D. Add the AssemblyKeyFile to the AssemblyInfo.vb file

E. Add the AssemblyName to the AssemblyInfo.vb file.

6. You are ready to install the serviced component you have developed to Component Services. What tool will you use to perform the installation?

A. Regsvr32.exe

B. Regsvcs.exe

C. The Component Services console

D. The Computer Management console

7. You have developed a serviced component that has the following class declaration:

```
<ClassInterfaceAttribute(ClassInterfaceType.AutoDual), _
  ObjectPooling(Enabled:=True, MinPoolSize:=5, MaxPoolSize:=42), _
```

```
ConstructionEnabled(True)>_
   Public Class MyClass
      Inherits ServicedComponent
 ...
 End Class
```

How many objects will be in the pool after one object has been instantiated and released?

A. 42

B. 5

C. 1

D. 0

Consume a Serviced Component

8. You are building a client that will make use of a serviced component. What steps must you take in order to be able to consume the serviced component? Select all the correct answers.

A. Import the namespace of the serviced component.

B. Set a reference to the Component.Services library.

C. Set a reference to the serviced component.

D. Set a reference to the System.EnterpriseServices.dll library.

E. Import the System.EnterpriseServices namespace.

9. When is the CanBePooled() method called in the following class?

```
<ClassInterfaceAttribute(ClassInterfaceType.AutoDual), _
   ObjectPooling(Enabled:=True, MinPoolSize:=5, MaxPoolSize:=42), _
   ConstructionEnabled(True)>_
   Public Class MyClass
      Inherits ServicedComponent
 ...
      Protected Overrides Function CanBePooled() As Boolean
         Return False
      End Function
   End Class
```

A. Never

B. During instantiation of the object

C. Every time the object is about to be put back to the pool

D. During installation, and as it returns False, the method will never be called again

10. You have developed the serviced component in this code segment. The class is in a component named MyComp:

```
<ClassInterfaceAttribute(ClassInterfaceType.AutoDual), _
  ObjectPooling(Enabled:=True, MinPoolSize:=5, MaxPoolSize:=42), __
 Public Class MyClass
    Inherits ServicedComponent
    Public Function MyFunc() As String
       Return "Hello World"
    End Function
End Class
```

What code segment correctly consumes the `MyFunc()` function?

A. Will you use this code?

```
Imports MyComp
. . .
    Dim x As New MyClass()
    MsgBox(x.MyFunc())
. . .
```

B. Will you use this code?

```
Imports MyClass
. . .
    Dim x As New MyComp()
    MsgBox(x.MyFunc())
. . .
```

C. Will you use this code?

```
Imports MyComp
. . .
    Dim x As MyClass()
    MsgBox(x.MyFunc())
. . .
```

D. Will you use this code?

```
Imports MyClass
. . .
    Dim x As MyComp
    x = New MyComp()
    MsgBox(x.MyFunc())
. . .
```

SELF TEST ANSWERS

Building a Serviced Component

1. ☑ **B.** The process to avoid using the SetComplete and SetAbort calls is to mark the method with the `<AutoComplete()>` attribute. Then you can remove the Try/Catch construction. The method will automatically vote for success if the method completes successfully; if an exception is thrown, the vote is for failure.
   ☒ **A, C, and D.** Answer **A** is incorrect because the <AutoComplete()> attribute does not take a parameter. Answer **C** is incorrect because the <Transaction()> attribute is missing. Answer **D** is incorrect because the <Transaction()> attribute is missing and the <AutoComplete()> attribute is wrong.

2. ☑ **B and D.** By marking the method with the <ConstructionEnabled(True)> attribute and implementing the overridden `Construct()` method, you can pass a string to the class during instantiation. The correct syntax to implement an overridden method is: Protected Overrides Construct(ByVal s As String).
   ☒ **A and C.** Answer **A** is incorrect because the attribute is incorrect. Answer **C** is incorrect because the signature is wrong.

3. ☑ **B.** The Shared Property Manager is the mechanism that is supplied through Component Services for this kind of shared data between components in an application.
   ☒ **A, C, and D.** **A** is incorrect because an Application object is not part of Components Services. **C** is incorrect because using the Registry for this type of data is dangerous and might lead to corruption of the Registry. **D** is incorrect because the Shared Property Manager performs just that service.

4. ☑ **D.** The `Deactivate()` method is derived from the ServicedComponent class that is part of the System.EnterpriseServices namespace.
   ☒ **A, B, and C.** **A** is incorrect because that is the namespace, not the class. Answer **B** is incorrect because that is the wrong class, and answer **C** is incorrect because that is the wrong class.

5. ☑ **A and D.** You need to create a strong-name file for the AssemblyKeyFile attribute of the AssemblyInfo.vb file.
   ☒ **B, C, and E.** Answer **B** is incorrect because there is no such utility. Answer **C** is incorrect because the sn.exe utility produces a strong-name file that is used with the AssemblyKeyFile attribute. **E** is also incorrect because the AssemblyName attribute is not mandatory.

6. ☑   **B.** The correct tool to use is Regsvcs.exe, which is specially built to ease the management of Component Services for Visual Basic .NET developers.

   ☒   **A, C,** and **D.** Answer **A** is incorrect because that is the utility that is used to register COM components and .dll libraries in the Windows Registry. Answers **C** and **D** are incorrect; these are management consoles that are used with legacy components.

7. ☑   **B.** The pool will be filled with the number of objects indicated in the MinPoolSize parameter.

   ☒   **A, C,** and **D.** These answers are incorrect because the pool will be filled with the number of objects indicated in the MinPoolSize parameter.

Consuming a Serviced Component

8. ☑   **A, C,** and **D.** The client application must have a reference to the System.EnterpriseServices.dll library and the serviced component; only the serviced component's namespace need be imported.

   ☒   **B** and **E.** Answer **B** is incorrect because there is no such namespace. Answer **E** is incorrect because there is no need to import the namespace of the System.EnterpriseServices library.

9. ☑   **C.** The `CanBePooled()` method is called every time the object is about to be returned to the pool; if the return value is True, the object is returned to the pool; if False, it is discarded.

   ☒   **A, B,** and **D.** These answers are incorrect because the `CanBePooled()` method is called every time the object is about to be put back in the pool.

10. ☑   **A.** The namespace imported is the same as the component's, and the object is correctly instantiated; the method call is correct as well.

   ☒   **B, C,** and **D.** Answer **B** is incorrect because the namespace imported is the class name and the object is assigned to the component. Answer **C** is incorrect because the object is never instantiated. Answer **D** is incorrect because the class and component are switched.

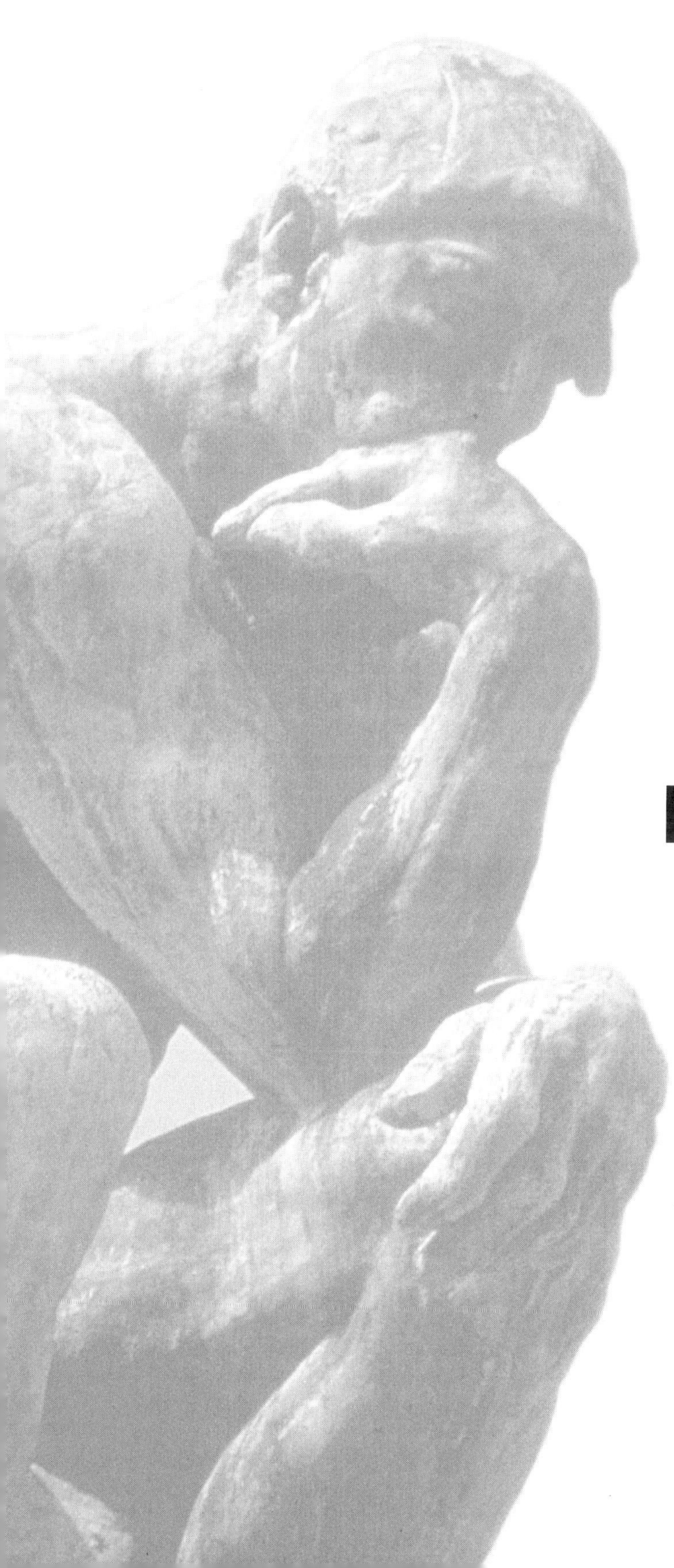

MCAD/MCSD

MICROSOFT® CERTIFIED APPLICATION DEVELOPER
& MICROSOFT® CERTIFIED SOLUTION DEVELOPER

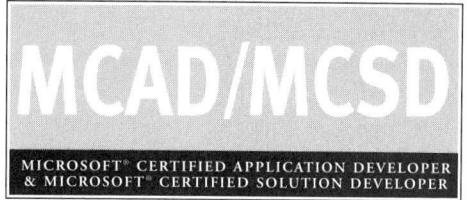

4

Creating and Managing Microsoft .NET Remoting Objects

CERTIFICATION OBJECTIVES

4.01	Overview of .NET Remoting
4.02	Create a .NET Remoting Object Using a TCP Channel
4.03	Create a .NET Remoting Object Using an HTTP Channel
4.04	Client-Activated Objects
4.05	Asynchronous Methods
✓	Two-Minute Drill
Q&A	Self Test

I n this chapter, you will explore the distributed object system called .NET Remoting that is built into the .NET Framework. The short description of .NET Remoting is that it enables you to interact with software objects that are running under the Common Language Runtime on a remote host on the network as if it were a local software object running in the same Common Language Runtime.

CERTIFICATION OBJECTIVE 4.01

Overview of .NET Remoting

The process for using software components (objects) was traditionally one where you as a developer had to code the location of the component and how you were to use that component. There are two distinct ways to use a component in an application—*in process* and *out of process*. In process is when a component is executing inside the same application domain as the application that is using the component. All calls to the component are local to the application. Out of process is when the component is located in a different execution process, either on the local host or on a remote host. The client application uses a proxy component that encapsulates the out-of-process component.

The system called .NET Remoting is the .NET Framework's method for providing built-in support for out-of-process components. In this section, you will learn about the building blocks of .NET Remoting—server objects, the channel formatter, well-known objects, and how to register the objects, as well as the application communication.

The exam will test your knowledge on how to design, build, configure, and use .NET remote software components. The language that is used in the exam is Visual Basic .NET, but the questions are focused on the concepts rather than on the language.

Communication Issues

The process that a .NET application executes in is called an *application domain*. The boundaries of this application domain are such that the application cannot access any resources directly through that boundary.

In order for an application located in one application domain to communicate with another application in a separate application domain, there must be some communications facility between the two applications, as you can see in Figure 4-1.

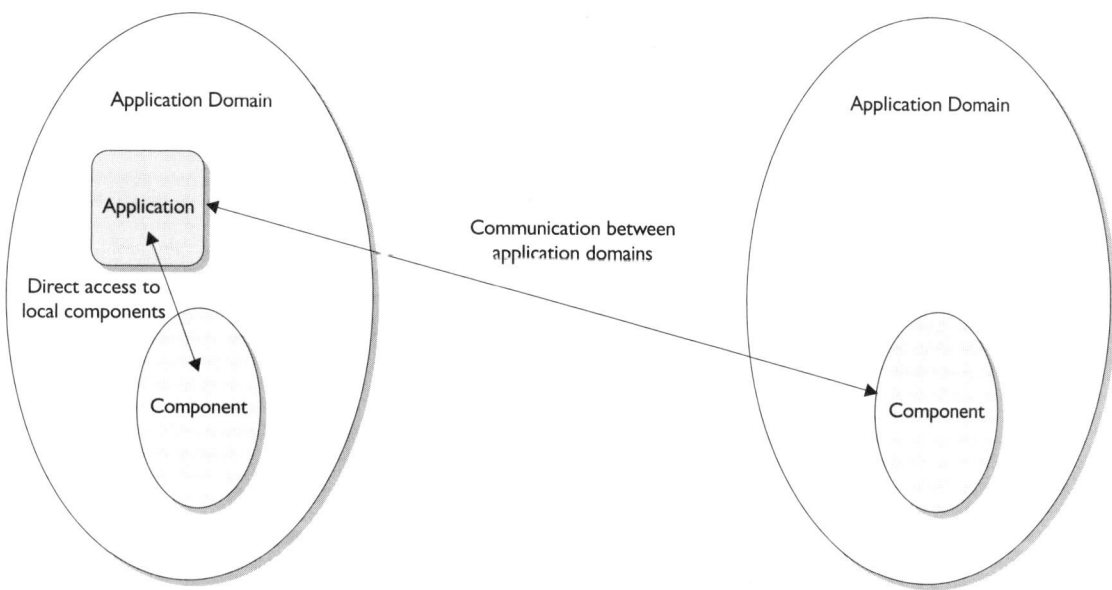

FIGURE 4-1 Communication between two application domains

The problem with the architecture in Figure 4-1 is that the developer must fully define the communication and thus know at design time where the remote object is located and how the network is configured to allow for communication. The first attempt to solve this communications dilemma was to define a protocol that allowed two processes to communicate through process boundaries. The generic name for this protocol is Remote Procedure Call (RPC), and there are a number of implementations of the RPC protocol. Microsoft uses Distributed Component Object Model (DCOM) to refer to their version, for example, but DCOM is not compatible with the RPC used by CORBA.

DCOM uses a proprietary binary protocol to communicate between the different processes. To alleviate the need for the developer to know the communication code, DCOM uses a proxy in the client process that encapsulates the remote process and a stub in the server process that encapsulates the client—the proxy and stub are classes that encapsulate the networking code. In Figure 4-2, you can see where the proxy and stub are inserted.

FIGURE 4-2 **FIGURE 4-2**   The DCOM model

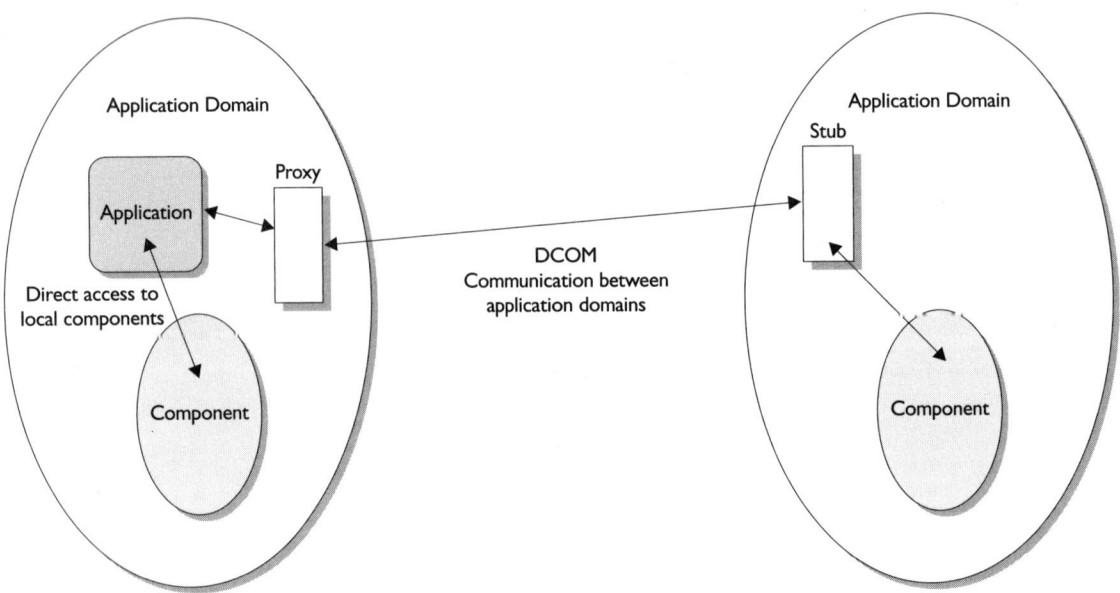

DCOM is a very secure protocol, but it is also proprietary and closed, making DCOM a Microsoft-only protocol that is tied to the Windows operating system. DCOM uses a number of TCP/IP ports in order to work and thus poses a security threat if DCOM is used through a firewall, because those extra ports will have to be enabled in the firewall.

The answer to these issues (proprietary nature and security) is to use standard protocols that can be used securely on the Internet for the communication. That is what .NET Remoting uses for communication. In Table 4-1, you can see how .NET Remoting and DCOM compare.

exam
ⓌatchWatch   *You can expect to need to know some things about DCOM for the exam, such as determining what is the best technology to use in a given situation. Remember that DCOM needs multiple ports open on the firewall for access on the Internet.*

TABLE 4-1   .NET Remoting Versus DCOM

.NET Remoting	DCOM
No built-in security—relies on other components to provide the security.	DCOM is secure and can use encrypted transmissions.
There is a many-to-one relationship between clients and the server.	There is a one-to-one relationship between client and server.
Open architecture that can be expanded and extended at will.	Closed architecture.
The client manages the lifetime of the server.	The server manages its own lifetime—resulting in the server having to ask the client if it can unload.

The .NET Remoting Architecture

The objects (building blocks) that are used in the .NET Remoting architecture appear in the following list:

- **Server object**   Located at the server, provides the service to the client.
- **Channel**   Connects the server and the client. Used to send request messages from the client and response messages from the server.
- **Formatter**   Performs the encoding and decoding of the messages sent between client and server.
- **Registration of well-known objects**   The server object is registered to make it known on the network.
- **Configuration of remoting**   The server object can also be made known on the network by configuration at the client rather than through registration.
- **Activation**   The client activates the server object.

In the following sections, you will learn more about these objects.

Server Object

Before you start coding the server object, you need to determine how the server object will be marshaled during its remoting. The term *marshal* refers to the process of packaging up method calls with parameters and return values, and passing them across process boundaries. You can select from one of the two marshaling methods—by reference and by value. You use the *by reference* method when you want to send a reference to the object rather than a copy of the object to the client. *By value* is the opposite—a copy of the object is sent to the client.

Many server objects cannot or should not be copied and moved to some other process for execution. Extremely large objects with many methods can be poor choices for copying, or passing by value, to other processes. Usually, a client needs only the information returned by one or a few methods on the server object. Copying the entire server object, including what could be vast amounts of internal information or executable structures unrelated to the client's needs, would be a waste of bandwidth as well as of client memory and processing time. In addition, many objects expose public functionality but require private data for internal execution. Copying these objects could enable malicious clients to examine internal data, creating the potential for security problems. Finally, some objects use data that simply cannot be copied in any understandable way. A FileInfo object, for example, contains a reference to an operating system file, which has a unique address in the server process's memory. You can copy this address, but it will never make sense in another process.

The alternative is that the server process passes the client process a reference to the server object, not a copy of the object. Clients can use this reference to call the server object. These calls do not execute in the client process. Instead, the remoting system collects all information about the call and sends it to the server process (marshals), where the call is made to the server object on the client's behalf. The result of the call is then sent back to the client. Thus, resources are used for only the critical information—the call, call arguments, and any return values or exceptions.

exam
ⓦatch
Remember that operating system resources should always be marshaled by reference.

To configure the server object to be marshaled by reference, your class inherits from System.MarshalByRefObject.

```
Public Class RemoteHello
       Inherits MarshalByRefObject
```

```
. . .
End Class
```

To select the marshal by value model, the class does not inherit from System.MarshalByRefObject, as in this example.

```
Public Class RemoteHello
. . .
End Class
```

exam
Watch

If the remote class is not derived from `MarshalByRefObject`, the object will be passed by value.

Channel

Applications in the .NET Framework communicate using either HTTP or TCP channels. When a client calls a method on a remote object, the parameters as well as other details related to the call are transported through the channel to the remote object.

The HTTP channel uses the SOAP protocol to pass messages between the client and the server. These are the features of the HTTP channel:

- It provides communication between client and server using the HTTP protocol.

- It provides encoding of data in SOAP.

- The server receives HTTP requests and sends HTTP responses in ASP.NET and on a TCP socket (port 80 by default).

- It opens by default a maximum of two concurrent connections on the server. This number can be adjusted.

The TCP channel uses a binary stream to pass SOAP-encoded messages between client and server; these are the features of the TCP channel:

- It provides communication between client and server using the TCP protocol.

- It provides encoding of data in a binary stream and SOAP.

- It opens as many connections as there are threads.

on the **job**

If you are developing a number of applications using .NET Remoting, it is easy to make the mistake of using an HTTP channel to connect to a server application domain that listens with a TCP channel. If you do, the client will receive the following exception: "The underlying connection was closed: An unexpected error occurred on a receive." If you receive this exception, you should check for mismatched channels.

To support the channels, you will need to import the namespace System.Runtime .Remoting.Channels, as well as one of the following namespaces: for the HTTP channel, System.Runtime.Remoting.Channels.Http, or for the TCP channel, System.Runtime.Remoting.Channels.Tcp.

To use a channel, you need to create an object based on the channel object, as in this example for a TCP channel:

```
Imports System.Runtime
Imports System.Runtime.Remoting
Imports System.Runtime.Remoting.Channels.Tcp
...
Dim chan as TCPChannel
chan = new TCPChannel()
```

You then register the channel using the
`System.Runtime.Remoting.ChannelServices.RegisterChannel()`
method as in this example:

```
...
ChannelServices.RegisterChannel(chan)
...
```

The equivalent code for an HTTP channel is as follows:

```
Imports System.Runtime
Imports System.Runtime.Remoting
Imports System.Runtime.Remoting.Channels.Http
...
Dim chan as HTTPChannel
chan = new HTTPChannel()

ChannelServices.RegisterChannel(chan)
```

Formatter

The role of the formatter is to encode and decode the messages that are sent between the client and the server on the channel. Some default formatters are based on the channel that is selected, as is shown in Table 4-2.

The SOAP formatter is found in the following class:

```
System.Runtime.Serialization.Formatters.SOAP.SoapFormatter.
```

And the binary formatter is found here:

```
System.Runtime.Serialization.Formatters.Binary.BinaryFormatter.
```

Registration of Well-Known Objects

The server object needs to be known to the network, and that task is performed by calling the `RegisterWellKnownServiceType()` method of System.Runtime .RemotingConfiguration. This method is called with information about the server object as the parameters, as you can see in the following code segment:

```
RemotingConfiguration.RegisterWellKnownServiceType(Type.GetType _
        ("RemotingSamples.HelloServer, object"), "SayHej", _
        WellKnownObjectMode.SingleCall)
```

After calling `RegisterWellKnownServiceType()`, the server object should wait for a request from a client, a blocking call.

TABLE 4-2   The Default Formatters

Channel	Default Formatter
HTTP	SOAP
TCP	Sockets

Configuration of Remoting

An alternative to using the preceding method is to use a text file that contains the information on where the server object can be found. The following example shows the structure of the configuration file that is used by the server object:

```
Name#<Application_Name>
WellKnownObject#<Full_Type_Name>#<Assembly_Name>#<Full_Type>
         #<Activation_Mode>
Channel#<Channel_Assembly_Name>#<Channel_Full_type_name>
       #[Port=<port_number>]
```

The Server calls the method

```
System.Runtime.Remoting.RemotingServices.RemotingConfiguration.Configure()
```

passing the name of the configuration file to the method. The server should now wait for a request from the client.

The client program can also use the same method to control where the server object can be found. The following configuration file is used by the client:

```
Name#<application_name>
Assembly#<Assembly_Name>#<Remote_Application_Name>
        #<Full_Type_Name>=<Object_URI>
RemoteApplication#<Remote_Application_Name>#<Remote_Application_URI>
Channel#<Channel_Assembly_Name>#<Channel_Full_type_Name>
        #[port-<Port_Number>]
```

At this point, the client application is all set to call the server application.

Activation

The server object has two distinct ways of being activated—SingleCall and Singleton. These activation modes can be defined as follows:

- **SingleCall mode**   This mode creates a new instance of the server object for every client connection. Use this mode for server objects that don't share data.

- **Singleton mode**   This mode is where one server object is used by all clients. The Singleton mode is used when the data is to be shared between all clients.

The client application uses the `System.Activator.GetObject()` method to get a proxy that represents the remote object. The same call is used for both the Singleton and SingleCall modes. The Type parameter indicates the activation type of the remote object, and the URL is the location of the object as shown in the following code segment:

```
System.Activator.GetObject(Type, URL)
```

A second way of activating the remote object is to use the `System.Activator`
`.GetInstance()` method. The client must be configured for this practice to work.
Given that the client is configured to use the remoting object RemHello, the remote
object can be activated using either of the following lines:

```
remObj As RemHello = new RemHello()
```

or

```
remObj = System.Activator.GetInstance(TypeOf RemHell)
```

Now put it all together so that you can see how all these parts fit in the .NET
Remoting architecture. Figure 4-3 shows you how the parts interact.

The proxy that is located in the client environment is also called a transparent
proxy because the client process is not aware that the method calls to the remote
object actually pass through the proxy. The transparent proxy looks exactly like the
remote object to the client application. There is a real proxy (called the RealProxy)
that actually performs the communication between the client and the server. In
Figure 4-4, you can see the different objects and their communication.

FIGURE 4-3 The .NET Remoting Interactions

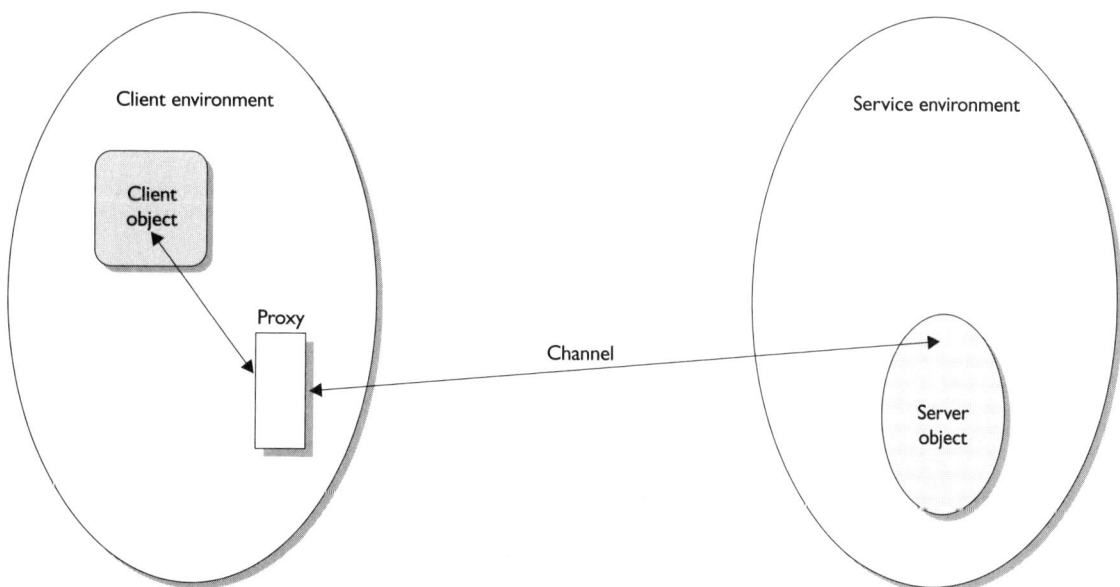

FIGURE 4-4 The remoting communication process

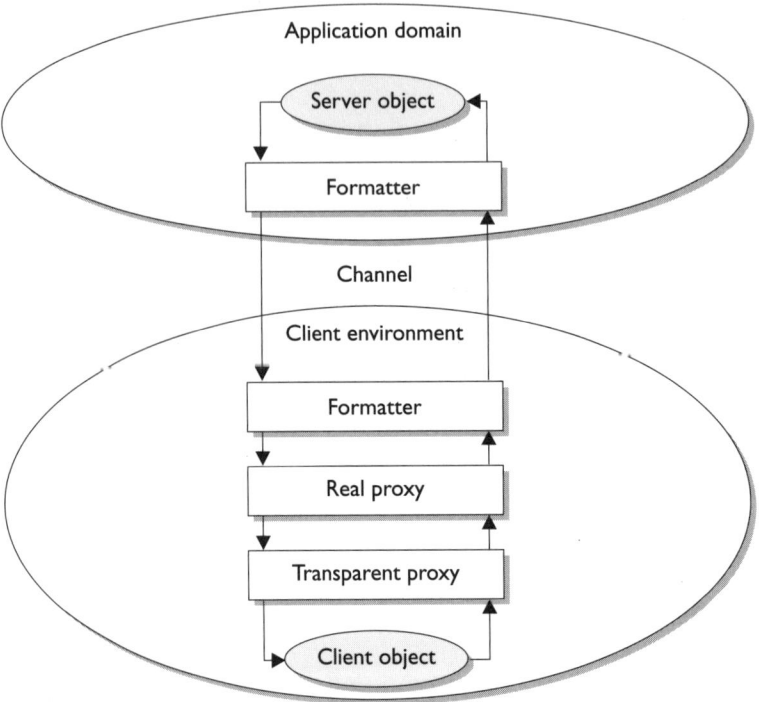

That is all the theory about .NET Remoting. Now you are going to create a couple of remote servers and then consume them.

CERTIFICATION OBJECTIVE 4.02

Creating a .NET Remoting Object Using a TCP Channel

Start by building a Hello World .NET Remoting server—this particular server will use a TCP channel.

EXERCISE 4-1

A .NET Remoting Server Using a TCP Channel

This exercise is built using a text editor and the command-line compiler for Visual Basic .NET.

1. Open the Visual Studio .NET command prompt from Start | Programs | Microsoft Visual Studio .NET | Microsoft Visual Studio .NET Tools | Visual Studio .NET Command Prompt.

2. Change to the VB directory on the C: drive.

```
Setting environment for using Microsoft Visual Studio .NET tools.
(If you also have Visual C++ 6.0 installed and wish to use its tools
from the command line, run vcvars32.bat for Visual C++ 6.0.)
C:\>cd \VB
C:\VB>
```

3. Create a new directory named **Hello** and change to that directory.

```
C:\VB>md Hello
C:\VB>cd Hello
C:\VB\Hello>
```

4. Using your favorite editor (Notepad is used in this example), create a Visual Basic .NET source file named HelloObj.vb. When you are prompted to create a new file, click Yes.

```
C:\VB\Hello>Notepad HelloObj.vb
```

5. Create the remote object by defining a new class as follows:

```
' HelloObj.vb
Imports System
Namespace HelloWorld
Public Class HelloServer
    Inherits MarshalByRefObject

   ' The constructor only writes something on the console
   Public Sub New()
     ' Uncomment the following line to see diagnostics
     ' System.Console.WriteLine("Building Hello...")
   End Sub
```

```
' This is where we do some work greeting our caller
Public Function HelloMethod(str As String) As String
    ' Uncomment the following line to see diagnostics printed
    ' Print diagnostics on the console
    ' Console.WriteLine("Saying Heja to " + str)
    ' Return the greeting to the client
    Return "Hello " + str + " nice to see you in my World!"
  End Function
 End Class
End Namespace
```

The class contains a default constructor and one method (HelloMethod()) that takes a String as a parameter and returns a String to the caller. The String returned is a greeting with the String parameter concatenated into it.

6. Save the HelloObj.vb source file.

7. Compile the source file into a library using the vbc.exe command-line compiler.

```
C:\VB\Hello>vbc /t:library HelloObj.vb
Microsoft (R) Visual Basic .NET Compiler version 7.00.9466
for Microsoft (R) .NET Framework version 1.00.3705.209
Copyright (C) Microsoft Corporation 1987-2001. All rights reserved.
C:\VB\Hello>
```

The result is that a library (HelloObj.dll) is created in the C:\VB\Hello directory. I have commented out the two lines that write diagnostics in the console. You would uncomment those lines (and recompile) to see what is going on.

EXERCISE 4-2

Building the Remote Server

The next step is to build the remote server that will use our HelloObj.dll library to give us HelloWorld functionality:

1. Open the Visual Studio .NET command prompt.

2. Navigate to the C:\VB\Hello directory.

3. Using your favorite editor, create a new Visual Basic .NET source file, named **HelloServer.vb.**

4. Enter the following code in the HelloWorld.vb source file:

```
' HelloServer.vb
Imports System
Imports System.Runtime.Remoting
Imports System.Runtime.Remoting.Channels
Imports System.Runtime.Remoting.Channels.Tcp
Namespace HelloWorld
  Public Class RemoteHello
    <STAThread> _
    Public Shared Sub Main()

      ' Declare and create the channel object
      Dim chan As TcpServerChannel
      ' Make the TCP channel wait on port 4242
      chan = New TcpServerChannel(4242)

      ' Register the channel
      channelServices.RegisterChannel(chan)

      ' Register the Remote object
      RemotingConfiguration.RegisterWellKnownServiceType( _
          Type.GetType("HelloWorld.HelloServer, HelloObj"), _
          "SayHello", WellKnownObjectMode.Singleton)

      ' We must wait here, so ask the user to press the any key
      Console.WriteLine("Press <enter> to stop the server.......")
      Console.ReadLine()
      End Sub
  End Class
End Namespace
```

The code that performs the work here is the line

```
chan = New TcpServerChannel(4242)
```

that defines the port to be 4242, and then registers the channel

```
channelServices.RegisterChannel(chan)
```

and registers the server by calling

```
 RemotingConfiguration.RegisterWellKnownServiceType( _
   Type.GetType("HelloWorld.HelloServer, HelloObj"), _
   SayHello", WellKnownObjectMode.Singleton)
```

5. Compile the server using the following command-line compile command.

```
vbc /r:System.Runtime.Remoting.dll /r:HelloObj.dll  HelloServer.vb
```

Visual Basic .NET requires that the libraries that are part of the application be added on the command line. This way, the Server application is correctly compiled.

If you want to see the server in action, you can execute it from the command line at this point; it will not do anything except prompt us to press ENTER to exit. Go ahead and exit from the server now.

Next you need a client application that uses the .NET Remoting server.

EXERCISE 4-3

Building a Client Application Using a TCP Channel

The client application is built in the same directory as the server:

1. Open a Visual Studio .NET command prompt.

2. Navigate to the C:\VB\Hello folder.

3. Using your favorite editor, create a new Visual Basic .NET source file and call it HelloClient.vb.

4. Enter the following code in the source file:

```
Imports System
Imports System.Runtime.Remoting
Imports System.Runtime.Remoting.Channels
Imports System.Runtime.Remoting.Channels.TCP

Namespace HelloWorld
    Public Class Client
        Shared Sub Main
            Dim chan As New TCPChannel()
            ChannelServices.RegisterChannel(chan)
            Dim obj As HelloServer
            obj = CType(Activator.GetObject(Type.GetType _
                    ("HelloWorld.HelloServer,HelloObj"), _
                    "tcp://localhost:4242/SayHello"), HelloServer)
            If obj Is Nothing Then
                System.Console.WriteLine("Could not locate server")
            Else
                Console.WriteLine(obj.HelloMethod("Kornette"))
            End If
        End Sub
```

```
     End Class
   End Namespace
```

5. Build the client application by running the following command-line compiler.

```
vbc /r:System.Runtime.Remoting.dll /r:HelloObj.dll  HelloClient.vb
```

Now you can test your very first .NET Remoting application.

EXERCISE 4-4

Using the .NET Remoting Server and Client

1. Open two Visual Studio .NET command prompts.

2. Navigate to C:\VB\Hello in both of the command prompts.

3. In one command prompt window, start the server by entering **HelloServer** followed by pressing ENTER. The result is shown here:

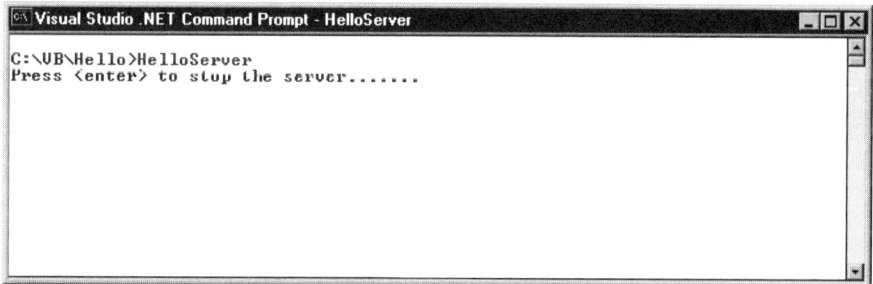

4. Switch to the second command prompt window and start the client by typing **HelloClient** followed by ENTER; the result should be as shown next:

5. The server process should indicate that you said Hello to a client as is shown next:

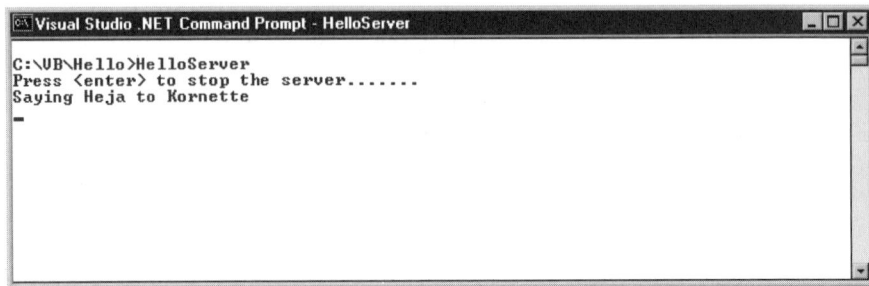

That concludes the TCP channel exercises. Next you are going to build a more involved application using the HTTP channel.

CERTIFICATION OBJECTIVE 4.03

Creating a .NET Remoting Object Using an HTTP Channel

This section will explore the use of Internet Information Services (IIS) and the HTTP channel and how you can build .NET Remoting components using the Visual Studio .NET.

Projects that will be used for remoting are started as class libraries. That way the project template will contain the needed settings. Build the server first.

EXERCISE 4-5

Building a Remote Object Using an HTTP Channel

Develop a remote server object by following these steps.

1. Start Visual Studio .NET.

2. Select a Visual Basic Project from the Project Type menu.

3. Select Class Library from the Templates menu.

4. Name the new project **HelloAgain**. The New Project dialog should look like this:

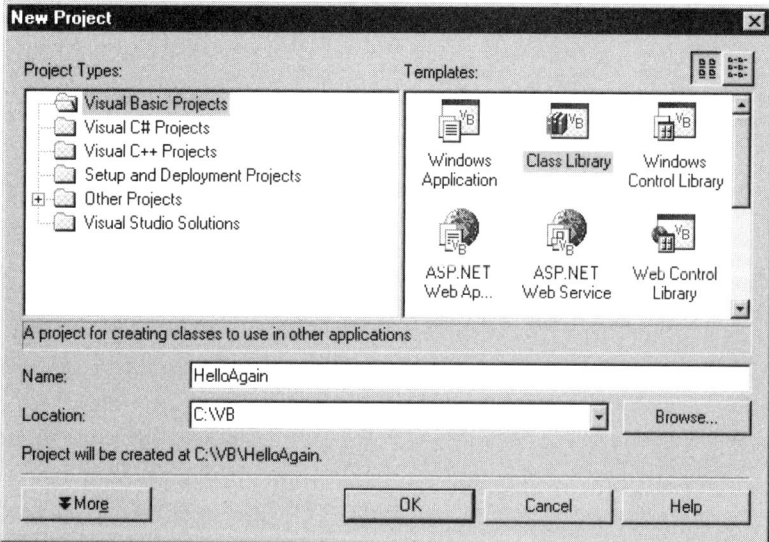

5. Click OK to create the project. The result is a project that contains a Visual Basic .NET source file named Class1.vb with one class named Class1. You will need to change the name of the file and the class to better reflect the purpose of the projects.

6. Rename the Class1.vb file to **Hello.vb**.

7. Change the name of the class in the Hello.vb file to **Hello** in the code designer.

8. Inherit the Hello class from the System.MarshalByRefObject class.

9. Create a default constructor for the `Hello` class. The code should look as follows:

```
Public Class Hello
    Inherits System.MarshalByRefObject

    Public Sub New()
        ' Default constructor
    End Sub
End Class
```

The method that will be the actual service is the Greeting function. The Greeting function should return a greeting that is personalized. Add the Greeting method as follows:

```
Public Function Greeting(ByVal name As String) As String
    Return String.Concat("Hello, ", name)
End Function
```

10. Build the class library, and make a note of the directory the Hello.dll file is located in (\bin).

That is all the work involved in building the entire .NET Remoting object. In order to make this object available to client applications, you will have to create a configuration file and locate that configuration file in the same directory as the class library.

The name of the configuration file is web.config, and that name cannot be changed. The web.config file contains the configuration for the remote object in an XML format. The root element is <configuration> as in all configuration files that are used in the .NET Framework. The service that is configured is <system .runtime .remoting>, and you need to make an entry under the <application> <service> element that describes the <Wellknown> service. The following is the procedure for adding web.config for the HelloAgain .NET Remoting object.

EXERCISE 4-6

Creating the Server Configuration

1. Open the HelloAgain project from Exercise 4-5.

2. Click the Show All Files button in the Solution Explorer.

3. Right-click the \bin directory in the Solution Explorer, and select Include In Project from the context menu.

4. Select the \bin directory in the Solution Explorer. Add an XML file to the project by using the Project | Add New Item. . . menu, as is shown next.

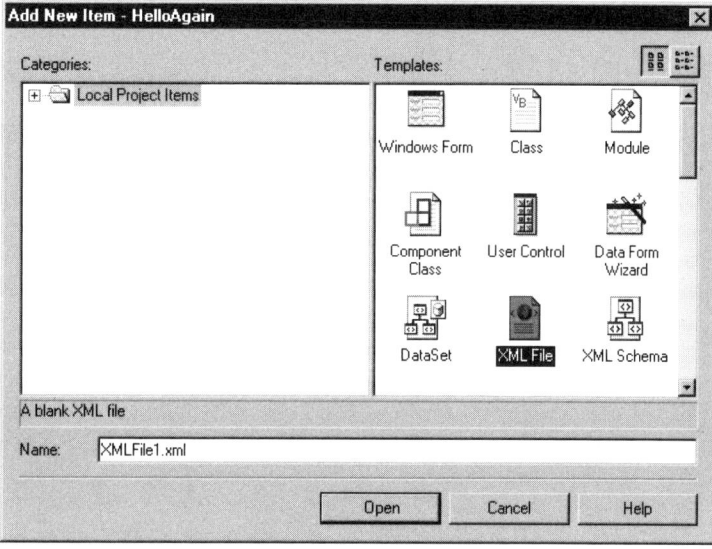

5. Change the name of the XML file to **web.config**.

6. After you click Open, the XML file is created in the \bin directory as is shown here:

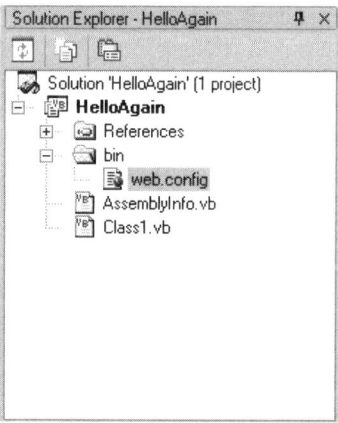

7. The new item is opened in the XML Editor, and the normal XML processing directive is inserted as is shown next:

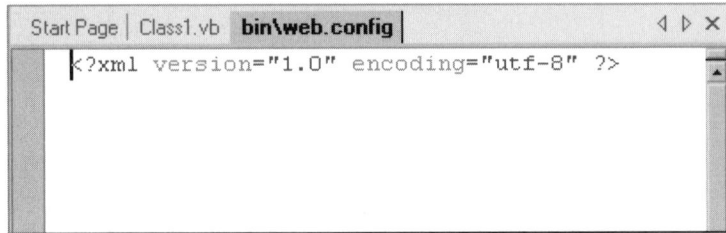

8. Change the content of the web.config file to the following:

```
<configure>
    <system.runtime.remoting>
        <application>
            <service>
                <Wellknown mode="Singleton"
                            type="HelloAgain.Greeting, Greeting"
                            objectUrl="Greeting.soap">
                </Wellknown>
            </service>
        </application>
    </system.runtime.remoting>
</configure>
```

The configuration is set to use the Singleton mode. This mode uses one object that serves all client calls, by contrast with SingleCall mode, in which each client will have a private object.

Now you have the configuration for the server. The next task is to build the client.

EXERCISE 4-7

Building the Client Application

You will build a Windows Form client to call the .NET Remoting server HelloAgain.

1. Start a new Windows Application project, naming the project
   RemoteHello:

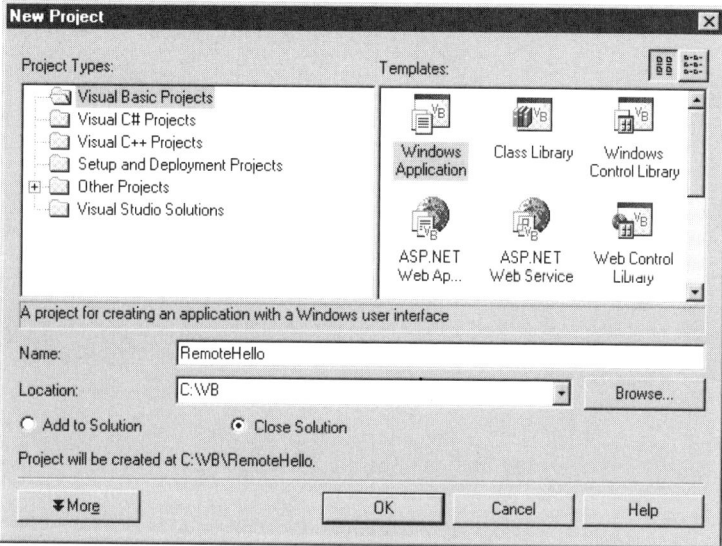

2. Rename the form from Form1 to **frmHello**, and change the Text property
   to "Remote Hello".

3. Open the Project properties and change the startup object to
   frmHello.

4. Add a button to the form, and name the button **btnRemoteHello**.
   Change the Text property to **Remote Click**.

5. Add a label to the form, and name the label **lblRemoteHello**.
   Change the Text property to "   ". The form should look like the following.

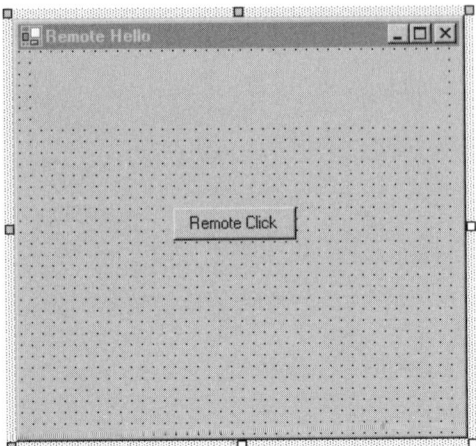

6. Add a reference to the HelloAgain server by choosing Project | Add Reference. . . . You need to use the Browse button and find the directory that the HelloAgain.dll is located in.

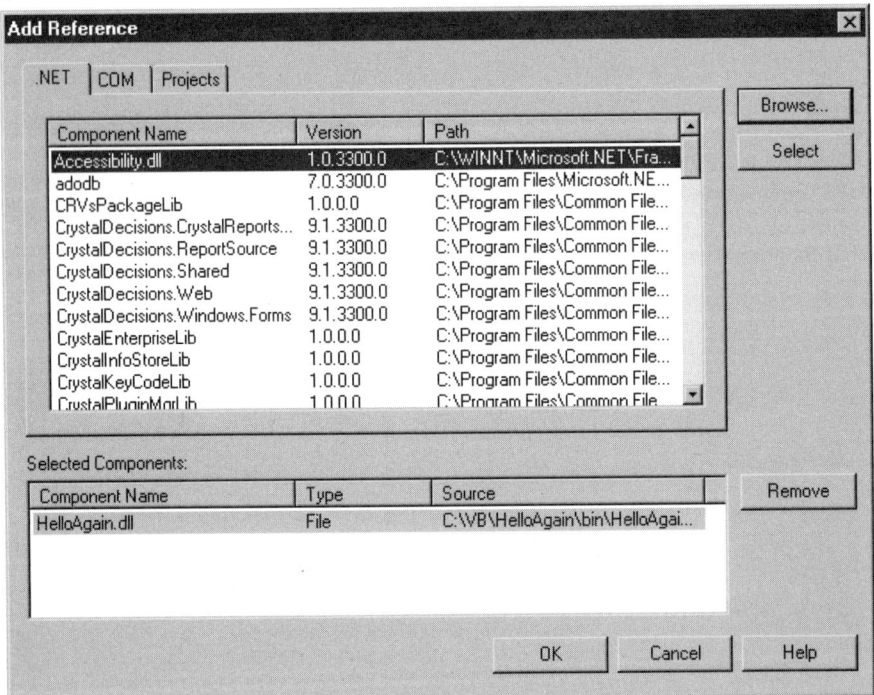

7. Add a reference to the System.Runtime.Remoting.dll library.

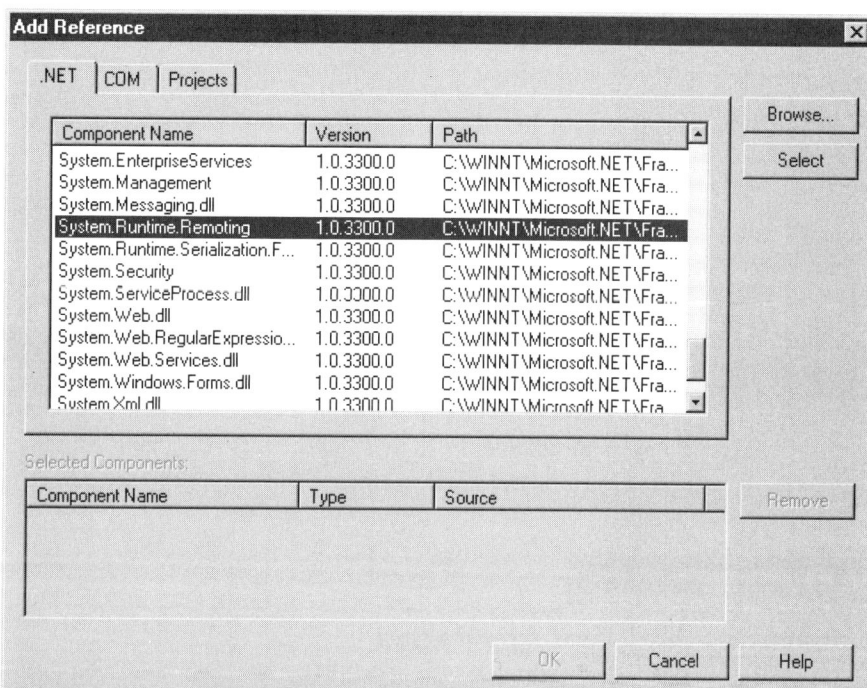

8. Import the following namespaces into the code module for the frmHello form:

```
Imports System
Imports System.Runtime.Remoting
Imports System.Runtime.Remoting.Channels
Imports System.Runtime.Remoting.Channels.http
Imports HelloAgain
```

9. Modify the constructor for the form to initialize the channel.

```
Public Sub New()
    MyBase.New()
    'This call is required by the Windows Form Designer.
    InitializeComponent()
    'Add any initialization after the InitializeComponent() call
    Dim ch As HttpChannel = New HttpChannel()
    ChannelServices.RegisterChannel(ch)
End Sub
```

10. Implement the click event for the btnRemoteHello button. In this event handler, you will activate the remote server and then call the `Greeting()` method to use it.

```
Private Sub btnRemoteHello_Click(ByVal sender As System.Object, _
        ByVal e As System.EventArgs) Handles
btnRemoteHello.Click
    Dim he As Hello = Activator.GetObject(Type.GetType("Hello"), _
                "http://localhost:8181/HelloAgain", _
                WellKnownObjectMode.Singleton)
    lblRemoteHello.Text = he.Greeting("Kenneth")
End Sub
```

You have now built both the server and the client, but there are still two tasks that must be completed for the system to work: the client must be configured, and the server must be deployed to IIS.

EXERCISE 4-8

Configuring the Client Application

The client must be configured much as the server was earlier in this chapter. The client's configuration file is named according to the executable's name—if the executable is named RemoteHello.exe, the configuration file will be named RemoteHello.exe.config and located in the same directory as the executable. This is how you create the configuration file:

1. Add an XML document to the directory where the Hello.exe file is located. Name the file RemoteHello.exe.config.

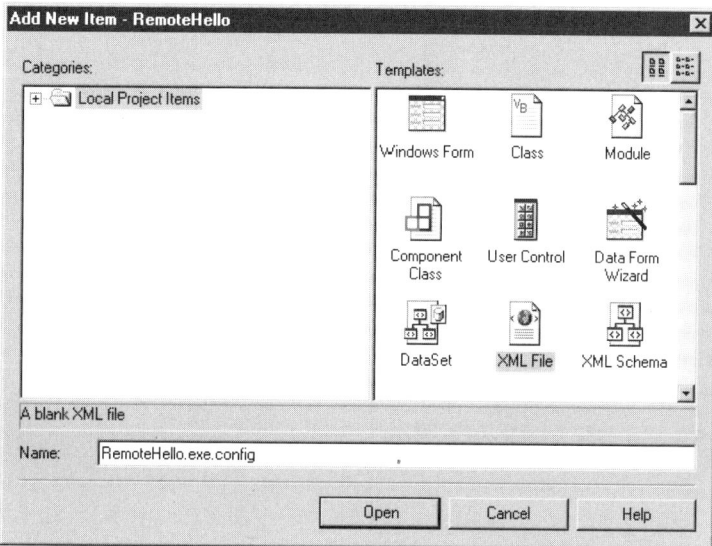

Ensure the file is located in the same directory as the RemoteHello.exe program, normally in the \bin directory.

2. Edit the client configuration file to include the following:

```
<configuration>
  <system.runtime.remoting>
    <application name="RemoteHello">
      <channels>
        <channel
type="System.Runtime.Remoting.Channels.Http.HttpChannel, _
                  System.Runtime.Remoting">
        </channel>
      </channels>
    </application>
```

```
    </system.runtime.remoting>
</configuration>
```

The configuration file identifies the application in the <application> element, as well as the channel type and namespace.

3. Save the project.

Now there is only one task left, and that is to deploy the server to IIS.

EXERCISE 4-9

Configuring IIS for Remoting

In order for IIS to be able to respond with the correct remoting object, there must be a proper mapping of the files that are used on the server. In our case, all the files are located under the C:\VB directory.

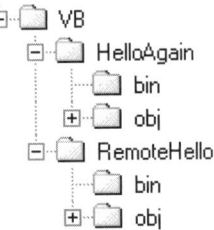

In order for IIS to be able to serve the server object, you need to configure a virtual directory that is mapped to the physical location of the server object. Here's how to do that:

1. Start the Internet Services Manager. It can be found in the Administrative Tools folder in the Control Panel.

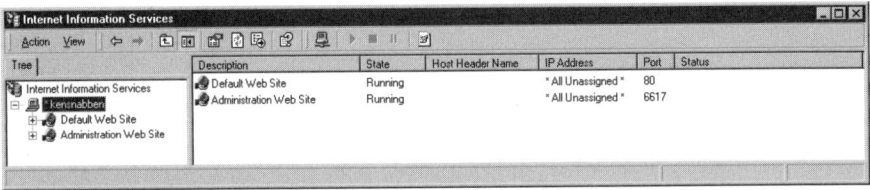

2. Double-click the computer name in the left pane, and then double-click the Default Web Site in the left pane to expand the web folders.

3. Right-click the Default Web Site and select New | Virtual Directory, and click Next on the welcome screen.

4. Create an alias for the virtual directory. For this exercise, the name should be RemHello as is shown here:

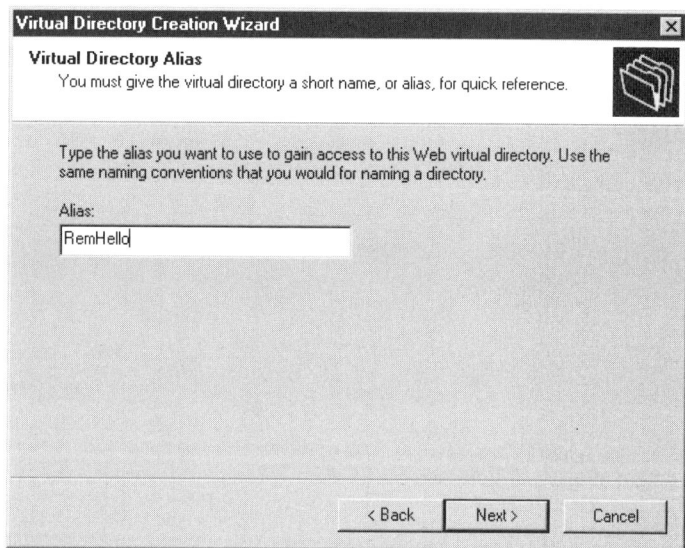

5. Click Next and set the physical directory that contains the remote server (C:\VB\HelloAgain\bin) as shown here:

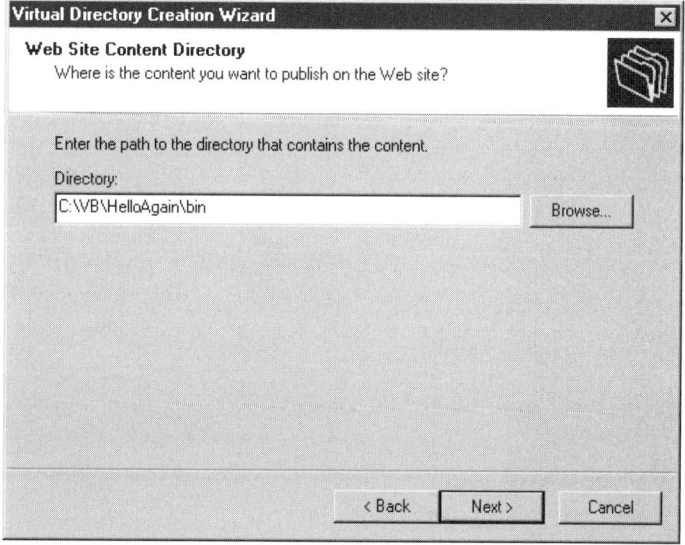

6. Click Next and set the Permissions for the virtual directory as shown next:

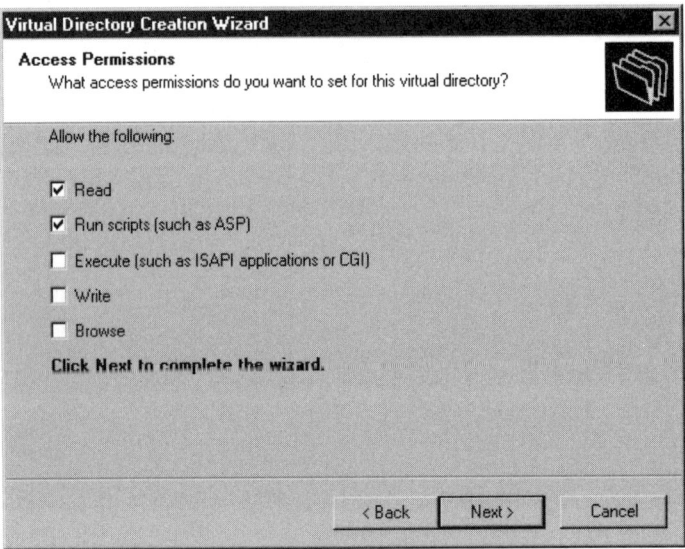

7. Click Next and then Finish to complete the wizard.

8. The final step is to run the client from Exercise 4-8. You do that by opening the RemoteHello project and run the application (press F5). The following illustration shows the final application.

FROM THE CLASSROOM

The concept of remote software objects is one that sometimes baffles the student of Visual Basic .NET. In VB 6, you used the COM model for client-activated objects and Microsoft Transaction Server (MTS) for server-activated objects. MTS changed name with the release of Windows 2000 and is now called Component Services. Now with the .NET Framework, you have .NET Remoting.

The most important point to remember about all the remote object technologies is that the client software uses a proxy to hide the remoteness of the object. This way, you don't have to hard-code the communication between the software components.

Another feature of .NET Remoting is that you can take advantage of the Internet Information Services (IIS) to host our remote software components using the HTTP protocol. You can think of HTTP in terms of browsing a web page—the browser sends a GET request to IIS and IIS replies with a POST response. With remoting, the request is for a method in a server object. IIS will call the method on our behalf and respond with the result of the method call.

CERTIFICATION OBJECTIVE 4.04

Client-Activated Objects

The two types of server activation that you have seen so far are Singleton and SingleCall activation. There is a third mode that is very close to the mode used with legacy COM components—the client-activated object (CAO).

The CAO mode creates an object for the exclusive use of the client. The object will not be destroyed at the end of the method call; it will stay instantiated for the client until the client application destroys the CAO. This is in contrast to the SingleCall mode for server-activated objects (SAOs), where the object is destroyed at the end of the method call.

So how do you know what mode to use? Should you use server-activated objects or client-activated objects? The following Scenario & Solution sidebar might come in handy to answer those questions.

SCENARIO & SOLUTION

How do I decide whether I need to use a Singleton or SingleCall server-activated object?	In the case of server-activated objects, the decision between Singleton and SingleCall activation mode is one of scalability. There is a fine line between what is scalable and what is not. For the best scalability, use SingleCall activation, where each client has its own object for the duration of the method call. If the need for concurrent access is minimal, use of Singleton activation can make the load on the server less, although the scalability might not be as great.
How do I determine if I need a client-activated object?	If every client needs to save its own data in the object between method calls, you need a client-activated object. This is called *maintaining state.* If the answer is that if the client does not need to maintain its own data in the object, use a server-activated object.
How do I build a .NET Remoting object when I need to maintain state between method calls?	The client-activated objects are private to the client for the duration. The client manages the lifetime of the object.
How do I increase scalability?	Scalability is when you can serve an increasing number of clients simply by adding hardware to the solution. The best activation model for scalability is the SingleCall server-activated object.

CERTIFICATION OBJECTIVE 4.05

Asynchronous Methods

One of the central tenets of VB .NET programming is event-driven development and the capability for components to invoke an event handler based on the occurrence of a specific action. You have seen how to bind code to such events as the click of a button control, or the loading of a form. These types of events and event handlers should be familiar to all VB and VB .NET developers.

The event and event handler can be used as a method of communicating between components. The process enables components to work together on a problem while being totally disconnected from each other—we call this *asynchronous programming,* or loose binding.

The process is started by the calling component informing the called component where to return a message (the callback address) when the process is complete. The called component starts the processing while the caller continues with other tasks rather than waiting for the called component to finish. When the called component is finished, it sends a message to the caller by calling the callback address. The end result of this type of processing is that to the user of the system, there are very few times when the system is blocked and the user needs to wait.

Think of a situation where you have a software component that retrieves information for a sales report from a database. Now, say the average time needed to retrieve the information is 20 seconds. A synchronous version of the application would call the software component and wait for the component to return the data. The GUI would be frozen while the application waited for the data to be returned. Changing the model to an asynchronous communications model will leave the GUI functional while the data is being retrieved, allowing you to work on other tasks.

There are a number of scenarios in the real world where waiting times are involved—file and database access, network I/O, Web access, and so on. You will be able to take advantage of asynchronous solutions in your software that will keep the application's user productive.

The .NET Framework provides a design pattern (object model) that provides a uniform environment for asynchronous calls across the .NET Framework. There are a couple of methods that are included in classes that provide built-in support for asynchronous calls; for example, the Stream class (System.IO.Stream) provides the Read() method for synchronous calls and the `BeginRead()` / `EndRead()` pair of methods for asynchronous access. For the most part, the details of asynchronous calls and multithreading are hidden from the VB .NET developer.

In the next part of this chapter, you will learn how to create and use the Delegate model to create callbacks that will provide asynchronous event handling.

Handling Events

As you look at asynchronous programming using VB .NET and .NET Framework, you must look at event handling. The first item on the agenda must be the definition of the event, so that is where you will start your journey.

The examples used to describe event handling are based on the concept of a car object—I have found that this type of example, rather than a more code-based example, makes this topic easier to comprehend.

When I use the term *event*, I refer to something that is important for an object's processes to communicate to the world. For example, if you imagine the car object, the specific object you have is red in color with a black top. The object has four methods, `accelerate()`, `coast()`, `brake()`, and `refill()`—and one parameter, gasLevel (indicates how much gas is in the gas tank). This is a very common, everyday car, or it can be a software object that emulates a car; either way, you can interact with the car object.

Here is the problem: If you want to make sure you never run out of gas, you want to refill the car object's gas tank as soon as it is near empty. In order to establish when it nears empty, you need to perform a loop asking, Is it empty? By reading the gasLevel parameter every so many seconds, and then refilling the gas tank object when the gasLevel parameter indicates that the gas tank is nearly empty, you achieve your goal. You would also produce a procedural software structure similar to this pseudocode:

```
do while (true)
{
  if (car.gasLevel <= 0)
  {
    car.refill()
  }
}
```

This type of looping structure was the mainstay of the procedural world. You used to draw lovely flowcharts so that you would know the flow through the application. This type of processing is synchronous—everything happens in the predetermined order, and only in that order. In our car example, the end result of all that checking would be that the car would most likely not be able to perform any other computations than checking the level in the gas tank.

The natural question is whether there is a better way to communicate between objects than procedural loops, and fortunately there is. The event model gives you the ability to have two or more objects communicate with each other in an asynchronous manner.

You will bestow on your car two events. You will define an event as something that is important to the object, so you will give your car the gasAlmostEmpty event and the `gasFull` event. The car will cause the `gasAlmostEmpty` event when the car's gas tank has one gallon left and the gasFull event when the car's gas tank is close to overflowing. To take advantage of this new, better model of the car, you need to do one extra thing. You need to inform the car that you would like to be told when the event takes place. The request is a registration of interest. In effect, you give the car a sticky note that says: "Tell me when the gasAlmostEmpty event happens" and an address where it can call you. That address is the callback. Now you can go about your day doing what you do best, and when the car is running out of gas, you will get a message from the car to your callback address telling you that the tank is almost empty.

As with previous Windows languages, this process is performed in the .NET environment every time you use an event. In the software world, we call the event *routing a callback.* The receiver of the event registers an address (the callback address) that should be called when the event fires (happens). The address of the code that is called when the event fires is the callback, and the code is the event handler.

Now take a look at how you perform the event handling in the .NET environment. The steps in setting up the event communication between the source and the handler involve adding the delegate to connect the two sides. The following section discusses the delegate and how to declare it.

Delegates

One option for referring to methods and other items uses the address where the item is stored in memory. This concept of being able to refer to a function by its address (the function pointer) is a very powerful one, but it is also fraught with dangers. For example, if the address changes, the call to the location of the address will most likely run code that will crash the application, or even the operating system. The designers of the .NET Framework made it possible for you to have the equivalent of the function pointer in an object-oriented way: the delegate.

The one-sentence description of a delegate is

The delegate encapsulates a reference to a method in the Delegate object.

The process of configuring the delegate is as follows:

1. Declare the event argument class that will communicate the data for the event.

2. Declare the delegate.

3. Declare the event to be of the `Delegate` data type.

4. Instantiate the event argument object and populate the attributes.

5. Raise the event.

Take a look at how to declare and instantiate a delegate. The first step is to declare a class that will represent the event information. In the following segment, that class is defined:

```
' Class that contains the data for
' the Char event. Derives from System.EventArgs.
'
Public Class CharEventArgs
   Inherits EventArgs
    Dim _Character As Char
    'Constructor.
    '

...

' The Character property that contains the character for the event.
    '
   Public ReadOnly Property Character() As Char
     Get
        Return _Character
     End Get
   End Property

End Class
```

The event argument class defines the data that the event will communicate between the processes in the asynchronous model. Note the use of the private variable (_Character) and public property procedures.

The second step is to declare the delegate, defining two parameters: sender As Object and e As CharEventArgs. The second data type is the event argument class you just defined. The following code sequence declares a delegate:

```
' Delegate declaration.
' Pass variables by value
   Public Delegate Sub CharEventHandler(ByVal sender As Object,
                            ByVal e As CharEventArgs)
```

Once you have declared the event argument class and the delegate, you need to add code that declares the event and raises the event when needed.

```
' The event member that is of type CharEventHandler.
   '
   Public Event Chars As CharEventHandler
```

```
' The protected OnChar method raises the event by invoking
' the delegates. The sender is always Me, the current instance
' of the class.
'
    Protected Overridable Sub OnChar(ByVal e As CharEventArgs)
        RaiseEvent Chars(Me, e)
    End Sub
```

e x a m
ⓦa t c h

The sender in the event is a reference to the object that raised the event.

The RaiseEvent statement will raise the event as described by the method. The sender parameter is always the current object (Me), and the event argument is the object passed to communicate the data for the event.

```
Dim e As New CharEventArgs(Chr(i))
OnChar(e)
```

The event argument class will pass the character to the OnChar method, which in turn will raise the event.

The preceding steps have defined the event argument class, delegate, and event and have raised the event. But you did not handle the event! The next step is to create and register the callback to handle the event for us.

Callbacks

When an event is raised, the handlers that are registered to receive the event will be called according to the address of the event handler. The first step is to declare the event handler class and a method to receive the event, as in this code segment.

```
' Declare the event handler class and method
Public Class CharHandler
  Public Sub CharEvent(sender As Object, e As CharEventArgs)
    Console.out.Write(e.Character)
  End Sub
End Class
```

Please note that the signature of the method defines the same parameters as the delegate did. With the handler defined, you need to instantiate the event handler object and the event source, as in this segment.

```
' Instantiates the event receiver.
Dim w As New CharHandler()

' Instantiates the class that is the source of the event.
Dim CharMaker As New charFactory()
```

To connect the two together, use the AddHandler statement, which takes two properties—the event from the source object and the address of the event handler, as in the following code segment:

```
' Connects the CharEvent method to the Char event.
AddHandler CharMaker.Chars, AddressOf w.CharEvent
```

e x a m
ⓌatCh

The event model can register multiple handlers to the same event.

The next (and last) step is to start the processing in the source object. The following exercise will have you build an application to illustrate asynchronous processing.

The delegates you create can have multiple delegates registered to receive notification of the event. This is known as the multicast delegate.

e x a m
ⓌatCh

The multicast delegate cannot guarantee the order in which the multiple event handlers will be called.

<hr>

EXERCISE 4-10

Asynchronous Processing

In this exercise, look at the difference between synchronous and asynchronous communication between objects. The application generates random digits where each generation takes a random amount of time to complete. The synchronous version of the application is illustrated in the following code listing:

```
Imports System
Imports Microsoft.VisualBasic

Namespace Sync
Public Class Sync
  Public Shared Sub Main()
    Dim c As CharFactory
    c = New CharFactory
```

```
        Console.out.WriteLine(c.makeChars())
    End Sub
End Class


Class charFactory
  ' Generate random characters, using a random delay
  '
  Private Function makeChar() As Char
    Dim i, j As Integer
    '
    ' Delay a random number of iterations between 1 and 424,242
    '
    For j = CInt(Int((424242 * Rnd()) + 1)) To 424242
      ' Generate an integer between 48 and 47 for every iteration
      ' That range defines the ASCII code for the digits 0-9
      '
      i = CInt(Int((9 * Rnd()) + 48))
    Next j
' return the character based on the ASCII value after the last iteration
  '
    Return Chr(i)
  End Function

  Public Function makeChars() As String
    Dim i As Integer
    Dim s As String
    ' Generate 424 random digits, concatenate them to the string
    '
    For i = 0 To 424
      s += makeChar()
    Next
    ' Return the string to the caller
    '
    Return s
  End Function
End Class
End Namespace
```

This program is a console (command-line) application that will print the digits in the console. To compile this program, follow these instructions:

1. Open a Visual Studio .NET command prompt (Start | Program Files | Microsoft Visual Studio .NET | Visual Studio .NET Tools | Visual Studio .NET Command Prompt).

2. Create a new directory on the C:\ drive and call it **C:\SyncTest** (MD **C:\SyncTest**).

3. Change to that new directory (**CD \SyncTest**).

4. Save the source as Sync.vb in that directory, or copy from the Chapter 4 directory on the CD-ROM.

5. Compile the Sync.vb file by typing the following command:

```
vbc /r:System.dll sync.vb
```

6. Run the sync.exe program and note that the numbers will not appear until after a very long time. The following shows the compilation and execution of the application:

```
C:\SyncTest>vbc /r:System.dll sync.vb
Microsoft (R) Visual Basic .NET Compiler version 7.00.9466
for Microsoft (R) .NET Framework version 1.00.3705.209
Copyright (C) Microsoft Corporation 1987-2001. All rights reserved.


C:\SyncTest>sync
3632571403385866686105013216670234534841885254010162836681542155 6166
...
5755523781884248205040383
C:\SyncTest>
```

The delay before all the digits appear depends on the speed of your computer. You can change the number of generated digits to adjust the delay.

7. In order to build an asynchronous version of the digit-generating program, you will modify the sync program. Copy the sync.vb file to asynch.vb (**xcopy sync.vb asynch.vb**).

8. Open asynch.vb in your favorite editor (**notepad asynch.vb**).

9. Edit the Imports section to refer to System, System.ComponentModel, and Microsoft.VisualBasic.

```
Imports System
Imports System.ComponentModel
Imports Microsoft.VisualBasic
```

10. Change the namespace declaration to be Async.

```
Namespace Async
```

11. Declare the event argument class directly after the namespace declaration. The class declaration must have a constructor that takes a character as its parameter.

```
' Class that contains the data for
' the Char event. Derives from System.EventArgs.
'
  Public Class CharEventArgs
    Inherits EventArgs
      dim _Character as Char
'Constructor.
'
    Public Sub New(Character As Char)
      Me._Character = Character
    End Sub

    ' The Character property that contains the
    ' character for the event.
    Public ReadOnly Property Character() As Char
      Get
          Return _Character
      End Get
    End Property
  End Class
```

12. Declare the delegate after the CharEvents class.

```
Public Delegate Sub CharEventHandler(sender As Object,
                                     e As CharEventArgs)
```

13. Delete the Sync class.

14. Declare a Public Async class, with the following Main() method.

```
Public Class Async
    Public Shared Sub Main()
        ' Instantiates the event receiver.
        Dim w As New CharHandler()

        ' Instantiates the event source.
        Dim CharMaker As New charFactory()

        ' Wires the CharEvent method to the Char event.
        AddHandler CharMaker.Chars, AddressOf w.CharEvent
```

```
            CharMaker.makeChars()
        End Sub
    End Class
```

15. At the top of the declaration for the charFactory class, insert the event declaration.

```
' The event member that is of type AlarmEventHandler.
'
Public Event Chars As CharEventHandler
```

16. Declare a member method of the charFactory class to raise the event.

```
Protected Overridable Sub OnChar(e As CharEventArgs)
    RaiseEvent Chars(Me, e)
End Sub
```

17. Modify the makeChar() method to raise the Chars event (highlighted text is added), change the type from Function to Sub, and remove the Return statement.

```
Private Sub makeChar()
    Dim i, j As Integer
    For j = CInt(Int((424242 * Rnd()) + 1)) To 424242
        i = CInt(Int((9 * Rnd()) + 48))
    Next j
    Dim e As New CharEventArgs(Chr(i))
    OnChar(e)
End Sub
```

18. Modify the makeChars() method to be a Sub rather than a Function and call makeChar() as a Sub; do not return a string.

```
Public Sub makeChars()
    Dim i As Integer
    Dim s As String
    For i = 0 To 424
        makeChar()
    Next
End Sub
```

19. Declare a new class called CharHandler. Declare a public method to act as the event handler.

```
Public Class CharHandler
   Public Sub CharEvent(sender As Object, e As CharEventArgs)
      Console.out.Write(e.Character)
   End Sub
End Class
```

Save the source file in the C:\SyncTest directory as Async.vb.

20. Compile the program.

```
vbc /r:System.dll Async.vb
```

21. Execute the program and note that the digits are printed as they are generated.

The full code for this exercise can be found in the Chapter 4 code folder on the CD-ROM. There are a number of ways this exercise can be modified and extended—I leave it up to you to explore the opportunities.

See the following Scenarios & Solutions sidebar. It might come in handy when studying for the Microsoft exam.

SCENARIO & SOLUTION

How do I make more than one event handler execute when the event fires?	By using the AddHandler statement once for each event handler that should be registered.
When I register multiple event handlers to an event, will the handlers execute in the order they were defined?	No. There is no guarantee that event handlers will execute in the order they were defined.
Once I have registered an event handler, can I unregister it when it is not needed anymore?	Yes. Use the RemoveHandler statement to disconnect an event handler from a specific event.
Why do I need to inherit my event argument class from EventArgs class?	The System.EventArgs class provides the necessary functionality for the Event Arguments class. That way, you will not have to reinvent the class every time.

CERTIFICATION SUMMARY

In this chapter, you explored the .NET Remoting architecture as well as asynchronous method calls. The exam will test your knowledge of how the .NET Remoting works—not so much about the code as about the channels and what channel to use under what circumstance. Remember that the TCP channel requires that the port you use be open on all firewalls, where the HTTP channel works with port 80, which is normally open by default.

The asynchronous method calls were contrasted with the procedural call model, and you also looked at how you can take advantage of events, delegates, and callbacks to give components the ability to communicate asynchronously. One of the issues when developing modern form-driven applications is that some processing has the side effect of blocking the user's interaction with the application—we call this effect modal or synchronous behavior. Another term is blocking processing. In order to avoid this synchronous behavior, you learned about the asynchronous programming model of the .NET Framework and how to take advantage of the built-in support in the .NET Framework for asynchronous calls to methods. You also learned how to add support for asynchronous calls to any method.

TWO-MINUTE DRILL

Client-Activated Objects

❏ A client-activated object's lifetime is controlled by the client, thus allowing the object to maintain state between method calls.

❏ A server-activated object's lifetime is controlled by the host. The object is destroyed after the method call (SingleCall) or has no local storage (Singleton).

Creating a .NET Remoting Object Using an HTTP Channel

❏ The HTTP channel is derived from the System.Runtime.Remoting .Channels.Http namespace.

❏ In order to successfully compile a project that uses the HTTP channel, you need to have a reference to the System.Runtime.Remoting.dll library.

Creating a .NET Remoting Object Using a TCP Channel

❏ The TCP channel is derived from the System.Runtime.Remoting .Channels.Tcp namespace.

❏ In order to successfully compile a project that uses the HTTP channel, you need to have a reference to the System.Runtime.Remoting.dll library.

Overview of .NET Remoting

❏ Remoting hosts are required to run the remote object.

❏ Internet Information Services (IIS) can be a host, but only when using the HTTP channel.

❏ The object that is remoted can inherit from System.MarshalByRefObject to ensure that references are used for the marshaling; if the object does not inherit from System.MarshalByRefObject, the object is passed by value.

❏ The configuration of both the clients and the server is performed by using an XML file that is named web.config.

❏ You do not have to recompile after changing the configuration of a client or server.

---

*Please be aware that the questions and answers at the end of this chapter for the Two-Minute Drill, the Self Test Questions, and the Self Test Answers may *not* match the order of those found in the corresponding chapter on the CD-ROM.

Asynchronous Methods

❏ Asynchronous processing allows different processes to run independently—nonblocking.

❏ Events are represented by an event argument object.

❏ Event sources raise the event—event sinks handle the event.

❏ The delegate represents the event handler's address in a type-safe way.

❏ The event handler must be registered with the event source to be able to receive the event.

❏ The event model has some statements that are used to control the event model—AddHandler, RemoveHandler, RaiseEvent, and so on.

❏ Multiple event handlers can be registered with one event source—multicast delegate.

SELF TEST

Overview of .NET Remoting

1. You have been given a project that was started by another developer in your company. The project contains a remoting object that is served by a console application. The application compiles, but when the client attempts to connect, there is an exception. The following is the code for the server application:

```
Imports System
Imports System.Runtime.Remoting
Imports System.Runtime.Remoting.Channels
Imports System.Runtime.Remoting.Channels.Tcp
Namespace HelloWorld
Public Class RemoteHello
    <STAThread> _
    Public Shared Sub Main()
        Dim chan As TcpServerChannel
        chan = New TcpServerChannel(4242)
        ChannelServices.RegisterChannel(chan)
        RemotingConfiguration.RegisterWellKnownServiceType( _
            Type.GetType("HelloWorld.HelloServer, HelloObj"), _
            SayHello", WellKnownObjectMode.Singleton)
        Console.WriteLine("Press <enter> to stop the server.......")
        Console.ReadLine()
    End Sub
End Class
End Namespace
```

This is the code for the remote object:

```
Imports System
Namespace HelloWorld
Public Class HelloServer
    Public Sub HelloServer()
        System.Console.WriteLine("Building Hello...")
    End Sub
    Public Function HelloMethod(str As String) As String
        Console.WriteLine("Saying Heja to " + str)
        Return "Hello " + str + " nice to see you in my World!"
    End Function
End Class
End Namespace
```

What is the most likely reason for the exception?

A. The remote object needs to import the System.Runtime.Remoting namespace.

B. The HelloMethod() function is not marked with the <Remote> attribute.

C. The remote object must inherit from System.MarshalByRefObject.

D. The remote server must import the HelloServer namespace.

Client-Activated Objects

2. You are developing a remote object (GetData.dll) that will return customer records from the Sales database. The remote object must be able to keep a running total of all the calls to the server by incrementing an attribute of the object. Which activation mode will you use?

A. Server activated

B. Singleton

C. Client activated

D. SingleCall

Creating a .NET Remoting Object Using an HTTP Channel

3. You are developing a remote object (Howdy.dll) that will be deployed to IIS. You need to create a configuration file that is used to set the location and type information. What configuration file will you create?

A. Howdy.dll.config

B. machine.config

C. Howdy.ini

D. web.config

4. You are developing a remote object that will use the HTTP channel. What formatters can be used on the HTTP channel? Select all answers that apply.

A. Binary formatter

B. RPC formatter

C. SOAP formatter

D. DCOM formatter

Creating a .NET Remoting Object Using a TCP Channel

5. You are developing a remote object that raises an exception when executed. The following listing shows the code for the remote server:

```
Imports System
Imports System.Runtime.Remoting
Imports System.Runtime.Remoting.Channels
Imports System.Runtime.Remoting.Channels.Tcp
Namespace HelloWorld
Public Class RemoteHello
   <STAThread> _
   Public Shared Sub Main()
      Dim chan As TcpServerChannel
      chan = New TcpServerChannel(4242)
      RemotingConfiguration.RegisterWellKnownServiceType( _
          Type.GetType("HelloWorld.HelloServer, HelloObj"), _
          SayHello", WellKnownObjectMode.Singleton)
      Console.WriteLine("Press <enter> to stop the server.......")
      Console.ReadLine()
   End Sub
End Class
End Namespace
```

What is the most likely reason for the exception?

A. The channel is not registered.

B. The channel type is wrong.

C. The activation mode is wrong.

D. The System.Activation namespace is missing.

Asynchronous Methods

6. You must add a delegate to a program you are working on. Which of the following statements will correctly add the delegate?

A. `Public Delegate Sub ChEh(ByVal sender as Object, ByVal e As ChEa)`

B. `Public Event Sub ChEh(ByVal sender as Object, ByVal e As ChEa)`

C. `Private Delegate Sub ChEh(ByVal sender as Object, ByVal e As ChEa)`

D. `Private Event Sub ChEh(ByVal sender as Object, ByVal e As ChEa)`

7. You have created a custom event in a class you are currently developing—now you need to raise the event. The following code segment is the code you developed. What code segment should go in place of `<<Insert code here>>`?

```
Public Event Tjabo As TjEventHandler
Protected Overridable Sub OnTja(ByVal e as TjaEventArgs)
  <<Insert code here>>
End Sub
```

   A. `AddHandler TjaEventHandler(AddressOf Tjabo, Me)`

   B. `RaiseEvent TjaEventArgs(Me)`

   C. `RaiseEvent Tjabo(Me, e)`

   D. `AddHandler Tjabo(AddressOf Me.e)`

8. You have been assigned an application that was started by another developer in your company. The users of the application are reporting that the generation of the daily reports is very slow—they ask for the report and have to wait while the report is generated, and during this time the application is not responding to any user requests. You must improve the speed of the report generation so that the users can become more productive. What strategy will give you the most improvement with the least effort?

   A. Change the application to use a distributed relational database manager (RDBM) that load-balances the report requests between any of the database nodes. Use a distributed n-tier application model.

   B. Change the application so that the report generation is performed by an object that operates in an asynchronous manner.

   C. Change the application to use an n-tier model, and upgrade the server the database is on.

   D. Change the application to take advantage of the load-balancing features of Windows 2000 Application Center Server, and implement clustering.

9. Which namespace must be included in order for custom event handling to be possible? Choose all that apply.

   A. `System`

   B. `System.ComponentModel`

   C. `Microsoft.VisualBasic`

   D. None of the above

10. You have built a form that uses a class that retrieves data from a database and returns the data by using an event that your form has registered. The event handler has two parameters, `sender` and e. What object does `sender` represent?

A. The base object in the .NET Framework

B. The object that is the instance of the `Delegate` class

C. The object that is the instance of the class that retrieves the data

D. The object that is the instance of the `Form1` class

SELF TEST ANSWERS

Overview of .NET Remoting

1. ☑ **C.** The remote object must inherit from `System.MarshalByRefObject` in order to be able to respond to method calls.

   ☒ **A** is incorrect because the remote object does not need any additional namespaces;. **B** is incorrect because there is no such attribute. **D** is incorrect because the remote server needs a reference to the remote object, but not the namespace, at compile time.

Client-Activated Objects

2. ☑ **B.** The Singleton activation model is the best answer; it maintains state between method calls.

   ☒ **A** is incorrect because server-activated objects include both the Singleton and SingleCall modes. **C** is incorrect because the client-activated objects keep state for each client, but not for the process as a whole. **D** is incorrect because the SingleCall mode does not keep state.

Creating a .NET Remoting Object Using an HTTP Channel

3. ☑ **D.** The correct filename for the configuration file is web.config.

   ☒ **A** is incorrect because no such configuration filename is recognized in the .NET Framework. **B** is incorrect because that filename is the serverwide configuration file. **C** is incorrect because that filename extension is not used in .NET Framework.

4. ☑ **A and C.** SOAP and binary formatters are the only ones supported in the .NET Framework.

   ☒ **B** is incorrect because RPC is the protocol for DCOM. **D** is incorrect because DCOM is the RPC protocol.

Creating a .NET Remoting Object Using a TCP Channel

5. ☑ **A.** In order for the remote object to be able to communicate, the channel must be registered.

   ☒ **B** is incorrect because the channel is correct according to the code. **C** is incorrect because the activation mode does not affect the behavior of the remote object. **D** is incorrect because that is an object, not a namespace.

Asynchronous Methods

6. ☑ **A.** The correct signature needed to declare a delegate is to declare the delegate public.
☒ **B** is incorrect because the `Event` keyword will not declare a delegate. **C** is incorrect because the delegate must be declared public. **D** is incorrect because the delegate must be declared public, and the `Event` keyword will not declare a delegate.

7. ☑ **C.** The event must be raised. The `RaiseEvent` statement performs that action, and the name of the event is Tjabo, so answer **C** is the only answer that correctly performs the action requested.
☒ **A** is incorrect because you need to raise the event, not register the handler, and the name of the event is Tjabo, not TjaEventHandler. **B** is incorrect because the `TjaEventArgs` class is not the event. **D** is incorrect because you need to raise the event, not register a handler.

8. ☑ **B.** The issue here is that you want to speed up the report generation without spending a lot of effort. It is stated in the question that the users find the speed to be poor because they have to wait. To increase the speed, you will use asynchronous techniques to have the report generator use events to communicate back with us.
☒ **A** is incorrect because it does not fall under the category "least effort"; changing the database platform and the applications architecture is a major effort. **C** is incorrect because **B** will produce the speedup with less effort. **D** is incorrect because although it might produce a speedup, there is no inherent speedup in changing to this product, and it does not fall under the least-effort category.

9. ☑ **D.** This is a trick question. The keyword is *must*, and there are no rules that say you *must* import any namespaces. However, you must supply fully qualified class names if you don't import the `System` namespace.
☒ **A** is incorrect because the `System` namespace can be explicitly supplied for the event support classes that are in the `System` namespace, for example, `System.EventArguments`. **B** is incorrect because the `System.ComponentModel` namespace is not needed to implement event handling. **C** is incorrect, since the `Microsoft.VisualBasic` namespace is used for legacy VB syntax, not event handling.

10. ☑ **C.** The `sender` variable is a reference to the object that raised the event.
☒ **A** is incorrect because the sender is a reference to the object that raised the event. **B** is incorrect because the Delegate is used for the encapsulation of the event handler's address, not as part of the event handler's signature. **D** is incorrect because the object instantiated from the `Form1` class is the parent class for the form, not the object that raised the event.

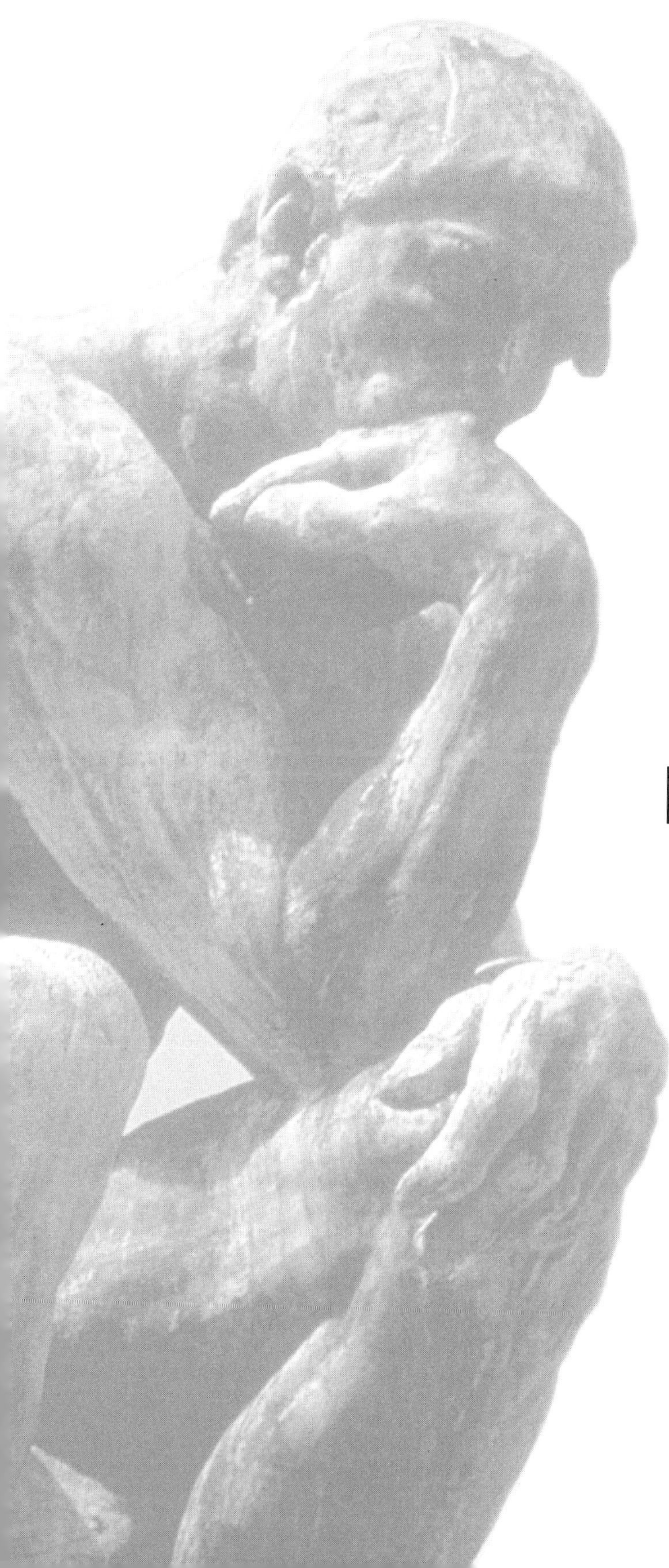

MCAD/MCSD

MICROSOFT® CERTIFIED APPLICATION DEVELOPER & MICROSOFT® CERTIFIED SOLUTION DEVELOPER

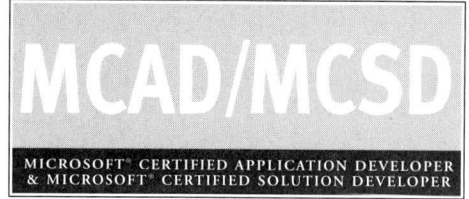

5

Creating and Managing Microsoft XML Web Services

CERTIFICATION OBJECTIVES

5.01	Explain XML Web Services
5.02	Know XML Web Services Architecture
5.03	Create an XML Web Service
5.04	Set the Web Method Attributes
5.05	Consume an XML Web Service
5.06	Discover XML Web Services
5.07	Build an XML Web Service Consumer
5.08	Create Asynchronous Web Methods
5.09	Create and Use SOAP Extensions
✓	Two Minute Drill
Q&A	Self Test

I n this chapter, you will learn how to design, create, and use XML web services, and most important from the exam point of view, you will learn how to control the environment of particular XML web services. You will work with both static and dynamic discovery of XML web services, and use the UDDI protocol to publish and locate an XML web service. The exam draws heavily from material in this chapter, so be certain that you are familiar with the terms and concepts I discuss.

CERTIFICATION OBJECTIVE 5.01

XML Web Services Explained

This chapter starts with the theory behind the XML web services. After you have covered the basics, you will get to the fun part: building XML web services and then consuming them. In this section, you will look at distributed applications and where XML web services fit. This section focuses on distributed applications and the protocols that are used to communicate between components, some of which are RPC, message-based systems, and web standards like XML.

Distributed Applications

Distributed applications are made up of many software components that are distributed between multiple computers connected by a network. This decentralization of the software components offers a number of benefits when the sum of the processing power of the different physical computers is available to the application and the data can be physically distributed across many different systems.

The Web is one of the architectures that have grown almost overnight, and it is one natural environment where distributed applications can reside. The standardized protocols that components can use to communicate over the Web are the foundation for distributed applications on the Web.

The protocols that are used on the Web include the latest interoperability protocols to be released (XML and SOAP, for example), along with Remote Procedure Call (RPC) and message-based protocols.

FROM THE CLASSROOM

Loose Coupling

One of the important concepts in computer engineering is that software components should be loosely coupled. That translates into a design where the components have knowledge only of each other's public methods, and the calls to those methods are asynchronous.

In order to be able to set up asynchronous method calls, you need to be able to register a callback method—that is, a method that is called when the work is complete. One option for referring to methods and data items uses the address where the item is stored in memory. This concept of being able to refer to a function by its address (the function pointer) is a very powerful one, but it is also fraught with dangers. For example, if the address changes, the call to the location that the address points to will most likely end up running code that will crash the application, or even the operating system. The designers of the .NET Framework made it possible for us to have the equivalent of the function pointer in an object-oriented way: the *delegate*. The delegate hides the problem by hiding the address in a class that is used to refer to the object whose address in stored in the delegate.

The one-sentence description of a delegate is, *The delegate encapsulates a reference to a method in the Delegate object.*

The asynchronous call is central to being able to build a distributed application using software components. The steps involved in setting up an asynchronous call are as follows:

- Instantiate a delegate object that will encapsulate the address of the callback method.

- Call a `Beginxxx()` method of the proxy, and pass a reference to the delegate as well as to any parameters to the asynchronous method.

- When the callback method is called, use the `IAsyncResult` parameter that is passed in order to access the return data from the asynchronous method.

- Call `Endxxx()` to complete the asynchronous call.

This technique of loosely coupling components is very resistant to network problems and can be used to provide scalable solutions where the objects must be load balanced.

Web Standards and XML

RPC-based environments have been successfully implemented by many different organizations in the form of the Distributed Component Object Model (DCOM) from Microsoft, the Common Object Request Broker Architecture (CORBA) from HP et al., and Remote Method Invocation (RMI) from Sun. These implementations are designed around binary protocols; however, binary protocols as a group have inherent problems:

- **Interoperability**   The binary protocols are not interoperable, because they were developed to be monolithic standards within the context of the specific distributed environment. Translation services can and have been developed, but these services are not only unwieldy, they also tend to lose some information as is normal in any translation process. The problems arise when different partners have selected a different binary protocol, resulting in translation problems.

- **Firewalls**   Firewalls are network components that control what network traffic is allowed to pass between the internal and external networks. RPC communication is point to point and uses ranges of TCP ports that must be opened (made available) in the firewall for communication to function. Opening ports in the firewall is considered to be a security risk by most organizations.

- **Data types**   The different binary protocols encode data in different ways, which creates a huge problem when the call must be translated. If there is no direct relationship between the data types in the systems, the result is inevitable data loss.

The solution to the binary protocol quandary is to use standard protocols that can be used and understood by all parties who want to participate in the distributed application. A quick refresher list of the different web protocols includes

- **HTTP**   Hypertext Transfer Protocol is the protocol that transfers any kind of document across the Web from client to web server and back again. HTTP traffic uses only one TCP port, making the firewall configuration more secure.

- **HTML**   Hypertext Markup Language is the language that is used to describe the web pages you see and use on the Web. They are delivered to the browser from the web server using HTTP.

- **XML**   Extensible Markup Language is the standard that gives you the ability to package data and the structural definition (metadata) of that data in one document. XML documents offer the following benefits:
  - It is easy to use across the Internet.
  - It is easy to process.
  - It is easy to create.
  - It is extensible.
  - It is platform independent.
  - It is easy to localize.
  - It offers a clear data model.

For a full discussion of the protocols, refer to Appendix D.

The adoption of XML by web server and web solution vendors has brought XML to the forefront as the most important web technology of this decade. XML is also the technology that is the solution to transmitting documents between partners in most e-commerce scenarios. Some developers think that XML has yet to prove itself, but the web world seems to have adopted XML, and you are not likely to go back to the monolithic environments of the past with their vendor-specific protocols.

That being said, there are some problems involved in transmitting information on the Internet that must be solved. Two of the most important concerns are

- **Performance**   The client still connects to the Internet mostly through dial-up connections, resulting in the need to send small amounts of data back and forth between the client and the web server. This is not a major concern when you develop for intranets, as they run on high-bandwidth networks; however, it should be considered when developing for Internet or extranet use.

- **Security**   The Internet is a public place, presenting opportunities for shadowy individuals to intercept, modify, spoof, or steal data using any one of many hacking techniques. You will deal with the defenses against these attacks in Chapter 8.

XML is an excellent choice when it comes to solving these two problems. XML transmits data and the structure of that data in a compact text format. This data can be encrypted for security.

XML Web Services in a Nutshell

XML Web Services is the end result of research into the problems with distributed applications based on binary protocols. The fast adoption of web protocols was one of the factors that made XML Web Services possible. XML Web Services is based on the XML standard, as the name implies, but there are a number of other standard protocols, including HTTP and Simple Object Access Protocol (SOAP), that are instrumental in making XML Web Services functional. The standard protocols are detailed in Appendix D.

An *XML web service* is a URL-addressable set of functionalities that is exposed over a network to serve as a part of a distributed application. All communication between a client and the XML web service server uses the HTTP protocol.

The XML web service acts as a building block of a distributed application and, as such, acts as a component, a black box. The design for the XML web service uses common object-oriented (OO) techniques that encapsulate the implementation and the data of the XML web service, thus making the XML web service suitable for building distributed applications.

An XML web service can be a very simple static service that provides information to the user, or a fully aggregated system of XML web services that provide a dynamic, complex software system. Aggregated XML web services are also known as *federated* XML web services.

The standards that support XML virtually guarantee that XML web services will be one of the major development environments for years to come. The level of adoption of the XML standard and of the technologies that support XML has not been seen in the Information Systems sector before. For example, an XML web service written in Visual Basic .NET and exported in IIS can be used by a Common Gateway Interface (CGI) application written in C++, and the usage is seamless.

Microsoft has made tools and technologies available that enable developers to take software components and expose them (make them available) as XML web services without rewriting them through Visual Studio .NET and the .NET Framework.

The use of SOAP guarantees that XML web services are interoperable with CORBA, DCOM, and any other binary protocols. XML web services can be hosted and accessed by any computer that supports HTTP and XML. HTTP is the only communication protocol that is needed, and XML is a markup language that allows the XML web services to communicate with the XML-based protocols such as SOAP.

XML web services can be written in any .NET language (C# .NET, Visual Basic .NET, COBOL .NET, and so on), enabling the developer to be productive in a familiar language, rather than having to learn yet another new language.

Wire Protocols

The term *wire protocol* is used to describe the protocol that is used for components to communicate with each other. XML web services can use the legacy binary wire protocols (RPC) that were used to let components communicate via DCOM, or a number of different Internet protocols.

The following wire protocols are available to developers when creating XML web services:

- **HTTP-GET and HTTP-POST**   These are standard protocols that have been evolving since the Web was invented. They use HTTP encoding to pass name-value pairs as part of the request. All nontext characters must be quoted and encoded. Both of these protocols are very low weight (low use of processing and transmission resources) but can be cumbersome to work with due to the URL encoding that must take place to put data in the request.

- **SOAP**   The Simple Object Access Protocol is XML based. Messages sent using SOAP can be passed between nodes using HTTP packets without requiring any special encoding. Because SOAP uses XML, the data and the structure are very clear. SOAP is the protocol of choice. For a refresher on SOAP, see Appendix D.

exam
ⓦatch   *When faced with a choice about the wire protocol to use, consider SOAP first because it is the most portable and can be encrypted at will.*

CERTIFICATION OBJECTIVE 5.02

XML Web Services Architecture

The architecture used for XML Web Services is one in which the XML web service is loosely coupled to the clients that will use it—the resources of the service and the client are separate and distinct. The communication to and from the service must meet the Internet standards, and the methods that will be called from a client of the XML web service must be published for public use and be publicly accessible.

There are three services in the XML Web Services architecture, as is shown in Figure 5-1.

The service provider hosts the XML web service and is responsible for providing access to the public interface of the software service. The service consumer is the client that will bind to the interface of the service provider. Note that in this architecture, the service consumer is not the end user—it is a software node in an application. The service broker is a node that is used to locate the service provider of a specific XML web service.

The interactions in Figure 5-1 are as follows:

- **Publish service**   The service provider publishes the XML web service to a service broker.

- **Find service**   The service consumer uses the service broker to find the service provider.

- **Bind to service**   The service consumer binds to the service from the service provider.

FIGURE 5-1

The objects in the XML Web Services architecture

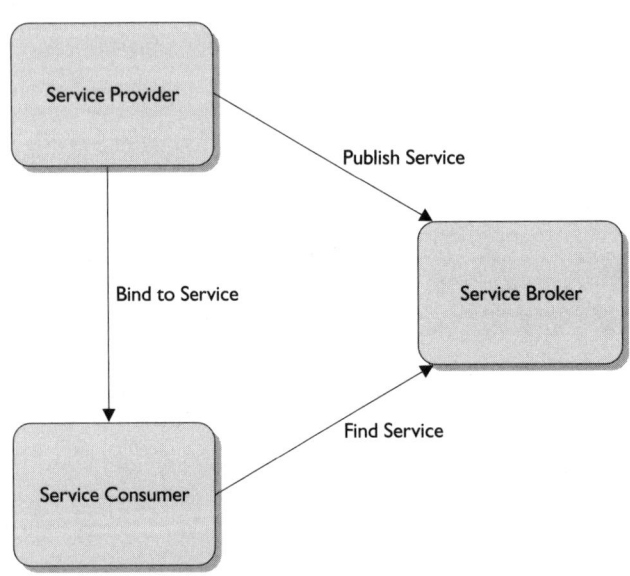

The find and bind actions can be dynamic, giving applications the ability to be configured dynamically at run time.

Figure 5-2 shows the protocols that are used between the three services in the XML Web Services architecture.

The service broker is a node in the network that implements a Universal Description, Discovery, and Integration (UDDI) registry. Universal Description, Discovery, and Integration is the yellow pages of web services. As with traditional yellow pages, you can search for a company that offers the services you need, read about the service offered, and contact someone for more information. You can, of course, offer a web service without registering it in UDDI, just as you can open a business in your basement and rely on word-of-mouth advertising, but if you want to reach a significant market, you need UDDI so that your customers can find you (see Appendix D for a description of UDDI). The service provider exposes (provides) XML services through an ASP.NET file that has the file extension .asmx. The service consumer can be any node in the network that can communicate using SOAP or HTTP, can supply the required authentication, and understands the service interface.

exam
ⓦatch

The service consumer does not have to be a client application—it can be another XML web service.

FIGURE 5-2

The protocols in the XML Web Services architecture

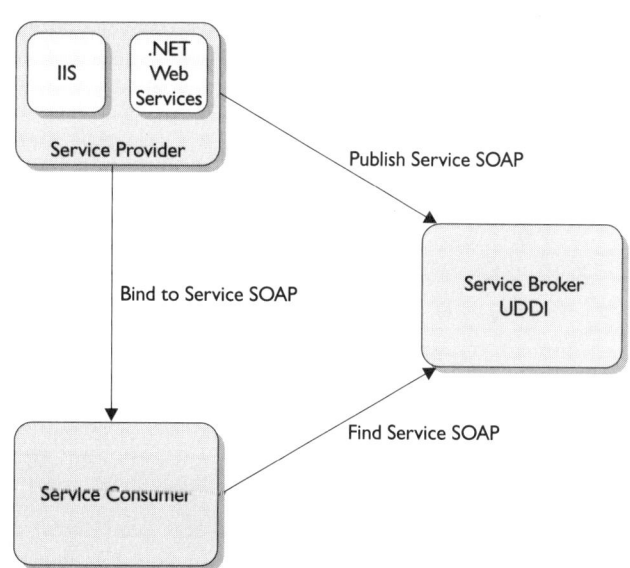

In the following sections, you will look more closely at the nodes in the XML Web Services architecture.

XML Web Service Provider

The central role of the XML Web Services architecture is that of an XML web service provider (I will use the term service provider for short). The service provider should supply HTTP protocol handling and authentication services. If the service provider can't supply these infrastructure services, the XML web service must implement them on behalf of the provider.

The minimum requirement for the service provider is that it must supply a protocol listener for the HTTP protocol. A *protocol listener* is a software component that waits (listens) for connections using a specific protocol, in this case HTTP. The service provider must also be able to distinguish between calls to different XML web services that are hosted on the same service provider, as well as provide basic security at the protocol level.

The service provider that Microsoft offers is Internet Information Services (IIS). IIS is a web server that provides all the services required of a service provider. IIS has the ability to redirect client calls to invoke service components on the server according to the configuration of IIS and the extension of the file being requested on the web server. For example, IIS can invoke CGI applications, Active Server Pages (ASP), and ASP.NET applications, as well as ISAPI (Internet Server Application Programming Interface) applications, and this is not an exhaustive list.

XML Web Service Consumer

The XML web service consumer (service consumer) is the node in the network that uses XML Web Services to provide its functionality. The service consumer is usually not the client application—rather, it is one node in the network that aggregates other services to provide some specific part of the distributed application. The minimum requirement of a service consumer is that it can call the XML web service using the wire protocol that the service supports—this can be any of the standard protocols. The .NET Framework provides classes that encapsulate the details of building custom communications packages in any of the protocols.

The service consumer uses the XML web service broker to locate the service provider that exposes the XML web service. The XML web service can be found dynamically at run time from a service broker, or it can be hard-coded at design time. Using the dynamic process makes the application configurable at run time and allows it to handle load balancing. XML web services and the endpoints (the service providers) are found by using the UDDI registry. For a full discussion on how to use UDDI, see Chapter 9.

The service consumer implements a proxy class that is used on the consumer to hide the details of the XML web service. This makes it possible for the developer to use the methods of the XML web service as if they were local methods.

XML Web Service Broker

XML web service brokers (service brokers) are used by service providers to publish the XML web services in the UDDI registry. The service broker provides the following:

- Contact information for the XML web service
- A text description for the XML web service
- Classification of the XML web service
- Links to documentation about the XML web service
- The location of the endpoints of the XML web service, stored as URLs

The service consumer uses the service broker to search for an XML web service and then discover the information that is needed to bind to that XML web service.

The method used by the service broker to make XML web service information available to service consumers uses the UDDI, which is a distributed registry. It allows service providers to publish their XML web services, and service consumers to find information about those published services. UDDI consists of three parts—business addresses, a list of categories, and technical information. Any XML web service can be described using these three parts.

XML Web Services Programming Model

The programming model used to build XML web services is based on some key features:

- **Statelessness** The XML web service is stateless. By not storing information between method invocations, the service becomes more scalable, even if the burden on the developer to design the stateless component can be quite high: because of the need to always keep the lack of state in mind, the application design will get more complicated.

- ■ **Use of web protocols** XML web services are totally programmed around the standard web protocols: HTTP, XML, SOAP, and UDDI.
- ■ **Loose coupling** By avoiding shared storage and data, XML Web Services makes the distributed application more resistant to service failures or to services being unavailable.
- ■ **XML data types** The data type used with XML Web Services is XML. XML is used in all areas of XML Web Services. For a refresher in XML, see Appendix D.

e x a m
ⓌⓐⓉ⓬ⓗ

Loose coupling is a key term that usually points to the right answer. Making components loosely coupled makes the components scalable, which is usually the optimum goal.

CERTIFICATION OBJECTIVE 5.03

Creating an XML Web Service

Although you'll be focusing on the use of VISUAL BASIC .NET for your examples, XML web services can be built using any of the .NET languages. An XML web service is an ASP.NET project saved with the file extension .asmx, for which the methods have been marked to be published as web methods.

An XML web service is made up of four separate parts:

- ■ The processing directive
- ■ The namespaces
- ■ The public class
- ■ Methods that are web callable

In the next sections, you will look at how to create an XML web service, as well as identify the parts of the project. You will create an XML web service that will convert between metric and imperial measurements.

The First XML Web Service

In this exercise, you will build and test a default XML web service; you are going to continue using this XML web service in other exercises in this chapter.

Step 1. Create a new Visual Basic .NET Project in Visual Studio .NET.

Step 2. Select the ASP.NET Web Service template.

Step 3. Name the project **CConverter**.

Step 4. Locate it on the localhost server, as shown next.

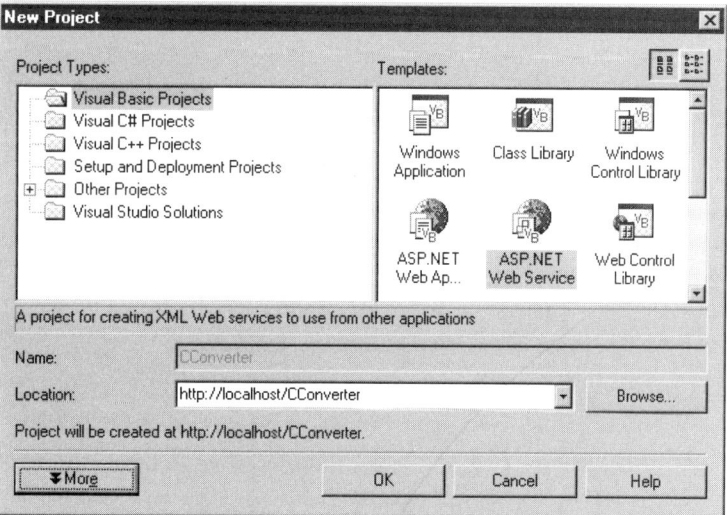

Step 5. Click OK, and the project will be created as shown here.

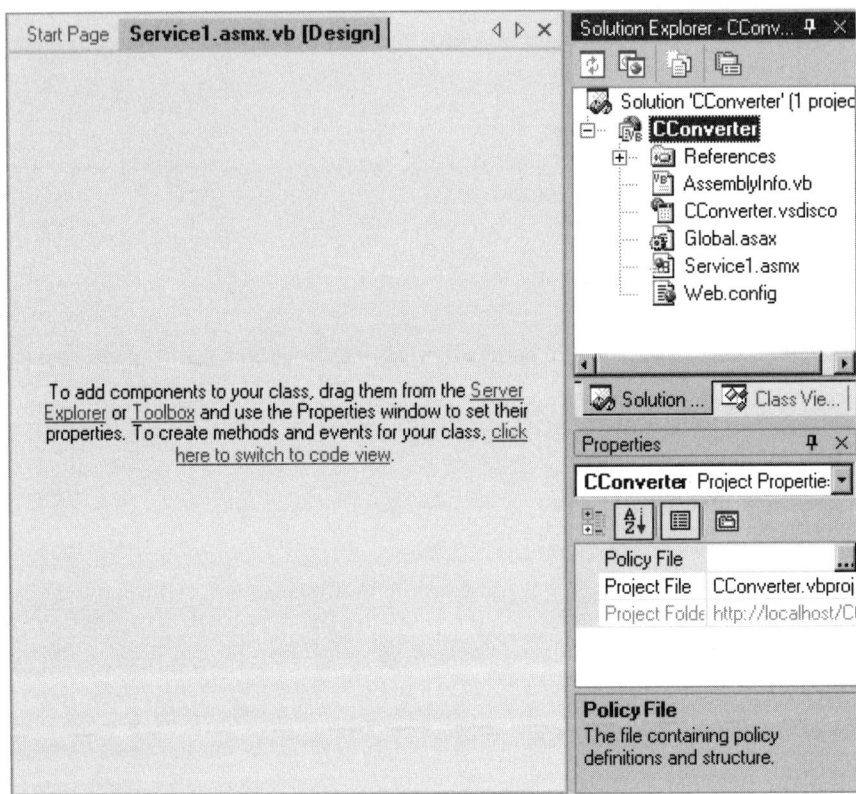

Step 6. Rename the project files to reflect your names rather than use the default names created by the New Project Wizard. Change the name of the Service1.asmx file to **Converter.asmx**.

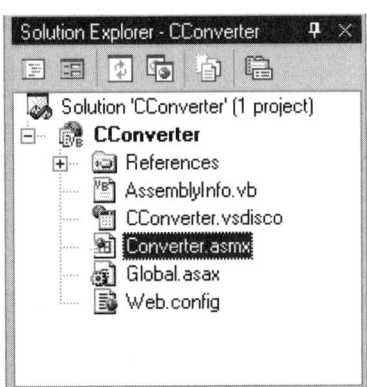

The note in the middle of the display in the following illustration prompts you to drag objects from the Toolbox or the Project Explorer onto the view, for the object to be part of the service. You can also click on the Converter.asmx.vb tab to see the source code for the project.

```
Imports System.Web.Services

<WebService(Namespace := "http://tempuri.org/")> _
Public Class Service1
    Inherits System.Web.Services.WebService

    Web Services Designer Generated Code

    ' WEB SERVICE EXAMPLE
    ' The HelloWorld() example service returns the string Hello World.
    ' To build, uncomment the following lines then save and build the project.
    ' To test this web service, ensure that the .asmx file is the start page
    ' and press F5.
    '
    '<WebMethod()> Public Function HelloWorld() As String
    '    HelloWorld = "Hello World"
    ' End Function

End Class
```

The source code module has some items added by default, as shown in the following code segment. The following is the complete code generated by the wizard; I have inserted some explanations to highlight the features.

```
Imports System.Web.Services
```

The System.Web.Services namespace provides support for the XML Web Service architecture and must be included with the namespaces that are imported. Other namespaces can be imported as needed to support additional services.

```
<WebService(Namespace := "http://tempuri.org/")> _
Public Class Service1
    Inherits System.Web.Services.WebService
```

The preceding segment declares the public class `Service1` and inherits from `System.Web.Services.WebService`. This makes the class an implementation of an XML web service.

```
Public Sub New()
    MyBase.New()

    'This call is required by the Web Services Designer.
```

```
InitializeComponent()

'Add your own initialization code after the InitializeComponent() call

End Sub
```

on the
①ob

The constructor in Visual Basic .NET is the New() method; use the constructor to initialize the class.

The preceding constructor calls the base class's constructor (`MyBase.New()`) and then `InitializeComponent()` to perform any custom initialization. The default implementation of `InitializeComponent()` is an empty body.

```
'Required by the Web Services Designer
Private components As System.ComponentModel.IContainer
```

The preceding line declares a private member of type System.ComponentModel .Container to hold references to any components that are added to the XML web service, and it initializes the member to null.

```
'NOTE: The following procedure is required by the Web Services Designer
'It can be modified using the Web Services Designer.
'Do not modify it using the code editor.
<System.Diagnostics.DebuggerStepThrough()> _
Private Sub InitializeComponent()
    components = New System.ComponentModel.Container()
End Sub
```

The preceding initialization function is used by the Visual Studio .NET designer to initialize any components that are added to the XML web service project.

```
Protected Overloads Overrides Sub Dispose(ByVal disposing As Boolean)
    'CODEGEN: This procedure is required by the Web Services Designer
    'Do not modify it using the code editor.
    If disposing Then
        If Not (components Is Nothing) Then
            components.Dispose()
        End If
    End If
    MyBase.Dispose(disposing)
End Sub
```

The preceding code is the clean-up code that will iterate through the `IComponent` member, calling the `Dispose()` method on all components that have been added to the project. Finally the base class's `Dispose()` method is called.

```
' WEB SERVICE EXAMPLE
' The HelloWorld() example service returns the string Hello World.
' To build, uncomment the following lines then save and build the project.
' To test this web service, ensure that the .asmx file is the start page
' and press F5.
'
'<WebMethod()> Public Function HelloWorld() As String
'     HelloWorld = "Hello World"
'     End Function
```

The preceding code is the last part of the generated code. It is a sample declaration of a web method that will return the string "Hello World" to the caller of the method. The `<WebMethod>` attribute marks the public `HelloWorld()` method to be published and callable. Let's continue the exercise to see the XML web service in action.

Step 7.   Remove the comments from the `HelloWorld()` method as shown in the following code segment:

```
...
' WEB SERVICE EXAMPLE
' The HelloWorld() example service returns the string Hello World.
' To build, uncomment the following lines then save and build the project.
' To test this web service, ensure that the .asmx file is the start page
' and press F5.
'
<WebMethod()> Public Function HelloWorld() As String
    HelloWorld = "Hello World"
End Function
...
```

Step 8.   Save the project. Press F5 to build and run the XML web service. The result is that your web browser will start up and display the information page about the XML web service. This page is the start of the XML help application that will help you test and use your XML web service, as shown in the following illustration. The note about the default namespace is important, as it makes sure you use your namespace rather than the http://tempuri.org/ URI that Microsoft has designated as the testing namespace for XML web services. A Universal Resource Indicator (URI) is a unique string that is used to avoid name conflicts between services that have the same name.

Service1

The following operations are supported. For a formal definition, please review the <u>Service Description</u>.

- <u>HelloWorld</u>

on the job

The URI is a unique string that identifies an entity; there does not have to be a web site that matches the URI.

The name of the only declared web method is listed at the top of the page—click the HelloWorld link to review the SOAP request and response headers that are used to call the web method; you can use these headers to build custom communication between your XML web service and the consumer application, as shown next.

Service1

Click <u>here</u> for a complete list of operations.

HelloWorld

Test

To test the operation using the HTTP GET protocol, click the 'Invoke' button.

    Invoke

exam watch

The XML web service Help pages are great for getting the WSDL document (the WSDL document will be explained in the "WSDL" section of this chapter).

Click Invoke to see the XML document that represents the return value from the web method.

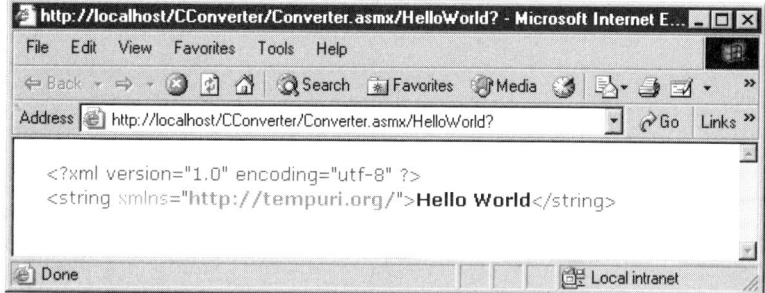

The default behavior when you call an XML web service directly from a browser is for the .NET Framework to render the service as an information page, listing all the web methods that are defined in the service. This Service page forms the basis for unit testing of the XML web service. For more information on unit testing and debugging of XML web services, see Chapter 7. One thing you need to do with the XML web service is to change the namespace from http://tempuri.org/ to http://*xxx.yyy/*, where *xxx.yyy* represents your domain name; you would replace the URI with one for your organization to ensure that you have a unique namespace.

Step 9. Open the code editor, and locate the <WebService...> element.

Step 10. Modify the <WebService> element by adding the attribute shown in bold in the following listing to the class definition. This will change the namespace of the XML web service.

```
...
<WebService(Namespace:="http://xxx.yyy/")> _

Public Class Service1

    Inherits System.Web.Services.WebService
...
```

Step 11. Press F5 to compile and execute the helper application. Here is the display that results when the revised project is executed:

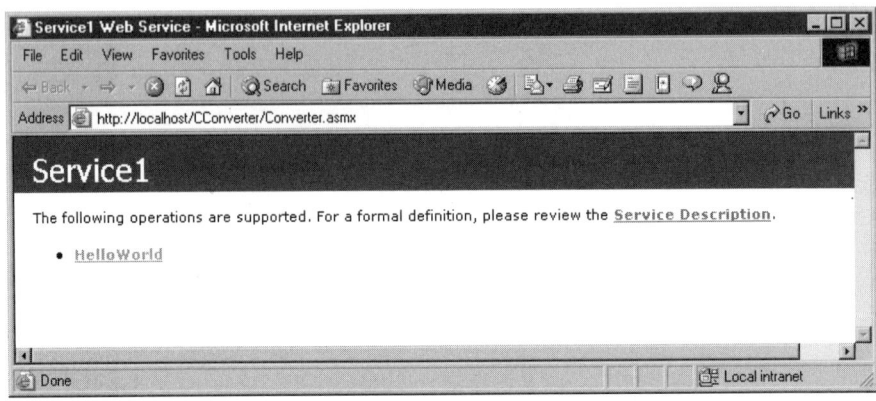

Now that you have your first basic XML web service, you will add some custom behavior to it to truly make it a converter.

EXERCISE 5-2

The Web Method

In order to make a method visible through an XML web service, you need to define the methods that are callable as web methods. You will continue the metric and imperial conversion XML web service from the preceding section. In order to make a method available to be called, it must be exposed as a web method.

1. Comment out the `HelloWorld()` web method used in the preceding exercise.

2. At the end of the `Service1` class definition, insert a web method named `Cmi` (Convert to miles) as shown in the following code segment:

```
<WebMethod()> Public Function Cmi(ByVal km As Double) As Double
    Return (0.621371 * km)
End Function
```

3. Add three more web methods after the definition of `Cmi`; they are named `Ckm` (Convert to kilometers), `Cfa` (Convert to Fahrenheit), and `CCe` (Convert to Celsius). The following code segment shows how the code should look:

```
<WebMethod()> Public Function Ckm(ByVal mi As Double) As Double
    Return (1.609344 * mi)
End Function

<WebMethod()> Public Function CFa(ByVal c As Double) As Double
    Return (((c * 9) / 5) + 32)
End Function

<WebMethod()> Public Function CCe(ByVal f As Double) As Double
    Return (((f - 32) * 5) / 9)
End Function
```

4. The methods must be public in scope and marked with the `<WebMethod>` attribute to be available to XML web service consumers.

```
The conversions used are: 1 mi = 1.609344 km, 1 km = 0.621371 mi, 1 F =
(C*9/5) + 32, and 1 C = (F - 32) * 5/9.
```

5. Save and execute the XML web service by pressing F5. The resulting display should be as shown next.

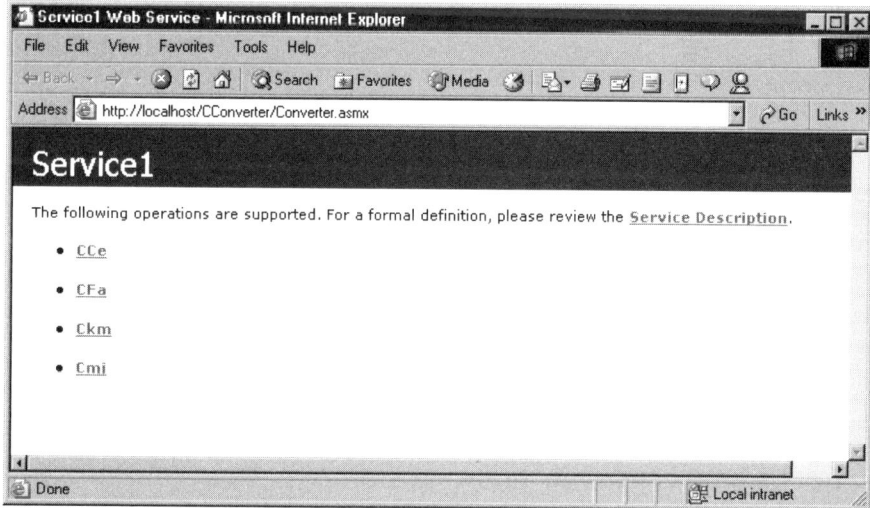

6. Select the Ckm conversion function, and a page requesting the value of the parameter will be displayed.

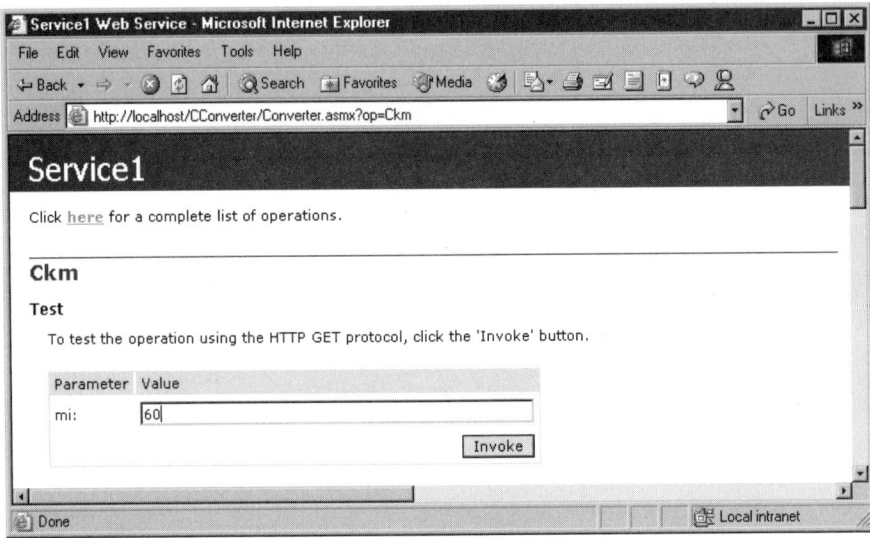

7. Enter the parameter value (60 miles in this example), and click Invoke to display the resulting calculation.

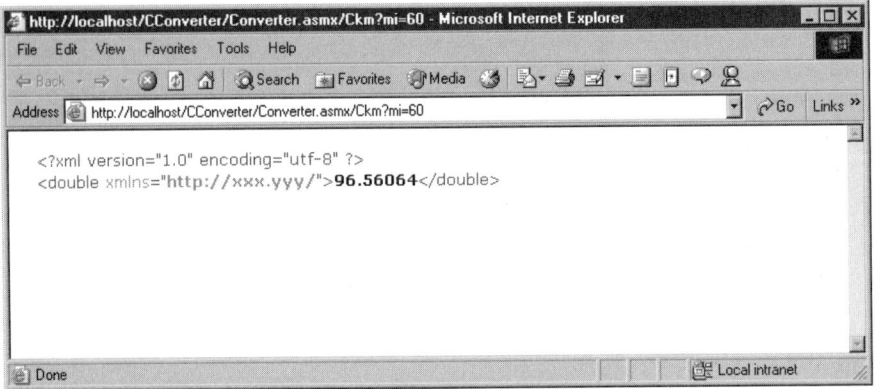

8. Perform a test of all four methods using a range of values to ensure that the conversion methods work. Some interesting numbers to test with are: 212 F = 100 C, 37.7 C = 100 F, 50 km = 31 mi.

Now you have a functional conversion XML web service. The next topic is how to control the web methods using the <WebMethod> attributes.

Setting the Web Method Attributes

The <WebMethod> attribute you used in the preceding section has a number of properties that are used to customize the way the <WebMethod> operates. Table 5-1 describes those properties.

TABLE 5-1   Attributes for the <WebMethod> Attribute

Property	Description
BufferResponse	The BufferResponse property controls how the response from the <WebMethod> is returned to the client. If the property is set to True (the default setting), ASP.NET will buffer the entire response before returning anything to the client. This type of buffering is very efficient. If the BufferResponse property is set to False, ASP.NET will send the response in 16KB packets.
CacheDuration	The CacheDuration property controls the lifetime of the cached response. The default setting is 0, which means that caching is disabled for results. The property is in seconds with 0 turning it off, and any other value indicating the amount of time the result should be cached.
Description	This property supplies the description of the <WebMethod> that will be supplied on the XML web service Help page.
EnableSession	When the EnableSession property is set to True, the <WebMethod> can use the Session object of WebService.Session to maintain state between calls. The default setting is False.
MessageName	You can uniquely identify an overloaded <WebMethod> by using the MessageName as an alias. The default value of the MessageName property is the name of the WebMethod, and changing the property will publish the new name.
TransactionOption	This property enables the XML web service method to participate as the root object in a transaction using the Microsoft Distributed Transaction Coordinator (MS DTC).

To use the properties with the `<WebMethod>` attribute, you include the properties in a list as part of the attribute. The following example sets the `CacheDuration` to 600 seconds:

```
<WebMethod(CacheDuration = 600)>
```

To add additional parameters, use a comma to separate the properties, as in the following example:

```
<WebMethod(CacheDuration = 600, Description="This is a test")>
```

You are now going to use these attribute properties to modify how the conversion XML web service is defined.

EXERCISE 5-3

In this Exercise, you are going to modify the conversion XML web service from Exercise 5-2 by applying attributes to the web methods.

1. Open up the CConvert project from the preceding exercise.

2. Create a second `Ckm` web method that takes an Integer as the parameter and returns an Integer.

3. Add to the web method definition for the `Ckm` web method to set the `CachDuration` to 3 seconds.

4. Add to the web method definition a description for the `Ckm()` method to read "This is the miles to km Integer Conversion".

5. Add to the web method definition a `MessageName` to `CkmInt`.

6. The code for the Integer version of `Ckm` should look like the following code listing:

```
<WebMethod(CacheDuration:=3, _
    Description:="This is the miles to km Integer Conversion", _
    MessageName:="CkmInteger")> _
Public Function Ckm(ByVal mi As Integer) As Integer
    Return (1.609344 * mi)
End Function
```

7. Modify the original `Ckm` web method by adding attributes to make it unique as is shown in the following code segment.

```
<WebMethod(CacheDuration:=3, _
    Description:="This is the miles to km Double Conversion", _
    MessageName:="CkmDouble")> _
Public Function Ckm(ByVal mi As Double) As Double
    Return (1.609344 * mi)
End Function
```

8. Perform the same actions to the Cmi(), CFa(), and CCe() web methods as well. The resulting code segment should look as follows:

```
<WebMethod(CacheDuration:=3, _
    Description:="This is the km to miles Integer Conversion", _
    MessageName:="CmiInteger")> _
Public Function Cmi(ByVal km As Integer) As Integer
    Return (621371 * km) / 1000000
End Function

<WebMethod(CacheDuration:=3, _
    Description:="This is the km to miles Double Conversion", _
    MessageName:="CmiDouble")> _
Public Function Cmi(ByVal km As Double) As Double
    Return (0.621371 * km)
End Function

<WebMethod(CacheDuration:=3, _
    Description:="This is the miles to km Integer Conversion", _
    MessageName:="CkmInteger")> _
Public Function Ckm(ByVal mi As Integer) As Integer
    Return (1609344 * mi) / 1000000
End Function

<WebMethod(CacheDuration:=3, _
    Description:="This is the miles to km Double Conversion", _
    MessageName:="CkmDouble")> _
Public Function Ckm(ByVal mi As Double) As Double
    Return (1.609344 * mi)
End Function

<WebMethod(CacheDuration:=3, _
    Description:="This is the Celsius to Fahrenheit Integer Conversion", _
    MessageName:="CFaInteger")> _
Public Function CFa(ByVal c As Integer) As Integer
    Return (((c * 9) / 5) + 32)
End Function

<WebMethod(CacheDuration:=3, _
    Description:="This is the Celsius to Fahrenheit Double Conversion", _
    MessageName:="CFaDouble")> _
Public Function CFa(ByVal c As Double) As Double
```

```
      Return (((c * 9) / 5) + 32)
  End Function

  <WebMethod(CacheDuration:=3, _
      Description:="This is the Fahrenheit to Celsius Integer Conversion", _
      MessageName:="CCeInteger")> _
  Public Function CCe(ByVal f As Integer) As Integer
      Return (((f - 32) * 5) / 9)
  End Function

  <WebMethod(CacheDuration:=3, _
      Description:="This is the Fahrenheit to Celsius Double Conversion", _
      MessageName:="CCeDouble")> _
  Public Function CCe(ByVal f As Double) As Double
      Return (((f - 32) * 5) / 9)
  End Function
```

9. The use of the `Description` and `MessageName` properties in the preceding code illustrates how you can overload methods in an XML web service.

10. Save and execute the project by pressing F5. The result should look like what is shown in the following illustration. Test the web methods to ensure that they truly work as overloaded functions and that the conversion works.

Service1

The following operations are supported. For a formal definition, please review the <u>Service Description</u>.

- **CFaDouble**
  This is the Celsius to Fahrenheit Double Conversion

- **CmiInteger**
  This is the km to miles Integer Conversion

- **CmiDouble**
  This is the km to miles Double Conversion

- **CkmInteger**
  This is the miles to km Integer Conversion

- **CkmDouble**
  This is the miles to km Double Conversion

- **CCeInteger**
  This is the Fahrenheit to Celsius Integer Conversion

- **CFaInteger**
  This is the Celsius to Fahrenheit Integer Conversion

- **CCeDouble**
  This is the Fahrenheit to Celsius Double Conversion

The Project Files

The different files that are included in the Solution Explorer are part of the XML web service project and perform important tasks during the design-time and runtime phases of the XML web service. These files are listed in Table 5-2.

e x a m

ⓦ a t c h

The /bin directory is very important. Any assemblies copied into the /bin directory are available to the application without any registration in the GAC.

TABLE 5-2	File	Description
Files Used by an XML Web Service	Global.asmx	This file is located in the root directory of the web application and is used to configure handlers for events raised by the ASP.NET application or session objects. The Global.asmx file cannot be returned to a client browser because the .NET Framework is configured to reject any request for the file. Should a new version of the Global.asmx file be saved into the root directory of the application, Global.asmx will be recompiled when all current connections are closed. The use of the Global.asmx is optional; the Visual Studio .NET wizard creates it, but it can be deleted if not needed.
	Web.config	This is the configuration file for the XML web service. By using this file, you can configure all aspects of the service, including security. For more information about the Web.config file, see Chapter 9.
	.vsdisco file	This is the dynamic discovery document that is used to publish the XML web service. To use dynamic discovery, publish the .vsdisco file rather than the XML web service.
	AssemblyInfo.vb	This file contains project information and will be compiled into the XML web service assembly.
	/bin folder	This folder off the root of the application is where the compile output of the application will be stored. The /bin folder is also important in that any assembly added to it will be available to the application without any registration.

CERTIFICATION OBJECTIVE 5.05

Consuming an XML Web Service

Now look at how you can create an application that will consume an XML web service. There are a number of different steps, and you will look at them in turn. First, revisit the Web Service Description Language (WSDL) and the structure of a WSDL document. Then look at the XML web service discovery process. Also look at the XML web service proxy and how it is generated using wsdl.exe, and then implement the consumer using Visual Studio .NET and Visual Basic .NET.

WSDL

The Web Service Description Language (WSDL) is an XML grammar that describes an XML web service by defining the messages it accepts and sends. The WSDL document forms a contract between the service provider and the service consumer.

The WSDL document is a list of definitions—indeed the root element of the WSDL document is named `<definitions>`. Table 5-3 describes the elements that must be present in the `<definitions>` element.

The best way to see WSDL in action is to look at an XML web service and then describe it using WSDL. You will look at the different stages of creating a WSDL file in the next examples. The following source code has been tagged with attributes and defines a storage-only class (`Weather`) that has been marked with the

TABLE 5-3	Element	Description
Some of the Elements in a WSDL Document	type	Defines the data types that are used to exchange messages
	message	Describes the messages that are exchanged
	portType	Lists a set of operations and the messages for those operations
	binding	Describes the protocol binding for service operations
	service	Groups ports to provide the web service

<XmlRoot> attribute to be called "forecast". Each of the data members is marked with the <XmlElement> attribute, identifying it as a public entity.

```
<XmlRoot("forecast")>
Public Class Weather
    <XmlAttribute("city">
    Public City As String
    <XmlElement("state">
    Public State As String
    <XmlElement("country">
    Public Country As String
    <XmlElement("windspeed">
    Public WindSpeed As Decimal
    <XmlElement("winddirection">
    Public WindDirection As String
    <XmlElement("temperature">
    Public Temperature As Decimal
    <XmlElement("airpressure">
    Public AirPressure As Decimal
    <XmlElement("sky">
    Public Sky As String
End Class 'Weather

Public Class WeatherForecast
    <WebMethod>
    Public Function GetForecast(city As string) As Weather
        Dim w As Weather = new Weather()
        w.City = "Mimico"
        w.State = "Ontario"
        w.Country = "Canada"
        w.WindSpeed = 5.0
        w.WindDirection = "NNW"
        w.Temperature = 33.0
        w.AirPressure = 960.4
        w.Sky = "Partly cloudy"
        return(w)
    End Function
End Class 'WeatherForcast
```

Given the Visual Basic .NET source code with XML web service attributes, you can now start building the WSDL document. The first step is to define the data types that are used in the messages the XML web service supports. This is done by describing them using the Extensible Schema Definition language (XSD). The namespaces used in this example are s (which is xmlns:s=http://www.w3.org/2001/XMLSchema), and s0, which refers to the namespace of the <WebService>. The data-type definition for the Weather class would be as follows:

```
<s:complexType name="Weather">
  <s:sequence>
    <s:element minOccurs="1" maxOccurs="1" name="state" type="s:string" />
    <s:element minOccurs="1" maxOccurs="1" name="country" type="s:string" />
    <s:element minOccurs="1" maxOccurs="1" name="windspeed" type="s:decimal" />
    <s:element minOccurs="1" maxOccurs="1" name="winddirection"
      type="s:string" />
    <s:element minOccurs="1" maxOccurs="1" name="temperature"
      type="s:decimal" />
    <s:element minOccurs="1" maxOccurs="1" name="airpressure"
      type="s:decimal" />
    <s:element minOccurs="1" maxOccurs="1" name="sky" type="s:string" />
  </s:sequence>
  <s:attribute name="city" type="s:string" />
</s:complexType>
```

The preceding XSD document represents the following XML document:

```
<?xml version="1.0" encoding="utf-8"?>
<forecast city="Mimico">
    <state>Ontario</state>
    <country>Canada</country>
    <windspeed>5.0</windspeed>
    <winddirection>NNW</winddirection>
    <temperature>33.0</temperature>
    <airpressure)960.4</airpressure>
    <sky>Partly Cloudy</sky>
</forecast>
```

Once the data types are defined, you need to define the structure of the messages that are exchanged. In this example, the GetForecast() method is the only <WebMethod> defined, so inbound messages will have the same name as the method, while outbound messages will have the same name as the method with the word "Response" appended. The following XML segment would be nested inside the type element, and it defines the two messages for this example:

```
<s:element name="GetForecast">
   <s:complexType>
      <s:sequence>
         <s:element minOccurs="1" maxOccurs="1" name="city"
                    nillable="true" type="s:string" />
      </s:sequence>
   </s:complexType>
</s:element>
<s:element name="GetForecastResponse">
   <s:complexType>
      <s:sequence>
         <s:element minOccurs="1" maxOccurs="1" name="forecast"
                    nillable="true" type="s0:Weather" />
      </s:sequence>
   </s:complexType>
</s:element>
```

The next step in building the WSDL document is to define the message elements based on the structure just defined. When the message element is defined, it will have one or more part child elements. The part child element is similar to a parameter in a method call. The definition of a request message has all the in and inout parameters, while the response message contains all out and inout parameters as well as the return value. The following code segment defines the request and response messages:

```
<message name="GetForecastIN">
   <part name="parameters" element="s0:GetForecast" />
</message>
<message name="GetForecastOut">
   <part name="parameters" element="s0:GetForecastResponse" />
</message>
```

Now you can start putting the pieces together by declaring the portType element that will define the XML web service and the messages that the service handles. In other words, you define the endpoints for the service. The following lines perform that operation:

```
<portType name"WeatherService">
   <operation name="GetForecast">
     <input message="s0:GetForcastIn" />
     <output message="s0:GetForecastOut" />
   </operation>
</portType>
```

The preceding definition declares the logical endpoints of the service. The next step is to specify how you can bind to the port where the GetForecast operation is available. That is done using the binding element, as in the following code segment:

```
<binding name="WeatherService" type="s0:WeatherService">
  <soap:binding transport=http://schemas.xmlsoap.org/soap/http
               style="document" />
  <operation name="GetForecast">
   <soap:operation soapAction="http://xxx.yyy/GetForecast"
                            style="document"/>
    <input>
      <soap:body use="literal" />
      </input>
    <output>
      <soap:body use="literal" />
      </output>
    </operation>
</binding>
```

The final step you need to take to create the WSDL document is to specify the protocol endpoints that are used to connect to the XML web service. To do this, define the service element as in the following code lines:

```
<service name="WeatherService">
   <port name="WeatherService" binding="s0:WeatherService">
      <soap:address
             location="http://localhost/Weather/Forecast.asmx" />
   </port>
</service>
```

The complete code for the preceding WSDL document is available in the companion Chapter 5 folder on the accompanying CD-ROM.

There may seem to be a lot of work involved in producing the WSDL document, but even that can be automated. By opening the XML web service in a browser and selecting Service Description, you make the entire WSDL file available. The exam will not test you on how to create the file automatically, though—you will just need to know about the parts that make up the WSDL document.

exam

ⓦatch

The parts of the WSDL document are type, message, portType, binding, *and* service. *Remember that the order is important.*

CERTIFICATION OBJECTIVE 5.06

Discovering XML Web Services

As you saw in the preceding section, the WSDL document describes all the aspects of how a consumer should communicate (exchange messages) with an XML web service. In order to use an XML web service, the consumer must be able to find the WSDL document that defines the service. XML web service discovery is the process that a consumer goes through to find an XML web service and learn how to communicate with it.

Earlier in this chapter, you were introduced to the three nodes that make up the architecture of an XML web service—the service provider, the service consumer, and the service broker. It is the role of the service broker to help service consumers find the description of the XML web service and assist in learning about the service. If the service isn't published through a service broker, you need a method to discover the XML web services that are available at an endpoint. To that end, there is disco, a discovery tool that enumerates the XML web services that are available at a particular endpoint.

You can make the discovery information available either statically through a .disco document, or dynamically, which means the discovery document is generated at run time.

Static Discovery of XML Web Services

Static discovery is based on a discovery file that is made available to the consumer. The static discovery file is an XML document that contains the references to the entry points where discovery and contract information can be found. The file usually has the extension .disco, but that is not required.

The following is an example of a static discovery document in which you can see the two main elements: `discoveryRef`, which supplies additional information, and `contractRef`, which points to the document that can supply the contract information.

```
<?xml version="1.0"?>
<discovery xmlns:xsi="http://www.w3.org/2000/10/XMLSchema-instance"
           xmlns:xsd="http://www.w3.org/2000/10/XMLSchema/"
           xmlns="http://schemas.xmlsoap.org/disco/">
    <discoveryRef ref="http://localhost/WeatherService/Weather.disco"/>
    <contractRef ref="http://localhost/WeatherService/Weather.asmx?wsdl"
           docRef="http://localhost/WeatherService/Weather.asmx"
           xmlns="http://schemas.xmlsoap.org/disco/scl/"/>
</discovery>
```

Note that the parameter that is passed to the `contractRef` element (`Weather.asmx?wsdl`) will retrieve the contract information from the XML web service. The `contractRef` can also be a separate XML file that defines the contract.

Dynamic Discovery

Dynamic discovery is not enabled by default. It must be turned on either in the machine.config .NET Framework configuration file (which is system-wide) or in the web.config application configuration file. Dynamic discovery is enabled by removing the comment from the .vsdisco `httpHandler` element, as shown in the following code segment from the machine.config file:

```
<httpHandlers>
    <add verb="*" path="*.vsdisco"
         type="System.Web.Services.Discovery.DiscoveryRequestHandler,
              System.Web.Services, Version=1.0.3300.0, Culture=neutral,
              PublicKeyToken=b03f5f7f11d50a3a"
         validate="false"/>
```

Once the dynamic discovery is enabled, a file named *<XML Web Service name>*.vsdisco must be placed in the root of the application. If Visual Studio .NET is used to create the XML web service, a default *<XML Web Service name>*.vsdisco is placed in the root of the application.

e x a m
ⓦ a t c h

It is illegal for you to place a .vsdisco file and a .disco file in the same directory. The result is that the client will not be able to discover the XML web service.

The following is an example of the file that Visual Studio .NET generated for the WeatherService. The file is called WeatherService.vsdisco.

```
<?xml version="1.0" encoding="utf-8" ?>
<dynamicDiscovery
 xmlns="urn:schemas-dynamicdiscovery:disco.2000-03-17">
<exclude path="_vti_cnf" />
<exclude path="_vti_pvt" />
<exclude path="_vti_log" />
<exclude path="_vti_script" />
<exclude path="_vti_txt" />
<exclude path="Web References" />
</dynamicDiscovery>
```

The default is to exclude the private directories from the discovery process. The dynamic discovery process is based on the .vsdisco extension being mapped to the Aspnet_isapi.dll that performs the discovery. The discovery process searches the folders for files with the extensions .asmx, .vsdisco, and .disco—the discovery process ends if one of these extensions cannot be found.

o n t h e
🛈 o b

Enabling dynamic discovery on production servers will expose information about your XML web services to anyone on the network, so you should use dynamic discovery only for development environments.

Proxies for XML Web Services

The consumer of an XML web service must be able to properly assemble the messages that are sent to the services, as well as understand how to disassemble the return messages. When you consume XML web services, you do so through a proxy class that performs the work of taking your method calls and packaging them up into messages, and vice versa with return messages.

The tool you use to create the proxy is wsdl.exe, along with the WSDL document that describes the service. The wsdl.exe utility tool has many command-line switches. To see a complete listing, execute this command:

```
wsdl /?
```

In order to generate the proxy, you will need to run the following command:

```
>wsdl /l:vb /o:Wproxy.vb http://localhost/Weather.asmx?WSDL
/n:WeatherService
```

This command produces a Visual Basic .NET language source file (the /l:vb part of the command) in the current directory and calls the file Wproxy.vb (the /o part). The information is gleaned from the Weather.asmx XML web service in the root of the localhost, and the namespace used is WeatherService.

The resulting source file needs to be compiled, and the following command performs the compilation:

```
>vbc /out:/bin/Wproxy.dll /t:library /r:system.web.dll,system.dll,
system.xml.dll,system.web.services.dll,system.data.dll Wproxy.vb
```

The command compiles and builds a library (/t:library), which is placed in the /bin directory and is called Wproxy.dll. All the namespaces that are listed after the /r command-line switch are the namespaces that will be imported. Finally, the name of the source file is listed.

CERTIFICATION OBJECTIVE 5.07

Building an XML Web Service Consumer

In this section, you will finally get to where you can consume the XML web service. You will use two exercises that will highlight how the service is consumed. The first example will use a console application to consume the imperial-to-metric converter service created earlier in the chapter. The second will use a Windows Form to do the same.

The procedure outlined in this section can be used to consume XML web services with Web Forms or other web services. Irrespective of the consumer application, the steps involved in consuming the XML web service are the same:

1. Create a proxy class for the XML web service.

2. Reference the proxy class in the consumer's code.

3. Instantiate the proxy in the consumer's code.

4. Call an XML web service method through the instance of the proxy class.

The XML Web Service Consumer

In this exercise, you will build a console application that uses the CConverter XML web service to convert between imperial and metric values.

1. Create a Visual Basic .NET project using the Console Application template and call the application **mikm**, as shown here:

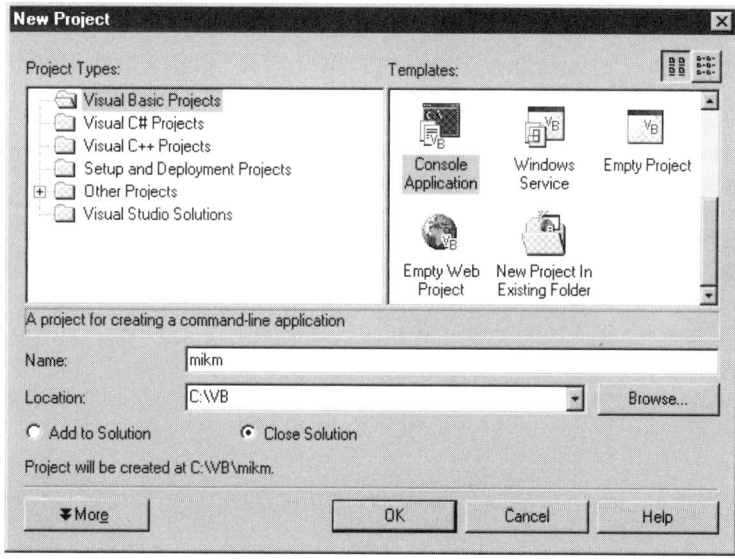

2. Add a reference by right-clicking the References node in the Solution Explorer and selecting Add Web Reference.

3. In the Add Web Reference dialog box, enter **http://localhost/CConverter/ Converter.asmx** in the address field and press ENTER. The Service help page will be displayed in the dialog.

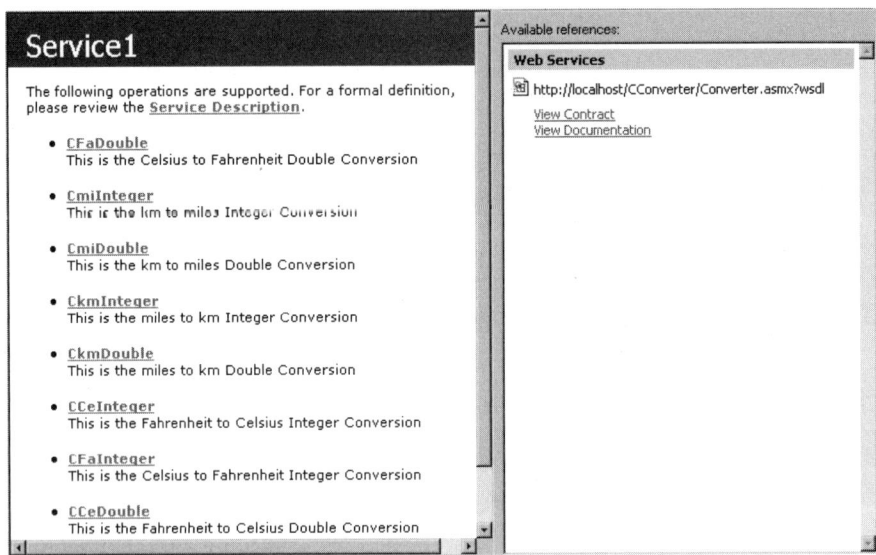

4. Click the Add Reference button to add the web reference. As you add the reference, the proxy class is automatically generated by Visual Studio .NET.

5. Expand the Web References node in the Solution Explorer. The node named `localhost` contains all the references found on the local server. Because the name `localhost` can be confusing, rename the node to **Converter**.

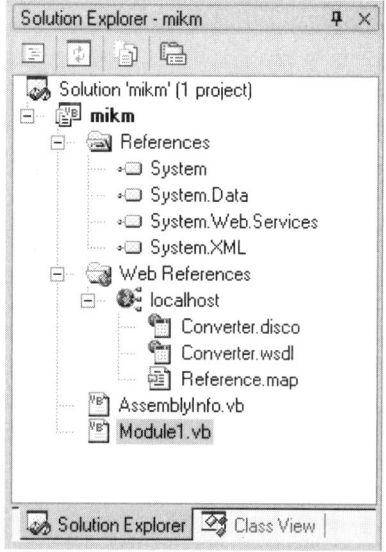

6. Enter the following code in the Module1.vb source file:

```
Module Module1
   Sub Main()
       Dim k As mikm.localhost.Service1 = New
mikm.localhost.Service1()
       Console.WriteLine(k.Cmi(100))
   End Sub
End Module
```

In the preceding code, the referenced XML web service is used by declaring a reference (k) to mikm.localhost.Service1 and then calling WebMethod (Cmi) on that reference.

7. Run the application by pressing CTRL-F5 (this way, the console will prompt you to press "any key" before closing the console).

As a result of this exercise, you consumed an XML web service, calling one of the web methods that the XML web service contains. Next you will learn how to consume a web service using a Windows form.

<hr>

EXERCISE 5-5

<hr>

A Windows Form Consumer

In this exercise, you will build a Windows form that will consume the XML web service you built earlier in this chapter.

1. Start a new Visual Basic .NET project, select the Windows Application template, and call the project **Convert**.

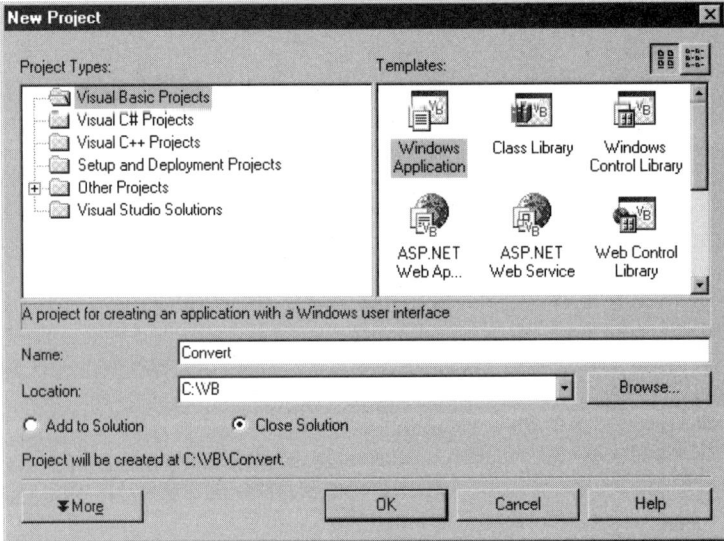

2. Add a reference by right-clicking the References node in the Solution Explorer and selecting Add Web Reference.

3. The Add Web Reference dialog will open. Type **http://localhost/ CConverter/Converter.asmx** in the Address field and press ENTER. The Service help page will be displayed in the dialog box.

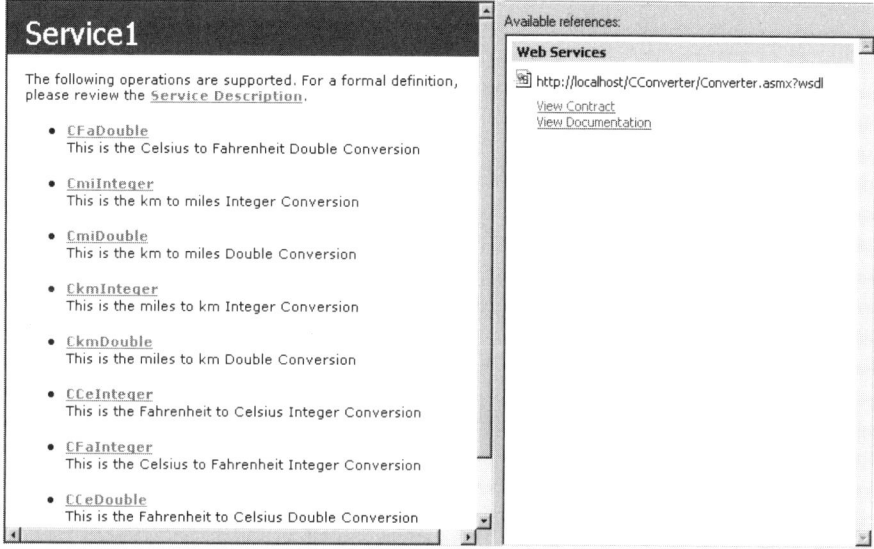

4. Click the Add Reference button to add the web reference. As you add the reference, the proxy class will automatically be generated by Visual Studio .NET.

5. Expand the Web References node in the Solution Explorer and rename the `localhost` node to **Conversion**.

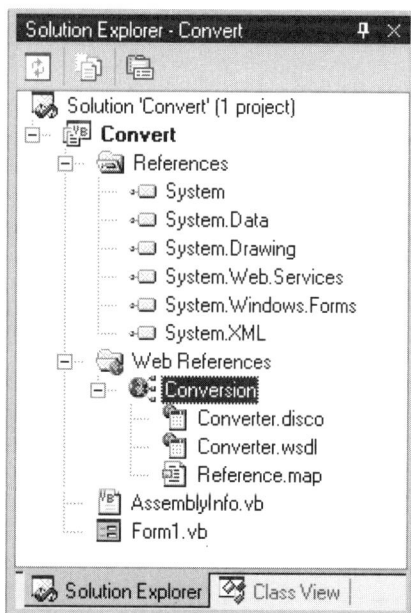

6. Add two text boxes and a button to the form. Change the names of the text boxes to **txtC** and **txtF** and clear the Text property. Change the name of the button to **btnConvert** and the Text for the button to **Convert**.

7. Add three labels to show what values are displayed and an equal sign (=) between the two text boxes. The form is shown next.

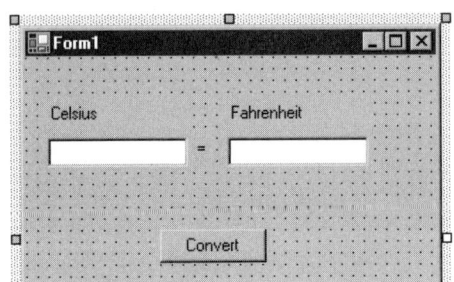

8. Implement the following code in the Button click event:

```
Private Sub btnConvert_Click(ByVal sender As System.Object, _
                            ByVal e As System.EventArgs) _
        Handles btnConvert.Click
    Dim k As Conversion.Service1 = New Conversion.Service1()
    Dim i As Integer
    Dim m As Integer
    m = Int32.Parse(txtC.Text)
    i = k.CFa(m)
    txtF.Text = i.ToString()
End Sub
```

9. Save and execute the application by pressing the F5 key.

10. Test the application by entering values in txtC and clicking the Convert button. Make sure the conversion works by testing different values. The final application is shown here.

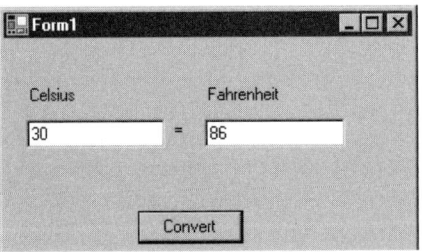

A theoretical discussion on where XML web services fit in the applications architecture and what they can be used for can be found later in this chapter.

Asynchronous Web Methods

Asynchronous method calls enable components to work together on a problem while being totally disconnected from each other—this is called *asynchronous programming*, or *loose binding*.

The asynchronous process is started by the calling component informing the called component where to send back a message (a callback) when the asynchronous process is complete. The called component starts the processing while the caller continues with other tasks, rather than waiting for the called component to finish. When the called component is finished, it sends a message to the caller by calling the callback. The end result of this type of processing is that there are very few times when the system is blocked and the user needs to wait. For a discussion on callbacks, see Chapter 4.

Consider a software component that retrieves information for a sales report from a database. The average time needed to retrieve the information is 20 seconds. A synchronous version of the application would call the software component and wait for the component to return the data. The client would be blocked until the data was returned. Changing the model to an asynchronous communications model will leave the client able to do other things while the data is being retrieved.

There are a number of scenarios in the real world where waiting times are involved—file and database access, network I/O, Web access, and so on. You can take advantage of asynchronous solutions in your software to keep users productive.

The object model of the .NET Framework provides a uniform environment for asynchronous calls across the .NET Framework. A couple of methods are included in classes to provide built-in support for asynchronous calls. For example, the Stream class (System.IO.Stream) provides the Read() method for synchronous calls and the BeginRead() and EndRead() pair of methods for asynchronous access.

The asynchronous method call is based on the use of delegates to encapsulate references to callback methods. The methods for creating asynchronous calls use an `AsyncCallback` delegate and two methods, `Beginxxx()` and `Endxxx()`, of the proxy class. The *xxx* in the `Beginxxx()` and `Endxxx()` refers to the method name. For example, the `GetForecast()` method would have a `BeginGetForecast()` and an `EndGetForeCast()`.

The following procedure describes how the asynchronous call is performed:

1. Instantiate an AsyncCallback delegate.

2. Call a `Beginxxx()` method of the proxy, and pass a reference to the proxy.

3. When the callback is called, use the `IAsyncResult` parameter that is passed in order to access the proxy.

4. Call `Endxxx()` to complete the asynchronous call.

EXERCISE 5-6

Console Consumer

The following exercise expands the functionality of the console consumer used in the preceding section.

1. Open the mikm project used in Exercise 5-4.

2. Change the Module1.vb source file to the following:

```
Public Class Class1
    Shared Sub Main()
        Dim k As mikm.localhost.Service1 = New mikm.localhost.Service1()
        Dim cb As AsyncCallback
        cb = New AsyncCallback(AddressOf Class1.Cback)
        k.BeginCmi(100, cb, k)
    End Sub
    Shared Sub Cback(ByVal ar As IAsyncResult)
        Dim k As mikm.localhost.Service1 = CType(ar.AsyncState,_
                                    mikm.localhost.Service1)
        Dim i As Integer = k.EndCmi(ar)
        Console.WriteLine(i)
```

```
Console.WriteLine("HELLO")
    End Sub
End Class
```

Run the application by pressing CTRL-F5, which will cause the console to prompt you to press "any key" before closing the console.

exam
ⓦatch

The Beginxxx() method is called to start the asynchronous process. The callback method calls the Endxxx() method to end the call and retrieve the return data.

CERTIFICATION OBJECTIVE 5.09

SOAP Extensions

The .NET Framework includes ways and means for us to process raw SOAP messages either before they are deserialized into objects within the Framework, or after they are serialized but before they are sent on to the consumer. This functionality is included in the SOAP extensions, which allow us to work with the data outside of the SOAP environment. In order to take advantage of the SOAP extensions, you need to derive one class from System.Web.Services.Protocols.SoapExtension and one class from System.Web.Services.Protocols.SoapExtensionAttribute.

One common reason for using SOAP extensions is security. By using SOAP extensions, it's possible to encrypt and decrypt the SOAP headers for transmission. For a full discussion on encryption and SOAP extensions, see Chapter 9.

In order to understand how you can access the raw SOAP messages, you need to understand how the .NET Framework routes SOAP messages. The Framework uses event stages to decide on the routing—when a SOAP message comes in, the server determines which method it will route to, and then it checks to see if there are any extensions, in which case it invokes the extensions with the event stage BeforeSerialize. When the extension returns, the server deserializes the SOAP stream and invokes the methods with the AfterDeserialize stage.

SCENARIO & SOLUTION

How do I overload web methods?	By giving web methods unique `MessageName` properties:
	`<WebMethod (MessageName:="One")>`
	`Public Function O(x as Integer) as Integer`
	`...`
	`End Function`
	`<WebMethod (MessageName:="Two")>`
	`Public Function O(x as Double) as Integer`
	`...`
	`End Function`
	The two methods `O()` are overloaded and exposed as web methods through the different `MessageName` properties.

How do I create a proxy for an XML web service?	There are two ways of creating XML web service proxies: manually by using the wsdl.exe utility, or by using the Add Web Reference dialog in Visual Studio .NET.
How do I expose a class as an XML web service?	You expose a class as an XML web service by adding the `<WebService>` attribute to the class declaration.
What is the .disco file used for?	The .disco file in the root of your XML web service directory is the manual discovery file; by using the .disco file, you can configure discovery of the XML web service.
How do I enable automatic discovery for my XML web service?	Uncomment the .vsdisco httpHandler section in the servers configuration file (machine.config). Implement a .vsdisco file in the root of the XML web service.
What is the XML web service help application?	When you navigate directly to an XML web service, the .NET Framework delivers an application to the browser that encapsulates the XML web service so that it can be tested. The help application also provides the SOAP headers as well as HTTP-GET and HTTP-POST messages that can be copied into the client application.

CERTIFICATION SUMMARY

In this chapter, you have been introduced to one of the .NET distributed components: the XML web service. You have learned how to create a web service and how to consume it. From the standpoint of the exam, this chapter forms the basis of a handful of the questions, but the concept of how to build XML web services and how to consume them is central in the majority of the exam questions.

You also learned about the WSDL document that forms the contract for the XML web system and about the five parts that make up the WSDL document: `type`, `message`, `portType`, `binding`, and `service`.

When connecting from a consumer to the XML web service, you need to create a proxy class to encapsulate the web service, and the tool that performs that task is wsdl.exe. Visual Studio .NET created the proxy for you when you set a web reference to the service.

SOAP extensions are used to give you raw access to the SOAP stream before it is deserialized.

The 70-310 Exam will test you on the .NET Framework and how it is used to build XML web service. The code used will be written using Visual Basic .NET, but stay focused on the fact that it is the .NET Framework and XML web services that are tested.

TWO-MINUTE DRILL

Creating an XML Web Service

❏ Web services are VB .NET applications that are made available through web servers.

❏ When you write a web service, you expose public methods by adding the `<WebMethod>` attribute to the method definition.

❏ The protocol that is used for a VB .NET application to communicate with a web service is XML based, making it network neutral.

❏ The codebehind file is the VB .NET file that defines the behavior of the web service. It will execute on the server on behalf of the client application.

❏ The processing directive for the web service declares the language, the public class name, and the name of the codebehind file.

❏ The namespace that defines a web service is `System.Web.Services`.

❏ The XML web service class inherits from `System.Web.Services.WebService`.

Setting the Web Method Attributes

❏ The proxy describes the methods that are marked as `<WebMethod>` in the web service and the mechanism that will be used to communicate with the web service.

❏ The `<WebMethod>` properties are used to control the web method: `CacheDuration` specifies how long the web method will be cached in seconds, the `MessageName` specifies an alias for the web method, and the Description is used to provide help with the web method.

❏ The `MessageName` property is used to provide method overloading.

Consuming an XML Web Service

❏ To add a web service to an application, use the Add Reference dialog from the Project menu in Visual Studio .NET.

❏ The Help application is used to test the XML web service.

Discovering XML Web Services

❑ The .disco file is used for static discovery of the XML web service.

❑ To enable dynamic discovery, you will need to uncomment the `httpHandler` for .vsdisco in the server's machine.config file.

❑ It is illegal to have both a .disco and .vsdico file for the same XML web service.

Building an XML Web Service Consumer

❑ When the reference to the web service is added to the application, a proxy is created that abstracts the web service for the application.

❑ To create the proxy manually, use the wsdl.exe utility.

❑ The utility that Visual Studio .NET uses to create the proxy for a web service is wsdl.exe.

❑ The language that defines the proxy is web service Description Language.

Creating Asynchronous Web Methods

❑ Asynchronous programming is sometimes referred to as loose binding.

❑ The `Beginxxx()` and `Endxxx()` methods are used to start and end the asynchronous call.

Creating and Use SOAP Extensions

❑ The SOAP extensions are commonly used to process the raw SOAP headers.

SELF TEST

Creating an XML Web Service

1. Your manager has asked you about interoperability between XML web services and an existing CORBA environment. What wire protocol will you tell your manager about that will interoperate with CORBA?

   A. RPC

   B. DCOM

   C. COM+

   D. SOAP

2. When you create an XML web service, it is stored in a source file. What is the extension of that source file?

   A. .asmx

   B. .asxm

   C. .asmxl

   D. .xmls

3. True or false: XML documents contain the data model of the data they contain.

   A. True

   B. False

Setting the Web Method Attributes

4. You have developed an XML web service that calculates an index that determines the current state of the air in your city. You have coded the following web methods, but when you compile the class, you receive error messages. What code will you change to be able to successfully compile your project?

```
<WebMethod>
Public Function GetIndex(x As Integer, y As Double) As Double
...
End Function
<WebMethod>
Public Function GetIndex(x As Integer, y As Integer) As Double
...
End Function
```

    A. Add unique `MessageName` properties to the two `<WebMethod>` attributes.

    B. Change the return data type of the two overloaded methods to be different.

    C. Add the `System.Web.Service.Overload` namespace to the project.

    D. Change the names of the two web methods to be unique.

5. You want to ensure that your web method uses the cache for results, and so you change the web method attribute to `<WebMethod(BufferResponse = true)>`. When you investigate, you find that your web method still is not using the cache. What is the most efficient way of ensuring that your web method uses the cache?

    A. Add `CacheTime=300` to the `<WebMethod>` attribute.

    B. Add `Cache=true` to the `<WebMethod>` attribute.

    C. Add `EnableCache=true` to the `<WebMethod>` attribute.

    D. Add `CacheDuration=300` as a parameter to the `<WebMethod>` attribute.

Consuming an XML Web Service

6. After creating a proxy class, you compile it. What type of file will the proxy be compiled to?

    A. .asxm

    B. .dll

    C. .aspx

    D. .proxy

Discovering XML Web Services

7. You need to configure dynamic discovery for your XML web service. What two steps must be performed to enable dynamic discovery? Select two answers.

    A. Provide a .vsdisco file in the root folder of the application.

    B. Uncomment the .vsdisco `httpHandler` entry in the machine.config file.

    C. Provide a .disco file in the root folder of the application.

    D. Uncomment the .dyndisco `httpHandler` in the machine.config file.

8. The XML web service Broker stores information about the XML web services that have published their services to the Broker. What structure does the Service Broker store the information in?

   A. The Broker Registry

   B. An XML document

   C. The Windows Registry

   D. A UDDI Registry

Building an XML Web Service Consumer

9. You need to build a proxy class for an XML web service; what tool will you use? Please select all that apply.

   A. proxy.exe

   B. wsdl.exe

   C. disco.exe

   D. vbc.exe

Creating Asynchronous Web Methods

10. What sentence best describes loosely coupled components?

    A. Both components use asynchronous methods to communicate.

    B. Both components use only public methods to communicate.

    C. Both components use public variables and methods to communicate.

    D. Both components use a common event model to communicate.

SELF-TEST ANSWERS

1. ☑ **D.** SOAP is the protocol.
   ☒ **A, B,** and **C.** Answers **A** and **B** are incorrect because RPC and DCOM are the same and are available only in the Windows environment. Answer **C** is incorrect because COM+ is the service in the Windows environment that provides the object request broker (ORB) functions.

2. ☑ **A.** The extension used for XML web service source files is .asmx.
   ☒ **B, C,** and **D.** These file extensions are not used by the XML web service.

3. ☑ **A.** XML documents contain the data and the schema (the data model) for the data.
   ☒ **B.** Answer **B** is incorrect because the XML document contains the data model of the data.

4. ☑ **A.** The way to separate the two functions is to give them different `MessageName` properties.
   ☒ **B, C,** and **D.** Answer **B** is incorrect because the return data type is not used to determine the uniqueness for overloaded functions. Answer **C** is incorrect because that namespace does not exist. Answer **D** is incorrect because that action would not produce the overloading required.

5. ☑ **D.** The `CacheDuration` is used to control when data is aged out of the cache; the parameter takes a value in seconds.
   ☒ **A, B,** and **C.** Answer **A, B,** and **C** are incorrect because those parameters do not exist.

6. ☑ **B.** The proxy is compiled to a .dll library that will be used by the client.
   ☒ **A, C,** and **D.** Answer **A** is incorrect because .asmx files are XML web service source files. Answer **C** is incorrect because .aspx files are Web Form source files, and **D** is incorrect because that extension is not used.

7. ☑ **A** and **B.** In order to configure dynamic discovery, you need to provide a .vsdisco file for the application as well as uncomment the .vsdisco `httpHandler` entry in the server's configuration file (machine.config).
   ☒ **C,** and **D. C** is incorrect because the .disco file is used with static discovery. Answer **D** is incorrect because there is no .dyndisco entry in the server's configuration file.

8. ☑ **D.** The Service Broker uses UDDI to store the Published XML services.
   ☒ **A, B,** and **C.** Answer **A** is incorrect because there is no such registry. Answer **B** is incorrect because even though an XML document could be used, the data is stored using UDDI. Answer **C** is incorrect because the Windows Registry is not used with .NET Framework XML Web Services.

9. ☑ **B.** The proxy is built using the wsdl.exe utility. You can use the utility directly from the command line, or through Visual Studio .NET by using the Add Web Reference dialog.
    ☒ **A, C,** and **D.** Although all these answers sound great, they are wrong. There is no proxy.exe utility; disco.exe is used for discovery of XML web services, and vbc.exe is the Visual Basic .NET compiler.

10. ☑ **A.** By using asynchronous method calls, the two components are truly loosely coupled.
    ☒ **B, C,** and **D.** Answer **B** is a possible answer, but the question asked for the best answer, and public methods are not the best answer. Answer **C** is incorrect because that is exactly how you don't write loosely coupled software components. Answer **D** is incorrect because that would be tightly coupled.

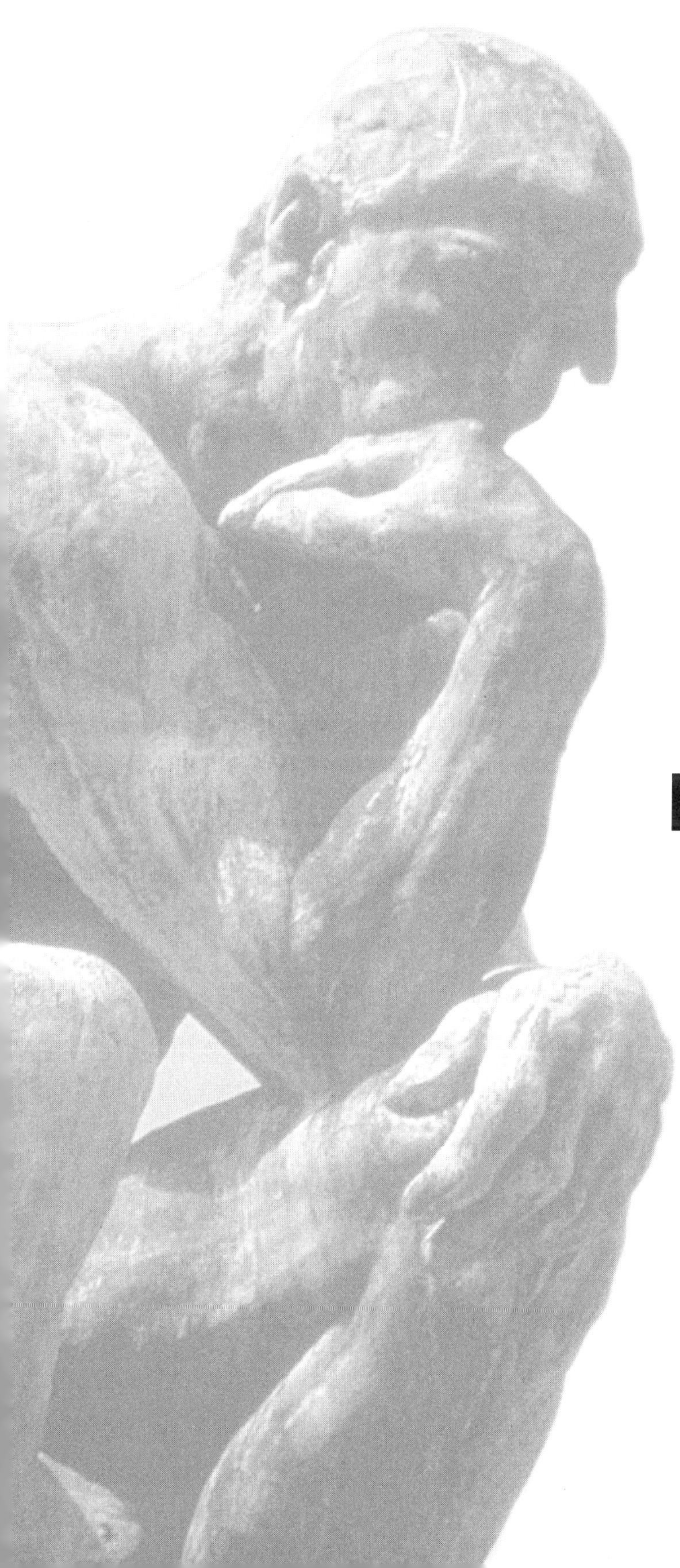

6

Consuming and Manipulating Data

T he data-driven application is the most common type of application that you will be working with, and this importance is echoed in the XML Web Services exam. In this chapter, you will round out your coverage of data technologies by looking at how you can implement XML web services that both expose and consume data.

The move to use XML documents both as the source and the client storage of data means that you need to look at how you can create an XML document from an existing ADO.NET DataSet and directly from Microsoft SQL Server.

This chapter focuses mainly on the theory of ADO.NET and SQL. Exercises are included to show the code and techniques needed to understand the questions on the exam.

CERTIFICATION OBJECTIVE 6.01

Data Access with ADO.NET

ADO.NET has evolved from a combination of DAO (Data Access Objects), VBSQL (Visual Basic SQL), RDO (Remote Data Objects), and ADO (ActiveX Data Objects), but it does not share the same programming model as these technologies, even though most of the functionality is the same. The different data-access technologies represent the history of how Microsoft has supported database developers over the different versions of development tools and operating systems. DAO was introduced with VB 3 to support Access development, VBSQL was a technology that allowed VB programmers to access SQL Server data, RDO provided for disconnected recordsets, and ADO gave us COM and data.

ADO.NET is based on a disconnected `DataSet` that is stored with the client, while earlier technologies were connection oriented through the recordset. If you are familiar with ADO, the transition to ADO.NET will be one of learning to work with disconnected data as well as how to update data on the data source while solving any conflicts.

ADO.NET Architecture

Microsoft defines ADO.NET as being "A set of classes for working with data." In other words, the ADO.NET "package" is an object model that helps you work with data: any data, from anywhere, using any storage technology.

These are some of the advantages of ADO.NET:

- **Interoperability** The format used to transfer data between the data source and the in-memory copy of the data is the standard XML document, which allows seamless data interoperability between dissimilar systems.

- **Maintainability** ADO.NET maintains local in-memory caches of the data, making it possible to spread the application logic between many tiers in an n-tier application. This makes the application more scalable.

- **Programmability** ADO.NET is based on the .NET Framework, which uses strongly typed data types. Strongly typed data makes the source code more concise and less prone to "undocumented features" (bugs).

- **Performance** Because ADO.NET is strongly typed, it also helps you avoid data conversions that can be costly to the performance of the application.

- **Scalability** ADO.NET encourages programmers to minimize resource use by maintaining a local in-memory copy (cache) of the data, enabling you to disconnect from the data source. By doing so, ADO.NET avoids keeping database locks and connections open between calls.

To use ADO.NET, you need to use its related namespaces, listed in Table 6-1.

exam
Watch

Commit these namespaces to memory. They will be needed.

The Object Model

Just as there are multiple `DataProvider` classes, a number of classes are derived (inherited) from the base `DataSet` class. The object model of ADO.NET contains two major components: the `DataSet` class and the .NET data provider classes.

The `DataSet` class manages data storage in a disconnected in-memory cache. The `DataSet` class is totally independent of the underlying data source. This way, the application can use all the features of the `DataSet` regardless of where the data came from (SQL Server, Access, Oracle, DB/2, and so on).

TABLE 6-1	Namespace	Description
ADO.NET Namespaces	`System.Data`	Contains the core classes of ADO.NET, including the classes that enable disconnected data (such as the `DataSet` class).
	`System.Data.Common`	Contains utility classes and interfaces that the data providers inherit and implement.
	`System.Data.SqlClient`	Contains the SQL Server .NET data provider.
	`System.Data.OleDb`	Contains the OLE DB .NET data provider.
	`System.Data.SqlTypes`	Contains classes and structures that encapsulate the native SQL Server data types. This is a type-safe faster alternative to native data types.
	`System.Xml`	Contains the support for the XML standard, including classes for processing and encapsulating an XML document (such as the `XmlDataDocument` class).

A .NET data provider class is specific to the type of data source and is custom-built for that particular data source. The .NET data provider classes can include the ability to connect to, retrieve data from, modify data in, and update data sources.

The DataSet Class   The `DataSet` is a collection of `DataTable` objects that represent the underlying data of a data source. A `DataSet` has zero or more tables associated with it. These tables are accessed through a `Tables` property that refers to a collection of `DataTable` objects in the `DataSet`. If the tables have relationships between them, those relationships are available through the `Relations` property, which refers to a collection of `DataRelation` objects in the `DataSet`. By using the `DataRelation` object, you can join two tables together to programmatically read the data in a parent/child relationship.

Let's look at the `DataTable` object and the collections that hold information on the data in the table and the cache. Table 6-2 contains information on the most important collections.

A `DataSet` can be bound to most controls in a Windows Form or a Web Form (data binding is the process by which a control is automatically synchronized with the `DataSet`). The data binding provides the underlying services needed to build data forms easily.

TABLE 6-2   Collections in the DataTable Object

Collection	Object in Collection	Description
DataColumnCollection	DataColumn	The DataColumn object contains data that describes the data in the column (metadata): the column name, the data type, whether the column can be NULL, and so on.
DataRowCollection	DataRow	DataRow encapsulates a row of data in the table. The DataRow objects also maintain the original row data before any changes were made, in addition to the current data.
ConstraintCollection	Constraint	Constraint is an abstract class. It represents the limit on one or more DataColumn objects. The collection can use any derived class or the two concrete subclasses: UniqueConstraint and ForeignKeyConstraint.
DataRelationCollection	DataRelation	DataRelation objects are used to represent relationships between columns in different tables. Use a DataRelation object to link (join) two tables on the primary and foreign keys.

.NET Data Providers   The ADO.NET classes contain .NET data providers that encapsulate a connection to a data source and the functionality to read, change, and update data in the data source. The .NET data providers are designed to be lightweight and include a minimal abstraction layer between the data source and your code. Microsoft supplies three .NET data providers for your use, as listed in Table 6-3.

There are four objects in each of the .NET data providers, as listed here (the prefix replacing the *Xxx* for each of these objects is specific to the provider):

- *XxxConnection* (for example, SqlConnection or OleDbConnection)
- XxxCommand (for example, SqlCommand or OleDbCommand)

TABLE 6-3	Data Provider	Description
The .NET Data Providers	SQL Server .NET	This is an optimized provider for use with Microsoft SQL Server 7.0 or higher databases.
	OLE DB .NET	This is the provider for all OLE DB provider connections. You can use this .NET data provider for connections to Oracle, DB/2, Informix, and Access. This is actually the .NET data provider that uses any traditional OLE DB provider.
	ODBC .NET	The ODBC .NET data provider is available as a download from Microsoft at http://msdn.Microsoft.com/downloads. The ODBC .NET provider is support for legacy ODBC data.

- ■ XxxDataReader (for example, SqlDataReader or OleDbDataReader)
- ■ XxxDataAdapter (for example, SqlDataAdapter or OleDbDataAdapter)

Table 6-4 provides a description of the objects.

e x a m
ⓦatch *The different providers and the products they service will be tested in the exam.*

TABLE 6-4	Object	Description
The Objects of the .NET Data Provider	XxxConnection	The XxxConnection object is used to encapsulate the connection between the code and a specific data source.
	XxxCommand	XxxCommand objects are used to execute commands on the data source. In the case of SQL Server, the SqlCommand is used to execute a stored procedure on the server.
	XxxDataReader	The XxxDataReader provides a forward-only read-only data stream from the data source. You can access the data stream through the ExecuteReader method of the XxxCommand object. The XxxCommand object is usually the result of a SQL SELECT statement or a stored procedure call.
	XxxDataAdapter	The XxxDataAdapter provides the services to connect a DataSet to an XxxCommand. It populates the DataSet and resolves any updates with the data source.

The `XxxDataAdapter` lets you manage the disconnected nature of the ADO.NET environment by acting as the manager of the *Xxx*Connection and DataSet objects. You use the `XxxDataAdapter` to populate the `DataSet` and to update the data source with any changes that have been made to the `DataSet`.

Some objects also have child objects associated with them. For example, the `XxxConnection` object has an `XxxTransaction` object and an `XxxError` object that expose underlying functionality. The `XxxTransaction` object represents a transaction of the underlying database, while the `XxxError` object represents any errors of warnings from the data source; this object is created by the .NET data provider when an error or warning is raised by the data source.

XML and ADO.NET

Over the last couple of years, the XML standard has emerged as the most important standard to date. It provides for the exchange of data, and most important, of metadata, between components. ADO.NET is tightly incorporated with XML. Both the object model and the services have XML at their core rather than as an add-on. With ADO.NET, you can easily convert from relational data to XML and back again.

XML is text based, making it instantly portable and universal. It is an open extensible standard that can be used for many different purposes. The following list identifies just some of the things you can do with XML support in ADO.NET:

- Read data from an XML document.

- Fill a `DataSet` with data from an XML document.

- Create an XML schema for the data in a `DataSet`, and then use the XML schema to write the data as XML.

- Use the XML schema to programmatically treat the XML document as a `DataSet`.

The most exciting fact about XML is that it is the standard format for exchanging data between dissimilar environments. XML is the basis for B2B (business-to-business) e-commerce and is rapidly replacing proprietary protocols for data exchange.

exam
ⓦatch

Extensible Markup Language is such an important technology for the .NET Framework that you can expect XML to be part of many exam questions not only on the 310 exam but on others as well.

CERTIFICATION OBJECTIVE 6.02

Accessing and Manipulating Data from a Microsoft SQL Server

SQL is a language, even though Microsoft calls their database server SQL Server, and in this section you will look at the Data Manipulation Language (DML) elements of the language (SELECT, INSERT, UPDATE, and DELETE) that are used to manipulate data stored in a relational database management system (RDBMS). Start with the SELECT statement, which returns information from a database, and then look at how to modify the content of the tables in a database by using INSERT, UPDATE, and DELETE statements.

All our examples will use the Northwind Traders sample database that is supplied by Microsoft as part of Access, SQL Server 7.0, and SQL Server 2000.

exam
ⓦatch

SQL statements will be used in many different questions. It is very important to have mastery over the SQL language.

SELECT

You use SELECT statements to retrieve data from tables in a database. The SELECT statement is the basic command for querying the database. In the statement, you specify the columns and tables you want data from, and you can optionally specify conditions and sorting instructions. The full syntax for the SELECT statement is rather complex; look at a shorter syntax listing with the most commonly used options:

```
SELECT [ALL | DISTINCT] select_list
FROM table_source
[ WHERE search_condition ]
[ ORDER BY order_expression [ ASC | DESC ] ]
```

The columns to be returned are listed in the select_list parameter. Use a comma to separate the column names or use the column wildcard character (*) to select all columns in the table. The ALL argument specifies that all rows in the table_source should be returned, even if there are duplicate rows. The DISTINCT argument removes all duplicates in the returned data. ALL is the default.

The FROM clause specifies the tables that the columns will be returned from. The FROM clause is mandatory, and you must provide at least one table name.

The following example returns all the staff from the Northwind Trading database (the query is executed against a SQL Server 2000 database):

```
/* Retrieve the First Name, Last Name, City and Country
   for all the staff */
USE Northwind
SELECT FirstName, LastName, City, Country
FROM Employees
```

The preceding SELECT statement produced the following result:

```
FirstName   LastName                    City              Country
----------  --------------------        ----------------  ----------------
Nancy       Davolio                     Seattle           USA
Andrew      Fuller                      Tacoma            USA
Janet       Leverling                   Kirkland          USA
Margaret    Peacock                     Redmond           USA
Steven      Buchanan                    London            UK
Michael     Suyama                      London            UK
Robert      King                        London            UK
Laura       Callahan                    Seattle           USA
Anne        Dodsworth                   London            UK
```

The SELECT statement returned all the rows in the table. If you want only the staff working in London, you can include a WHERE clause. The WHERE clause limits the number of rows that are returned to those that match the criterion supplied as part of the statement. Your SELECT statement looks like this with the new WHERE clause:

```
/* Retrieve the First Name, Last Name, City and Country
   for all the staff that live in London*/
USE Northwind
SELECT FirstName, LastName, City, Country
FROM Employees
WHERE City = 'London'
```

The result of this SELECT statement is as follows:

```
FirstName   LastName                City              Country
----------  --------------------    ----------------  ---------------
Steven      Buchanan                London            UK
Michael     Suyama                  London            UK
Robert      King                    London            UK
Anne        Dodsworth               London            UK
```

The WHERE clause can compare columns against literal values using the logical operators listed in Table 6-5. String literals in SQL are enclosed in single quotes (').

The WHERE clause has some additional features you can take advantage of. For example, to search for records where you know only part of the data in a column, you can use the LIKE argument, which lets you write string search patterns. The

TABLE 6-5   Comparisons Using the WHERE Clause

Logical Operator	Description	Sample and Explanation
=	Equality	WHERE City = 'London' Returns all records where the City is London.
<	Less than	WHERE Day < 21 Returns all records where Day is less than 21
>	Greater than	WHERE Day > 5 Returns all records where Day is greater than 5
<=	Less than or equal	WHERE Day <= 21 Returns all records where Day is less than or equal to 21
>=	Greater than or equal	WHERE Day >= 5 Returns all records where Day is greater than or equal to 5
!=	Not	WHERE City != 'London' Returns all records where the City is not London
AND	And	WHERE Day > 5 AND Day < 21 Returns all records where the Day is between 5 and 21; note that records where Day is 5 or 21 are not returned.
OR	Or	WHERE Day < 5 OR Day > 21 Returns all records where Day is less than 5 or greater than 21

following example shows how to use the LIKE argument in a search for all records where the FirstName column starts with "An":

```
/* Retrieve the First Name, Last Name, City and Country
   for all the staff that have
   First Names that start with 'An'*/
USE Northwind
SELECT FirstName, LastName, City, Country
FROM Employees
WHERE FirstName LIKE 'An%'
```

The percent sign (%) is the wildcard character that is used with all string and character comparisons in the SQL language, so 'An%' translates to any string that starts with "An." If you are looking for a substring, you can use multiple percent signs.

on the **Job**

Remember that character literals in SQL must be enclosed with single quotes.

The result of the preceding query is that only records that match the LIKE argument are returned:

FirstName	LastName	City	Country
Andrew	Fuller	Tacoma	USA
Anne	Dodsworth	London	UK

In your next example, you want to list all employees that have "ll" in their last names:

```
/* Retrieve the First Name, Last Name, City and Country
   for all the staff that have
   First Names that start with 'An'*/
USE Northwind
SELECT FirstName, LastName, City, Country
FROM Employees
WHERE LastName LIKE '%ll%'
```

This query results in the following output:

FirstName	LastName	City	Country
Andrew	Fuller	Tacoma	USA
Laura	Callahan	Seattle	USA

The other clause you haven't looked at yet is the ORDER BY clause. If you look back at the first result you received in this section, when you selected all the staff, you will find that it is not sorted on any of the columns, and it seems to have been returned in a random order. If you go back again and run the same query, you might get your results in the same order, but more likely you will not. Unless you specify an order, there is no guarantee as to what order the data will be returned in.

The ORDER BY clause lets us request that the result be returned in specific sorted order. The following example requests that the result be sorted on the LastName column:

```
/* Retrieve the First Name, Last Name, City and Country
   for all the staff and
   and sort on the LastName column*/
USE Northwind
SELECT FirstName, LastName, City, Country
FROM Employees
ORDER BY LastName
```

The preceding query returns the following result:

FirstName	LastName	City	Country
Steven	Buchanan	London	UK
Laura	Callahan	Seattle	USA
Nancy	Davolio	Seattle	USA
Anne	Dodsworth	London	UK
Andrew	Fuller	Tacoma	USA
Robert	King	London	UK
Janet	Leverling	Kirkland	USA
Margaret	Peacock	Redmond	USA
Michael	Suyama	London	UK

You can combine these SELECT clauses as you need them. Here are some recommendations for working with SELECT statements:

- Never use the column name wildcard (*) in the SELECT statement; list all the columns you need instead.

- Always include a WHERE clause to limit the number of rows returned.

- If you need the data sorted, use the ORDER BY clause.

JOIN

You will often need to combine data from two or more tables, and the JOIN clause allows you to perform this task. JOIN statements are used to query any number of tables and return a single result set that contains merged data from these tables. Joins are a central part of relational database theory and are used in the real world to implement relations between entities in a normalized data model.

There are three types of joins in SQL: *inner joins, outer joins,* and *cross joins.* These joins are described in Table 6-6.

The syntax for an inner join is as follows:

```
SELECT select_list
FROM first_table_name
[INNER] JOIN join_table_name
ON join_condition
```

The ON keyword defines the comparison that must be true for the inner join to return the row. The INNER keyword is optional, as it is the default join in the ANSI92 SQL standard.

Let's look at an example. Figure 6-1 shows the relationships between three tables.

The relationship is set up to enable us to join the three tables together. The EmployeeID column is used to connect the Employees and EmployeeTerritories

TABLE 6-6	Join Type	Description
The Different Join Types	Inner join	The inner join combines tables on the basis of the equality comparison of data values in common columns in the two tables. Only rows that match the comparison are returned in the result set.
	Outer join	The outer join combines rows from two tables on the basis of the equality comparison of data values in common columns in the tables. It returns all matching rows plus all the unmatched rows from one of the tables. The LEFT OUTER JOIN returns all the rows from the table that is named first, plus all the rows in the last named table that match the comparison. The RIGHT OUTER JOIN returns all the rows from the table that is named last, plus all rows from the first table that match the comparison.
	Cross join	A cross join produces a Cartesian product of the rows in both tables—it returns all possible combinations of rows. You do not specify any condition, as no comparison is used. The cross join is used to generate test data for databases.

FIGURE 6-1   Table relationships for an inner join example

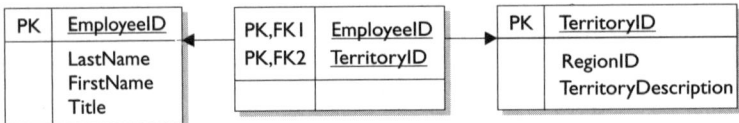

tables, and the TerritoryID column is used to connect the EmployeeTerritories and Territories tables.

If you needed to query this database and return TerritoryDescription, FirstName, and LastName for an employee with a last name of Buchanan, you could use the following query:

```
USE Northwind
SELECT TerritoryDescription, FirstName, LastName
FROM Employees
JOIN EmployeeTerritories
ON Employees.EmployeeID = EmployeeTerritories.EmployeeID
JOIN Territories
ON EmployeeTerritories.TerritoryID = Territories.TerritoryID
WHERE LastName = 'Buchanan'
```

This query will return all records for employees named Buchanan where there is an entry for a territory.

```
TerritoryDescription             FirstName   LastName
------------------------------   ----------  --------------------
Providence                       Steven      Buchanan
Morristown                       Steven      Buchanan
Edison                           Steven      Buchanan
New York                         Steven      Buchanan
New York                         Steven      Buchanan
Mellvile                         Steven      Buchanan
Fairport                         Steven      Buchanan
```

Let's look at what happened. The SELECT line specifies the columns that you need. Notice that you used the name of the column from the Territories table without specifying what table it came from, and as long as the column names are unique, you do not have to specify the table name as well. In the FROM clause, you added the JOIN clause to specify that you want the tables on either side of the JOIN clause to be connected. The ON statement sets the rules of the connection; in this case, you want the Employees table joined to the EmployeeTerritories table using the EmployeeID column in both tables.

When there are columns in two tables that have the same name, use a syntax that specifies the table and the column names in a dotted format: *table.column* (for example, Employees.EmployeeID). You must use this format in the ON clause unless the two columns have unique names.

Finally, join the Territories table to the result of the first JOIN. This results in the preceding output. The default behavior of the JOIN clause is to return all records that match the ON clause from the two tables, and this is known as an inner join.

e x a m
Ⓦa t c h

Remember the syntax for the JOIN operation, and remember that the inner join is the default JOIN.

In the next example, you will use aliasing—shorthand names for columns and tables—to make the code easier to read. Figure 6-2 shows the model for the example. You want a query that will return category name, product name, and supplier for the beverages category, and you want to sort the output on the product name. The following query performs that task:

```
USE Northwind
SELECT CategoryName, ProductName, CompanyName
FROM Categories c
JOIN Products p
ON c.CategoryID = p.CategoryID
JOIN Suppliers s
ON p.SupplierID = s.SupplierID
WHERE CategoryName = 'Beverages'
ORDER BY ProductName
```

The biggest difference between this example and the preceding one is that you used aliases to identify the tables rather than long table names that can be hard to

FIGURE 6-2   Relationships for the aliasing example

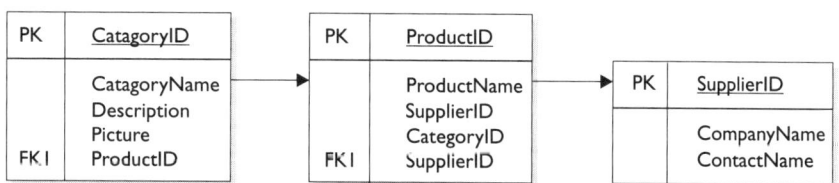

PK	CatagoryID		PK	ProductID				
	CatagoryName			ProductName		PK	SupplierID	
	Description			SupplierID				
	Picture			CategoryID			CompanyName	
FK I	ProductID		FK I	SupplierID			ContactName	

read in complicated join statements. The following code segment defines c as the alias for the Categories table and p as the alias for the Products table:

```
FROM Categories c
JOIN Products p
```

You can now use c and p to refer to the tables, simplifying the query.

The result of the preceding query is as follows:

```
CategoryName   ProductName                CompanyName
------------   -------------------------  ---------------------------------------
Beverages      Chai                       Exotic Liquids
Beverages      Chang                      Exotic Liquids
Beverages      Chartreuse verte           Aux joyeux ecclésiastiques
Beverages      Côte de Blaye              Aux joyeux ecclésiastiques
Beverages      Guaraná Fantástica         Refrescos Americanas LTDA
Beverages      Ipoh Coffee                Leka Trading
Beverages      Lakkalikööri               Karkki Oy
Beverages      Laughing Lumberjack Lager  Bigfoot Breweries
Beverages      Outback Lager              Pavlova, Ltd.
Beverages      Rhönbräu Klosterbier       Plutzer Lebensmittelgroßmärkte AG
Beverages      Sasquatch Ale              Bigfoot Breweries
Beverages      Steeleye Stout             Bigfoot Breweries
```

INSERT

There are a number of different ways of inserting data into tables in a database; these are all based on the INSERT statement. Next, look at how to insert one row with new column values, and how to create a new table based on a query.

The INSERT statement is the fastest way of adding new data to the database. The syntax for the INSERT statement is as follows:

```
INSERT [INTO] table_name [(column1, column2, ..., column)]
VALUES (value1, value2, ..., value3)
```

The column list following the table_name allows you to specify the order in which data is inserted. If the column list is not used, the values must be listed in the column order of the table.

For example, to insert a new employee in the Employees table, you could use the following statement:

```
USE Northwind
INSERT Employees (FirstName, LastName)
VALUES ('Robert', 'Burns')
```

on the
job

*The column list of the **INSERT** statement is optional. If it is not used, the order of the values in the **VALUE** clause must match the column order of the table.*

To insert data from a query into an existing table, you can use the INSERT . . . SELECT statement. The syntax is as follows:

```
INSERT table_name
SELECT select_list
FROM table_source
[WHERE condition]
```

The resulting set from the SELECT statement will be added to the table_name table. There are some rules that you need to follow when using this technique:

- The data types of the columns in the result set should match the data types of the columns in the table.

- The result set must have data for all required columns in the destination table.

The following example takes all your employees and adds them to the Customers table so that your staff can also be your customers. You will build the CustomerID column data by taking the first three characters from the first name and the first two characters from the last name and concatenating them. The employee's first name is used as the contact name, and the last name as the company name:

```
USE Northwind
INSERT Customers
   SELECT substring(FirstName, 1, 3) + substring(LastName, 1, 2),
          LastName, FirstName, Title, Address, City,
          Region, PostalCode, Country, HomePhone, NULL
   FROM Employees
```

To create a new table from the query, you use this syntax:

```
SELECT select_list
INTO new_table
FROM table_source
[WHERE condition]
```

The new_table can be a local temporary table (#table_name), a global temporary table (##table_name), or a permanent table (table_name). One pound sign (#) indicates a local table that will be available as long as the session that created it is open; two pound signs (##) represent a globally available table that will exist until it is no longer used in any session. In order for you to be able to create a permanent table, the administrator of the database must have enabled SELECT INTO.

The select_list is commonly used to alias column names to new names for the new table. The AS keyword is used to change the name of a column (alias). In the following example, you will retrieve the price list from the Products table and save the product and the price in a new table. You will also calculate a 16 percent sales tax on the price:

```
USE Northwind
SELECT ProductName AS Product
      , UnitPrice AS Price
      , (UnitPrice * 0.16) AS SalesTax
      , UnitPrice + (UnitPrice * 0.16) AS NewPrice
   INTO #SalesTaxTable
FROM Products
```

The preceding example created a new local table named #SalesTaxTable. To query the new table, you could execute this query:

```
USE Northwind
SELECT *
FROM #SalesTaxTable
```

The partial result set is seen here:

```
Product                        Price        SalesTax        NewPrice
------------------------------ ------------ --------------- -----------
Chai                           18.0000      2.880000        20.880000
Chang                          19.0000      3.040000        22.040000
Aniseed Syrup                  10.0000      1.600000        11.600000
Chef Anton's Cajun Seasoning   22.0000      3.520000        25.520000
...
(77 row(s) affected)
```

UPDATE

You can use the UPDATE statement to make changes to one or more rows at a time. The syntax for the UPDATE statement is as follows:

```
UPDATE table_name
  SET column_name = expression, ...
  [WHERE condition]
```

As you use the UPDATE statement, you should be aware of some rules and recommendations:

- Use the WHERE condition to control which rows are updated; if you don't use a WHERE condition, every row in the table is updated.
- Use the SET keyword to specify the new value for a column in the row.
- The UPDATE statement will work only on one table at a time.

If you wanted to increase the unit price for the products that were supplied by New Orleans Cajun Delights (SupplierID = 2) by 25 percent, you could use the following:

```
USE NorthWind
UPDATE Products
  SET UnitPrice = UnitPrice * 1.25
  WHERE SupplierID = 2
```

on the
Job

*Always include a **WHERE** clause in the **UPDATE** statement; otherwise, all rows will be updated, not just the one you were targeting.*

DELETE

Use the DELETE statement to remove rows from a table. The DELETE statement has the following syntax:

```
DELETE table_name
  [WHERE condition]
```

If you issue the DELETE statement without a WHERE clause, the statement will remove all the rows in the table.

To remove rows representing products that were shipped before November 1, 2001, you could use this code:

```
USE Northwind
DELETE Orders
  WHERE shippeddate < '11/1/2001'
```

on the
Job

*Always include a WHERE clause in the **DELETE** statement; otherwise, all rows in the table will be deleted.*

Stored Procedures

The stored procedure is very much like a method in Visual Basic .NET except that it is built from Transact-SQL statements (the language of Microsoft SQL Server) and stored in the database for reuse. Stored procedures are like methods in a database; they can receive parameters and then return values to the caller. There are a number of reasons for using stored procedures:

- Stored procedures are stored in the procedure cache of the database server, resulting in faster execution if the stored procedure is called repeatedly.
- Stored procedures are used to centralize the data-access logic on the server.
- Stored procedures will minimize the use of the network for large queries.

The way to create a stored procedure is to use the CREATE PROCEDURE statement There are three parts to the declaration: CREATE PROCEDURE defines the name and parameters of the stored procedure, and the AS and GO keywords enclose the code block. The basic statement takes this form:

```
CREATE PROCEDURE <name>
AS
    <definition of the stored procedure>
GO
```

To create a stored procedure that returns customers from the Customers table, you would write this code:

```
CREATE PROCEDURE procGetCustomers
AS
    SELECT * FROM CUSTOMERS
GO
```

This stored procedure returns all the customers. If you want to pass a parameter to the stored procedure, you do so by inserting the parameter definition between the CREATE statement and the AS keyword, as in this example:

```
CREATE PROCEDURE procGetCustomers
    @C_NAME nvarchar(40) = '%'
AS
    SELECT * FROM CUSTOMERS
    WHERE CompanyName LIKE @C_NAME
GO
```

In the preceding example, the parameter @C_NAME was added to the stored procedure. Parameters must have a data type; I used an nvarchar with a default value of '%' (the wildcard for searches).

Stored procedures are usually more involved than what you saw in this section, typically involving CURSORS, IN, and OUT parameters. The exam will not test you on building complicated stored procedures, but you will need to remember that they are server based and are built using the CREATE PROCEDURE statement.

on the
Ϳob

The Transact-SQL language allows that the CREATE PROCEDURE statement be written as CREATE.

Transactions

When you work with data on central database servers, there are two main areas of concern: allowing multiple users access to the same data in a safe way, and guaranteeing that any data modification performed will maintain the integrity of the data. To attempt to solve both these issues, use *transactions*.

A transaction is a group of related operations that either succeed or fail as one unit—the transaction will either *commit* or *roll back,* respectively. In order for a transaction to commit, all parts of the transaction must succeed. In other words, transactions provide all-or-nothing processing.

A popular example of a transaction is the ATM (automatic teller machine), where you might transfer $100.00 from your checking account to your savings account. You can reasonably expect that the $100.00 was transferred, or if something went wrong with the ATM or the banking system that the money would still be in the checking account. Either the transfer takes place (commits) or, if there is a problem (any problem) with the transfer, the accounts are returned to the original state (the transaction rolls back).

A transaction is tested against its *ACID* properties, named for the four key concepts of a transaction (Atomicity, Consistency, Isolation, and Durability):

- **Atomicity** A transaction is said to be atomic when it is one unit of work containing many steps. It will execute exactly one time and will either commit or roll back.

- **Consistency** A transaction maintains the integrity (consistency) of the data when the transaction either commits or rolls back. In this case, there is never any chance of undefined states after the transaction executes.

- **Isolation**   A transaction is isolated from all other transactions on the system, making the process look as if it were the only transaction running. This isolation guarantees that no transaction will ever be able to "see" intermediate values from any other transaction (meaning there are no *dirty reads*).

- **Durability**   A transaction that commits is guaranteed to have its values persist even if the system crashes directly after the transaction commits.

The ACID properties ensure predictable behavior and the all-or-nothing nature of a transaction. A database system that does not provide transactions or can't meet the ACID properties is considered unsuitable for anything beyond personal use.

In SQL, you can control transactions using the transaction control statements shown in Table 6-7. They can be used as part of any SQL process.

The following example uses the traditional bank example—you are going to move $100.00 from one account to another. This example will not execute against the Northwind database because the BankAccount table is not part of the database, but the code is included as an example of transactions:

```
BEGIN TRANSACTION
INSERT INTO BankAccount (AccountNUM, Amount, Type)
  VALUES (424242, 100, 'debit')
INSERT INTO BankAccount (AccountNUM, Amount, Type)
  VALUES (121212, 100, 'credit')
IF (@@ERROR > 0) ROLLBACK TRANSACTION
  ELSE COMMIT TRANSACTION
```

TABLE 6-7	Statement	Description
SQL Transaction Control Statements	BEGIN TRANSACTION	Starts the transaction; all statements after the BEGIN TRANSACTION statement are part of the transaction.
	COMMIT TRANSACTION	Ends the transaction, indicating success; all processing will be persisted in the database.
	ROLLBACK TRANSACTION	Ends the transaction, indicating failure; all processing will be rolled back to the state it was in when the transaction started.

There are two data-modification statements in this example that insert debit and credit rows in the specific accounts. If any errors occur during this processing, the global @@ERROR variable will be set to a nonzero value. A nonzero value will cause a rollback; otherwise, you should commit.

exam
Ⓦatch

*The transactions are focused on the connection to the database and are exposed through the **XxxTransaction** object.*

CERTIFICATION OBJECTIVE 6.03

Creating and Manipulating DataSets

The DataSet object in ADO.NET represents data in a local in-memory cache and provides the functions for accessing the data regardless of where the data originated. It is a disconnected representation of the data, and it does not have to be connected to the data source for the data to be available.

The data in a DataSet is organized much as data is represented in a relational database. The DataSet uses the DataTable collection to represent the tables—a DataTable represents one table of in-memory data, and it uses the DataColumn collection to represent the columns of the DataTable. The DataSet presents a relational view of the data, and the data can optionally be represented in XML format. You will look at the XML representation later in this chapter.

DataSet Schemas

The terms schema and data model are used interchangeably to describe how the DataSet is built. They describe how the data is separated into tables. The schema ensures that the data in the DataSet is presented in a normalized fashion. The process of designing the schema is called *data modeling,* a mathematical process that takes any data and breaks it into entities (tables) in such a way that the data is stored only once in the schema. The end result of the data-modeling design is that the database is normalized.

The exam will not test your data-modeling skills; rather, the questions will focus on the implementation of the schema and the use of the DataSet. Follow this process by looking at the different objects and at how they are used with the DataSet.

Database Objects

The basic objects you need to work with are the DataSet, DataTable, and DataColumn objects. Using these three objects, you can implement any schema. Let's start by looking at where the DataSet fits into the scheme of things. Figure 6-3 shows the relationship between the database and the DataSet object that is built from DataColumns.

When you model (design the schema for) a DataSet, you can use constraints to guarantee that the data that is inserted into or deleted from a DataTable meets the business rules for that data. Two types of constraints are available: a UniqueConstraint ensures that the data entered into a DataColumn of a DataTable is unique, and the ForeignKeyConstraint verifies that data entered in the DataColumn already exists in a referenced DataColumn.

FIGURE 6-3   The relationship between the database and the DataSet object

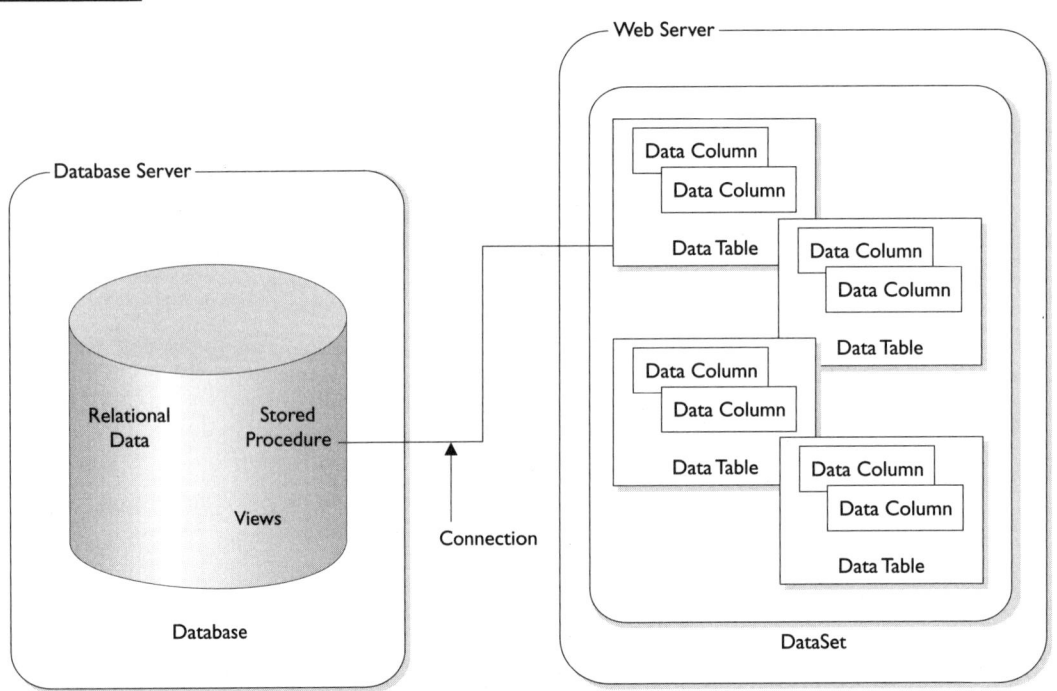

Constraints

Constraints are added to the Constraints collection of the DataTable object, as you can see in the following code segment:

```
' Create an UniqueConstraint on the OrderID column on the Orders table
Dim dcOrderID As DataColumn = ds.Tables("Orders").Columns("OrderID")
Dim ucOrderID As UniqueConstraint
ucOrderID = New UniqueConstraint("UC_OrderID", dcOrderID)
ds.Tables("Orders").Constraints.Add(ucOrderID)

' Create a ForeignKeyConstraint
Dim parentCol As DataColumn
Dim childCol As DataColumn
Dim dsFKC As ForeignKeyConstraint

' Set parent and child column variables.
parentCol = ds.Tables("Orders").Columns("OrderID")
childCol = ds.Tables("Orders").Columns("OrderID")
dsFKC = New ForeignKeyConstraint("OrderIDFKConstraint", parentCol, childCol)
' Set null values when a value is deleted.
dsFKC.DeleteRule = Rule.SetNull
dsFKC.UpdateRule = Rule.Cascade
dsFKC.AcceptRejectRule = AcceptRejectRule.Cascade
' Add the constraint, and set EnforceConstraints to true.
ds.Tables("Order Details").Constraints.Add(dsFKC)
ds.EnforceConstraints = True
```

The constraints fill the same function as do their database counterparts—if one of the constraints is violated, the operation will throw an exception that can be caught using a `Try...Catch` construction.

The Data Model

When you implement a schema, you need to create the DataSet object and then add DataTable objects to it. Finally, the DataColumn objects are added to the DataTable.

The first thing you need before you create the DataSet is a data model (schema) to implement. Figure 6-4 shows the data model for the DataSet you will work with in the next section. In this DataSet, you have removed the relationships between the tables to make the model easier to read.

The four tables contain the core data describing a customer order. Each table has columns with properties like name, data type, and length, and you will use these values when you build the objects.

FIGURE 6-4 The data model

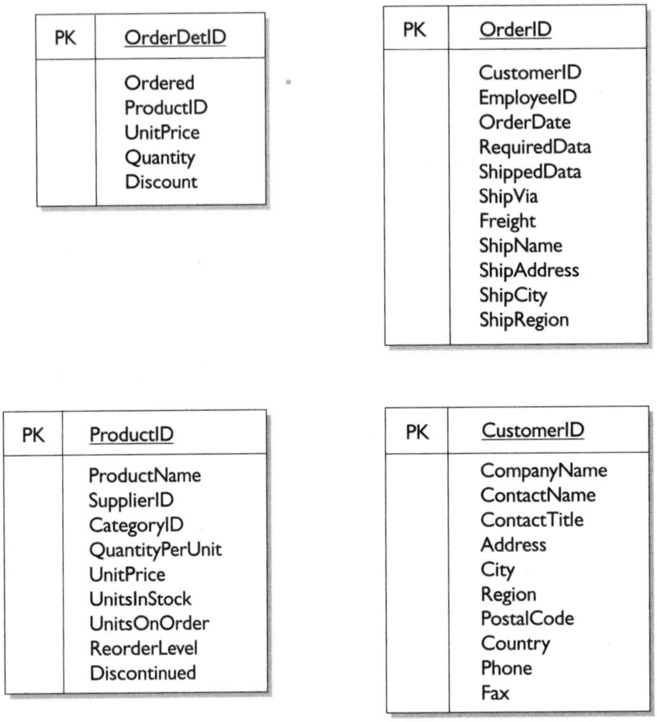

PK	OrderDetID
	Ordered
	ProductID
	UnitPrice
	Quantity
	Discount

PK	OrderID
	CustomerID
	EmployeeID
	OrderDate
	RequiredData
	ShippedData
	ShipVia
	Freight
	ShipName
	ShipAddress
	ShipCity
	ShipRegion

PK	ProductID
	ProductName
	SupplierID
	CategoryID
	QuantityPerUnit
	UnitPrice
	UnitsInStock
	UnitsOnOrder
	ReorderLevel
	Discontinued

PK	CustomerID
	CompanyName
	ContactName
	ContactTitle
	Address
	City
	Region
	PostalCode
	Country
	Phone
	Fax

Building a DataSet

In this section, you will build a DataSet object that reflects the data model (schema) in Figure 6-4. The resulting XML web service will deliver the DataSet to any application that needs to consume it.

EXERCISE 6-1

Building a DataSet

1. Create a new Visual Basic .NET project in Visual Studio .NET, and select the ASP.NET Web Service template. Name the project DataSetTest, and locate it on the localhost server, as shown here:

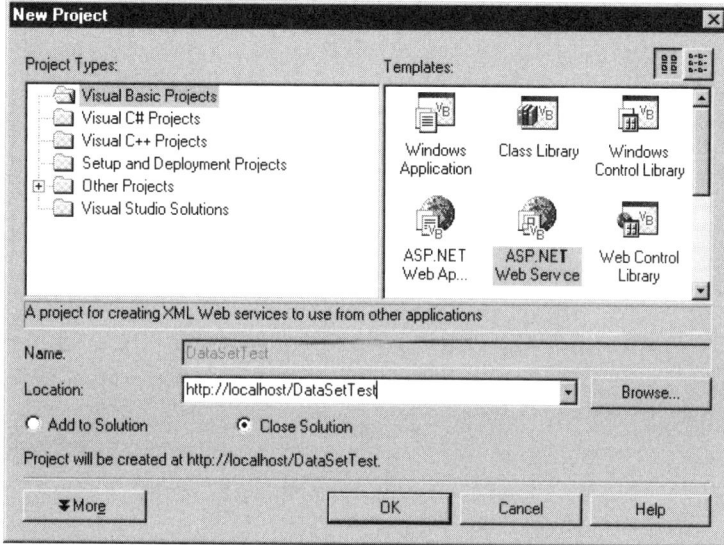

Once the project is created, open the code module for the XML web service. You will need to add some code to the code module that will create the DataSet, as detailed in the next steps.

2. Import the System.Data namespace by adding it to the list of namespaccs at the start of the code module—System.Data is the namespace needed to support DataSet objects. You will also need to add additional namespaces to support specific ADO.NET providers, but that can wait until you set up the database connection.

3. Declare a private variable to represent the DataSet. Call the variable ds.

4. Create a public method in the Service1 class named makeDataSet() with a signature as shown here:

```
Imports System.Web.Services
Imports System.Data

<WebService(Namespace := "http://tempuri.org/")> _
Public Class Service1
    Inherits System.Web.Services.WebService
    Dim ds As DataSet
...
Public Sub makeDataSet()
End Sub
```

Now that you have a variable for the DataSet, you can go ahead and create the DataTable objects and add them to the DataSet.

5. Create the DataTable objects for the DataSet by using the Add() method of the Tables collection in the DataSet. The following code segment creates the DataSet by passing the name of the DataSet to the constructor and then creates the four DataTable objects.

```
...
Public Sub makeDataSet()
    ds = New DataSet("OrderSet")
    Dim dtOrderDetails As DataTable = ds.Tables.Add("Order Details")
    Dim dtCustomers As DataTable = ds.Tables.Add("Customers")
    Dim dtProducts As DataTable = ds.Tables.Add("Products")
    Dim dtOrders As DataTable = ds.Tables.Add("Orders")
End Sub
...
```

The next step is to add the columns to the DataTable objects. The technique for this is similar to adding the DataTable objects to the DataSet.

6. The DataTable object has a Columns collection; use the Add() method to add the columns to the DataTable. The following code line shows a Column object being added to a DataTable object:

```
Dim colODOrderID As DataColumn = _
    dtOrderDetails.Columns.Add("OrderID", Type.GetType("System.Int32"))
```

The data type that is used for the dtOrderID column must be a valid data type in the .NET Framework. You need to use the typeof() method to pass the data type rather than just using the data type itself.

Adding the remaining columns to the DataTable objects results in the following code listing. Please note the .NET Framework data types and how they map to the Microsoft SQL Server data types:

```
...
Public Sub makeDataSet()
    ds = New DataSet("OrderSet")
    Dim dtOrderDetails As DataTable = ds.Tables.Add("Order Details")
    Dim dtCustomers As DataTable = ds.Tables.Add("Customers")
    Dim dtProducts As DataTable = ds.Tables.Add("Products")
    Dim dtOrders As DataTable = ds.Tables.Add("Orders")

    Dim colODOrderID As DataColumn = _
```

```
        dtOrderDetails.Columns.Add("OrderID", Type.GetType("System.Int32"))
Dim colODProductID As DataColumn = _
      dtOrderDetails.Columns.Add("ProductID", _
                                  Type.GetType("System.Int32"))
Dim colUnitPrice As DataColumn = _
      dtOrderDetails.Columns.Add("UnitPrice", _
                                  Type.GetType("System.Double"))
Dim colQuantity As DataColumn = _
      dtOrderDetails.Columns.Add("Quantity", _
                                  Type.GetType("System.Double"))
Dim colDiscount As DataColumn = _
      dtOrderDetails.Columns.Add("Discount", _
                                  Type.GetType("System.Double"))

Dim colCustomerID As DataColumn = _
      dtCustomers.Columns.Add("CustomerID", _
                                Type.GetType("System.String"))
Dim colCompanyName As DataColumn = _
      dtCustomers.Columns.Add("CompanyName", _
                                Type.GetType("System.String"))
Dim colContactName As DataColumn = _
      dtCustomers.Columns.Add("ContactName", _
                                Type.GetType("System.String"))
Dim colContactTitle As DataColumn = _
      dtCustomers.Columns.Add("ContactTitle", _
                                Type.GetType("System.String"))
Dim colAddress As DataColumn = _
      dtCustomers.Columns.Add("Address", Type.GetType("System.String"))
Dim colCity As DataColumn = _
      dtCustomers.Columns.Add("City", Type.GetType("System.String"))
Dim colRegion As DataColumn = _
      dtCustomers.Columns.Add("Region", Type.GetType("System.String"))
Dim colPostalCode As DataColumn = _
      dtCustomers.Columns.Add("OrderID", Type.GetType("System.String"))
Dim colCountry As DataColumn = _
      dtCustomers.Columns.Add("Country", Type.GetType("System.String"))
Dim colPhone As DataColumn = _
      dtCustomers.Columns.Add("Phone", Type.GetType("System.String"))
Dim colFax As DataColumn = _
      dtCustomers.Columns.Add("Fax", Type.GetType("System.String"))

Dim colProductID As DataColumn = _
      dtProducts.Columns.Add("ProductID", Type.GetType("System.Int32"))
Dim colProductName As DataColumn = _
      dtProducts.Columns.Add("ProductName", _
```

```
                                        Type.GetType("System.String"))
    Dim colSupplierID As DataColumn = _
        dtProducts.Columns.Add("SupplierID", Type.GetType("System.Int32"))
    Dim colCategoryID As DataColumn = _
        dtProducts.Columns.Add("CategoryID", Type.GetType("System.Int32"))
    Dim colQuantityPerUnit As DataColumn = _
        dtProducts.Columns.Add("QuantityPerUnit", _
                                    Type.GetType("System.String"))
    Dim colPUnitPrice As DataColumn = _
        dtProducts.Columns.Add("UnitPrice", Type.GetType("System.Double"))
    Dim colUnitsInStock As DataColumn = _
        dtProducts.Columns.Add("UnitsInStock", _
                                    Type.GetType("System.Int32"))
    Dim colUnitsOnOrder As DataColumn = _
        dtProducts.Columns.Add("UnitsOnOrder", _
                                    Type.GetType("System.Int32"))
    Dim colReorderLevel As DataColumn = _
        dtProducts.Columns.Add("ReorderLevel", Type.GetType("System.Int32"))
    Dim colDiscontinued As DataColumn = _
        dtProducts.Columns.Add("Discontinued", _
                                    Type.GetType("System.Boolean"))


    Dim colOrderID As DataColumn = _
        dtOrders.Columns.Add("OrderID", Type.GetType("System.Int32"))
    Dim colOCustomerID As DataColumn = _
        dtOrders.Columns.Add("CustomerID", Type.GetType("System.String"))
    Dim colEmployeeID As DataColumn = _
        dtOrders.Columns.Add("EmployeeID", Type.GetType("System.Int32"))
    Dim colOrderDate As DataColumn = _
        dtOrders.Columns.Add("OrderDate", Type.GetType("System.DateTime"))
    Dim colRequiredDate As DataColumn = _
        dtOrders.Columns.Add("RequiredDate", _
                                    Type.GetType("System.DateTime"))
    Dim colShippedDate As DataColumn = _
        dtOrders.Columns.Add("ShippedDate", _
                                    Type.GetType("System.DateTime"))
    Dim colShipVia As DataColumn = _
        dtOrders.Columns.Add("ShipVia", Type.GetType("System.Int32"))
    Dim colFreight As DataColumn = _
        dtOrders.Columns.Add("Freight", Type.GetType("System.Double"))
    Dim colShipName As DataColumn = _
        dtOrders.Columns.Add("ShipName", Type.GetType("System.String"))
```

```
        Dim colShipAddress As DataColumn = _
            dtOrders.Columns.Add("ShipAddress", Type.GetType("System.String"))
        Dim colShipCity As DataColumn = _
            dtOrders.Columns.Add("ShipCity", Type.GetType("System.String"))
        Dim colShipRegion As DataColumn = _
            dtOrders.Columns.Add("ShipRegion", Type.GetType("System.String"))
    End Sub
```

Now, look at a concept that you'll need before you complete this example later in the chapter. The `DataTable` objects in the `DataSet` are related to each other, and you can implement that relationship by using a couple of objects available in the `DataSet` object.

DataSet Relationships

The relationship between tables in a schema is modeled using primary key and foreign key constraints that are combined using a `DataRelation` object. Let's start with a refresher of the relationship terminology.

Using Primary and Foreign Key Constraints

The *primary key* is a structure in a table that can consist of one or more columns that are guaranteed not to have any duplication of data. The primary key is usually implemented as a unique index. One common candidate for a primary key is a column that represents the ID of the data stored in the table, such as an OrderID. The primary key is used to ensure the uniqueness of the data stored in the rows of that table.

The *foreign key* is a constraint on a table that references one or more columns in that table to a primary key on a different table in the database. The reference is such that no entry of data is allowed in the table if there is no corresponding entry in the primary key column of the other table. For example, you could not enter data into the Orders Details table for an order that had not been entered into the Orders table first (the OrderID must already be inserted in the Orders table).

In the context of foreign keys, the table that has the primary key constraint is called the *parent table,* and the table that has the foreign key constraint is called the *child table.* The relationship between the tables is a one-to-many relationship, where the parent table represents the "one" side and the child table represents the "many" side. Figure 6-5 shows the relationships in the `DataSet` you have been building.

FIGURE 6-5   The DataSet with relationships

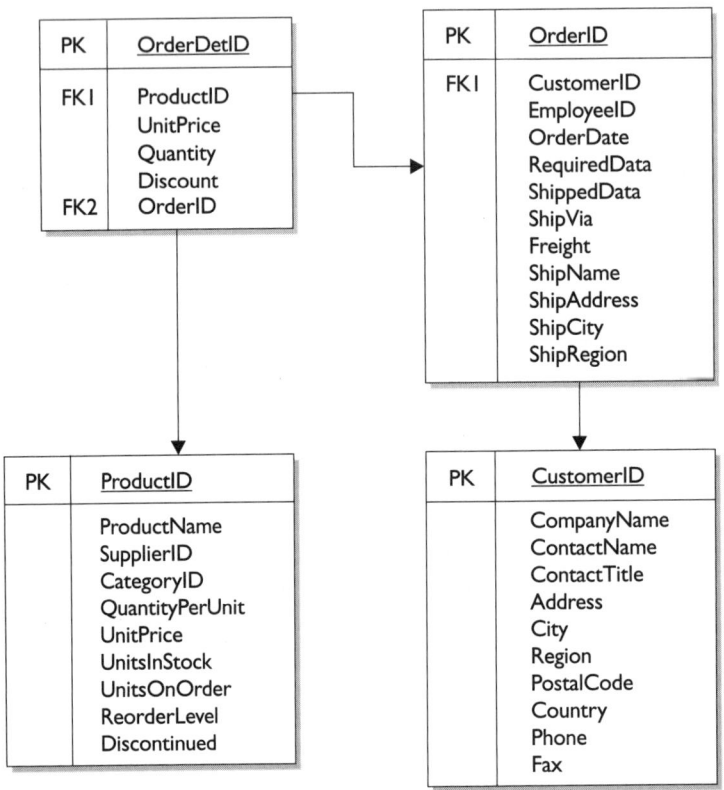

The foreign key constraint can be used to restrict what actions can be performed on the two tables that are connected through this relationship of primary key and foreign key. There are two operations that have actions defined for the relationship—delete and update. The delete operation has a `DeleteRule` property in the foreign key constraint, and the update operation has an `UpdateRule` property. These properties can be set to one of the four Rule values:

- **Cascade**   When a value in the primary key changes, the corresponding action is performed in the foreign key. This is the default behavior.

- **SetNull**   Sets the value in the foreign key to DBNull in order to maintain the rows in the child table.

■ **SetDefault**   Sets the value in the foreign key to the default value for the column(s).

■ **None**   Performs no action but raises an exception so that you can customize the processing.

exam
ⓦatch   *Remember that the primary key is the one (unique) side of the relationship, and the foreign key is the many side. There is one Customer (one side) that has many Orders (many side).*

EXERCISE 6-2

Foreign Key Constraint

1. To set the specific action for the foreign key constraint, add this code to the end of the makeDataSet() method:

```
Dim parentCol As DataColumn
Dim childCol As DataColumn
Dim dsFKC As ForeignKeyConstraint
' Set parent and child column variables.
parentCol = ds.Tables("Orders").Columns("OrderID")
childCol = ds.Tables("Orders").Columns("OrderID")
dsFKC = New ForeignKeyConstraint("OrderIDFKConstraint", parentCol, childCol)
' Set null values when a value is deleted.
dsFKC.DeleteRule = Rule.SetNull
dsFKC.UpdateRule = Rule.Cascade
```

2. Save and build the project.

Navigating Related Data

The DataSet object represents data in tables and columns but does not provide the functionality to retrieve and work with data using relationships—the DataRelation object performs that task, as well as enforcing referential constraints.

The DataRelation object is the final object to look at in the DataSet. It is used to define the relationship between two tables in a DataSet. The typical relationship is that two tables are linked by one column in each table that represents the same data, such as an OrderID column.

To create a `DataRelation` object, you add it to the `Relations` collection of the `DataSet` object as in the following code segment:

```
ds.Relations.Add("FK_CustOrder", dtCustomers.Columns("CustomerID"),
    dtOrders.Columns("CustomerID"))
```

The `DataRelation` object was added by providing the primary and foreign key constraints to the `Add()` method of the `Relations` collection.

The benefit of creating the `DataRelation` is that you can now navigate the parent/child structure programmatically—without the `DataRelation` object, that would not have been possible. The following code segment iterates through the `DataSet` using the `DataRelation` you just created:

```
Dim drCustomer As DataRowDim drOrder As DataRow
For Each drCustomer In ds.Tables("Customer").Rows
    For Each drOrder In drCustomer.GetChildRows("FK_CustOrder")
        ' Process the data in the row
    Next
Next
```

EXERCISE 6-3

Constraints

In this exercise, you will add constraints and work with the data in the `DataSet`.

Now, go back to the exercise you started earlier in the chapter. We'll add data to the `DataSet` and retrieve the data through the XML web service help application.

1. If you closed the project earlier, open the DataSetTest project now.

2. Add constraints to the end of the `makeDataSet()` method to relate the four DataTable objects in the `DataSet`. The constraints are listed in Table 6-8.

The code that adds these constraints should be added to the end of the `makeDataSet()` method. It should look like the following code:

```
Public Sub makeDataSet()
...
    ' add the constraints to the dataset
    Dim ucProdID As UniqueConstraint = _
        New UniqueConstraint("UC_ProdID", dtProducts.Columns("ProductID"))
    dtProducts.Constraints.Add(ucProdID)
    Dim ucCustID As UniqueConstraint = _
        New UniqueConstraint("UC_CustID", dtCustomers.Columns("CustomerID"))
    dtCustomers.Constraints.Add(ucCustID)
```

```
    Dim ucOrdID As UniqueConstraint = _
        New UniqueConstraint("UC_OrdID", dtOrders.Columns("OrderID"))
    dtOrders.Constraints.Add(ucOrdID)
    Dim cCol As DataColumn = dtOrderDetails.Columns("ProductID")
    Dim pCol As DataColumn = dtProducts.Columns("ProductID")
    Dim fcProdID As ForeignKeyConstraint = _
                New ForeignKeyConstraint("FK_ProdID", pCol, cCol)
    dtOrderDetails.Constraints.Add(fcProdID)
    cCol = dtOrderDetails.Columns("OrderID")
    pCol = dtOrders.Columns("OrderID")
    Dim fcOrdID As ForeignKeyConstraint = _
                New ForeignKeyConstraint("FK_OrdID", pCol, cCol)
    dtOrderDetails.Constraints.Add(fcOrdID)
    cCol = dtOrders.Columns("CustomerID")
    pCol = dtCustomers.Columns("CustomerID")
    Dim fcCustID As ForeignKeyConstraint = _
                New ForeignKeyConstraint("FK_CustID", pCol, cCol)
    dtOrders.Constraints.Add(fcCustID)
    ds.Relations.Add("FK_Cust", dtCustomers.Columns("CustomerID"), _
                        dtOrders.Columns("CustomerID"))
    ds.Relations.Add("FK_Ord", dtOrders.Columns("OrderID"), _
                        dtOrderDetails.Columns("OrderID"))
    ds.Relations.Add("FK_Prod", dtProducts.Columns("ProductID"), _
                        dtOrderDetails.Columns("ProductID"))
End Sub
```

TABLE 6-8   The Constraints for the DataSetTest Project

Constraint	On Object	Constraint Name
UniqueConstraint	dtProducts.Columns("ProductID")	ucProdID
UniqueConstraint	dtCustomers.Columns("CustomerID")	ucCustID
UniqueConstraint	dtOrders.Columns("OrderID")	ucOrdID
ForeignKeyConstraint	dtOrderDetails.Columns("ProductID") to dtProducts.Columns("ProductID")	fcProdID
ForeignKeyConstraint	dtOrderDetails.Columns("OrderID") to dtOrders.Columns("OrderID")	fcOrdID
ForeignKeyConstraint	dtOrders.Columns("CustomerID") to dtCustomers.Columns("CustomerID")	fcCustId
DataRelation	ucCust to fcCust	
DataRelation	ucOrdID to fcOrdID	
DataRelation	ucProdID to fcProdID	

3. Save and build the project. Once you have defined the schema (data model) for the `DataSet`, you need to enter some data. For this example, enter only a few rows for each `DataTable` so that you have some data to test with. The following list shows the data you will enter into the Customers `DataTable`:

- CustomerID: 42
- CompanyName: Vineyard 12
- ContactName: Merl Ot
- ContactTitle: Chief Bottle Washer and CEO
- Address: Rue Bordeaux
- City: Lyon
- Region:
- PostalCode: FR-110 15
- Country: France
- Phone: +FR 08 113 45
- Fax: +FR 08 113 46

Also, add some other customers to your `DataSet`—you can pick random information for this example.

You can insert information into a `DataTable` using one of two methods. The first method uses the `DataRow` object and an index into the `DataRow` to identify the `DataColumn`. The following code segment will insert some columns into a row; the new row is created by the utility method `NewRow()`, which is part of the `DataTable`:

```
Dim drCustomer As DataRow = dtCustomers.NewRow()
drCustomer(0) = 42
drCustomer(1) = "Vineyard 12"
...
drCustomer(10) = "+FR 08 113 46"
```

The index of the `DataRow` object can also be used with the `DataColumn` name, as in the following line of code:

```
drCustomer("City") = "Lyon"
```

After the data is added to the `DataRow` object, the `DataRow` must be added to the `DataTable` object's `Rows` collection, as shown in this code segment:

```
dtCustomers.Rows.Add(drCustomer)
```

The second method of inserting data is by using the `Add()` method of the `Rows` collection of the `DataTable` object. In this method, you create a new object that will represent the entire row; it is initialized by passing a comma-delimited list of data values, as shown in the following code segment:

```
Dim dtCustomers As DataTable = ds.Tables("Customers")
dtCustomers.Rows.Add(New Object() {42, "Vineyard 12", "Merl Ot", _
    "Chief Bottle Washer and CEO", " Rue Bordeaux", "Lyon", "", _
    "FR-110 15", "France", "+FR 08 113 45", "+FR 08 113 46"})
```

on the Job *You can also load data from an XML document received from another source into the DataSet; check out that topic in the section "Accessing and Manipulating XML Data," later in this chapter.*

EXERCISE 6-4

Populating the DataSet

Now that you know how to add data, you will populate the `DataSet` in the DataSetTest project.

1. Create a new method in the `Service1` class with the following signature:

```
Public Sub populateDataSet()
End Sub
```

2. Implement the `populateDataSet()` method to add some customers to the `DataSet` (`ds`) as in the preceding code segment, and feel free to add more customers.

```
Public Sub populateDataSet()
Dim dtCustomers As DataTable = ds.Tables("Customers")
dtCustomers.Rows.Add(New Object() {42, "Vineyard 12", "Merl Ot", _
    "Chief Bottle Washer and CEO", " Rue Bordeaux", "Lyon", "", _
    "FR-110 15", "France", "+FR 08 113 45", "+FR 08 113 46"})
End Sub
```

3. Once you have populated the Customers table, the next table you will need to populate is the Products table. Use the data in Table 6-9 to populate the `DataSet`. The columns that are not listed should be set to 0 (zero) for numeric data types and `""` (empty string) for string types. This code also goes in the `populateDataSet()` method.

The resulting code that is added to the end of the `populateDataSet()` method should look like this:

```
Dim dtProducts As DataTable = ds.Tables("Products")
dtProducts.Rows.Add(New Object() {42, "Universal Answer", 0, 0, _
                                   "", 1242.34, 1, 0, 0, 0})
dtProducts.Rows.Add(New Object() {12, "Whitby Herring", 0, 0, _
                                   "", 4.12, 150, 0, 0, 0})
dtProducts.Rows.Add(New Object() {7, "Mimico Tuna", 0, 0, _
                                   "", 42.12, 65, 0, 0, 0})
```

Now you can create orders for those customers.

4. Define the order that will be inserted in the Orders `DataTable`. The data in Table 6-10 should be inserted, again using 0 (zero) for numeric values and empty strings for string values for columns that are not in the table.

The code that inserts the data in the Orders `DataTable` should look like this:

```
Dim dtOrders As DataTable = ds.Tables("Orders")
...
Dim dtNow As DateTime = DateTime.Today
dtOrders.Rows.Add(New Object() {1, 42, 0, dtNow, dtNow.AddDays(5), _
                                dtNow, 0, 0.0, "", "", "", ""})
```

TABLE 6-9	ProductID	ProductName	UnitPrice	UnitsInStock
The Data for the Product DataTable	42	Universal answer	1242.34	1
	12	Whitby herring	4.12	150
	7	Mimico tuna	42.12	65

TABLE 6-10	The Order Data for the Orders DataTable			
OrderID	**CustomerID**	**OrderDate**	**RequiredDate**	**ShippedDate**
1	42	Today's Date	5 days	Today's Date

5. The final step in populating the `DataSet` is to add the details of the order to the Order Details `DataTable`. The data is in Table 6-11.

The code should be similar to this code segment:

```
Dim dtOrderDetails As DataTable = ds.Tables("Order Details")
...

dtOrderDetails.Rows.Add(new Object() {1, 42, 4200.00, 1, 0.00})
dtOrderDetails.Rows.Add(new Object() {1, 12, 6.00, 40, 0.00})
dtOrderDetails.Rows.Add(new Object() {1, 7, 73.05, 6, 0.00})
```

Now, the XML web service is almost ready. All that is left is to create the web method and call your processing methods to generate the `DataSet`.

6. Enter the following code in the `Service1` class:

```
<WebMethod()> _
Public Function GetData() As DataSet
    makeDataSet()
    populateDataSet()
    Return ds
End Function
```

TABLE 6-11	The Data for the Order Details DataTable			
OrderID	**ProductID**	**UnitPrice**	**Quantity**	**Discount**
1	42	4200.00	1	0.00
1	12	6.00	40	0.00
1	7	73.05	6	0.00

7. Save and execute the XML web service by pressing F5. The resulting window is shown here:

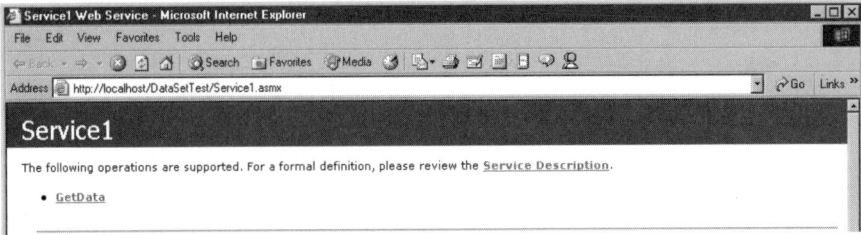

8. Click the GetData link to get the display shown next. In this display, you can see the SOAP code that will call the XML web service, along with your one control labeled Invoke.

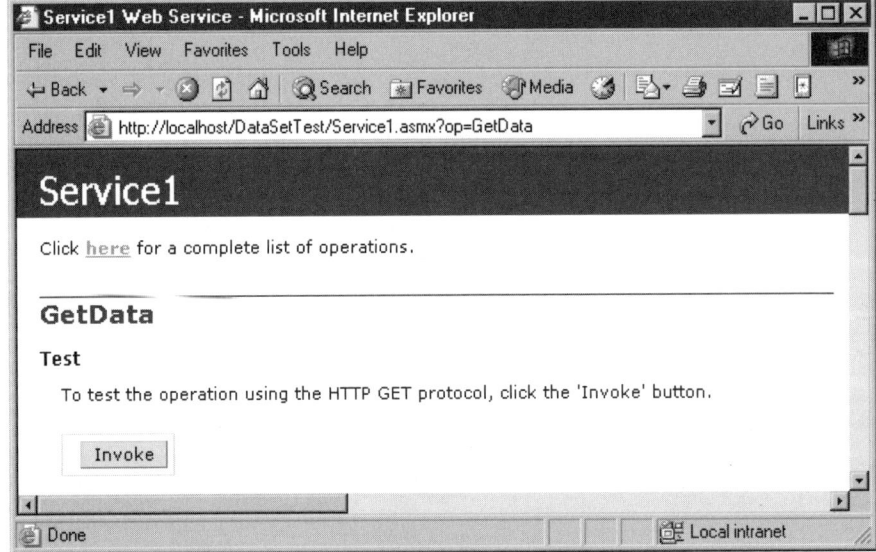

9. Click the Invoke button to execute the web method. The result is shown next, and the return data is in XML, as expected. That is it.

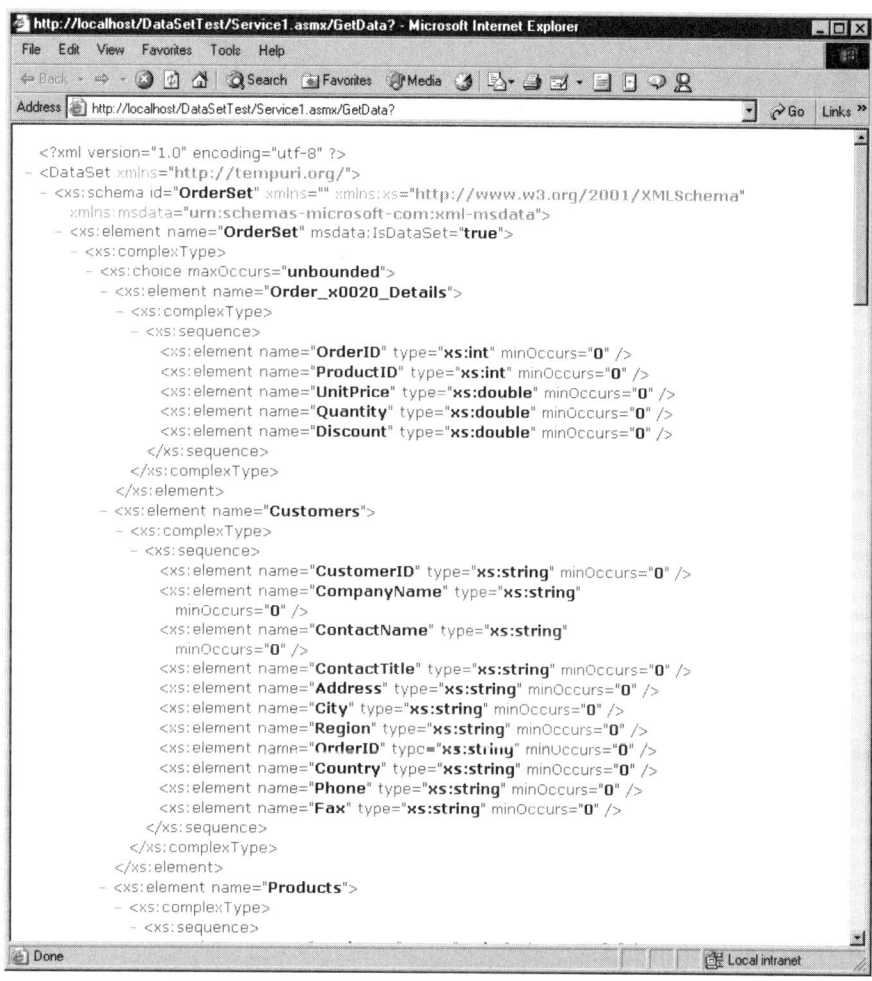

You have now looked at the code that makes it possible to work with `DataSet` objects to send data between XML web services and consumers of those services. You also saw how to work with the data programmatically. The next step is to look at how you can work with XML documents.

CERTIFICATION OBJECTIVE 6.04

Accessing and Manipulating XML Data

XML (Extensible Markup Language) is another acronym you will have seen used throughout this book. XML is discussed in Appendix D, so I will not detail the XML rules here. The purpose of this section is to show you how you can work with data in XML format programmatically by using the Document Object Model (DOM) for XML. This will include looking at the `XmlReader` object and the operations that can be performed with it.

Microsoft incorporated XML support into SQL Server 2000, and the exam will surely include questions on the extensions to the Transact-SQL language, so I have included information on those extensions in this section as well.

e x a m
ⓦa t c h

Be sure to know the six rules of well-formed XML: (1) there can be only one root element, and all elements require (2) matching opening and closing elements that are (3) case sensitive and must be (4) nested properly. Attributes must have their (5) values enclosed in quotes and (6) cannot be repeated.

Document Object Model (DOM)

XML is increasingly used to move data between processes, and as such, it is a very powerful language that simplifies the data exchange in a heterogeneous environment. It allows the sender and receiver of the data to operate on the data in a programmatic way. The object model that has become the standard (endorsed by the W3C) is the Document Object Model (DOM). This is the standard API for XML, but there is a second API that can be used to access XML documents called Simple API for XML (SAX). DOM uses an object model to operate on the data in the XML document, while SAX uses an event-driven API to work with the data. The standard is DOM, and that is what is tested in the exam, but that does not mean SAX should be ignored as a technology. SAX comes into its own when you need to process the XML document in a serial manner, and when the document is too large to fit in memory for use with DOM.

The standard way of accessing XML documents, however, is through DOM, and that is what the exam will test you on. The remainder of this chapter will work with DOM.

Let's have a look at the object model of DOM. In the true sense of the word, everything in DOM is a *node*. When you explore the objects, you will find that everything is a node in a b-tree, where the document is the root.

The XML document is parsed into a DOM tree when the document is read by the parser. Once the parser has loaded the document, it is available for you to manipulate. The tree structure of the DOM can be seen in Figure 6-6.

The XML document that was used in Figure 6-6 is as follows:

```xml
<?xml version="1.0"?>
<booklist>
  <book language="en">
    <isbn>007224436</isbn>
  </book>
...
</booklist>
```

FIGURE 6-6   The tree structure of DOM

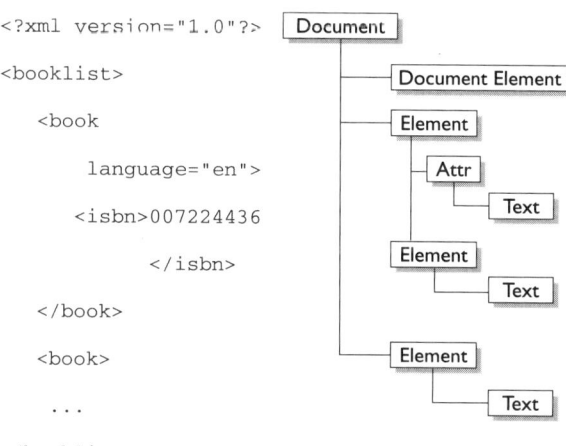

The following objects are in the DOM:

- **Document object** This is the topmost node of the DOM. This node contains the entire contents of the XML document.

- **Element objects** This node represents the elements in the XML document. The root element `<booklist>` is an element object, as are the `<book>` and `<isbn>` elements.

- **Attr objects** This node represents the attributes of the document, such as the `language` attribute.

- **Text object** This node represents the textual value stored in an element or attribute.

The DOM exposes a number of collections that makes it easy to work with multiple elements or attributes at the same time.

Every object in the DOM is a node that defines some properties that are available when you work with the document. For example, the navigation properties `firstChild`, `lastChild`, `nextSibling`, and `previousSibling` let you move through the node tree. Each node also has properties that you can query to find the type and name of the node: `nodeType` returns a number that defines what the node is, whereas the `nodeName` property returns the name of the node. The different node types are as follows:

1: element node

2: attribute node

3: text node

9: document node

Let's look at an example that will read the public domain XML version of Macbeth and then print it on the console. This example uses an XML file that is provided in the Chapter 6 folder of the CD-ROM that accompanies this book. We'll also use the `System.Xml` namespace, because that is where all support for XML in the .NET Framework comes from.

XML Access

1. Copy the Macbeth.xml file to a new folder on your C: drive.

2. Create a new Visual Basic .NET source file in that directory, and name the file **Dom.vb**.

3. Using your favorite editor, enter the following code into the Dom.vb file:

```vb
' Dom.vb
Imports System
Imports System.IO
Imports System.Xml
Imports Microsoft.VisualBasic    ' Support for IsNothing

Public Class Dom
    Public Shared Sub Main(ByVal args() As String)
        Dim XmlFileName As String = "Macbeth.xml"
        Dim myDom As Dom = New Dom()
        myDom.ParseTree(XmlFileName)
    End Sub
    Public Sub ParseTree(ByVal XmlFileName As String)
        ' use a try/catch block to ensure we handle any errors
        Try
            Console.WriteLine("\nLoading the {0} file, please wait", _
                                                    XmlFileName)
            Dim myDoc As XmlDocument = New XmlDocument()
            myDoc.Load(XmlFileName)
            ' after we have loaded the file display the content
            Console.WriteLine("/nDisplaying the content of the {0} file", _
                                                    XmlFileName)
            Dim node As XmlNode = myDoc
            ' go through and display all the nodes in the document
            PrintNodes(Console.Out, node)
        Catch e As Exception
            Console.WriteLine("Exception: {0}", e.ToString())
        End Try
    End Sub
    Public Sub PrintNodes(ByRef cOut As TextWriter, ByRef node As XmlNode)
        Try
            PrintNodeInfo(cOut, node)
            If node.HasChildNodes Then
                PrintNodes(cOut, node.FirstChild)
            End If
            If Not (IsNothing(node.NextSibling)) Then
```

```
                    PrintNodes(cOut, node.NextSibling)
              End If
        Catch e As Exception
              Console.WriteLine("Exception: {0}", e.ToString())
        End Try
    End Sub
    Public Sub PrintNodeInfo(ByRef cOut As TextWriter, ByRef node As XmlNode)
        cOut.Write("{0} [{1}] = {2} ", node.NodeType, node.Name, node.Value)
        Dim Attributes As Integer = 0
        If Not (IsNothing(node.Attributes)) Then
              Attributes = node.Attributes.Count
        End If
        Dim i As Integer = 0
        While I < Attributes
              cOut.Write("{0} [{1}] = {2} ", "Attr", node.Attributes(i).Name, _
                                              node.Attributes(i).Value)
              i += 1
        End While
        cOut.WriteLine()
    End Sub
End Class
```

This program makes use of the XML document, and it traverses the tree, printing information about the nodes as they are found. In order to compile the program, you need to execute the command-line Visual Basic .NET compiler as follows:

```
C:\VB\MacBeth>vbc /r:System.Xml.dll Dom.vb
Microsoft (R) Visual Basic .NET Compiler version 7.00.9466
for Microsoft (R) .NET Framework version 1.00.3705.209 Copyright (C)
Microsoft Corporation 1987-2001. All rights reserved.
```

4. Execute the program to get an output of the play on the console. A partial listing is shown here:

```
C:\VB\MacBeth>Dom
Loading the Macbeth.xml file, please wait
Displaying the content of the Macbeth.xml file
Document [#document] =
XmlDeclaration [xml] = version="1.0"
Element [PLAY] =
Element [TITLE] =
Text [#text] = The Tragedy of Macbeth
Element [fm] =
Element [p] =
Text [#text] = Text placed in the public domain by Moby Lexical Tools, 1992.
Element [p] =
Text [#text] = SGML markup by Jon Bosak, 1992-1994.
```

```
...
Element [LINE] =
Text [#text] = Took off her life; this, and what needful else
Element [LINE] =
Text [#text] = That calls upon us, by the grace of Grace,
Element [LINE] =
Text [#text] = We will perform in measure, time and place:
Element [LINE] =
Text [#text] = So, thanks to all at once and to each one,
Element [LINE] =
Text [#text] = Whom we invite to see us crown'd at Scone.
Element [STAGEDIR] =
Text [#text] = Flourish. Exeunt
```

FROM THE CLASSROOM

Over the last couple of years, I have seen an increase in the number of students who work with XML. There are a couple of ways to work with XML: either by directly hand-crafting the schema and the XML document (when nothing but human ingenuity can solve the business problem at hand) or by building the schema and document through software components like ADO.NET (when the transport requirements and the schema are defined by a standard).

I have found that the two "standards" for accessing XML documents create the most confusion. The Document Object Model (DOM) is what W3C has recommended, while Simple API for XML (SAX) is what has become the API by community process for accessing XML documents.

The DOM is based on XML documents being parsed and read into memory—you can then access the documents by traversing the node tree, as it were. This method works very well for smaller XML documents that are well formed. The process used is very procedural, but as I said, it lends itself very well to smaller documents. DOM is commonly used to create XML documents in memory based on the processing and then stream those documents to a consumer of the data.

SAX is based on event-driven parsers. As the parser reads the XML document, the registered events are fired and the code assigned to handle the events will execute. This event-driven nature of SAX makes it a more object-oriented approach to programmatic access to XML documents. SAX is very suitable to work with any size XML document.

As you can see, there is no real winner here. DOM versus SAX is a fight between two equals that produce the same output using different approaches. The two "standards" will both be with us for a long time to come.

In the previous exercise, you used the Load() method of the XmlDocument object to read the document into the DOM. Next, look at how to work with the XmlReader and XmlWriter classes.

XmlReader

With the XmlReader class, you can process the XML document using techniques similar to the ones available in the Simple API for XML (SAX) packages.

The XmlReader class is an abstract base class that provides the ability to read and parse an XML file in a forward-only, read-only, noncached manner for a number of classes that inherit from it. The following classes are derived from the XmlReader class:

- **XmlTextReader**   Reads character streams. This class has no support for schemas.

- **XmlNodeReader**   Parses XML DOM trees. This class has no support for schemas.

- **XmlValidatingReader**   Provides a fully compliant validating XML parser with schema support.

e x a m
ⓦ a t c h

The XmlReader class is the base class for a number of specialized readers.

EXERCISE 6-6

The XmlReader

To show the XmlReader in action, build a program that is based on the XmlTextReader class. This example will read, parse, and display an XML file.

1. Create a Visual Basic .NET source file in the same directory that contains the Macbeth.xml file, and name it **XmlReader.vb**.

2. Using your favorite editor, enter the following code into the XmlReader.vb file:

```
' XmlReader.vb
Imports System
Imports System.IO
Imports System.Xml
Imports Microsoft.VisualBasic   ' Support for IsNothing

Public Class ReadXml
```

```vbnet
Public Shared Sub Main(ByVal argh() As String)
    Dim stream As StreamReader
    Try
        Dim XmlFileName As String = "Employees.xml"
        If argh.Length > 0 Then
            XmlFileName = argh(0)
        End If
        Console.WriteLine("Reading XML ...")
        stream = New StreamReader(XmlFileName)
        Dim reader As XmlTextReader = New XmlTextReader(stream)
        reader.WhitespaceHandling = WhitespaceHandling.None
        ReadXml.ReadIt(reader)
    Catch e As Exception
        Console.WriteLine("Exception: {0}", e.ToString())
    Finally
        If Not (IsNothing(stream)) Then
            stream.Close()
        End If
    End Try
End Sub
Public Shared Sub ReadIt(ByVal r As XmlTextReader)
    Dim i As Integer = 0
    Try
        While (r.Read())
            i += 1
            Console.Write("Read[{0,3}]:", i)
            PrintInfo(Console.Out, r)
        End While
    Catch e As Exception
        Console.WriteLine("Exception: {0}", e.ToString())
    End Try
End Sub
Public Shared Sub PrintInfo(ByVal cOut As TextWriter, ByVal r As _
                                                    XmlReader)

    If (r.HasValue) Then
        cOut.Write("{0} [{1}] = {2} ", r.NodeType, r.Name, r.Value)
    Else
        cOut.Write("{0} [{1}] ", r.NodeType, r.Name)
    End If
    If (r.HasAttributes) Then
        While (r.MoveToNextAttribute())
            cOut.Write("{0} [{1}] = {2} ", r.NodeType, r.Name, r.Value)
        End While
    End If
    cOut.WriteLine()
```

```
        End Sub
End Class
```

The bold line in the preceding code specifies the handling of whitespace in the XML document. The `WhitespaceHandling` parameter is set to `WhitespaceHandling.None`, which ignores any whitespace.

3. Compile the program using the command-line compiler **vbc**.

```
C:\VB\MacBeth>vbc /r:System.Xml.dll XmlReader.vb
```

4. The XML file that is hard-coded in the program is Employees.xml, and it contains the following data:

```
<?xml version="1.0"?>
<employees>
    <employee>
        <name>John Smith</name>
        <salary>54000</salary>
    </employee>
    <employee>
        <name>Robert Jones</name>
        <salary>61000</salary>
    </employee>
    <employee>
        <name>Sue Brown</name>
        <salary>65000</salary>
    </employee>
</employees>
```

5. When you run the program, the output produced shows the document parsed into its nodes, as can be seen here:

```
C:\VB\MacBeth>xmlreader
Reading XML ...
Read[  1]:XmlDeclaration [xml] = version="1.0" Attribute [version] = 1.0
Read[  2]:Element [employees]
Read[  3]:Element [employee]
Read[  4]:Element [name]
Read[  5]:Text [] = John Smith
Read[  6]:EndElement [name]
Read[  7]:Element [salary]
Read[  8]:Text [] = 54000
Read[  9]:EndElement [salary]
Read[ 10]:EndElement [employee]
Read[ 11]:Element [employee]
Read[ 12]:Element [name]
Read[ 13]:Text [] = Robert Jones
```

```
Read[ 14]:EndElement [name]
Read[ 15]:Element [salary]
Read[ 16]:Text [] = 61000
Read[ 17]:EndElement [salary]
Read[ 18]:EndElement [employee]
Read[ 19]:Element [employee]
Read[ 20]:Element [name]
Read[ 21]:Text [] = Sue Brown
Read[ 22]:EndElement [name]
Read[ 23]:Element [salary]
Read[ 24]:Text [] = 65000
Read[ 25]:EndElement [salary]
Read[ 26]:EndElement [employee]
Read[ 27]:EndElement [employees]
```

In the preceding output, the whitespace was ignored. The default whitespace handling is to return all whitespace. To experiment with the whitespace handling, change the bold line in the earlier program code to read as follows:

```
reader.WhitespaceHandling = WhitespaceHandling.All
```

After compiling the program again, you can execute it, and you will get output as follows:

```
C:\VD\MacBeth>xmlreader
Reading XML ...
Read[  1]:XmlDeclaration [xml] = version="1.0" Attribute [version] = 1.0
Read[  2]:Whitespace [] =

Read[  3]:Element [employees]
Read[  4]:Whitespace [] =

Read[  5]:Element [employee]
Read[  6]:Whitespace [] =

...

Read[ 35]:Element [salary]
Read[ 36]:Text [] = 65000
Read[ 37]:EndElement [salary]
Read[ 38]:Whitespace [] =

Read[ 39]:EndElement [employee]
Read[ 40]:Whitespace [] =

Read[ 41]:EndElement [employees]
```

The whitespace in the XML document is now returned, as are the nodes.

The `XmlTextReader` is one of the objects that are used to parse XML documents and programmatically work with them. Once you have an XML document loaded, you can process the data in the nodes by using Visual Basic .NET, or you can take advantage of the transformations that can be performed. The next section will explore XML and transformations.

Transformations and XML

Using Extensible Stylesheet Language (XSL), you can transform the contents of an XML document into any other character-based format that is itself a well-formed XML document. The transformation is called XSL Transformation (XSLT). For example, you can transform an XML document to HTML for display in a browser, or you can transform the XML document to meet the formatting requirements of some other service. For a refresher on XSL, see Appendix D.

XSL support in the .NET Framework is found in the `System.Xml.Xsl` namespace. The `XslTransform` class in that namespace supports XML documents using XSL style sheets. The process of transforming an XML document starts with an instance of the `XslTransform` class. The XSL style sheet is read into the `XslTransform` object through the `Load()` method. Then the `Transform()` method is called with an `XPathDocument` as input, and the output can be either a writer, a stream, or an `XmlReader`. The `XPathDocument` is constructed from an XML document.

exam
ⓦatch

XSLT can transform only well-formed XML documents to other well-formed XML documents.

As an example, transform an XML document with employee information into an HTML table (the XML and XSL files are in the Chapter 6 folder on the accompanying CD-ROM). The XML document Empl.xml follows:

```
<?xml version="1.0" ?>
<empls>
   <employee id="42">
      <name>John Smith</name>
      <salary payperiod="Monthly">62000</salary>
      <department>Development
         <title>Sr. Developer</title>
      </department>
   </employee>
```

```
<employee id="43">
    <name>George Brown</name>
    <salary payperiod="weekly">53000</salary>
    <department>Customer Support
        <title>Customer care specialist</title>
    </department>
</employee>
<employee id="44">
    <name>Linda Philips</name>
    <salary payperiod="bi-weekly">52000</salary>
    <department>Development
        <title>Tester</title>
    </department>
</employee>
<employee id="45">
    <name>Guy Jones</name>
    <salary payperiod="monthly">72000</salary>
    <department>Accounting
        <title>Bookkeeper</title>
    </department>
</employee>
</empls>
```

The transformation will be performed by the following XSL style sheet that is also found in the Chapter 6 folder on the CD-ROM, Empl.xsl:

```
<xsl:stylesheet xmlns:xsl="http://www.w3.org/1999/XSL/Transform" version="1.0">
    <xsl:template match="/">
        <HTML>
        <TABLE border="1">
        <xsl:for-each select="empls/employee">
            <xsl:sort select="name"/>
            <TR VALIGN="top">
                <TD>
                    <xsl:value-of select="name" />
                </TD>
                <TD>
                    <xsl:value-of select="@id" />
                </TD>
                <TD>
                    <xsl:value-of select="salary" />
                </TD>
                <TD>
                    <xsl:value-of select="department" />
                </TD>
                <TD>
                    <xsl:value-of select="department/title" />
```

```
            </TD>
          </TR>
       </xsl:for-each>
       </TABLE>
       </HTML>
     </xsl:template>
  </xsl:stylesheet>
```

EXERCISE 6-7

XSLT

In order to transform the XML document, you need to write a command-line program.

1. Create a folder on your hard drive, and copy the XML and XSL files from the Chapter 6 folder on the CD-ROM to the folder. Then create a Visual Basic .NET source file in the same directory, and name the file **Trans.vb**.

2. Using your favorite editor, enter the following code:

```vb
' Trans.vb
Imports System
Imports System.IO
Imports System.Xml
Imports System.Xml.XPath
Imports System.Xml.Xsl

Public Class Trans
    Public Shared Sub Main()
        Dim xmlFile As String = "Empl.xml"
        Dim xslFile As String = "Empl.xsl"
        Dim transOut As String = "Empl.htm"
        Try
            Dim xslt As XslTransform = New XslTransform()
            xslt.Load(xslFile)
            Dim xpathDoc As XPathDocument = New XPathDocument(xmlFile)
            Dim xOut As XmlTextWriter = New XmlTextWriter(transOut, _
                Nothing)
            xOut.Formatting = Formatting.Indented
            xslt.Transform(xpathDoc, Nothing, xOut)
            xOut.Close()
        Catch e As Exception
            Console.WriteLine("Exception: {0}", e.ToString())
        End Try
```

```
    End Sub
End Class
```

3. Compile the program at the command line.

```
vbc /r:System.Xml.dll Trans.vb
```

4. Execute this program. The output is an HTML file (Empl.htm) located in the same directory as the program. The HTML that was generated through this transformation was indented. The HTML output code looks as follows:

```
<HTML>
  <TABLE border="1">
    <TR VALIGN="top">
      <TD>George Brown</TD>
      <TD>43</TD>
      <TD>53000</TD>
      <TD>Customer Support
                  Customer care specialist</TD>
      <TD>Customer care specialist</TD>
    </TR>
    <TR VALIGN="top">
      <TD>Guy Jones</TD>
      <TD>45</TD>
      <TD>72000</TD>
      <TD>Accounting
                  Bookkeeper</TD>
      <TD>Bookkeeper</TD>
    </TR>
    <TR VALIGN="top">
      <TD>John Smith</TD>
      <TD>42</TD>
      <TD>62000</TD>
      <TD>Development
                  Sr. Developer</TD>
      <TD>Sr. Developer</TD>
    </TR>
    <TR VALIGN="top">
      <TD>Linda Philips</TD>
      <TD>44</TD>
      <TD>52000</TD>
      <TD>Development
                  Tester</TD>
      <TD>Tester</TD>
    </TR>
  </TABLE>
</HTML>
```

When you open the Empl.htm file in a browser, the table is displayed as shown next.

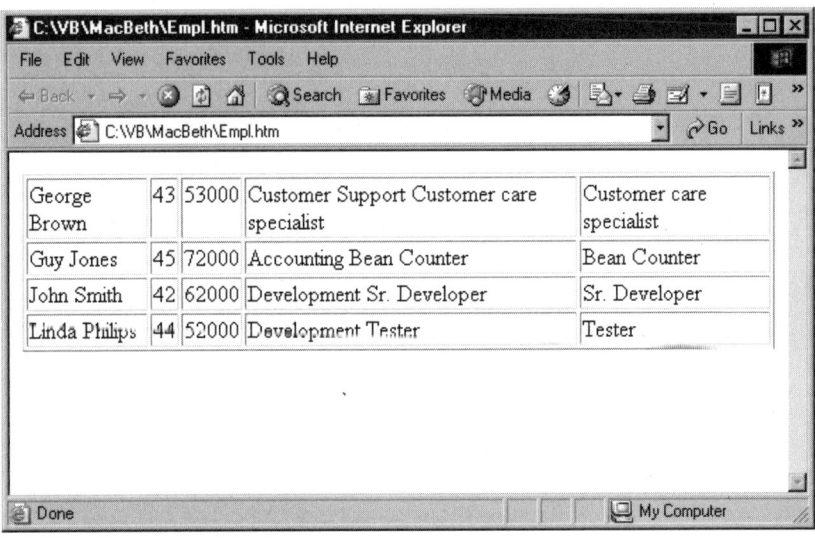

One issue that remains after you have transformed a document is validation—the process of guaranteeing that a document meets the rules. That's my next topic.

Validating XML

XML documents are designed to be passed between different services and processes, some of which are supplied by other entities and run on computers that you have no control over. This global reach means that you will need a way to guarantee that the document you just received from one of your vendors is correct in format. This is the process of validation. A valid XML document must meet the six rules for an XML document, and it must be validated against a schema. The schema is the definition of the elements, the attributes, the order of the nodes, the valid data types, the ranges of values, and how the nodes relate to each other.

The support for validation is provided through the `XmlValidatingReader` class that is created from an `XmlReader`—the `XmlValidatingReader` has a `ValidationType` property that controls how an XML document is to be validated. The possible values for the `ValidationType` property are

- **Auto**   Senses the type (Document Type Definition [DTD] or XML schema) of validation automatically

■ **DTD**   Forces DTD validation

■ **Schema**   Forces schema validation

■ **None**   Performs no validation

The first of the two types of validation is Document Type Definition (DTD), which is the original standard for validation formats. DTD has been considered a legacy type since the XML schema was turned into a standard. The `XmlValidatingReader` class is used to perform the validation; it uses the `ValidationEventHandler()` callback method that is called when a validation error has been found.

In order to explore validation, write an example that uses a DTD file to validate an XML document (both these files are found in the Chapter 6 folder on the accompanying CD-ROM). The XML document is the Emplo.xml file shown here:

```
<?xml version="1.0"?>
<!DOCTYPE emplo SYSTEM "Emplo.dtd">
<emplo>
    <employee>
        <fullname>Gregory Small</fullname>
        <remuneration>23500</remuneration>
        <title>Programmer</title>
        <location>Halifax</location>
    </employee>
    <employee>
        <fullname>Marg Simpson</fullname>
        <remuneration>51000</remuneration>
        <title>Tester</title>
        <location>Vancouver</location>
    </employee>
    <employee>
        <fullname>Patrik Soames</fullname>
        <remuneration>45000</remuneration>
        <title>System Architect</title>
        <location>Ottawa</location>
    </employee>
    <employee>
        <fullname>John Smith</fullname>
        <remuneration>112000</remuneration>
        <title>Project Manager</title>
        <location>Toronto</location>
    </employee>
</emplo>
```

The DTD file is Emplo.dtd:

```
<!ELEMENT emplo (employee*)>
<!ELEMENT employee (fullname, remuneration, title, location)>
<!ELEMENT fullname (#PCDATA)>
<!ELEMENT remuneration (#PCDATA)>
<!ELEMENT title (#PCDATA)>
<!ELEMENT location (#PCDATA)>
```

EXERCISE 6-8

DTD Validation

1. Create a folder on your hard drive, and copy the Empl.xml and Emplo.dtd files to that folder.

2. Create a Visual Basic .NET source file in the same folder, and name it **Valid.vb**.

3. Using your editor, enter the following code in the Valid.vb source file:

```
' Valid.vb
Imports System
Imports System.IO
Imports System.Xml
Imports System.Xml.Schema

Public Class Valid
  Private bOut As Boolean
  Dim reader As XmlValidatingReader
  Public Shared Sub Main(ByVal argh() As String)
      Dim Val As Valid = New Valid()
      Val.ValidateIt("Emplo.xml")
  End Sub

  Public Sub ValidateIt(ByVal xmlFile As String)
      bOut = True
      Try
          Console.WriteLine()
          Console.WriteLine("XML file: {0} is validating", xmlFile)
          reader = New XmlValidatingReader(New XmlTextReader(xmlFile))
          reader.ValidationType = ValidationType.DTD
          ' register the delegate for the event
          AddHandler reader.ValidationEventHandler, AddressOf ValHand
          Console.WriteLine("Validating using DTD")
          Dim doc As XmlDataDocument = New XmlDataDocument()
```

```
        doc.Load(reader)
        Dim str As String
        If bOut Then
            str = "success"
        Else
            str = "failure"
        End If
        Console.WriteLine("Validation finished.")
        Console.WriteLine("The outcome of the validation was a {0}", str)
        ' invalid XML exception
    Catch e As XmlException
        Console.WriteLine("Exception. {0}", e.ToString())
        ' all other exceptions
    Catch e As Exception
        Console.WriteLine("Exception: {0}", e.ToString())
    End Try
End Sub
Public Sub ValHand(ByVal sender As Object, _
                ByVal args As ValidationEventArgs)
    bOut = False
    Console.WriteLine()
    Console.Write("Validation error: {0}", args.Message)
    ' get a reference to the XmlTextReader
    Dim x As XmlTextReader = sender.Reader()
    ' print out the line with the error
    Console.WriteLine()
    Console.WriteLine("Line({0}) Character {1}", _
                                    x.LineNumber, x.LinePosition)
End Sub
End Class
```

4. To compile the program, you need to execute the command-line Visual Basic .NET compiler, like this:

```
vbc /r:System.Xml.dll /r:System.Data.dll Valid.vb
```

5. After you execute the program, the output should look like the following:

```
C:\VB\xml>Valid

XML file: Emplo.xml is validating
Validating using DTD
Validation finished.
The outcome of the validation was a success
```

6. Break the schema of the XML file by deleting the <location> element from one of the employees, and rerun the Valid.exe program. The result should be similar to the following, depending on which line you deleted:

```
C:\VB\xml>valid

XML file: Emplo.xml is validating
Validating using DTD

Validation error: Element 'employee' has invalid child element 'title'.
Expected: 'remuneration'.
An error occurred at file:///C:/VB/xml/Emplo.xml(13, 4).
Line(13) Character 4
Validation finished.
The outcome of the validation was a failure
```

XML is a very big topic, and it is used in every aspect of the .NET Framework. Expect to see multiple questions in the exam that present the question information in XML format.

CERTIFICATION OBJECTIVE 6.04

Write a SQL Statement That Retrieves XML Data from a SQL Server Database

When Microsoft SQL Server 2000 was released, there was almost no XML support built into any of the database products available. However, Microsoft included rudimentary XML support for SQL Server in the .NET Framework once the Framework was released.

The .NET SQL provider contains support for retrieving an XML stream from Microsoft SQL Server 2000. The SqlCommand object has the ExecuteXmlReader() method, which returns an XmlReader object populated with the result of the SQL statement specified for the SqlCommand.

The following code segment illustrates the use of the ExecuteXmlReader() method.

```
...
Imports System.Data.SqlClient
Imports System.Xml
...
Dim xmlCm As SqlCommand = new SqlCommand(
            "SELECT * FROM Customers FOR XML AUTO, ELEMENTS", dbCon)
Dim reader As XmlReader = xmlCm.ExecuteXmlReader()
```

The FOR XML clause specifies that the SELECT statement will return XML. The AUTO mode returns query results as nested XML elements, and the ELEMENTS option maps columns as elements rather than as attributes (for a refresher on XML, please see Appendix D).

Check out the corresponding Scenario & Solution sidebar about working with data sources.

SCENARIO & SOLUTION

How do I use the XxxDataAdapter object?	The *Xxx*DataAdapter object is used to build a DataSet object from *Xxx*Command objects. To use the *Xxx*DataAdapter, you will create *Xxx*Commands that will be used to populate the DataSet, update the data source from the DataSet, insert data in the data source, and delete data from the data source. If you supply only one *Xxx*Command that will populate the DataSet, the *Xxx*DataAdapter will use that *Xxx*Comand to update, insert, and delete as well.
What is a cross join?	The cross join effectively produces nonrelational output by matching all rows from one table with all rows in a second table. If Table A has 5 rows and Table B has 5 rows, the cross join between them will have 25 rows. Cross joins are mostly used to create data for testing databases.
What happens if I issue a DELETE command to a table without a WHERE clause?	All the rows in the table will be deleted. You should always include a WHERE clause in DELETE and UPDATE statements because the default is to affect all rows in the table.
Why should I use Try...Catch...Finally constructions in my data code?	Data sources are external resources to your program. Every time you access external resources, you must encapsulate that access in a Try block and handle any exceptions in a Catch block.

CERTIFICATION SUMMARY

This ends your visit to the land of data. The code you have worked with in this chapter is the type you will see in real-world applications that are built to give the developer full control of the process. This chapter looked at a number of special areas of the ADO.NET environment, especially the DataSet object and the use of XML, as well as the core concepts of one of the largest topic areas to be covered in the exam.

Data is the root of all applications, and the way you access data determines the success of your application. You were exposed to the ADO.NET concepts and the object models that make it possible to treat data in the same way irrespective of where it originated. The connection object encapsulates the data source to the point that you no longer need to know the specifics of the vendor's implementation. The DataSet makes the data available in a disconnected table, and it has moved the data architecture forward by leaps and bounds.

In the XML Web Services exam, there will be many questions that present similar code, and you must understand how to read that code to be able to answer the questions correctly. The exam questions may be on totally different topics from the ADO.NET DataSet code that was presented in the question.

The programmatic manipulation of XML documents through the DOM or through XmlReader objects is another skill that will be tested directly or indirectly. The topic of XML and of the use of XML as a generic data carrier is very large. Suffice it to say that at the time of writing this book, all major players in the data world have adopted the XML standards. The result should be that you see much better integration between products from different vendors, and in the end better opportunities for us as developers to work on some really cool products.

---

*Please be aware that the questions and answers at the end of this chapter for the Two-Minute Drill, the Self Test Questions, and the Self Test Answers may *not* match the order of those found in the corresponding chapter on the CD-ROM.

TWO-MINUTE DRILL

Consuming and Manipulating Data

- ADO.NET is a set of classes for working with data.
- `System.Data.OleDb` provides support for the Ole DB .NET provider.
- The .NET Framework ships with two .NET providers, one for Microsoft SQL Server 7.0 or higher, and one for Ole DB providers.

Accessing and Manipulating Data from a Microsoft SQL Server Database by Creating and Using *Ad Hoc* Queries and Stored Procedures

- `System.Data.SqlClient` provides support for the SQL .NET Provider.
- `System.Data.SqlTypes` provides support for the native data types for Microsoft SQL 6 Server.
- Use stored procedures to centralize business logic on the database server.

Creating and Manipulating DataSets

- `System.Data` contains the core classes for ADO.NET, for example, the `DataSet`.
- The `DataSet` class encapsulates `DataTables` to represent data disconnected from the data source.
- To access data from multiple `DataTables` in a related fashion, you need to create relation objects.

Accessing and Manipulating XML Data

- `System.Xml` provides support for XML documents.
- Everything in the DOM is a node—Document node, Element node, Attr node, Text node, etc.
- The only Reader class that supports the XML schema is the `XmlValidatingReader`.
- XSLT provides the support for transforming an XML document into any other XML document—HTML documents are also XML documents.

SELF TEST

Consuming and Manipulating Data

1. When would you not use the OleDbConnection object?

   A. To connect to a SQL 6.5 database

   B. To connect to an Access database

   C. To connect to a SQL 7.0 database

   D. To connect to a DB/2 database

2. What connection is used in ADO.NET to connect to a SQL Server 6.0?

   A. Upgrade the server to SQL 6.5 and use the SqlConnection class.

   B. Upgrade the server to SQL 2000 and use the OdbcConnection class.

   C. Upgrade the server to SQL 7.0 and use the OleDbConnection class.

   D. Use the OleDbConnection class.

Accessing and Manipulating Data from a Microsoft SQL Server

3. The following SQL INSERT statement fails. What is the most probable reason for the failure?

   ```
   INSERT INTO Employees VALUES (42,'Greta','Andersson', 12)
   ```

   A. The Employees database does not have a default table defined.

   B. Syntax error in the INSERT statement.

   C. The columns in the Employees table are not in the indicated order (int, char, char, int).

   D. The SELECT INTO permission is not set.

Creating and Manipulating DataSets

4. What is the SQL equivalent of the DataSet relation object?

   A. XOR JOIN

   B. CROSS JOIN

   C. INNER JOIN

   D. OUTER JOIN

5. You need to be able to retrieve data from a `DataSet` object that has four `DataTable` objects. There are currently `UniqueConstraint` and `ForeignKeyConstraint` objects on the `DataTable` objects to enforce the data rules. You find that you can retrieve data from the individual `DataTable` objects, but you are not able to retrieve data from the combination of `DataTable` objects in a parent/child manner. What should you do to be able to retrieve the data in a parent/child manner?

A. Set the `EnforceParentChild` parameter of the `DataSet` to True.

B. Set the `EnforceRelation` parameter of the `Relations` collection to True.

C. Add `DataRelation` objects to the `Relations` collection to make the `DataSet` present the data in a parent/child manner.

D. Add a primary key and a foreign key to each of the `DataTable` objects that should present the data in a parent/child manner.

6. You have been given a project that loads data into a `DataTable`, and you find that the project will not compile. You localize the problem to the statements that load the data into the `DataTable`, as shown in this code segment:

```
Dim dtProducts As DataTable = ds.Tables("Products")
dtProducts.Rows.Add(New RowSet{42,
                    "Universal Answer", 0, 0, "", 1242.34, 1, 0, 0, 0})
dtProducts.Rows.Add(New RowSet{12,
                    "Whitby Herring", 0, 0, "", 4.12, 150, 0, 0, 0})
dtProducts.Rows.Add(New RowSet{7,
                    "Mimico Tuna", 0, 0, "", 42.12, 65, 0, 0, 0})
```

What is the most efficient way to make the project compile?

A. Replace the curly braces {} with square brackets [].

B. Remove the new keyword from the `Add()` method.

C. Replace the reference to RowSet in the `Add()` method with `Object()`.

D. Change the `Add()` method to the `Load()` method.

Accessing and Manipulating XML Data

7. In what form is the data represented in an `XmlDataDocument`?

A. Flat

B. Relational

C. Hierarchical

D. Tabular

8. You are parsing an XML document using an `XmlReader`. You find that the resulting node tree is very large compared to the number of elements and attributes in the XML document. Why would the result of the parsing produce a large node tree?

   A. The WhitespaceHandling parameter is set to WhitespaceHandling.All.

   B. The WhitespaceHandling parameter is set to WhitespaceHandling.None.

   C. The WhitespaceHandling parameter is set to WhitespaceHandling.Auto.

   D. The WhitespaceHandling parameter is set to WhitespaceHandling.Special.

9. Which of the following classes supports XML schemas? Select all that apply.

   A. XmlReader

   B. XmlDocument

   C. XmlValidatingReader

   D. XmlNodeReader

10. You want to produce a form letter from an XML document. What method must you use?

   A. XSLT

   B. XSD

   C. Crystal Reports

   D. Visual Basic .NET

SELF TEST ANSWERS

Consuming and Manipulating Data

1. ☑ C. The `SqlDbConnection` object is used with Microsoft SQL Server 7.0 and higher.
    ☒ A, B, and D. Answer A, B, and D are incorrect because the `SqlDbConnection` object is used with Microsoft SQL Server 7.0 and higher.

2. ☑ D. The connection that will work with Microsoft SQL Server 6.0 is the OLE DB provider-based class (`OleDbConnection`).
    ☒ A, B, and C. A is incorrect because upgrading to Microsoft SQL Server 6.5 will not work with the `SqlConnection`; the SQL .NET providers work only with Microsoft SQL Server 7.0 or higher. B is incorrect because upgrading to Microsoft SQL Server 2000 will let you use the SQL .NET provider; the ODBC provider is an incorrect choice. C is incorrect because you can use the SQL .NET provider if you upgrade to Microsoft SQL Server 7.0; the `OleDbConnection` class is incorrect.

Accessing and Manipulating Data from a Microsoft SQL Server

3. ☑ C. The INSERT statement is correct and will execute without error if the Employees table has the four first columns that expect an int, a char, a char, and an int. Additionally, there cannot be any columns beyond the four first that have the NOT NULL property set.
    ☒ A, B, and D. A is incorrect because Employees refers to the table, not the database. Answer B is incorrect because the INSERT statement is syntactically correct. Answer D is incorrect, since there is no separate SELECT INTO permission.

Creating and Manipulating DataSets

4. ☑ C. The relation object is the equivalent of the INNER JOIN in the database; it represents a one-to-many relationship between two `DataTable` objects.
    ☒ A, B, and D. Answer A is incorrect because there is no XOR JOIN. Answer B is incorrect because the CROSS JOIN represents the Cartesian product between two tables, not the one-to-many relationship the relation object represents. Answer D is also incorrect because the OUTER JOIN represents the sum of two tables, not the one-to-many relationship the relation object represents.

5. ☑ C. The `DataSet` must have a `DataRelation` object for each pair of `DataTable` objects that should present their data in a parent/child manner.

☒   **A, B** and **D.** Answer **A** is incorrect because there is no `EnforceParentChild` parameter. Answer **B** is incorrect because there is no `EnforceRelation` parameter. Answer **D** is incorrect because `DataTables` cannot have primary or foreign keys.

6.   ☑   **C.** You must create an array of `Object` for this syntax to work; the correct line should be as follows (I show only one line here):

```
dtProducts.Rows.Add(new Object(){7,
                 "Mimico Tuna", 0, 0, "", 42.12, 65, 0, 0, 0})
```

☒   **A, B,** and **D.** Answer **A** is incorrect because changing the braces is syntactically wrong. Answer **B** is incorrect because removing the New keyword is also syntactically wrong. Answer **D** is incorrect because the `Load()` method will not create new rows for us.

Accessing and Manipulating XML Data

7.   ☑   **B.** The `XmlDataDocument` has a close affiliation with the `DataSet` class, which provides a relational view of the loaded XML data.
☒   **A, C,** and **D.** These answers are incorrect because the `XmlDataDocument` represents relational data.

8.   ☑   **A.** Setting the `WhitespaceHandling` property to `WhitespaceHandling.All` will return all `Whitespace` and `SignificantWhitespace` nodes. This is the default.
☒   **B, C,** and **D.** Answer **B** is incorrect because setting the property to `WhitespaceHandling.None returns no Whitespace and no SignificantWhitespace` nodes. Answer **C** is incorrect because there is no such value. Answer **D** is also incorrect. Setting the property to `WhitespaceHandling.Special` will return only `SignificantWhitespace` nodes.

9.   ☑   **C.** The only one of the listed classes that supports validation is `XmlValidatingReader`.
☒   **A, B,** and **D.** Answer **A, B,** and **D** are all incorrect because they do not support validation.

10.   ☑   **C.** Answer **C** is correct because Crystal Reports, included with Visual Studio .NET, provides the support for taking data from an XML document and using it in a form letter.
☒   **A, B,** and **D.** Answer **A** is incorrect because the resulting document must be a well-formed XML document, **B** is incorrect because this is the grammar for XML, not a formatting technology, and **D** is incorrect because Visual Basic .NET is not a letter generator.

MCAD/MCSD

MICROSOFT® CERTIFIED APPLICATION DEVELOPER
& MICROSOFT® CERTIFIED SOLUTION DEVELOPER

7

Testing and Debugging

CERTIFICATION OBJECTIVES

I n this chapter, you will learn about the testing process and specifically how unit testing fits into the overall testing of the application. You will also look at what tracing is and how you can make use of it, as well as how you implement your remote components and retrieve that information.

Debugging and especially how you debug remote components interactively will also be handled here. Another interesting area you will look at is how you can use SOAP extensions to debug the components.

Creating a Test Plan on the Evolutionary Model

This section will deal with software testing and the unit test in particular. Unit testing takes the smallest part of software practical and validates its function. The unit test must be planned and documented according to what is called the *unit test plan*. The software that usually is produced to perform the unit test is called the *test harness*—software that has stubs and functions that can call on and respond to any functionality in the unit being tested.

Software testing is a high-priority activity in the production of software applications. Among other things, the testing process

- **Measures the quality of the software** The assumption is that there will always be flaws in the software that are waiting to be discovered. By testing and debugging prior to release, you can ensure that your software is regarded as high-quality.

- **Validates that the application behaves as the user expects it to** The application is tested to ensure that it behaves as described in the documentation, and as the users expect the application to work.

- **Reduces the cost of development** Testing will reduce those costly last-minute errors that traditionally have delayed products and added to the cost. The unit test methodology results in individual software components being tested and validated before they are assembled into increasingly more complex units.

- **Reduces the cost of ownership by minimizing the cost of maintenance** Maintenance cost is determined by how much testing must be performed to validate the code after the maintenance. Because the testing plans are already written, the unit and integration tests are faster and more accurate.

■ **Replaces the traditional development and test planning process**   The
traditional process follows the waterfall model, where one task flows into
the next in an ordered manner as in the following list:

■ Analyze requirements

■ Create designs and specifications

■ Create the code

■ Test

■ Release

When you reach the testing phase in this model, the application is already finished,
and when problems are identified, there is a major issue. In order to make repairs, you
make changes, but those changes will modify the application, so you need to start
testing again. This cycle of testing and modifications on the finished application can be
never-ending. The development cost also increases enormously—there are estimates
that the cost can increase by 100 times when testing is delayed until the application
is finished.

on the
job   *Unit testing becomes almost automatic because the methodology leads us to*
test as you go along, building test harnesses to validate your implementation.

The waterfall model matched the development model for most procedural
environments, but when you moved into object-oriented development, the development
model changed to the evolutionary model where testing is an ongoing process that is
integrated into the development process.

The steps in the evolutionary model are to

1. Analyze requirements:

   ■ Discover classes

   ■ Develop classes

   ■ Test the classes

2. Repeat until the system is complete

The repetitious evolution of the application by building increasingly more complex
parts of the application on already tested units makes it possible to arrive at the end of
the development project with a fully tested application. The additional payback is that
at the end when the complete application is assembled from all the units, there will not
be any devastating errors that require rewriting parts of the application.

e x a m
ⓦatch

Expect questions that make you select between the waterfall model and the evolution model. You can rest assured that the evolution model will be the right answer.

The evolution model uses the iterative steps from object-oriented analysis and design (OOAD) to continuously analyze the application and build fully tested parts of that application before moving on to the next cycle, which starts with analysis again.

The unit test becomes a central task in the development of the application. As you move forward, you will have more and more fully tested units that can be assembled into larger units that are then tested, and so on until the application is finished.

Testing should be planned in a fashion similar to the main development effort. Planning for testing should be requirements based, drawing the test design from the requirements section of the software specification. Testing generally identifies defects (bugs) that allow, create, or cause unexpected behaviors in terms of the requirements. The requirements for the software must be written in such a way that they can be directly translated into test documentation. For example, requirements should be

- **Binding** The customer demanded them.
- **Testable** If you can't test the requirement, there is no way of proving compliance.
- **Clear** They must be unambiguous and interpretable in only one way.

Planning then proceeds by designing test cases that will validate each of the requirements. The test plan will outline the entire process with the individual test cases included. The development of a solid test plan is built on the systematic analysis of the application to make sure that everything is tested without repetitions. The plan ensures that testing procedures are known and do not depend on accidental or random testing.

One closely related task to testing is *optimization*. The optimization task is the process that removes bottlenecks (overuse of resources) in the software and hardware to produce the best combination that minimizes resource use. After performing optimization, you must perform the tests for each unit again to ensure that the optimization exercise did not break the application.

Testing

The testing exercise consists of three related tasks that together ensure the quality of the developed software. They are listed next.

- **The unit test**   Testing the smallest possible software unit
- **The integration test**   Testing combinations of software units
- **The regression test**   Retesting after modifications to the software units

The exam focuses on the unit test, but to fully understand the testing methodology, you will cover the other two as well.

Unit Testing

The goal of *unit testing* is to take the smallest possible testable software that is part of the application, remove it from the remainder of the software, and test to ensure it behaves as expected. Unit testing is a natural fit with the OOAD methodology used for modern software design because it flows naturally from the unit-by-unit iterative development that you are used to from the OOP world.

The testing process usually requires that you write a test harness that is used to communicate with the software unit. The terminology used to describe this scenario is that you will write a *driver* to simulate the caller and possibly a *stub* to simulate a called unit. The test harness becomes part of the applications code base and will be used for validation through the lifetime of the application.

The cost in time that is involved in writing the test harness makes it tempting to try to test larger units rather than identifying and testing the smallest possible unit. The problem with testing larger units is that it increases the difficulty in identifying where a problem is located. If you have two software units and you decide to test them together as one unit, you may face the following list of questions, which gives you an idea of the complexity of finding a bug:

- Is the error caused by a defect in the first unit?
- Is the error caused by a defect in the second unit?
- Is the error caused by a defect in the test harness?
- Is the error caused by a defect in both the first and second units?
- Is the error caused by a defect in the interface between the two units?

The complexity introduced makes it very hard to find the source of the defect—this is one compelling reason for implementing unit testing.

exam
ⓦatch   *Always select the smallest possible unit for the test.*

EXERCISE 7-I

Unit Testing

In this exercise, you will investigate writing a test harness. For this example, you have chosen a class as the unit you will test. The exercise is based on a console application to minimize the complexities.

1. Open a Visual Studio .NET Command Prompt (Start | Programs | Microsoft Visual Studio .NET | Visual Studio .NET Tools | Visual Studio .NET Command Prompt).

2. Change to the C:\VB directory, or create it if you do not have that directory.

3. Make a new directory named Testing (**md Testing**).

4. Change to the Testing directory (**cd Testing**).

5. Create a new Visual Basic .NET class file using your favorite editor. Name the file **Class.vb**.

6. Enter the following source code in the Class.vb source file:

```
Public Class Temperature
Private m_temperature As Integer

Public Property Temp As Integer
   Get
      Return m_temperature
   End Get
   Set(value As Integer)
      m_temperature = value - 273   ' Kelvin   End Set
End Property

Public Function Celsius() As Integer
   Return m_temperature
End Function

Public Function Fahrenheit() As Integer
   Return m_temperature
End Function
End Class
```

7. Next, write the test harness to test the Temperature class. The logic behind the test is that you will test the Celsius() and Fahrenheit() functions to ensure that the class returns the correct value. The test plan is to use a value of 30 Celsius and verify that it is correctly returned. Create a new source file in the Testing directory; name the file **Harness.vb**.

8. Enter the following Visual Basic .NET code in the Harness.vb file:

```vb
Public Class Tester

  Public Shared Sub Main()
    Dim t As Temperature = New Temperature()
    Static Thirty As Integer = 30

    t.Temp = Thirty ' assign the property 30 Celsius
    ' Now test the behavior when the temperature is set to 30 C

    Select Case t.Celsius()
      Case Thirty
        System.Console.Out.WriteLine( _
                  "The value is correct: {0} (Expected {1}C)", _
                  t.Celsius, Thirty)
      Case Else
        System.Console.Out.WriteLine( _
                  "The value is incorrect: {0} (Expected {1}C)", _
                  t.Celsius, Thirty)
    End Select
    Select Case t.Fahrenheit()
      Case ((Thirty* 9 / 5)+32)
        System.Console.Out.WriteLine( _
                  "The value is correct: {0} (Expected {1}F)", _
                  t.Fahrenheit, ((Thirty* 9 / 5)+32))
      Case Else
        System.Console.Out.WriteLine( _
                  "The value is incorrect: {0} (Expected {1}F)", _
                  t.Fahrenheit, ((Thirty* 9 / 5)+32))
    End Select
  End Sub
End Class
```

9. Save the source files and compile them using this command line:

```
C:\VB\Testing>vbc Harness.vb Class.vb
```

10. Run the harness program; the following is the output:

```
C:\VB\Testing>harness
The value is incorrect: -243 (Expected 30C)
The value is incorrect: -243 (Expected 86F)
```

As you can see, there is a problem, and if you look at the Temperature class, you will find that the temperature is stored using the absolute Kelvin scale, but there is no conversion in the Celsius() or Fahrenheit() functions. The next step provides the solution to the Celsius() function problem.

11. Correct the `Celsius()` function to correctly convert from Kelvin to Celsius. Here is the correct conversion:

```
Public Function Celsius() As Integer
    Return m_temperature + 273    ' convert from Kelvin to Celsius
End Function
```

12. Save and compile the harness program.

13. Execute the harness program. This should be the result:

```
C:\VB\Testing>harness
The value is correct: 30 (Expected 30C)
The value is incorrect: -243 (Expected 86F)
```

14. Correct the problem with the `Fahrenheit()` function using the following code segment:

```
Public Function Fahrenheit() As Integer
    Return (((m_temperature + 273) * 9 ) / 5 ) + 32
End Function
```

15. Save and compile the harness program.

16. Execute the harness program.

```
C:\VB\Testing>harness
The value is correct: 30 (Expected 30C)
The value is correct: 86 (Expected 86F)
```

Having tested the `Temperature` class, you can move on to other classes in the application.

Integration Testing

When the units of the application are completed and tested, they will be assembled (integrated) into larger units. These new integrated units need to be tested as well, in what is called *integration testing*. The most basic integration test takes two tested units and tests the interface between those two units. This process continues until all units have been integrated. By working with only two units at a time, the integration testing becomes manageable, and locating a defect will be much easier and faster.

There are three approaches to integration testing:

■ **The top-down strategy**   In this strategy, you start at the top of the application and integrate the units to ensure that high-level logic and dataflow are tested early in the development cycle. The top-down strategy minimizes the need for drivers (callers), but the need for stubs complicates management of the test. The low-level units are tested late in the development cycle. The top-down strategy has very poor support for early (proof of concept), limited-functionality releases of the application.

- **The bottom-up strategy** This strategy starts with the integration of the lowest-level units first, with the result that the utility level of the application is tested early in the process. This strategy minimizes the need for stubs while demanding drivers; the high-level logic and data flow are not tested until the later stages of the development cycle. The support for early releases is poor.

- **The umbrella strategy** In this strategy, you test along the lines of functional control and data-flow paths. The logic is to integrate low-level functions first—as in the bottom-up strategy—after which the output from each function is integrated in the top-down manner. This strategy minimizes the need for stubs and drivers but also makes management of the testing effort more complicated. The umbrella strategy leads to the possible early release of limited-functionality proof-of-concept versions.

The integration testing is completed when the application is ready to be shipped to the customer.

on the
job

The most common model for testing is a combination of the umbrella model and one of the other two models. That way, the early test versions can be brought together with the users to validate the design as well as the formalized top-down or bottom-up model. One word of advice, though: ensure that management of the testing is tightly controlled.

Regression Testing

Regression testing refers to the retesting of units after the unit has been modified. You perform the regression test by rerunning the original tests that were designed for that unit. The testing will determine if the modification broke the unit or not. Regression testing should not be a long process; rather, it should be a very quick go–no go test. Here are some strategies that can be used during the testing:

- Look out for side effects of fixes that have been incorporated.
- Write one regression test for each bug that was fixed.
- Test fixed bugs directly after the bug is fixed to ensure that the fix has no side effects.
- If multiple tests are similar, throw away the least efficient ones.
- Tests that always pass the program should be archived for historical reasons.
- Test functionality, not design.

- Vary the data for the test, look for data corruption. Try to overflow buffers, test for logical behavior.
- Track the memory use of the program.

The groups of tests that need to be maintained in order to be able to perform regression testing are most effectively stored in a library that constitutes a battery of standard tests that are used whenever the program has to be tested. One of the tricky aspects of the test library is to decide what to keep. Don't spend too much time analyzing the merits of a particular test case; if you can't make up your mind, add it to the library. The content of the library should be analyzed every so often to remove duplicated test cases as well as invalid tests.

Software testing is as much a science as is software design, and the preceding information is included as an overview of the topic. Remember that the exam will assume that you know how to write a test harness for a unit.

Providing Test Data to Components and Applications

The selection of test data for use with the test cases is as important as the design of the test cases themselves. The data that is used must be selected from the problem domain of the development project. The data is usually identified during the analysis phase of the project and should be verified with the domain experts of the project to ensure the data is valid.

When developing components that quite possibly will be used in an international environment, it is imperative that you provide for data that is valid for the different locales of the users of the component. To that end, work with the domain experts to identify the different locales that will be supported in the design and create data definitions for each locale.

The most important aspect of the localized component is that the tests must provide data in the format of the user locale and test that the component performs the correct conversions. For example, if the locale of the user presents dates in the *YYYY.MM.DD* format (2002.09.07), the test data must include that format to ensure that the conversions work.

CERTIFICATION OBJECTIVE 7.02

Logging Test Results

The performance of tests is one part of testing—but there is an equally important part that involves the logging or filing of the test data. The logging can be as low-tech as manually filing screen shots and handwritten notes in a filing system, or it can be as high-tech as using a versioning system that stores the test harness as well as the output together with the source code.

How you store the test results is not as important as that you store them in a searchable way. Remember that this involves the Quality Assurance (QA) records of the software application.

One product supplied by Microsoft as part of Visual Studio .NET is the Visual SourceSafe (VSS) product. You can use VSS to keep versioned copies of virtually anything. VSS is the application that makes team-based development possible.

exam
Watch

For the exam, you need to know that VSS is a product that is used to store versioned information about all aspects of the software development process in a project—including the test reports.

on the
Job

The storing of test results is one of the areas in software testing that usually is left to chance—which is a shame. You spend a lot of time designing and executing the tests, but then the results are just stored in a filing cabinet. Next year, when you need to return to the same application to test it after maintenance, you need those original results so that you can guarantee that the maintenance action did not break anything.

FROM THE CLASSROOM

One of the most ignored topics in any course is the importance of proper testing. I have made a point of introducing the concept of the test harness to the students that I teach. When you implement a class, you always write a small program—the test harness—that is used to exercise and test the class.

I have found that the software class is a manageable unit for testing, but that is based on the assumption that the classes are built as small single-use building blocks that will be assembled into larger classes that in turn are assembled into the application.

This brings us back to the proper class design that is the basis of OOAD. With a proper class design, the test cases will be easy to design and the iterative nature of OOAD will lend itself to providing a functional test plan.

CERTIFICATION OBJECTIVE 7.03

Instrumenting and Debugging a Service

Instrumentation is the process of collecting information about a program while it is running. A number of methods are available to us for collecting that information, ranging from online debugging to using the performance counters that can be monitored using operating system tools. The exam will test you on how to add trace statements and performance counters, and how to debug a remote component using these techniques.

Two different classes are available to us for getting information from the running application: the Trace class and the Debug class. These two classes are equivalent in all but one respect—the Debug class will not be available if the application has been compiled as a Release build, while the Trace class is available in both Debug and Release builds. As the two classes are equivalent in all but this respect, you will concentrate on the Trace class in this section. You will start with tracing to explore the different parts of the environment and how to use them.

Implementing Tracing

Tracing is the method used to monitor your application while it is running in production. The Trace class gives you the functionality you need to provide a very functional environment for production instrumentation of your application. The Trace class is located in the System.Diagnostics namespace. In order to add tracing to an application, you will need to include the System.Diagnostics namespace and use the methods of the Trace class.

The six methods in the Trace class that write output are listed in Table 7-1.

| **TABLE 7-1** | The Output Methods of the Trace Class |

Method	Output
Assert()	The output is written if the condition for the Assert is False. If no text is specified, Assert() outputs a stack trace.
Fail()	The text is output if present; else, the stack trace.
Write()	Outputs the specified text, no carriage return.
WriteIf()	Outputs the specified text, no carriage return, if the condition is True.
WriteLine()	Outputs the specified text followed by a carriage return.
WriteLineIfy	Outputs the specified text, followed by a carriage return, if the condition is True.

The output from the methods in Table 7-1 is written to TraceListeners. There is always a default TraceListener (`DefaultTraceListener`) that sends the trace information to the default error output for Windows. You can add additional TraceListeners to the TraceListenerCollection that the Listeners property of the `Trace` class refers to in order to enable custom tracing. Two TraceListeners are supported: the TextWriterTraceListener redirects output to an instance of the TextWriter class or to anything that is a Stream class, and the EventLogTraceListener redirects output to an event log.

e x a m
ⓦa t c h   *You can inherit from `TraceListeners` to build your own custom listener.*

The following code segment is an example of creating a `TextWriter TraceListener` and writing some trace information to it:

```
Imports System.Diagnostics
Imports System.IO
...
Dim outputFile As Stream = File.Create("OutputFile.txt")
' Add a new text writer to the trace listener collection
Dim tl As TextWriterTraceListener = New TextWriterTraceListener(outputFile)
Trace.Listeners.Add(tl)
' Write tracing information to the file
Trace.WriteLine("This line will be placed in the OutputFile.txt file")
```

Tracing can be controlled using the *trace switches* that are provided with the Trace class; this way, the application can have its trace capabilities modified at run time. The trace switches are as follows:

- 0 = None
- 1 = Errors only
- 2 = Warnings as well as errors
- 3 = Information messages (and warnings and errors)
- 4 = Verbose—as its name suggests, everything

By setting the TraceSwitch to one of the preceding levels, you can control the level of tracing that will take place. The following code segment shows how to use this technique:

```
Dim myTraceSwitch as New TraceSwitch("SwitchOne", "The first switch")
myTraceSwitch.Level - TraceLevel.Info
' This message box displays true, becuase setting the level to
' TraceLevel.Info sets all lower levels to true as well.
MessageBox.Show(myTraceSwitch.TraceWarning.ToString())
' This messagebox displays false.
MessageBox.Show(myTraceSwitch.TraceVerbose.ToString())
```

The TraceLevel enumeration is used to set the Level property of the TraceSwitch. Using this technique, you can use the `Main()` method and command parameters to indicate the detail of tracing that will take place, as is shown in the following code segment:

```
...
Public Shared Sub Main(ByVal Argh() As String)
    If Argh.Length > 0 Then
        Dim myTraceSwitch as New TraceSwitch("SwitchOne", "The first switch")
        Dim a as TraceLevel
        Select Case CType(Argh(0), Integer)
            Case 0
                a = TraceLevel.Off
            Case 1
                a = TraceLevel.Error
            Case 2
                a = TraceLevel.Warning
            Case 3
                a = TraceLevel.Info
            Case 4
                a = TraceLevel.Verbose
            Case Else
                a = TraceLevel.Off
        End Select
        myTraceSwitch.Level = a
    End If
End Sub
```

Let's look at an application that uses tracing to store trace information in the event log of the server.

exam
ⓦatch

Use the command-line parameters to configure tracing for components that are started with a command line. XML Web Services cannot use the command line but must use settings in the web.config file instead.

EXERCISE 7-2

Tracing

This exercise is based on an XML web service that uses the event log for tracing. For a refresher on XML Web Services, please see Chapter 5.

1. Start by creating an ASP .NET web service, using the localhost server. Name the service **TracerSample**, shown next.

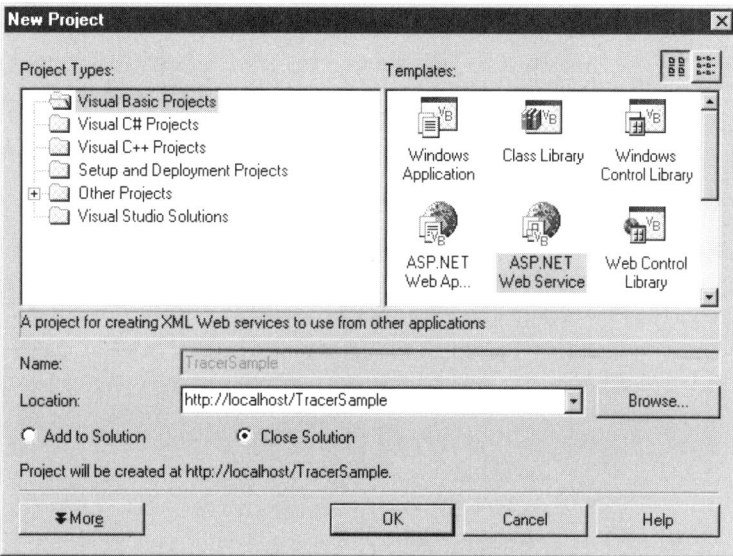

2. Once the project is created, you will need to provide some functionality. You will implement the temperature conversions you have seen many times already.

3. Create a WebMethod with the signature Public Function CtoF(c As Integer) As Integer to return a Celsius-to-Fahrenheit conversion ((c*9/5) + 32).

4. Create a WebMethod with the signature Public Function FtoC(f As Integer) As Integer to return a Fahrenheit-to-Celsius conversion ((f – 32)*5/9). These two methods are implemented as shown in the following code segment:

```
<WebMethod()> Public Function CtoF(ByVal c As Integer) As Integer
    Return ((c * 9 / 5) + 32)
End Function
<WebMethod()> Public Function FtoC(ByVal f As Integer) As Integer
    Return ((f - 32) * 5 / 9)
End Function
```

5. Save and test the XML web service to ensure the conversions are correct. The help page looks like this:

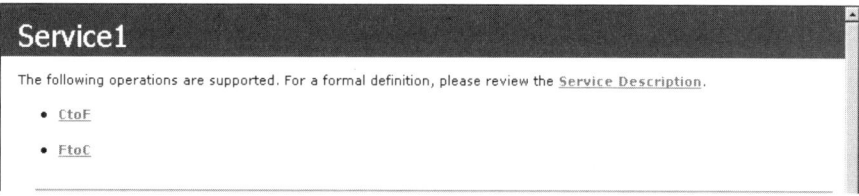

6. In order to add tracing, you will need to add code to the constructor of the web service. You will need to add code that creates an EventLogListener in the `New()` method as in the following code segment:

```
...
Dim myTraceListener As EventLogTraceListener
Public Sub New()
...

    'Add your own initialization code after the InitializeComponent() call
    ' Create a trace listener for the event log.
    If (Not System.Diagnostics.EventLog.SourceExists("ServiceOne")) Then
        EventLog.CreateEventSource("ServiceOne", "ServiceOneLog")
    End If
    myTraceListener = New EventLogTraceListener("ServiceOne")
    ' Add the event log trace listener to the collection
    Trace.Listeners.Add(myTraceListener)
End Sub
```

7. Add Trace output in the `CtoF()` and `FtoC()` methods to log the temperature that was converted, as is shown in the following code:

```
<WebMethod()> Public Function CtoF(ByVal c As Integer) As Integer
  Trace.WriteLine("CtoF: Converted " & c & "C to " & _
                  ((c * 9 / 5) + 32) & "F")
  Return ((c * 9 / 5) + 32)
End Function
<WebMethod()> Public Function FtoC(ByVal f As Integer) As Integer
  Trace.WriteLine("CtoF: Converted " & f & "F to " & _
                  ((f - 32) * 5 / 9) & "C")
  Return ((f - 32) * 5 / 9)
End Function
```

8. Save and execute the XML web service. Use the two conversion methods to convert some temperatures. I suggest that you try 30C (converts to 86F) and 32F (converts to 0C). If you receive an access error, you will need to change the security authorization for the TracerSample application to Integrated Windows Authentication; please see Chapter 8 for details.

9. Open the Event Viewer from Control Panel | Administrative Tools, open the ServiceOne Event Log, and locate the events for `CtoF()` and `FtoC()` respectively, as shown in the next two illustrations.

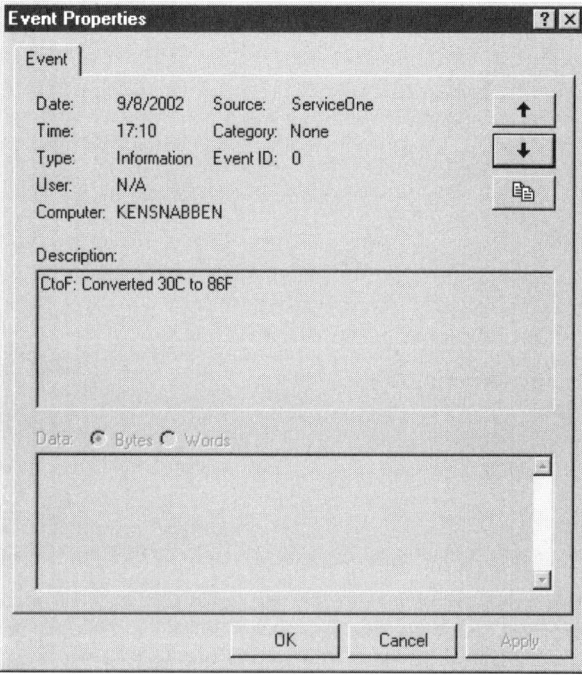

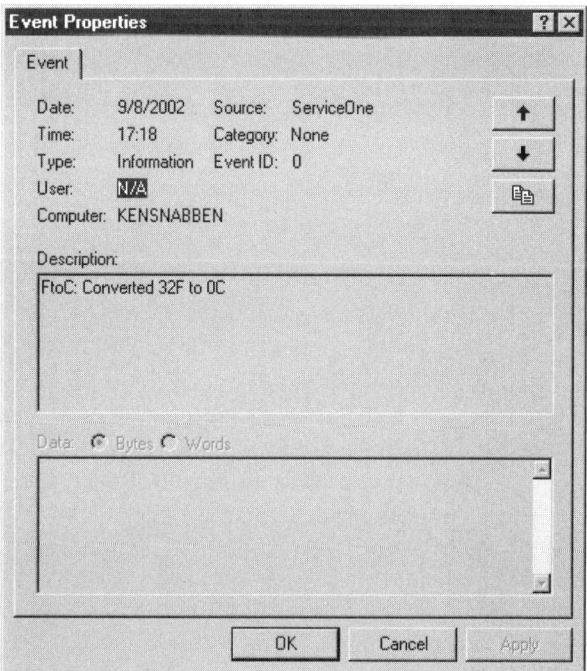

10. In order to turn off tracing, you should set the TraceSwitch to TraceLevel.Off in the constructor of the XML web service; to control it at run time, you would make an entry in the web.config application configuration file.

11. Open the web.config file for the project.

12. Add the following XML segment after the <configuration> element:

```
<configuration>
...
  <system.diagnostics>
    <switches>
      <add name="TraceSwitch" value="Off" />
    </switches>
  </system.diagnostics>
...
</configuration>
```

13. In the constructor for the XML web service, you need to create a TraceSwitch that uses the setting from the web.config file; the following code segment performs that task:

```
Public Class Service1
    Inherits System.Web.Services.WebService
    Dim myTraceListener As EventLogTraceListener
    Dim ts As TraceSwitch
...
    Public Sub New()
...
        If (Not System.Diagnostics.EventLog.SourceExists("ServiceOne")) Then
            EventLog.CreateEventSource("ServiceOne", "ServiceOneLog")
        End If

        ' Create a trace listener for the event log.
        myTraceListener = New EventLogTraceListener("ServiceOne")
        ' Add the event log trace listener to the collection.
        Trace.Listeners.Add(myTraceListener)
        ts = New TraceSwitch("TraceSwitch", "The TracerSample")
    End Sub
...
End Class
```

14. Modify the CtoF() and FtoC() methods to test the trace switch in the trace statements, using the Trace.WriteLineIf() method as shown in the following code segment:

```
<WebMethod()> Public Function CtoF(ByVal c As Integer) As Integer
  Trace.WriteLineIf(ts.TraceInfo, _
          "CtoF: Converted " & c & "C to " & ((c * 9 / 5) + 32) & "F")
  Return ((c * 9 / 5) + 32)
End Function
<WebMethod()> Public Function FtoC(ByVal f As Integer) As Integer
```

```
        Trace.WriteLine(ts.TraceInfo, _
              "FtoC: Converted " & f & "F to " & ((f - 32) * 5 / 9) & "C")
      Return ((f - 32) * 5 / 9)
    End Function
```

15. Save and execute the XML web service. Test it with a couple of conversions.

16. Review the event log to ensure no new events have been logged from the XML web service.

17. To test that you can turn on the tracing without recompiling the application, change the web.config file by updating the settings as in this code:

```
<configuration>
...
  <system.diagnostics>
    <switches>
      <add name="TraceSwitch" value="Info" />
    </switches>
  </system.diagnostics>
</configuration>
```

18. Execute the XML web application, and test the conversions.

19. Verify that there are new entries in the event log for the conversion.

This exercise has highlighted how to use tracing to get information from an application in production. The same operations are possible using the Debug class, with the one difference that the Debug class is not available in the Release build of the application, only in the Debug build.

exam

ⓦatch

*Use the **Trace.WriteIf** and **Trace.WriteLineIf** methods to produce selective trace output by setting **TraceSwitches**.*

*The **Debug** class is available only in Debug builds, while the **Trace** class is available in both Debug and Release builds.*

CERTIFICATION OBJECTIVE 7.04

Using the SOAP Extensions for Debugging

The .NET Framework includes ways and means for you to process raw SOAP messages either before they are deserialized into objects within the Framework or after they are serialized in preparation for sending on to the consumer. This

functionality, called the SOAP extensions, allows you to work with the data outside
of the SOAP environment.

In order to take advantage of the SOAP extensions, you need to derive
one class from System.Web.Services.Protocol.SoapExtension and one class from
System.Web.Services.Protocol.SoapExtensionAttribute. In order to understand how
you can get hold of the raw SOAP messages, you need to understand how the .NET
Framework routes SOAP messages. The Framework uses event stages to decide on
the routing: when a SOAP message comes in, the server determines which method
it will route to, then it checks to see if there are any extensions; if so, it invokes the
extensions with the event stage BeforeSerialize. When the extension returns, the
server deserializes the SOAP stream and invokes the methods with the
AfterDeserialize stage.

The best way to learn how to use the SOAP header extensions to debug an XML
web service application is to build an application that uses that technique.

EXERCISE 7-3

SOAP Headers

1. Create a new Visual Basic .NET project based on the ASP.NET Web Service
   template, naming the project **SOAPHeader**.

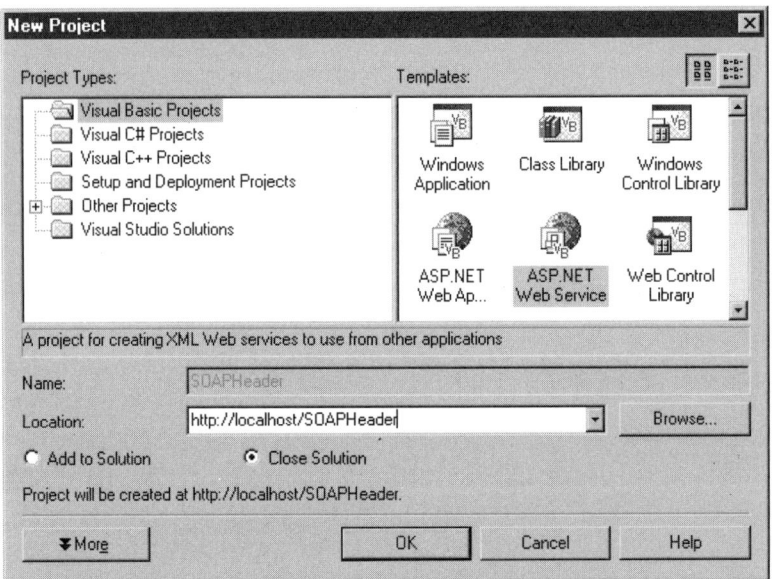

2. Add the following namespaces to the Service1.asmx.vb source file:

```
Imports System
Imports System.IO
Imports System.Text
Imports System.Web.Services
Imports System.Web.Services.Protocols
```

3. At the end of the code module, after the declaration of the Service1 class, you need to define a class that will be used as the data for this exercise. Call the class **Stuffer** and define it as follows:

```
Public Class Stuffer
    Public City As String
    Public Country As String
    Public Temperature As Integer
    Public WindSpeed As Integer
    Public WindDirection As String
End Class
```

4. Next you will need to implement the web method for this XML web service. Name it **GetStuff()** and implement it as follows. Note that the class SExt does not exist yet; it will be created to inherit from the SoapExtension class:

```
<WebMethod(), SExt()> Public Function GetStuff() As Stuff
    Dim s As Stuffer
    s = New Stuffer()
    s.City = "Mimico"
    s.Country = "Canada"
    s.Temperature = 31
    s.WindDirection = "SSW"
    s.WindSpeed = 8
    Return s
End Sub
```

The GetStuff() method only assigns values to the instance of the Stuff class and returns the instance to the caller; it is here only to perform the action of giving us some data.

5. The SExtAttr class will be implemented next. This class derives from SoapExtensionAttribute and overrides the ExtensionType() method. Implement the SExtAttr class as follows:

```
<AttributeUsage(AttributeTargets.Method)> Public Class SExtAttr
    Inherits SoapExtensionAttribute
    Public Overrides ReadOnly Property ExtensionType() As System.Type
        Get
            Return GetType(SExt)
```

```
        End Get
    End Property
End Class
```

The purpose of the `ExtensionType` property is to ensure the extension can be found.

6. Now comes the fun stuff. Define a class and name it **SExt**. It inherits from `SoapExtension`, as in the following code:

```
Public Class TraceExtension
    Inherits SoapExtension
...
End Class
```

7. Override the `ProcessMessage()` method in the `SExt` class as in the following code segment:

```
Public Overrides Sub ProcessMessage(ByVal message As
SoapMessage)
    Select Case message.Stage
        Case SoapMessageStage.AfterDeserialize
            'do nothing
        Case SoapMessageStage.AfterSerialize
            SendOutput(message)
        Case SoapMessageStage.BeforeDeserialize
            SendInput(message)
        Case SoapMessageStage.BeforeSerialize
            GetStream(message)
        Case Else
            Throw New Exception("invalid stage")
    End Select
End Sub
```

8. Override the `Initialize()` method with an empty body.

```
Public Overrides Sub Initialize(ByVal initializer As Object)

End Sub
```

9. Implement the `SendOutput()` method as in this code segment:

```
Public Sub SendOutput(ByVal message As SoapMessage)
        newStream.Seek(0, IO.SeekOrigin.Begin)

        Dim fs As New FileStream("C:\VB\Log.txt", _
                IO.FileMode.OpenOrCreate, IO.FileAccess.Write)
        Dim w As New StreamWriter(fs)
        w.BaseStream.Seek(0, IO.SeekOrigin.End)
```

```vbnet
            w.WriteLine("^^^^^")
            w.WriteLine("^^^^^     Response at {0}", DateTime.Now())
            w.WriteLine("^^^^^")

            Dim reader As TextReader = New StreamReader(newStream)
            Dim line As String

            line = reader.ReadLine()
            While Not line Is Nothing
                w.WriteLine(line)
                line = reader.ReadLine()
            End While

            w.Flush()
            w.Close()
            newstream.Seek(0, IO.SeekOrigin.Begin)
            Copy(newStream, oldStream)
        End Sub
```

10. Implement the `SendInput()` method as follows:

```vbnet
    Public Sub SendInput(ByVal message As SoapMessage)
        Dim m As New MemoryStream()
        Copy(message.Stream, CType(m, Stream))
        m.Seek(0, IO.SeekOrigin.Begin)
        Dim fs As New FileStream("C:\VB\Log.txt", _
                    IO.FileMode.OpenOrCreate, IO.FileAccess.Write)
        Dim w As New StreamWriter(fs)
        w.BaseStream.Seek(0, IO.SeekOrigin.End)

        w.WriteLine("^^^^^")
        w.WriteLine("^^^^^     Request at {0}", DateTime.Now())
        w.WriteLine("^^^^^")

        Dim reader As TextReader = New StreamReader(m)
        Dim line As String

        line = reader.ReadLine
        While Not line Is Nothing
            w.WriteLine(line)
            line = reader.ReadLine()
        End While

        w.Flush()
        w.Close()
        m.Seek(0, IO.SeekOrigin.Begin)
        message.Stream = m
    End Sub
```

11. Implement a utility function to copy information between two streams as in this code segment:

```
Private Sub Copy(ByRef sFrom As Stream, ByRef sTo As Stream)
    Dim reader As TextReader = New StreamReader(sFrom)
    Dim writer As TextWriter = New StreamWriter(sTo)
    Dim line As String
    line = reader.ReadLine
    While Not line Is Nothing
        writer.WriteLine(line)
        line = reader.ReadLine
    End While
    writer.Flush()
End Sub
```

12. Implement the `SetStream()` method to assign your stream.

```
Public Sub SetStream(ByRef message As SoapMessage)
    oldStream = message.Stream
    newStream = New MemoryStream()
    message.Stream = newStream
End Sub
```

13. Implement empty overrides for the `GetInitializer()` and `Initialize()` methods.

```
Public Overloads Overrides Function GetInitializer( _
    ByVal methodInfo As_
    System.Web.Services.Protocols.LogicalMethodInfo, _
    ByVal attribute As_
    System.Web.Services.Protocols.SoapExtensionAttribute) _
    As Object
    Return Nothing
End Function
Public Overrides Sub Initialize(ByVal initializer As Object)

End Sub
```

14. Save and build the XML Web Service.

15. Execute the service, invoke the web method, and note the information stored in the C:\VB\Log.txt file.

That concludes the exercise in the use of SOAP header extensions. Be sure to take a look at some common scenarios and solutions in the corresponding sidebar.

SCENARIO & SOLUTION

How do I find the test case for a unit?	The test case should be derived from the requirements of the project. The assumption in the exam is that all design and development is based on OOAD. The requirements document is then part of the project documentation.
How do I build an application that can be debugged while in production?	Use the `System.Diagnostics.Trace` class to enable tracing. The `Trace` class is available in the Release build.
What is needed in order to use the SOAP extensions?	You need to derive one class from `System.Web.Services.Protocols.SoapExtension` and one class from `System.Web.Services.Protocols.SoapExtentionAttributes`.
Why do I need to store test results?	Test results (as well as the tests themselves) will become very important when the application is changed during maintenance and you need to validate that the changes did not break the application.
How do I make use of trace switches?	Use trace switches to control the level of the tracing information that is provided through the output methods. You use the command-line parameters in the `Main()` method to set the trace switches when the application starts up, or in the case of applications that do not start from the command line, you use the web.config file to set the switch values.

CERTIFICATION SUMMARY

In this chapter, you have explored testing and debugging issues. From the point of the exam, unit testing is the most important form of testing. Remember that you want to test the smallest possible unit rather than risk having to try to find the location of any error between multiple units.

The evolution methodology maximizes test reuse and minimizes cost for testing in that the software units are tested and errors are found early in the development cycle when the costs of fixes are relatively low.

Debugging during development is achieved by using the Debug class and the methods available that will write debugging information to a file or the event log for further analysis. The same process can be used after the application has been deployed by using the Trace class and its methods. The Trace method calls can be included in the build of the application and then controlled by using the web.config application configuration file to change TraceSwitches that control what tracing, if any, takes place.

When working with components that use SOAP to communicate, you can use SOAP extensions to intercept the SOAP headers before they are encoded. This way, you can capture the raw SOAP information as it travels between the client and the server.

✓ TWO-MINUTE DRILL

Creating a Test Plan on the Evolutionary Model

❑ Ensure that test cases are based on the requirements of the project.

❑ Test the smallest possible software unit.

❑ Carefully design the test data to reflect the domain experts' input to the project.

Logging Test Results

❑ Store the test results with the project.

❑ Use a versioning system to store the results.

❑ Use Visual SourceSafe to store the test harness as well as the results.

Instrumenting and Debugging a Service

❑ The Debug class can be used only with Debug builds.

❑ The Trace class can be used with both Debug and Release builds.

❑ Control the output from the Trace class by using TraceSwitches.

❑ Trace listeners allow you to send the output to a text stream or the event log.

❑ Control the TraceSwitch setting by using command-line parameters or the web.config file.

Using the SOAP Extensions for Debugging

❑ The SOAP extensions have access to the raw SOAP header before encoding.

❑ In order to implement the SOAP extensions, you need two classes, one derived from System.Web.Services.Protocol.SoapExtension and the other from System.Web.Services.Protocol.SoapExtension Attributes.

SELF TEST

Using the SOAP Extensions for Debugging

I. You have found that you need to use the SOAP extensions to gain access to the SOAP messages before they have been deserialized. What namespaces must be imported? Select all that apply.

  A. `System.Web.Services.Protocol.SoapExtension`

  B. `System.Web.Services.Protocol.Soap.Extension`

  C. `System.Web.Services.Protocol.Soap.ExtensionAttribute`

  D. `System.Web.Services.Protocol.SoapExtensionAttribute`

Instrumenting and Debugging a Service

2. Trace switches can be set using which class?

  A. `System.Diagnostics.Trace`

  B. `System.Diagnostics.TraceSwitches`

  C. `System.Diagnostics.DefaultTraceListener`

  D. `System.Diagnostics.TraceSwitch`

3. What is the correct syntax for adding a trace listener to the `Listeners` collection?

  A. `Trace.Listeners.Add (new TextWriterTraceListener("myfile.txt"))`

  B. `TraceListeners.Add (new TextWriterTraceListener("myfile.txt"))`

  C. `Trace.Add (new TraceListener ("myfile.txt")`

  D. `Trace.Listener.Add (new TraceListener("myfile.txt")`

4. What code line correctly implements a trace switch (`ts`) to limit the output to error messages?

  A. `Trace.Write(ts.TraceError, "Error Message")`

  B. `Trace.WriteIf(ts.Error, "Error Message")`

  C. `Trace.WriteLineIf(ts.Error, "Error Message")`

  D. `Trace.WriteIf(ts.TraceError, "Error Message")`

5. You have designed an XML web service, and now you need to implement tracing. What method will you use to control the tracing?

  A. Implement the `Main()` method to take a command-line parameter that will be used to set a trace switch.

B. Implement the `Form_Load()` method to take a command-line parameter that will be used to set a trace switch.

C. Implement a `<TraceSwitch>` element in the web.config application configuration file.

D. Implement a `<switches>` element in the web.config applications configuration file.

Logging Test Results

6. You must log the test results from your current project. What else will you include with the test results? Select all that apply.

   A. Source code

   B. Use cases

   C. Test data

   D. The test program

Creating a Unit Test Plan on the Evolutionary Model

7. You are planning for the unit testing for the current project you are working on. What best describes what you will be testing?

   A. Base the tests on a random selection of approaches to ensure that all possible conditions that might break the unit are explored.

   B. Base the tests on the requirements identified in the project requirement document.

   C. Base the tests on the developer's notes for the unit to ensure that the developer has successfully followed the notes.

   D. Base the tests on standard tests as released for ISO 9001.

8. You have created an application that will be sending graphics and text to a printer. You have developed four classes that are aggregated. The classes are `Printer`, `GraphicsData`, `TextData`, and `Process`. The `Printer` is aggregated into the `Process` class, `GraphicsData` is aggregated into the `Printer` class, and the `TextData` class is aggregated into the `GraphicsData` class. What class will you perform unit testing on first?

   A. `Process`

   B. `Printer`

   C. `GraphicsData`

   D. `TextData`

9. You are reviewing the test harnesses for an application that is currently being changed. You must decide what to do with the test harnesses that perform the same test. What is the best strategy to deal with multiple similar test harnesses?

   A. Nothing—they were valid once and are still valid.

   B. Take all the test harnesses and combine them into one test harness. Implement a menu to select the individual test harness.

   C. Delete all but one of the test harnesses.

   D. Analyze the test harnesses. Select the one that best performs the test and delete the rest.

10. What model is unit testing based on?

   A. The waterfall model

   B. The common object model

   C. The ISO 9001 QA model

   D. The evolution model

SELF TEST ANSWERS

Using the SOAP Extensions for Debugging

1. ☑ A and D. The namespaces for the SOAP extensions are `System.Web.Services .Protocol.SoapExtension` and `System.Web.Services.Protocol .SoapExtensionAttribute`.
    ☒ B and C. Answers **B** and **C** are incorrect because there is no such namespaces.

Instrumenting and Debugging a Service

2. ☑ B. The trace switches are built from the `System.Trace.TraceSwitches` class.
    ☒ A, C, and D. Answer **A** is incorrect because that is the namespace for tracing, not the class for trace switches. Answer **C** and **D** are incorrect because the namespace is incorrect.

3. ☑ A. The `Trace` class has a collection of `Listeners`; you use the `Add()` method to add a listener to the collection.
    ☒ B, C, and D. **B** is incorrect; the `TraceListener` does not have an `Add()` method. **C** is incorrect because the listener must be added to the collection, not to the `Trace` class. **D** is incorrect because the collection is misspelled.

4. ☑ D. Use the `WriteIf()` or the `WriteLineIf()` methods to limit the output; the trace switch property that will be true when set to Error is `TraceError`.
    ☒ A, B, and C. **A** is incorrect because the `Trace.Write()` method does not take a parameter to determine the output. Answers **B** and **C** are incorrect, since the trace switch parameter is wrong.

5. ☑ Answer D. The configuration of trace switches for an XML web service is set in the `<switches>` element in the web.config configuration file.
    ☒ A, B, and C. Answer **A** is incorrect because XML web services do not start from the command line and do not have a `Main()` method. Answer **B** is incorrect because XML web services do not have `Form_Load()` methods and cannot be started from the command line. **C** is also incorrect because there is no `<TraceSwitch>` element defined for the web.config configuration file.

Logging Test Results

6. ☑ A, C, and D. You want to include all the information that is relevant to the test as it was executed, including the source code, the test data, the test harness, and the results from the test.
    ☒ B. **B** is incorrect because the use cases are not part of the test environment; they are part of the OOAD analysis.

Creating a Unit Test Plan on the Evolutionary Model

7. ☑ **B.** The tests should be based on the project's requirements to ensure that the unit performs the task envisioned when the project was designed.

☒ **A, C,** and **D.** Answer **A** is incorrect because the purpose of the test is not to make efforts at random to break the unit. Answer **C** is incorrect because the test is designed to ensure that the developer correctly implemented the design, not his own understanding of the design. Answer **D** is incorrect because the ISO does not have any knowledge of the project you are working on, and the tests must be based on the project.

8. ☑ **D.** You always start by testing the lowest class.

☒ **A, B,** and **C.** These classes contain other classes, so they are not suitable as the first class to test.

9. ☑ **D.** The number of duplicated or redundant test harnesses will grow through the development cycle of the project. When given a chance, you should analyze the harnesses and keep the best fit; the rest should be removed from the project.

☒ **A, B,** and **C.** Answer **A** is incorrect because the test harnesses evolve with the application, so the oldest ones are probably not valid anymore. Answer **B** is also incorrect. This is just another way of doing nothing in a very lengthy way. Answer **C** is also incorrect. This random selection will not meet the QA requirements of the test.

10. ☑ **D.** Unit testing is based on the evolution model, which is the basis of OOAD.

☒ **A, B,** and **C.** Answer **A** is incorrect because this is the legacy model that fails to provide for unit testing. Answer **B** is also incorrect because it is the basis for the distributed component model. Answer **C** is also incorrect; the ISO is not the model for the unit test.

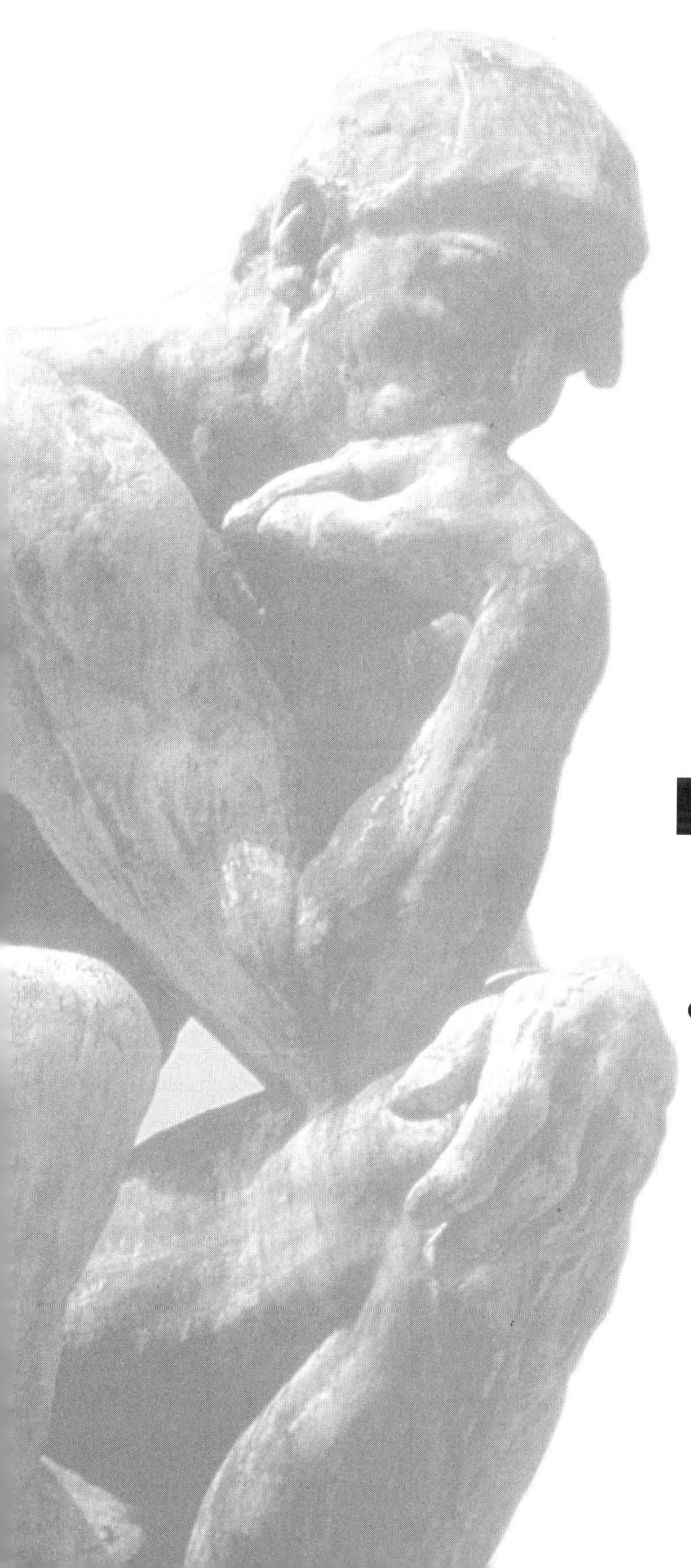

MCAD/MCSD

MICROSOFT® CERTIFIED APPLICATION DEVELOPER & MICROSOFT® CERTIFIED SOLUTION DEVELOPER

8

Security and Unmanaged Code

CERTIFICATION OBJECTIVES

8.01 Implement Security

8.02 Access Unmanaged Code

✓ Two-Minute Drill

Q&A Self Test

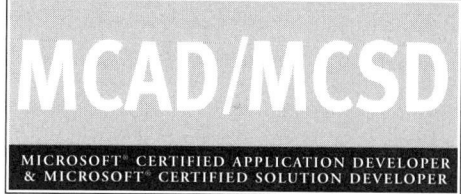

I n this chapter, you will learn about two topics: security for the Windows services, .NET Remoting objects, and XML Web Services and how to access legacy COM+ components.

The security implementation will cover how to configure and use the different security mechanisms available through the .NET Framework, and how to integrate the Windows authentication systems as well as the authorization needed to access resources.

A large number of existing COM and COM+ applications are in use today—it will take a long time to move beyond the use of them in all but total rewrite situations. You will look at how to make use of these components from a Visual Basic .NET application.

Implementing Security

You need to consider security for XML web services just as you do for any other software product on a network. As with other software products, there are three aspects of security that you must consider: authentication, authorization, and secure communication.

Authentication

Authentication is the process of verifying that the client is truly who he or she claims to be—this is done by collecting credentials (name and password) from the user. The credentials are validated against an authority like a database—if the credentials are valid, the client is an authenticated identity.

The authorization configuration is performed on IIS because IIS is the service that the consumer will interact with to get access to an XML web service. Internet Information Services (IIS) offers three security mechanisms:

- **Basic authentication**   The basic authentication method is a widely used standard method for collecting name and password information from the consumer. This method is part of the HTTP specification and is a standard that is widely supported by browsers. It transmits the security credentials in clear text, resulting in a possible security breach unless the transmission channel is encrypted using Secure Sockets Layer (SSL).

■ **Digest authentication** The W3C has introduced digest authentication as a replacement for the basic authentication method. In digest authentication, a binary hash is built from the name, password, requested resource, HTTP method, and some random values generated from the server.

To generate a hash, the browser applies an algorithm that is considered one-way, meaning that there is no known way of getting back to the clear text from the binary hash. This hash is then sent to the IIS server, which verifies that the hash is the same as it received when performing the same hash calculation on the user information as stored in the active directory.

Digest authentication is supported starting in HTTP 1.1.

■ **Integrated Windows authentication** This authentication is based on the consumer having a Windows account that can be used for authentication. The strength of integrated Windows authentication is that the username and password are not sent across the network. Rather, a hash of the credentials is used. In addition, the method can make use of the Kerberos V5 protocol to take advantage of the secret-key cryptography provided in Active Directory and Kerberos V5. The biggest problem with integrated Windows authentication is that the server and the client must have network communication over TCP/IP ports for the authentication—these ports are normally never left open on any devices that are used on the Internet because of the risk of intrusion into the system from Internet hackers.

You can also use custom SOAP headers, to add your own authentication mechanism instead of using the built-in solutions. An XML web service consumer can add credentials to the SOAP header that are then retrieved by the XML web service, which can use the credentials to authenticate the consumer. For a refresher on SOAP, see Appendix D.

IIS Authentication

In order to configure authentication for an XML web service, you need to configure IIS through the Internet Services Manager. To start the Internet Services Manager, select Start | Settings | Control Panel | Administrative Tools | Internet Services Manager. The program is shown in the following illustration.

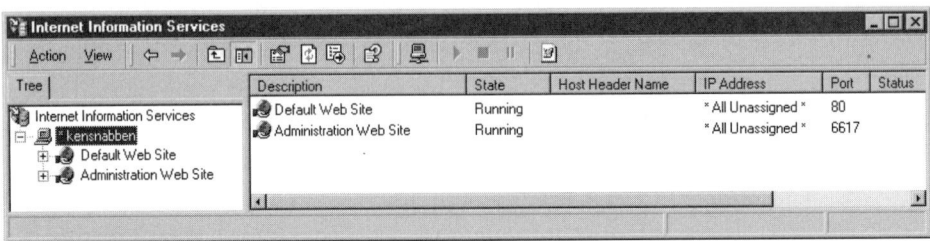

e x a m
ⓦ a t c h

Remember that the authentication method for Windows authentication is set in IIS.

In the Tree view, expand first the server and then the Default Web Site; you will see several entries, as shown in Figure 8-1.

Select the web site you want to configure, right-click it, and select Properties. This will open the Default Web Site Properties dialog box. Click the Directory Security tab as shown in Figure 8-2.

Security settings are configured under the Anonymous Access And Authorization Control section. Click Edit to open the Authentication Methods dialog box shown in the following illustration.

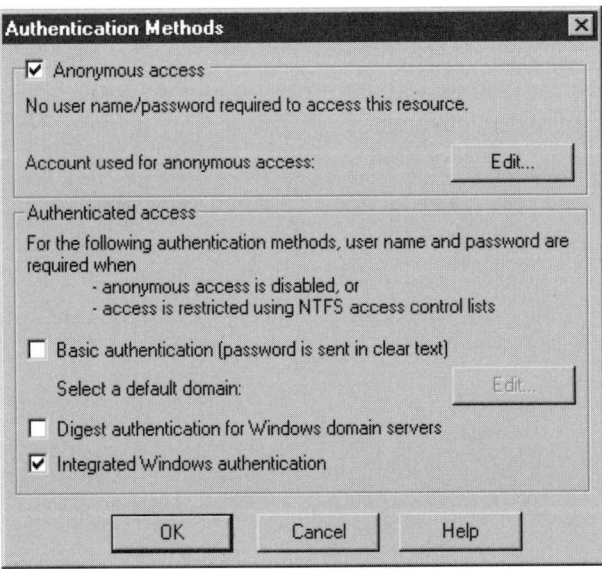

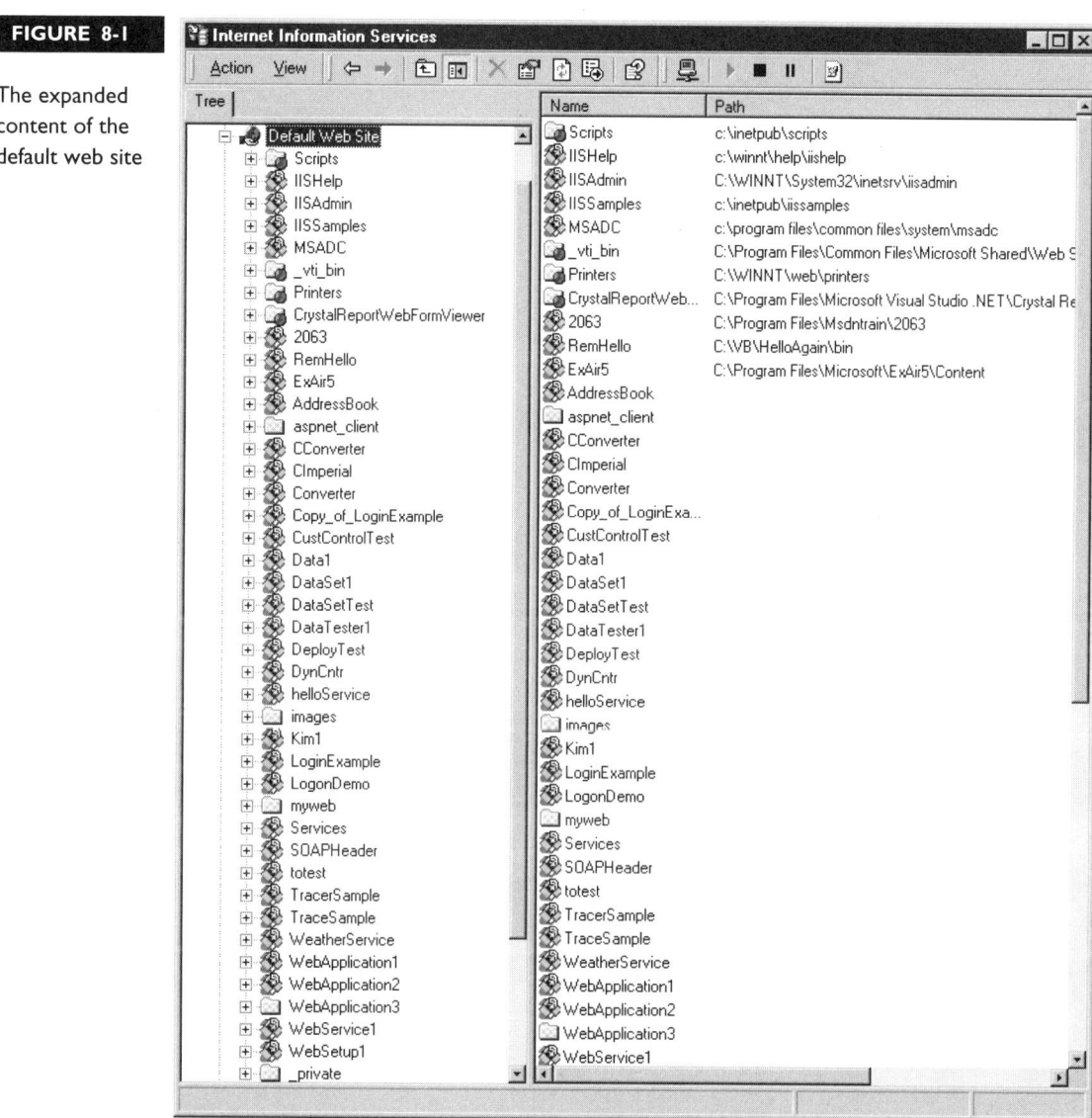

FIGURE 8-1

The expanded content of the default web site

You can configure authentication in this dialog box. The default setting is that anonymous access is permitted. You can change the anonymous authentication configuration with the proxy account in the Anonymous User Account dialog box,

FIGURE 8-2

The Properties
dialog box

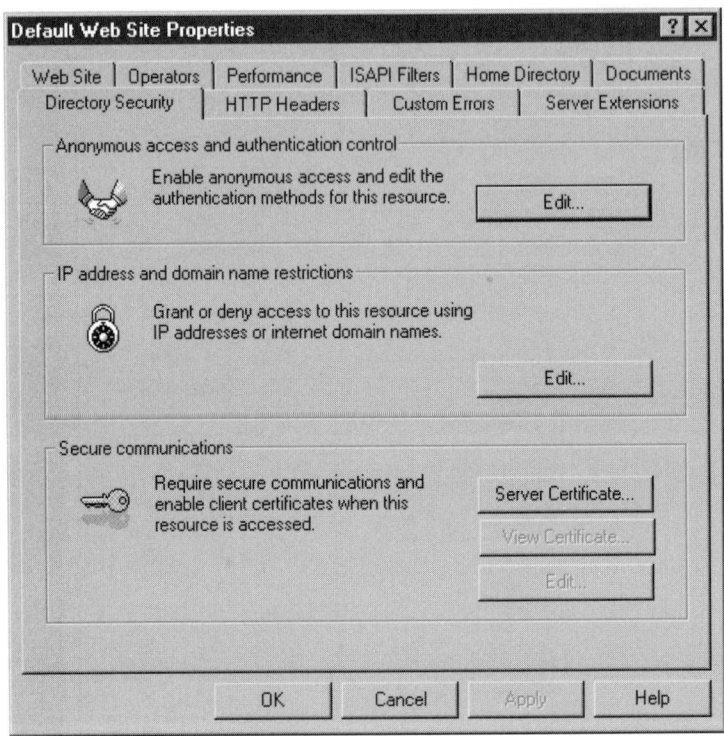

brought up when you click Edit in the Anonymous Access section. The proxy
account must be given the most restrictive access to the site possible.

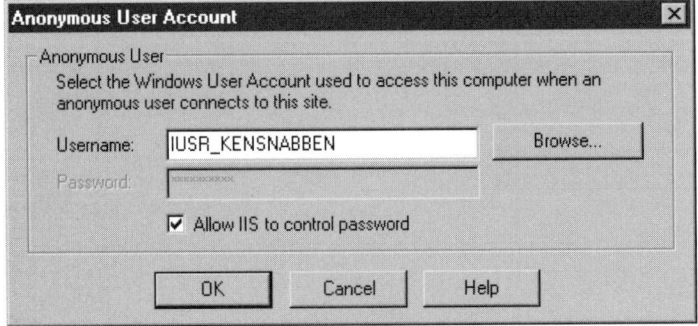

If you configure Basic Authentication in the Authentication Methods dialog box,
you must make sure that the accounts that will access the XML web service are
given permission to log on to the web server that is hosting the XML web service.

If you configure Digest Authentication For Windows Domain Servers, the domain controls must have a reversible encrypted (clear-text) copy of the account's password to be used when comparing against the hash the consumer sends in. You will be requested to agree to the clear-text passwords when you select digest authentication.

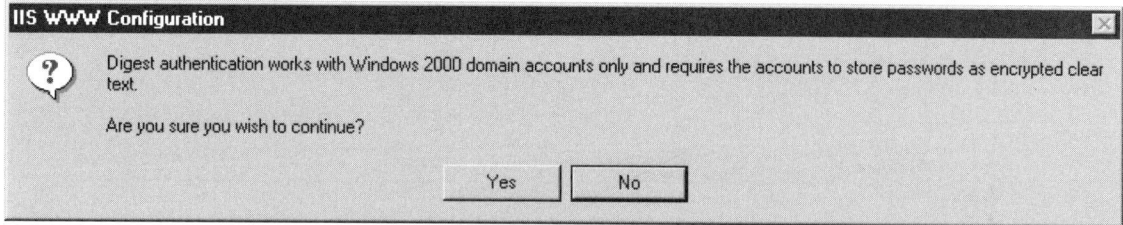

If you configure integrated Windows authentication, the user will not be prompted for credentials unless the integrated Windows authentication fails.

exam
Watch

Integrated Windows authentication cannot pass a firewall unless the administrator opens additional ports. It is highly unlikely that the administrator will do so because of the security risk involved.

Once the IIS configuration is complete, the XML web service must be configured to use the required authentication. This is done by editing the Web.config file that is located in the root directory for the XML web service. This file is also called the application configuration file. To enable the Windows-based authentication method (basic, digest, or integrated Windows) that was configured with IIS, add the following to the Web.config file:

```
<configure>
   <system.web>
      <authentication mode = "Windows" />
   </system.web>
</configure>
```

To access the user credentials programmatically, you can use the Context object as in this demo web method from Visual Studio .NET:

```
<WebMethod()> _
Public Function HelloWorld() As String
   return "Hello World " + Context.User.Identity.Name
End Function
```

The result of this web method is shown here:

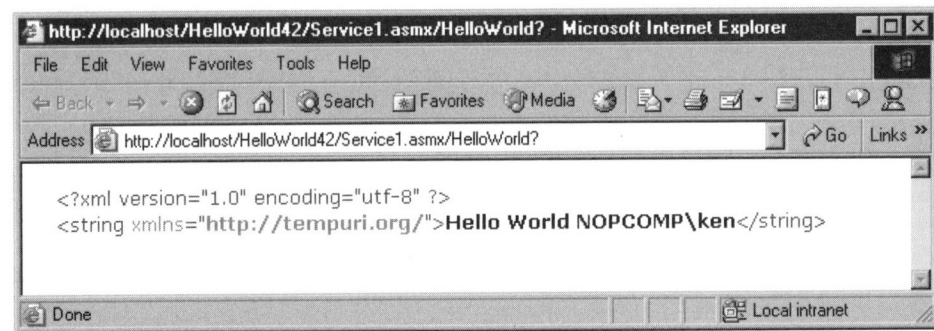

When you consume an XML web service by using the wsdl tool or by adding a web reference in Visual Studio .NET, the proxy class will inherit from the SoapHttpClientProtocol class. Through this class, you have access to the Credentials property that is used to read or set security credentials. In order to control the authentication process, you can use the NetworkCredential class as shown in the following code segment:

```
' instantiate the XML Web Service proxy
Dim ws As WService = New WService()
' get a NetworkCredential object
Dim cred As ICredentials
cred = New NetworkCredential("Ken", "password", "nop.com")
' configure the client credentials
ws.Credentials = cred
Dim s As String
Try
    s = ws.HelloWorld()
Catch
    Console.WriteLine("Authentication Failed!")
End Try
```

exam
Watch

*Use the **NetworkCredential** class to pass the authentication when calling an XML web service.*

EXERCISE 8-1

Using Network Credentials

In this exercise, you will build an XML web service and configure the authentication for it. You will also learn about how to create authentication accounts for the local server.

The second part of this exercise deals with the consumer of the web service, and how to use the `NetworkCredential` class to send authentication information to an XML Web Service.

1. Create a new Visual Basic .NET project based on the ASP.NET Web Service template. Name the project **HelloSecure**.

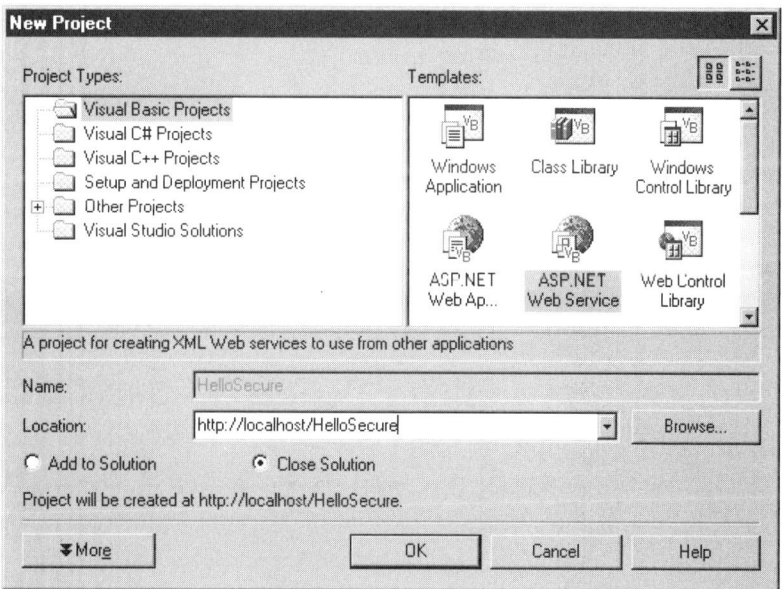

2. Open the code module and change the namespace of the web service from http://temuri.org to **http://secure.ws**.

3. Change the name of the class to **SHello**.

```
<WebService(Namespace:="http://secure.ws/")> _
Public Class SHello
    Inherits System.Web.Services.WebService
...
End Class
```

4. Implement a web method named `HelloWorld()` that returns a string.

```
<WebMethod()> Public Function HelloWorld() As String
...
End Function
```

5. In the return statement for the `HelloWorld()` web method, you need to append the name of the user that was authenticated to use the web method. The `Context.User.Identity.Name` property will give you that information.

```
<WebMethod()> Public Function HelloWorld() As String
    Return "Hello World " + Context.User.Identity.Name
End Function
```

6. Save and build the Web Service.

7. To test the web service, run the XML Web Service help application by pressing F5. The result of running the `HelloWorld()` web method should look like this:

Notice that the user identity is blank. That is because the web service at this moment is configured to use anonymous authentication. The next step is to change that to Windows integrated authentication, and the next few steps show how you do that.

8. Open the Internet Services Manager console from Control Panel | Administrative Tools.

9. Expand the `localhost` server.

10. Expand the Default Web Site.

11. Select the HelloSecure web site.

12. Right-click the HelloSecure web site, and select Properties from the context menu. This will open the HelloSecurity Properties dialog.

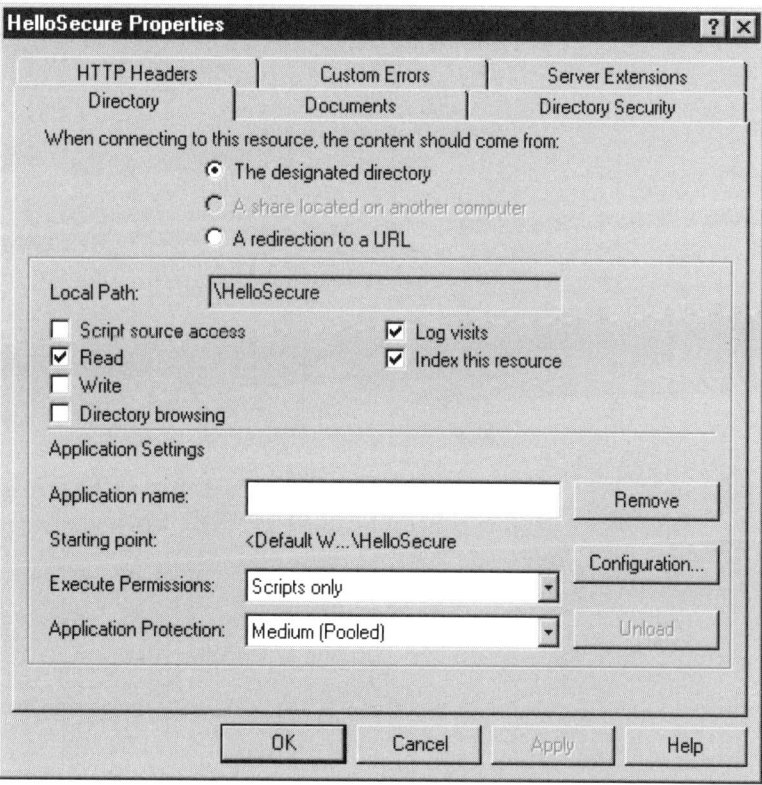

13. Select the Directory Security tab in the dialog.

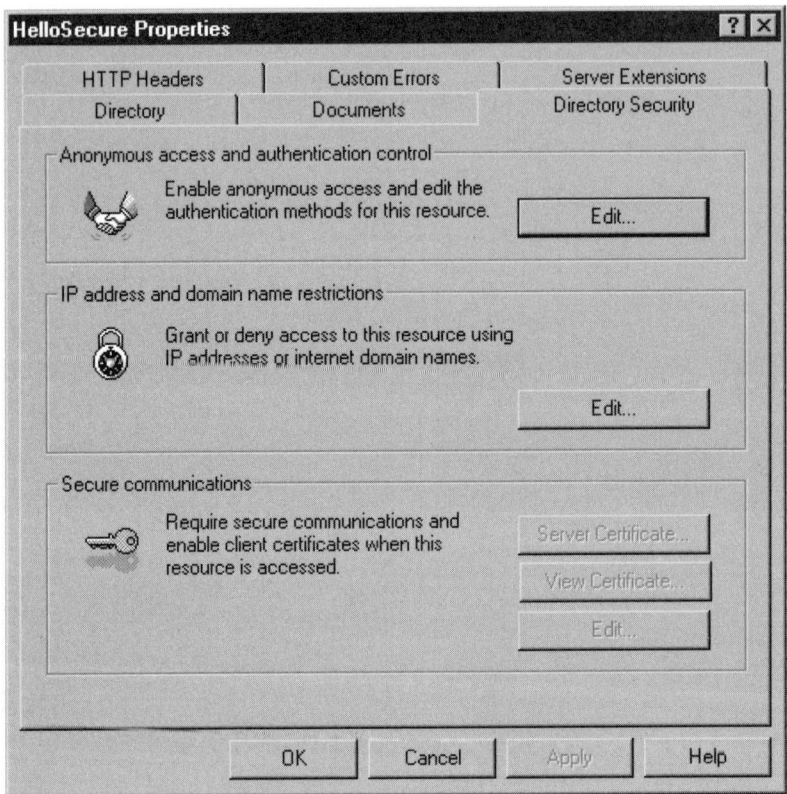

14. Click Edit in the Anonymous Access And Authentication Control section. This will open the Authentication Method dialog.

15. Clear the check box next to Anonymous access.

16. Make sure that the check box next to Integrated Windows Authentication is checked as shown here:

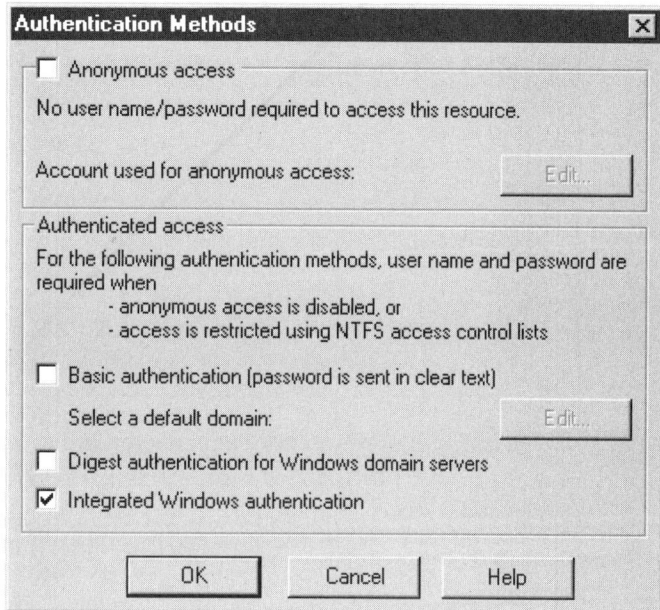

17. Click OK to close the Authentication Method dialog.

18. Click OK to close the HelloSecure Properties dialog.

19. Close the Internet Services Management console. To test that the security settings are in effect, you need to run the HelloSecure web service again.

20. Switch to the HelloSecure project. If you closed Visual Studio .NET earlier, you will need to start it first.

21. Execute the HelloSecure web service by pressing F5.

22. Invoke the `HelloWorld()` web method. The result should be similar to this image, apart from the username:

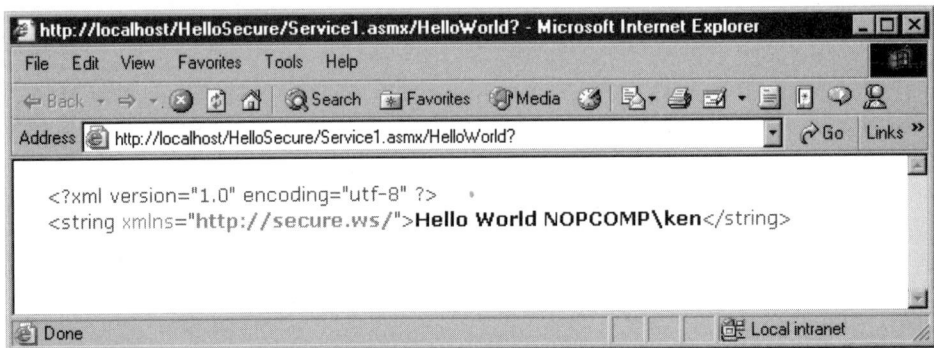

The addition of the security information indicates in this case that user ken from the NOPCOMP domain is the one that is currently authenticated to the web service.

The next step is to build a client that allows the user to select the login information needed—you will build a login form that uses the `HelloSecure` web service.

EXERCISE 8-2

Building a Security Client

For this exercise, you will build a Windows Form that will ask the user for login credentials. You will call the HelloSecure web service and use the return information to determine if the credentials you authenticated were valid.

1. Create a new Visual Basic .NET project based on the Windows Application template. Name the project HelloTest.

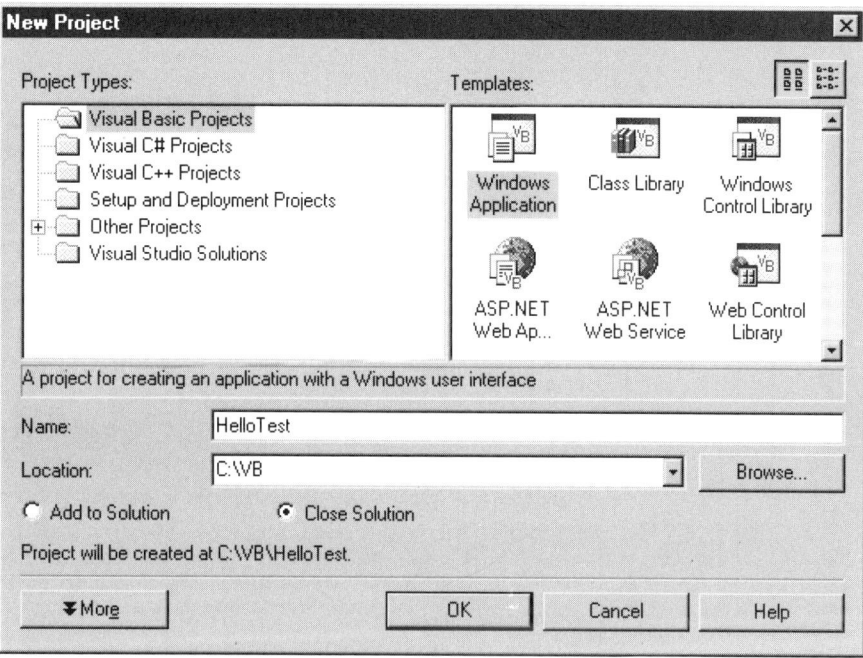

2. When the project is built, add two TextBox controls to the form. Change the name of the first to **txtUserName** and the second to **txtPassword**.

3. Position the `txtUserName` control and `txtPassWord` controls centered in the form.

4. Change the `PasswordCharacter` property of `txtPassword` to *.

5. Position a Button control directly under the `txtPassword` control.

6. Rename the Button control to **btnHello**.

7. Change the `Text` property of the `btnHello` control to `"Click Me!"`.

8. Position a Label control directly under `btnHello`; size the Label control to span the form.

9. Change the `TextAlign` property to `MiddleCenter`.

10. Clear the `Text` property of the Label control.

11. Change the name of the Label control to **lblHello**. The resulting form should look like this:

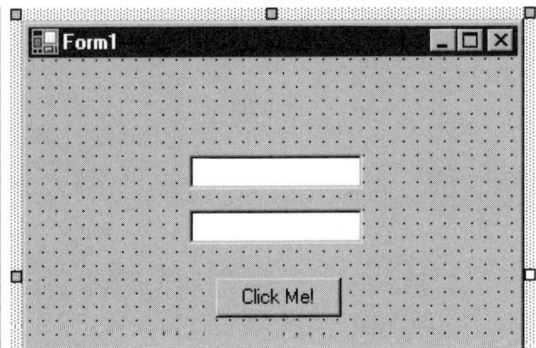

In order to be able to use the XML web service, you will need to add a web reference to the web service. Steps 12–16 show how you do that.

12. Select Add Web Reference from the Project menu to open the Add Web Reference dialog.

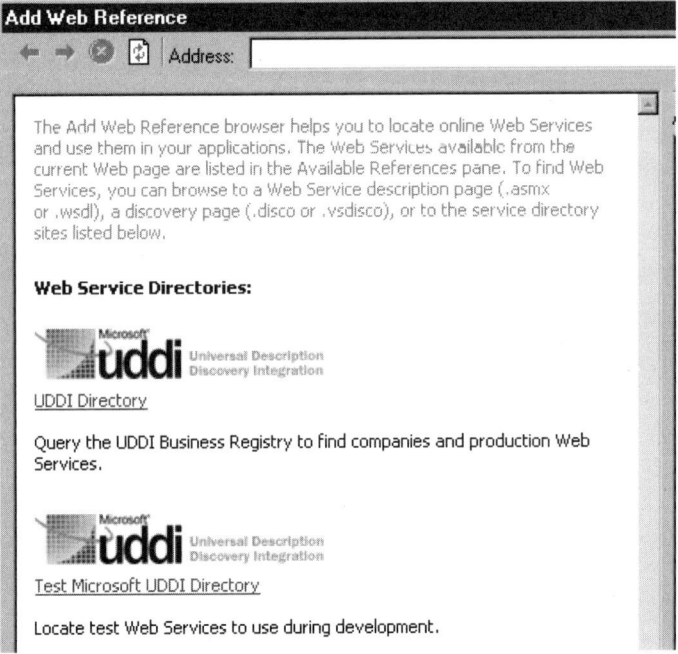

13. In the Address field, enter the URL of the HelloSecure XML web service you built in Exercise 8-1 (http://localhost/HelloSecure/Service1.asmx).

14. Press the ENTER key, or click the Enter button. The result is that the web service is shown in the Add Web Reference dialog.

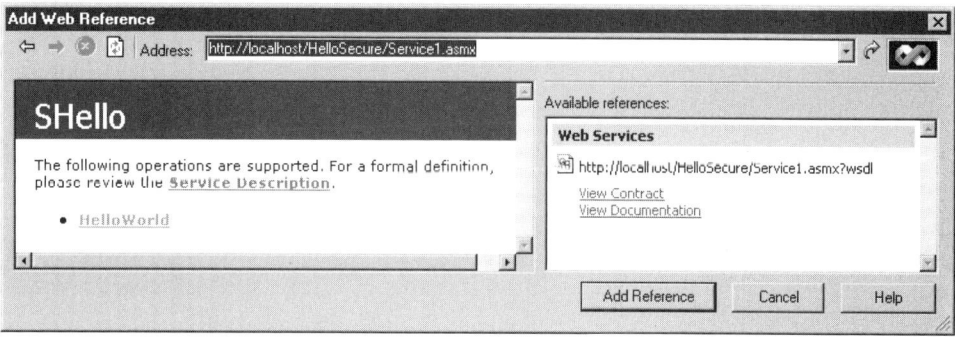

15. Click Add Reference to complete the action.

16. Expand the Web Reference tree in the Solution Explorer to ensure that the web service has been added.

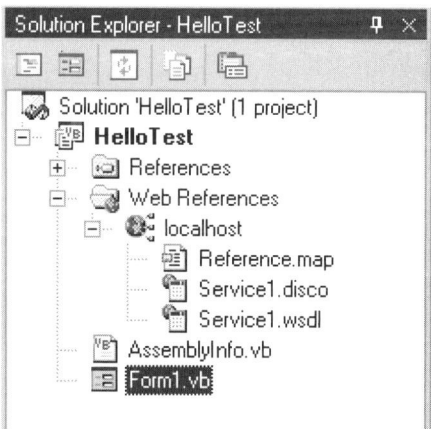

17. Open the code editor and add an import statement in the first line for System.Net to give access to the security classes.

```
Imports System.Net
```

18. Add an event handler for the `btnHello` control's click event.

19. In the click event handler, you will need to declare a variable (ws) that will be a reference to the web service and instantiate that service.

```
' instantiate the XML Web Service proxy
Dim ws As localhost.SHello
ws = New localhost.SHello()
```

20. Declare a variable to represent the security credentials (cred); it should be of type ICredentials. Instantiate the object as belonging to the NetworkCredential class. Pass two string parameters to the constructor; they should be the Text properties from the txtUsername and txtPassword controls.

```
' get a NetworkCredential object
Dim cred As ICredentials
cred = New NetworkCredential(txtUserName.Text, txtPassword.Text)
```

21. Assign the credentials to the web services Credentials property.

```
' configure the client credentials
ws.Credentials = cred
```

At this point, you have instantiated the web service and built network credentials that will be used when you execute the web service. The next step is to call the web method of the web service to see if it all works. The call to any web methods must be in Try...Catch blocks to ensure that you handle authentication exceptions.

22. Declare a variable for a String.

23. Declare a Try block, call the web method, and assign the return data to the string variable.

24. In the Catch block, assign the string literal "Authentication Failure, try again" to the String variable.

25. After the End Try statement, assign the string variable to the Text property of the lblHello control. The following code listing is the complete click event handler for the btnHello control:

```
Private Sub btnHello_Click(ByVal sender As System.Object, _
                    ByVal e As System.EventArgs) _
                    Handles btnHello.Click
```

```
' instantiate the XML Web Service proxy
Dim ws As localhost.SHello
ws = New localhost.SHello()
' get a NetworkCredential object
Dim cred As ICredentials
cred = New NetworkCredential(txtUserName.Text, txtPassword.Text)
' configure the client credentials
ws.Credentials = cred
Dim s As String
Try
    s = ws.HelloWorld()
Catch
    s = "Authentication Failure, try again"
End Try
lblHello.Text = s
End Sub
```

26. Save and execute the application. Enter a random username and password, click the button, and you should get the authentication error message shown next:

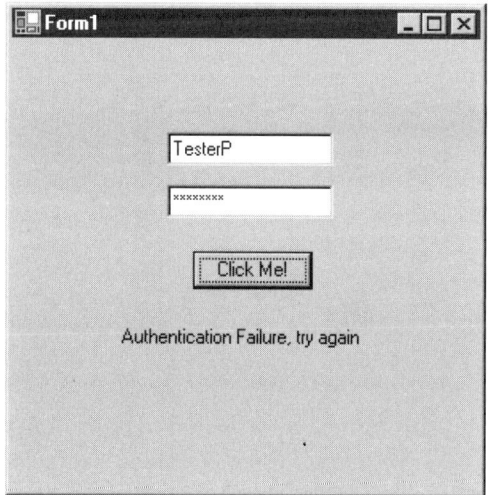

Before you can test the authentication, you will need to create some accounts that you can test against.

EXERCISE 8-3

Adding Accounts to the Server

In this exercise, you will create a number of security accounts for your server so that you can test the client for the HelloSecure web service. Note that computer and account names will vary because the servers will have different names. For an in-depth discussion on how to create accounts in different environments, please see Appendix E.

1. Open the Computer Management console from Control Panel | Administrative Tools.

2. Expand the System Tools.

3. Expand Local Users and Groups.

4. Click Users.

5. Review the users defined for your computer.

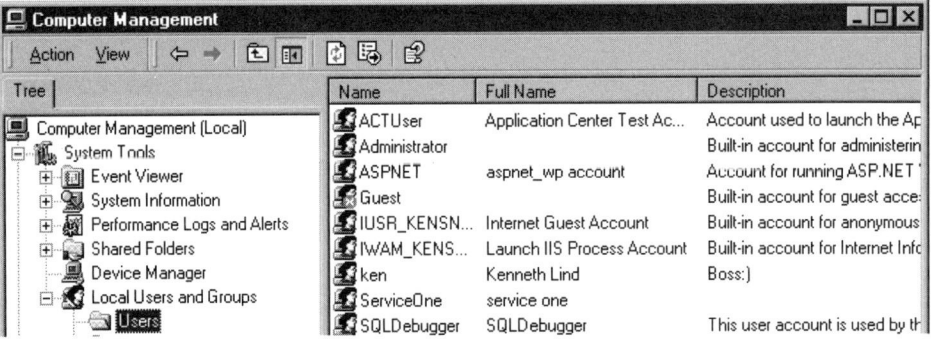

6. Right-click the Users folder; select New User from the context menu.

7. Fill in the information to create a new user account. The only mandatory piece of information needed is the login name; it must be unique within the server. The next image shows the New User dialog filled in.

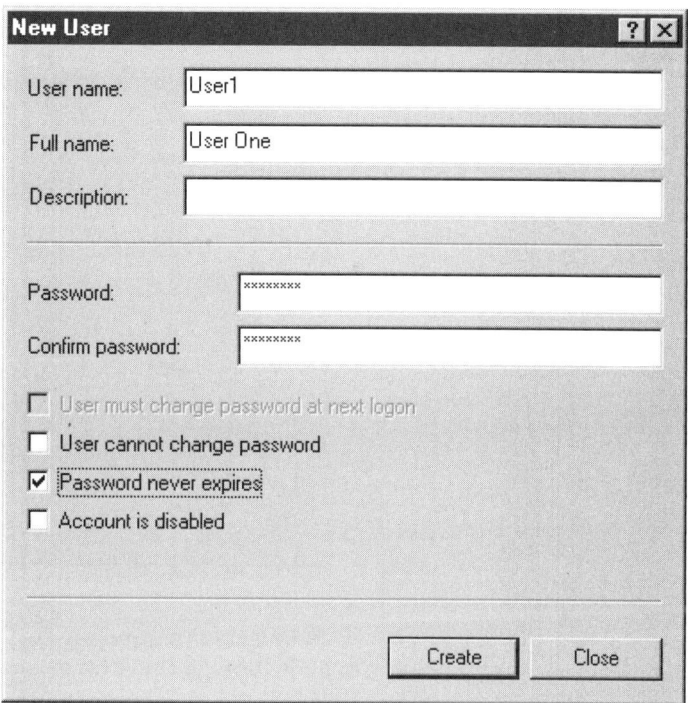

The password should be entered at this time, and as you will never log in to Windows with this account, you must clear the check box beside User Must Change Password At Next Logon.

8. Click Create, and the user account has been created.

9. Create the following user accounts: User1, User2, and User3. Set the password to be **password**.

10. Close the Computer Management console.

11. Open the HelloTest project in Visual Studio .NET.

12. Run the program.

13. Use the username User1 and password. The result is shown here:

The application you built through the three preceding exercises provides a good skeleton on which to build other secured applications.

The Windows authentication methods work well in intranets, but because of the additional ports that need to be opened to communicate through a firewall, these methods are not recommended for use on the Internet. The next section will deal with SOAP headers and how to customize them for authentication.

Custom SOAP Headers

For authenticating users on the Internet, you will most likely want to use a database that stores the account information of authorized users—there will potentially be too many users that need to be authenticated and that do not need to be maintained using an internal solution (Active Directory). Your authentication implementation then passes these credentials from the user to the XML web service so that the service can authenticate the user.

The SOAP header is a convenient area where additional information can be passed between the consumer and the server. When you want to pass usernames and passwords in the SOAP header, you need to be concerned about the security of the information, and the best solution is to use strong encryption on the header only.

To customize the SOAP headers, you need to derive a class from `SoapHeader` as in the following code segment:

```
Imports System.Web.Services
Imports System.Web.Services.Protocols
Public Class AuthenticationHeader
        Inherits SoapHeader
    ' declare storage for username and password
    Public username As String
    Public password As String
End Class
' declare the XML Web Service
Public Class HelloService
        Inherits WebService
    ' declare a reference to the header
    public AuthenticationHeader m_header;
    <WebMethod()> _
    <SoapHeader("m_header", Required=false)> _
    Public Function HelloWorld() As String
        ' do something interesting
        Return "Hello World"
    End Function
End Class
```

Because you are implementing a custom authentication method, you need to turn off the authentication in the XML web service's Web.config file, as shown in the following code segment. Otherwise, the settings in the Web.config file would override the custom authentication:

```
<configuration>
    <system.web>
        <authentication mode = "None" />
    </system.web>
</configuration>
```

Authentication ensures that you know the identity of the entity that is accessing the service. The other side of the coin is *authorization*—ensuring that the entity has been granted the right to perform the actions requested. Authorization is your next topic.

FROM THE CLASSROOM

One of the vexing issues with Windows native authentication is that it is based on protocols that require the use of additional TCP/IP ports. Depending on the client and whether Active Directory is installed, these ports might be the ones used by NTLM authentication or Kerberos V5 authentication.

The biggest problem using Windows authentication is on the Internet where the additional ports must be made available through any firewalls. The existence of ports that are used solely for authentication is an invitation to would-be hackers. This is why there is a global rule that Windows authentication never is used on the Internet.

Any of the authentication modes that transmit their traffic via HTTP (port 80) are considered when needing authentication on the Internet. You must always remember that some of these authentication modes send the credentials in clear text, whereas others use SSL or digest authentication to encrypt the transmission of the credentials.

Authorization

The Three Amigos in the authorization game are ASP.NET, the .NET Framework, and the Windows operating system. These three provide many techniques that combine to build a secure environment. When an XML web service consumer wants to access a resource, the effective permissions for that resource are the combination of the authenticated consumer's Windows permissions, the assembly's declarative access security, and the role-based security for the XML web service. These are the key factors to remember about this combination:

- The Windows operating system's security is based on the ability of the administrator to control access to resources. All resources in the Windows operating system have Discretionary Access Control Lists (DACLs) associated with them. Only administrators can modify these DACLs to control the access for the users (consumers).

- Code-access security, or the assembly's declarative access security, is the programmatic method for ensuring that a user is authenticated before giving access to resources or running specific code.

■ Role-based security groups users into roles that give identical access to users with similar needs. When a user is added to a role, it is not the user's credentials that are used but the role's. Using role-based security makes the administration of security easier.

Authorization can also be controlled as part of the XML Web Services URI namespace by modifying the <authorization> section of the Web.config file that is located in the root of the application. The statements in the <authorization> section take this form:

```
<[allow|deny] [users] [roles] [verbs] />
```

The following example highlights the use of this element:

```
<configuration>
   <system.web>
     <authorization>
         <allow users="MIMICO\Dan"/>
         <deny users="MIMICO\Des"/>
         <deny users="?"/>
         <allow roles="service"/>
     </authorization>
   </system.web>
</configuration>
```

The users="?" part in the preceding code matches the anonymous user that is the default web user.

EXERCISE 8-4

Authorization

In this exercise, you will continue to work with the HelloSecure and HelloTest projects you created in Exercises 8-1 and 8-2. You will explore authorization and the use of web.config to allow and deny access.

1. Open the HelloSecure project from Exercise 8-1 in Visual Studio .NET.

2. Open the web.config configuration file.

3. Edit the <authorization> element to look as follows:
```
<authorization>
    <allow users="User1, User2" /> <!-- Allow all users -->
```

```
    <deny users="User3" />
        <!-- <allow    users="[comma separated list of users]"
                        roles="[comma separated list of roles]"/>
            <deny       users="[comma separated list of users]"
                        roles="[comma separated list of roles]"/>
        -->
    </authorization>
```

The users that log in using User1 or User2 as their login names are allowed, while User3 is denied access to the web service.

4. Save the web.config file. This file is not compiled, so you do not need to make any further changes to the XML Web Service.

5. Open the HelloTest project from Exercise 8-2 in Visual Studio .NET.

6. Run the application.

7. Use the login for User1 (the password is "password"). This image shows the outcome:

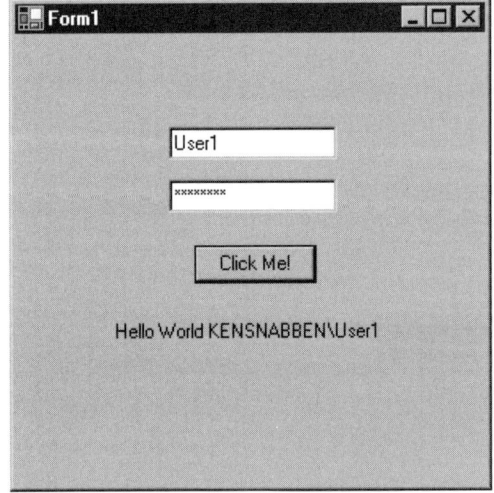

8. Use the login for User3 and click Click Me!. The result is shown next:

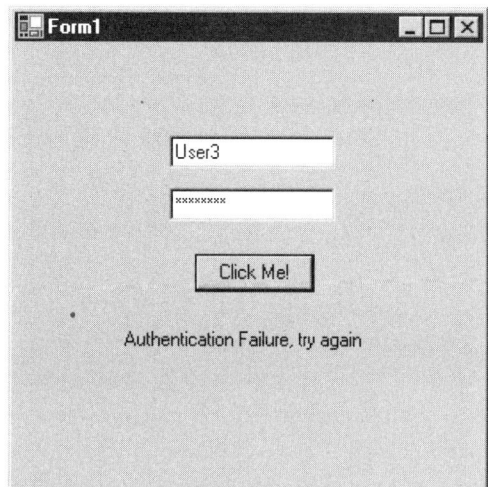

This exercise shows how to limit access to a web service using the settings in web.config. The point here, as well, is that the web service did not have to be recompiled after making changes to the configuration file.

A new concept that has been introduced into software engineering over the last number of years is role-based security. In the next section, you will look at how to configure roles and authorization.

Role-Based Security

Role-based security was introduced in Microsoft Transaction Server (MTS) and moved into the Component Services. By using roles, you define what jobs or tasks the user performs rather than who the user is. For example, in working with a database application, there are entry clerks who will perform data entry, and they will be given insert permission. Another role is the analyst, who requires read-only access to the data. Another role refers to the administration of the data, and the users in this role are given full control over the database.

The .NET Framework adds to this task-oriented role environment by adding two new concepts: *principals* and *identities*. The principal represents the security context that the code is running under, and the identity encapsulates information about the user and the entity that has been authenticated.

The .NET Framework has four classes that are used to encapsulate the identities:

- `WindowsIdentity`
- `FormsIdentity`
- `GenericIdentity`
- `PassportIdentity`

XML web services can only work with the `WindowsIdentity` and `GenericIdentity` classes. The `WindowsIdentity` class is based on the Windows authentication methods, and it can impersonate a user other than the one that is connected to the current thread. This ability makes it possible to access resources on behalf of a user. The `GenericIdentity` class represents the user that has been authenticated through a custom authentication method.

Two principals are used in role-based security:

- `WindowsPrincipal`
- `GenericPrincipal`

The `WindowsPrincipal` class represents the Windows users and the roles those users belong to. The `GenericPrincipal` represents an identity and a list of roles that the identity belongs to.

You use the `WindowsIdentity` and `WindowsPrincipal` objects to access information on the consumer through the `Context.User` object. For example, to find out whether a user is in a specific role, you can use the `IsInRole()` method as shown in the following code segment:

```
If Context.User.IsInRole("BUILTIN\\Developers") Then
    ...
End If
```

This segment tests to see if the currently authenticated user belongs in the Windows group called Developers on the local server. However, it's probably better style to use the `WindowsBuiltInRole` enumeration than to hard-code the role.

In this next example, the same test is performed, but you use the enumeration instead.

```
If Context.User.IsInRole(WindowsBuiltInRole.Developers) Then
    ...
End If
```

The use of authentication and authorization gives us the ability to control who can access your XML web services. The problem is that the data, and possibly the authentication credentials, can be stolen in transit if the communication is in clear text. Encryption is one way to help secure that information, and in the next section you will explore encryption.

Secure Communication

You can encrypt messages as they are sent between the XML web service and the consumer of the service. Encryption takes a lot of resources and is considered an expensive operation, so you need to pick the right level of encryption. There are several strategies:

- **Encrypt the whole message**   This is the sledgehammer method, as it is very unlikely that all messages require encryption. It is easy to implement sthis method, but it makes a high demand on the computers involved in the communication.

- **Encrypt only the body of the message**   This puts slightly less load on the servers than encrypting the whole message, but it is still probably more than is needed.

- **Encrypt only the header of the message**   SOAP headers contain authentication information, so it is a good thing to encrypt them. The load on the servers that this involves is rather light.

- **Encrypt only some select messages**   From the system's point of view, this is the best trade-off—it puts a light load on the servers, and it offers security only when it is needed. The other side of the coin is that the developer will need to spend more time developing the processing for this model, creating an algorithm that decides what messages to encrypt.

- **No encryption**   You must ask yourself if you really need to encrypt any traffic, and if the answer is no, then don't encrypt.

- **Partition the XML web service**   If you find that part of your XML web service requires encryption while another part doesn't, you can build two

XML web services—one for secure communication and one for open communication. This is a very functional solution.

There are a number of options that can be used to encrypt the traffic between the XML web service and the consumer. Look at two of those options that provide encryption:

- **Secure Sockets Layer (SSL)**   Using SSL for the communication is an easy way to configure encryption. With SSL, the entire message is encrypted.

- **Custom SOAP extensions**   Using custom SOAP extensions gives you (the developer) full control over how the messages are encrypted and what messages are encrypted.

Now that you have identified the options, you will look at how to implement SSL and custom SOAP extensions.

Implementing SSL

SSL is based on *security certificates*. A security certificate is a binary structure that has been issued by a trusted certificate authority (CA). The standard certificates are called X.509 certificates, after the standard number.

You need to request a certificate from a CA, who will verify that you are who you claim to be by verifying names, addresses, and so on. The certificate is created by the CA signing the certificate with its *private key*.

Private keys are binary numbers that are prime numbers. The private key is called *private* because it is stored in such a fashion that it cannot be accessed by anyone but the owner of the key. Anything signed with a private key can be verified to have been signed with that key by using the public key that corresponds to the private key. This pair of keys makes up the basis for most encryption in the public sphere today.

The fact that you can verify that the certificate was signed by the CA means that you can trust the certificate without having to contact the CA every time, and by proxy the entity that the certificate was made out for can also be trusted to be who he or she claims to be.

In order to enable SSL in IIS, you need to open the properties for the web site that requires SSL, as shown in Figure 8-3. In the Directory Security tab, click the Server Certificate button to manage the certificates for the server. Adding the certificate received from the CA enables SSL for that web site. In order to be able to use certificates for virtual sites, the default web site must have a certificate first.

FIGURE 8-3

The Web Site
Properties dialog
box, Directory
Security

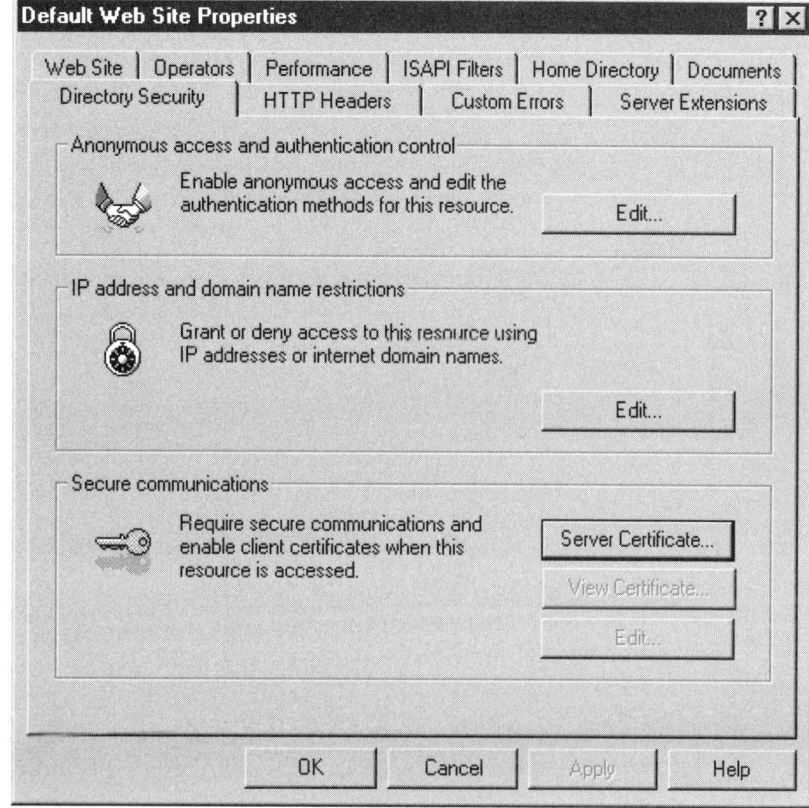

One problem with SSL is that it provides only all-or-nothing encryption. You
do not have the control to encrypt only some messages, or just the headers. For this
type of control, you need to use the custom SOAP header extensions.

Using Custom SOAP Extensions

SOAP extensions allow you to get to the raw SOAP envelope before or after the
serialization of the data. By working with the raw data, you can control how it
is encrypted during transmission. To create the extensions, you need to create
a class that inherits from the `System.Web.Services.Protocols`
`.SoapExtensions` class.

The encryption support comes from the `DESCryptoServiceProvider` class.
This class provides access to the cryptographic service provider (CSP) that provides

Data Encryption Standard (DES) support. The following code segment shows how to use the class:

```
Dim cryptographer As ICryptoTransform
Dim decryptographer As ICryptoTransform
cryptographer = des.CreateEncryptor(key, IV)
decryptograph = des.CreateDecryptor(key, IV)

Dim cStream As CryptoStream
cStream = new CryptoStream(message, cryptographer,
CryptoStreamMode.Write)
' perform some interesting processing here
cStream = new CryptoStream(message, decrytpographer,
CryptoStreamMode.Read)
```

To encrypt and decrypt messages, you need to apply the custom attributes that reference the SOAP extensions. For a discussion on SOAP headers and attributes, please see Appendix D.

The corresponding common Scenario & Solution might be helpful when you are studying security.

SCENARIO & SOLUTION

Why do I need IIS to get access to Windows authentication?	Web services are hosted by IIS, and IIS provides the interface to the Windows authentication models.
How do I control access to my XML Web Service?	Access is controlled by using the web.config application configuration file for the Web service. Modify the `<authorization>` section by inserting `<allow>` and `<deny>` elements.
What is role-based authorization?	Role-based authentication is based on the UML actor. Each actor is defined in terms of the task performed, for example, Customer, Sales Rep, and Supervisor. The roles are named the same as the actors, and the security for each role is defined by what processes the role performs.
My IIS server is not part of Active Directory. What are my authentication options?	Without Active Directory, the only authentication methods left are Anonymous, Basic, and SSL.

CERTIFICATION OBJECTIVE 8.02

Accessing Unmanaged Code

The distributed environment that has been, and still is, the leading distributed environment for Microsoft systems is the COM environment. Even though XML web services are slated to replace COM components, it will not happen overnight.

You can expect to incorporate COM components from existing systems into your designs. There are some issues with the COM components, though. The first is that they are native code for the platform, and they execute in their own unmanaged process spaces. In order to effect communication between the managed code in your XML web service and the unmanaged code in the COM component, you need to marshal the method call and the data between the two environments. This is accomplished using InterOp, or more correctly COM InterOp.

There is also an issue with deployment. COM components must be registered in the Registry database in order for client software to be able to locate them. During deployment, either the component must be deployed with the XML web service, or the Registry database on the production server must be updated with the Registry setting for the COM component. The utility that is used to register COM components is regsvr32.exe. Let's look at how you can incorporate COM components in your XML web service.

Using a COM Component

The advent of the .NET Framework and Web Services will not translate into an immediate worldwide change to the new technology. You will be faced with the need to interoperate with existing COM and COM+ objects that are already deployed in your environments. Fortunately, the Framework contains the capability to let you use existing components in your VB .NET applications. In this section, you are going to take a look at the interoperability between COM(+) and .NET Framework. The term used to describe how you interoperate between the two environments is COM InterOp.

e x a m
ⓦ a t c h

Expect to be tested on how to register and use a COM component in your Visual Basic .NET application. There are a very large number of COM components in use around the world right now, and Microsoft wants to make sure that they are still usable with new applications.

In order for Visual Basic .NET code to reference and access a COM component, you will need to include a wrapper class (also called a proxy) for the COM component. This wrapper class encapsulates the COM objects and the interfaces in Visual Basic .NET classes. The wrapper class, technically called the Runtime Callable Wrapper (RCW), is the part that makes the component self-describing. It wraps the COM component in a layer of XML called the *manifest*, so that the component looks like a .NET assembly to the application.

The utility tool that actually performs the proxy creation is the Type Library Importer (tlbimp.exe), which is included with the .NET SDK. You can execute tlbimp.exe manually to control the generation of the .NET proxy. If you execute the tlbimp.exe utility with the /? command-line switch, it will give you a brief help display.

e x a m
ⓦ a t c h

Use the tlbimp.exe utility to generate the proxy for a COM component.

Even though it looks as if you have hidden the COM component (with all its problems) behind the RCW, that is not the case. The COM component is still the part that needs to perform the work. COM components that are used by .NET applications still have to be deployed in the same careful and meticulous way as always. They must even be registered using the regsvr32.exe utility as in this example:

```
regsvr32 tconv.dll
```

e x a m
ⓦ a t c h

The regsvr32.exe utility is used only to register COM components in the Registry.

The tlbimp.exe utility converts the COM component's internal objects as follows:

- COM `CoClass` classes (COM classes that implement the interfaces of the COM component) are converted to Visual Basic .NET classes.
- COM `structs` are converted to Visual Basic .NET `structs`.

e x a m
ⓦ a t c h *COM components used by .NET applications must be registered in the*
Windows Registry.

Once you have built the RCW, you can proceed to use the COM component in the XML web service.

Another way to create the RCW is to use the Add Reference dialog in Visual Studio .NET, which lets you add and remove references to objects that are part of the project. The Add Reference dialog, which is shown in Figure 8-4, is opened by selecting Project | Add Reference. The three tabs of the dialog are used for different types of object references. The first tab (.NET) is used for .NET assemblies, the second tab (COM) is used for COM components, and the third tab (projects) lists all the projects that are referenced from the current project.

To be able to add references to a COM object, you need to select the second tab. The content of the tab is shown in Figure 8-4. You use the Select button to select a COM component that will be added to the project, or use the Browse button to add

---

FIGURE 8-4

The COM
tab in the Add
Reference dialog

Add Reference   ☒

.NET   COM   Projects

Component Name	TypeLib Ver...	Path	
HomePage14 1.0 Type Library	1.0	C:\Program Files\Microsoft Ha...	
HomerDB 1.0 Type Library	1.0	C:\PROGRA~1\MI4F93~1\ho...	
hosting 1.0 Type Library	1.0	C:\Program Files\Common File...	
hosting 2.0 Type Library	2.0	C:\Program Files\Common File...	
hosting 7.0 Type Library	1.0	C:\Program Files\Common File...	
HSMADMINLib	1.0	C:\WINNT\System32\rsadmin...	
HTML Dialogs 1.0 Type Library	1.0	C:\Program Files\Microsoft Vis...	
HTML Inline Multimedia	1.0	C:\Program Files\Microsoft Offi...	
HUtility 1.0 Type Library	1.0	C:\PROGRA~1\MI4F93~1\hu...	
IAS Core Components 1.0	1.0	C:\WINNT\System32\iassvcs...	
IAS DataStore2 1.0	1.0	C:\WINNT\System32\iasads.dll	
IAS Network Access Policy 1.0	1.0	C:\WINNT\System32\iasnap.dll	

Browse...

Select

Selected Components:

Component Name	Type	Source	

Remove

OK   Cancel   Help

an unregistered COM component as shown in Figure 8-5. After you click the Open button, the COM component is added to the Add Reference dialog. Click OK and the COM component is added to the project.

After adding the reference to the component, you can now proceed to use it in your Visual Basic .NET code. Visual Studio .NET has created a namespace for the component and added the classes from the COM component into that namespace. You will use the component in the same manner that you use native Visual Basic .NET objects—by setting a reference and instantiating and invoking component methods.

The following code segment creates an instance of the TConv COM component that was added to the project:

```
Dim tc As TConv.CConverterClass
tc = New TConv.CConverterClass()
```

For the following exercise to work, you need to have a copy of the TConv.dll COM component. A copy is included in the code directory for Chapter 8 on the

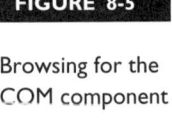

FIGURE 8-5

Browsing for the COM component

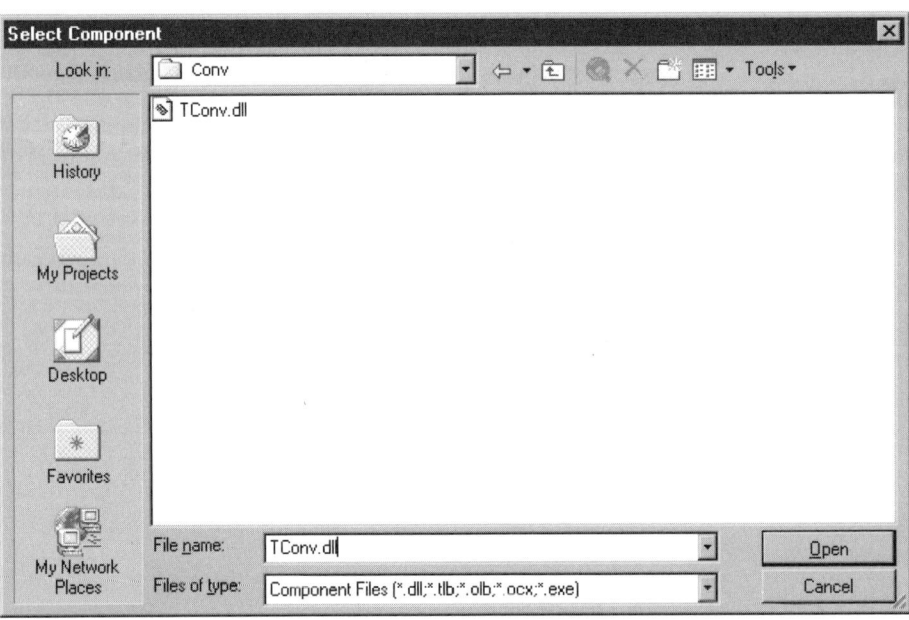

CD-ROM that accompanies this book. Copy this file to a directory on your hard drive and call this directory Conv. Open a command window, navigate to the C:\Conv directory, and register the component using the following command:

```
Regsvr32 TConv.dll
```

EXERCISE 8-5

Using a COM Component

In this exercise, you will use a COM component that converts from Celsius to Fahrenheit and vice versa.

1. Create a new Visual Basic .NET ASP.NET Web Service project, and call the project TempConv.

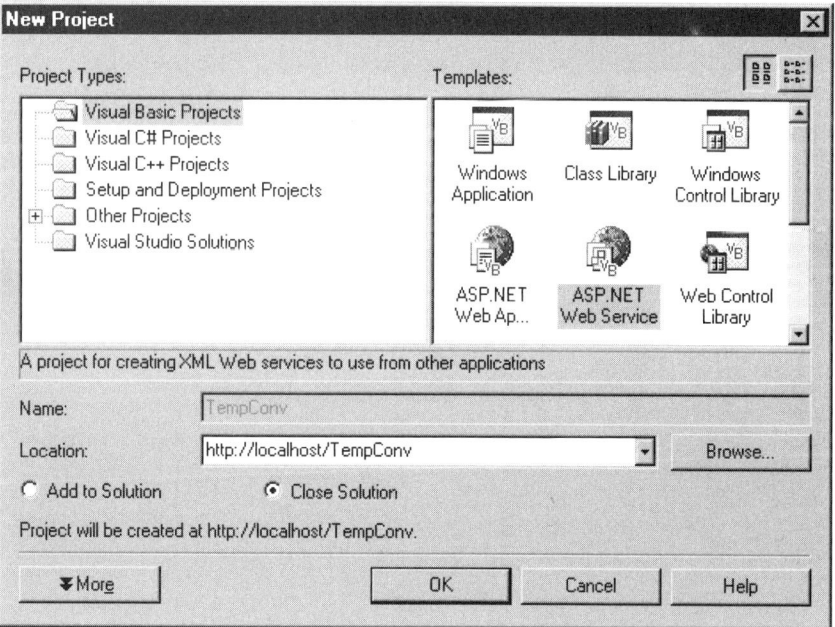

2. Open the Add Reference dialog by selecting Project | Add Reference.
3. Select the COM tab, and click Browse.
4. Browse to the TConv.dll COM component (C:\Conv\TConv.dll).

5. Select TConv.dll and click Open. When you are back in the Add Reference dialog, click OK. The resulting changes to the project appear next:

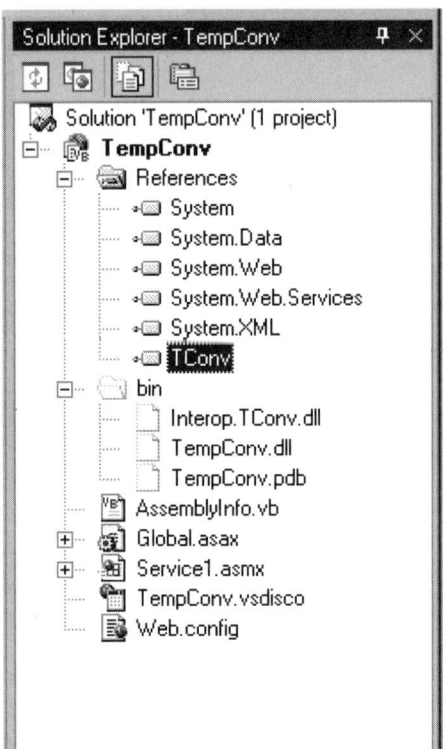

6. Implement a Web method named CtoF().

```
<WebMethod()> Public Function CtoF(ByVal c As Double) As Double
...
End Function
```

7. Enter the following code for the CtoF() Web method:

```
<WebMethod()> Public Function CtoF(ByVal c As Double) As Double
    Dim tc As TConv.CConverterClass
    tc = New TConv.CConverterClass()
    Return tc.CtoF(c)
End Function
```

8. Implement a Web method named FtoC().

```
<WebMethod()> Public Function FtoC(ByVal f As Double) As Double
...
End Function
```

9. Enter the following code for the `FtoC()` Web method:

```
<WebMethod()> Public Function FtoC(ByVal f As Double) As Double
    Dim tc As TConv.CConverterClass
    tc = New TConv.CConverterClass()
    Return tc.FtoC(f)
End Function
```

10. Save, compile, and test the application by pressing F5. Test by using different temperature values. Test using known values, for example 100C = 212F. This should be the resulting display:

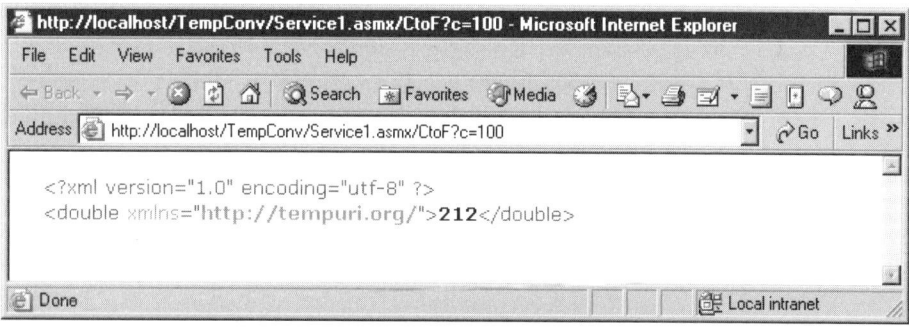

Use the companion common scenario questions and their solutions as a quick reference.

SCENARIO & SOLUTION

How do I make a COM component available to my application?	Use the Add Reference dialog to add a reference to the COM component.
How do I generate the proxy for a COM component?	Use the TlbImp.exe utility to generate proxies from COM components, or add a reference in Visual Basic .NET.
How do I register a COM component in the Registry?	Use the Regsvr32.exe utility to register COM components in the Registry.

CERTIFICATION SUMMARY

In this chapter, you explored security for your XML Web Services and how you could use different authentication and authorization methods to achieve the security you require.

You were introduced to role-based authentication, and how you can access the role the component is executing under programmatically.

The exam will test your knowledge of where and how you specify authentication and authorization. Remember that authentication is specified using IIS, while authorization is controlled using the application web.config file.

The mechanics of using COM(+) components are very straightforward—you register the COM component in Windows Registry, create a proxy, and use the component. The proxy can be generated using two different procedures—either by adding a reference to the project or by using the Tlbimp.exe utility.

In the exam, you can expect to see a couple of COM questions, specifically testing your knowledge of how to interoperate with COM components.

TWO-MINUTE DRILL

Implementing Security

❏ Use integrated Windows authentication on your Intranet.

❏ Use W3C standard authentication on the Internet.

❏ Configure authentication using the IIS Internet Services Manager.

❏ Secure the Internet anonymous account.

❏ Passwords must be stored using reversible encryption in order to work with digest authentication.

❏ Use the `NetworkCredential` class to pass credentials to called components.

❏ Place all files on NTFS volumes to take advantage of Windows Discretionary security.

❏ Use role-based authorization to simplify the administration of security.

❏ The `<authorization>` element in the web.config file is used to `<allow>` or `<deny>` access to the component.

❏ To deny anonymous users, use `<deny users="?"/>`.

❏ Use SOAP Header Extensions to encrypt the headers of the SOAP messages.

Accessing Unmanaged Code

❏ COM components must be registered before they can be used in a Visual Basic .NET application.

❏ Register COM components with the Regsvr32.exe utility.

❏ Generate a proxy for the COM component with the Tlbimp.exe utility, or by adding a reference in Visual Studio .NET.

SELF TEST

Implementing Security

1. You have located the following lines in the Web.config file for the XML web service you are currently working on. What is the function of the lines?

```
<configuration>
  <system.web>
    <authentication mode = "Windows" />
  </system.web>
</configuration>
```

A. The authentication mode is set to Windows NT authentication.

B. The authentication mode is set to what IIS is set to.

C. The authentication mode is set to Windows 2000 Active Directory.

D. The authentication mode is set to integrated Windows.

2. You are investigating the XML web service shown in this code segment:

```
' instantiate the XML Web Service proxy
Dim ws As WService = new WService()
' get a NetworkCredential object
Dim cred As ICredentials
cred = new NetworkCredential("Ken", "password", "nop.com")
' configure the client credentials
ws.Credentials = cred
Dim s As String
```

You need to assign the return value from the XML web service to the string s. Which code segment correctly assigns the return value to s?

A. This code?

```
s = HelloWorld()
```

B. This code?

```
Try
   s = ws.HelloWorld()
Catch
   Console.WriteLine("Authentication Failed!")
End Try
```

   C. This code?

```
s = ws.cred.HelloWorld()
```

   D. Or, this code?

```
s = ws.HelloWorld()
```

3. You are developing an XML web service that will use custom SOAP headers, and you need to correctly define the SOAP header. In the following code, which snippets of code do you need to insert at the marks?

```
Imports System.Web.Services
Imports System.Web.Services.Protocols
<<< Insert code here >>>
   ' declare storage for user-name and password
   Public username As String
   Public password As String
End Class
' declare the XML Web Service
<<< Insert code here >>>
   ' declare a reference to the header
   public AuthenticationHeader m_header;
   <WebMethod()> _
   <<< Insert code here >>> _
   Public Function HelloWorld() As String
      ' do something interesting
      Return "Hello World"
   End Function
End Class
```

   A. `Public Class AuthenticationHeader`
      `Inherits SoapHeader`

   B. `Public Class AuthenticationHeader`
      `Inherits WebService`

   C. `<SoapHeader("m_header", Required=false)>`

   D. `Public Class HelloService`
      `Inherits SoapHeader`

   E. `Public Class HelloService`
      `Inherits WebService`

   F. `<SoapHeader(username, password)>`

4. You have implemented an XML web service that uses custom SOAP header authentication. When you test the XML web service, you find that the custom SOAP header authentication does not work. What is the most efficient way of making the XML web service use the custom SOAP header authentication?

   A. Add or change the `<authentication mode="None"/>` element to the Web. config file.

   B. Add or change the `<authentication mode="Custom"/>` element to the Web.config file.

   C. Add or change the `<authentication mode="SOAP"/>` element to the Web.config file.

   D. Add or change the `<authentication mode="IPP"/>` element to the Web.config file.

5. You have configured authorization for the XML web service you are currently developing. The configuration can be seen in the following segment:

```
<configuration>
    <system.web>
        <authorization>
            <allow users="MIMICO\Dan"/>
            <deny users="MIMICO\Des"/>
            <allow users="?"/>
            <allow roles="service"/>
        </authorization>
    </system.web>
</configuration>
```

   What users have access to the XML web service? Select all that apply.

   A. Des from Mimico

   B. Dan from Mimico

   C. Andy from Mimico

   D. Anonymous users

   E. The Service role

6. You need to encrypt the SOAP header. What is the correct method to use?

   A. Inherit the web service class from the `SoapHeaderEncrypt` class.

   B. Enable SSL for the XML web service and configure it to encrypt the headers.

   C. Use custom SOAP headers.

   D. Use SOAP header extensions.

7. You are configuring security for an XML web service. The authentication should use the users' login credentials from their workstations. What steps do you have to perform to configure the security? Select all correct answers. Each answer makes up part of the solution.

   A. Configure integrated Windows authentication in IIS.

   B. Include `<authentication mode="Integrated" />` in the Web.config file in the root of the XML web service.

   C. Include `<authentication mode="NTLM" />` in the Web.config file in the root of the XML web service.

   D. Include `<authentication mode="SSL" />` in the Web.config file in the root of the XML web service.

   E. Include `<authentication mode="Windows" />` in the Web.config file in the root of the XML web service.

   F. Disallow anonymous access in IIS.

Accessing Unmanaged Code

8. You are using Visual Studio .NET to set up a Reference to a COM component, but the Reference operation fails. What is one possible solution?

   A. Register the COM component with .NET using TlbImp.exe.

   B. Register the COM component using wsdl.exe.

   C. Move the COM component to the bin directory of the application.

   D. Register the COM component in the Registry using Regsvr32.exe.

9. You need to call a method located in a Web Service named TService on the localhost server that has been correctly registered in your application. The method is in the class `Tconv` and is named `CtoF` with the signature `CtoF(dd As Double) As Integer`. What code segment correctly calls the `CtoF()` method?

   A.
```
Dim tc As localhost.TService.Tconv
Dim x As Integer
tc = new TService.Tconv
x = tc.CtoF(42.12)
```

   B.
```
B.Dim tc As TService.Tconv
tc = new TService.Tconv
x = tc.CtoF(42.12)
```

C.
```
C.Dim tc As TService.Tconv
tc = new TService.Tconv()
x = tc.CtoF(42.12)
```

D.
```
D.Dim tc As TService.Tconv
Dim x as Integer
tc = new TService.Tconv()
x = tc.CtoF(42.12)
```

10. Where must a COM component be registered to be used by an XML web service?

A. Locally on the server where the XML web service is installed.

B. On a domain controller in the domain the XML web service is installed in.

C. On the client computer that will consume the XML web service.

D. On a middle-tier server accessible by both the client and the XML web service.

SELF TEST ANSWERS

Implementing Security

1. ☑ **D.** Authentication is set to be integrated Windows.

   ☒ **A, B,** and **C.** Answer **A** is incorrect because Windows NT authentication is not part of the supported models. Answer **B** is incorrect because the mode is set to the integrated Windows mode. Answer **C** is incorrect because there is no such authentication mode.

2. ☑ **B.** In this case, "correctly" means that you must handle the exceptions thrown by incorrect credentials.

   ☒ **A, C,** and **D.** Answer **A** is incorrect because you need to reference the web service in the call. Answer **C** is incorrect because of the superfluous `cred` in the call. Answer **D** is incorrect because the code segment does not handle the exceptions.

3. ☑ **A, C,** and **E.** The `AuthenticationHeader` class inherits from `SoapHeader`, and the `HelloService` class inherits from `WebService`, plus the web method must be marked with the `SoapHeader` attribute that links in the header.

   ☒ **B, D,** and **F.** **B** is incorrect because the inherited class is wrong. **D** is incorrect because the inherited class is wrong. **F** is incorrect because the attribute uses the wrong parameters.

4. ☑ **A.** The authentication mode must be turned off for custom methods to work.

   ☒ **B, C,** and **D.** These answers are incorrect, because the authentication mode must be turned off for the custom method to work.

5. ☑ **B, D,** and **E.** Des is explicitly denied; Andy is not in the list, and if he does not change his login to anonymous, he will not have access.

   ☒ **A** and **C.** Answer **A** is incorrect because Des is explicitly denied access. Answer **C** is incorrect because Andy will need to change to anonymous authentication before he can get access.

6. ☑ **D.** You would use SOAP header extensions to encrypt the SOAP headers.

   ☒ **A, B,** and **C.** These are wrong; they cannot be used to encrypt SOAP headers.

7. ☑ **A, E,** and **F.** In order to configure integrated Windows authentication, you need to configure it in IIS as well as disable anonymous authentication; the final step is to configure the web.config file.

   ☒ **B, C,** and **D.** These answers are incorrect because they describe authentication modes that are incorrect for integrated Windows authentication. The answer in **C** is also incorrect because you cannot control whether NTLM or Kerberos V5 authentication will be used.

Accessing Unmanaged Code

8. ☑ **D.** To successfully reference a COM component, the component must be registered in the Registry of the host operating system. Remember that the COM component is where the work will be performed, so the operating system must be able to find it, and COM components use the Registry for all registration information. The Regsvr32.exe utility is used to request COM components to register themselves in the registry.

   ☒ **A, B,** and **C.** Answer **A** is incorrect because the TlbImp.exe utility is used to create the XML wrapper that provides the manifest that VB .NET uses. Answer **B** is incorrect because the wsdl.exe utility is used to create the proxy for a web service. Answer **C** is incorrect because moving the COM component will not register it in the Registry.

9. ☑ **D.** To correctly call the `CtoF()` method, you need to declare the reference to the web service and instantiate the object, and then the method can be called using the reference to the object.

   ☒ **A, B,** and **C.** Answer **A** is incorrect because the instantiation of the object is wrong; the line must read `tc = new TService.Tconv()`. Answer **B** is incorrect because the instantiation of the object is wrong and the variable `x` is not declared; all variables must be declared before use. Answer **C** is also incorrect because the variable `x` is not declared.

10. ☑ **A.** This statement is true. COM components are still managed by the Windows operating system and must be registered in the Windows Registry.

   ☒ **B, C,** and **D.** Answer **B, C,** and **D** are incorrect because the component must be locally registered.

MCAD/MCSD

MICROSOFT® CERTIFIED APPLICATION DEVELOPER
& MICROSOFT® CERTIFIED SOLUTION DEVELOPER

9

Deployment

T he last task in any software project is to deploy the application to the production environment—server or client computer. Deployment can be as easy as copying the application to the target computer or can involve building an installation application that takes care of all the details.

In this chapter, you will learn how to deploy a .NET Remoting Object and an XML web service. The deployment of a Windows service was handled in Chapter 2, and serviced components were covered in Chapter 3.

Deploying a .NET Remoting Object

In order to deploy a .NET Remoting object, you need to add an installation project to the solution. Installation projects produce as their output a Windows Installer file that has the .msi extension. Microsoft Windows Installer is an installation and configuration service that ships as a part of Windows 2000, Windows Me, and Windows XP.

Windows Installer is based on a model that provides all installation data and instructions in a single package. Traditional scripted setup programs focused on how to install an application—Windows Installer focuses on what to install.

Windows Installer keeps track of what has been installed and verifies that no software component is uninstalled if there are any applications that rely on the component. The data that is kept on each computer includes Registry keys and dependencies. Windows Installer also supports self-repair—the ability of an application to automatically reinstall missing files that may have inadvertently been deleted by the user.

exam
ⓦatch

The Setup and Deployment projects add support for Windows Installer to a solution.

Windows Installer is the base that the deployment tools in Visual Studio .NET are built on—providing a comprehensive set of tools that you can use to manage the deployment and maintenance of your applications.

EXERCISE 9-1

Deploying a .NET Remoting Object

In this exercise, you will deploy a .NET Remoting object. The remoting object is the HelloAgain project you built in Chapter 4. The HelloAgain solution is available on the accompanying CD-ROM in the Chapter 9 directory.

1. Copy the HelloAgain solution from the CD-ROM to the C:\VB directory.

2. Navigate to the C:\VB\HelloAgain directory.

3. Double-click the HelloAgain.sln solution file to open the project in Visual Studio. NET. The result should look like this:

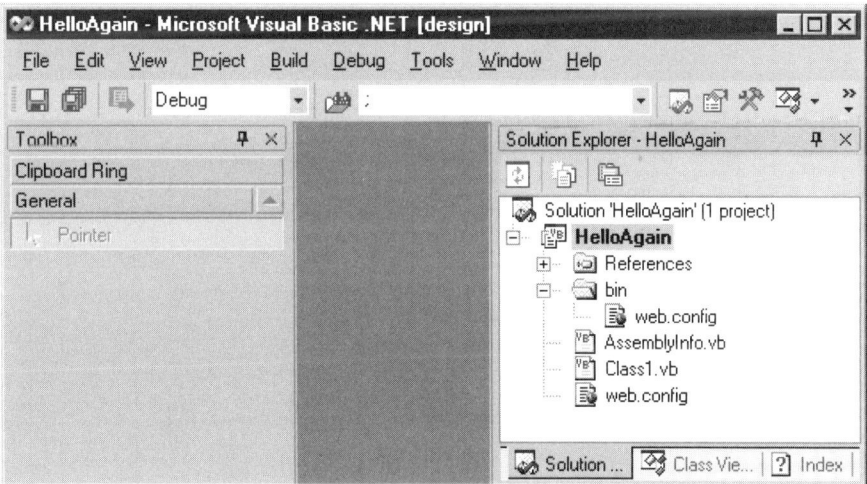

4. Right-click the HelloAgain solution in Solution Explorer. Select Add | New Project from the context menu.

5. Add a new Setup and Deployment project based on the Setup project template. Name the project HelloSetup.

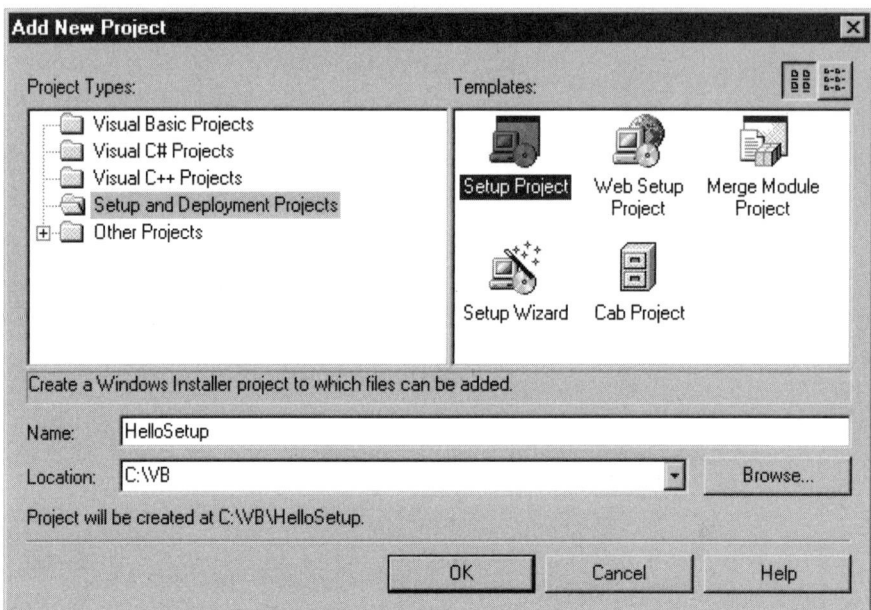

The resulting solution is shown next:

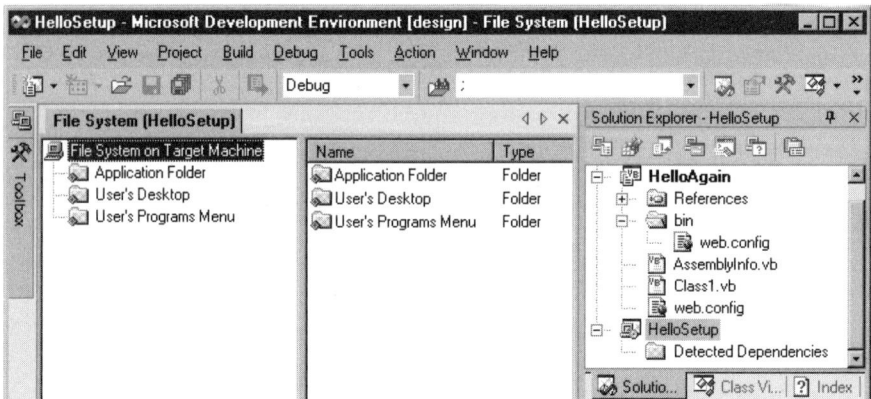

6. Add the HelloAgain project output to the Setup project by right-clicking Application Folder in the File System window. Select Add | Project Output from the context menu. This step will identify the application (either .exe or .dll) files that will be deployed with the setup application.

7. Change the Configuration to be Release .NET and select Primary Output.

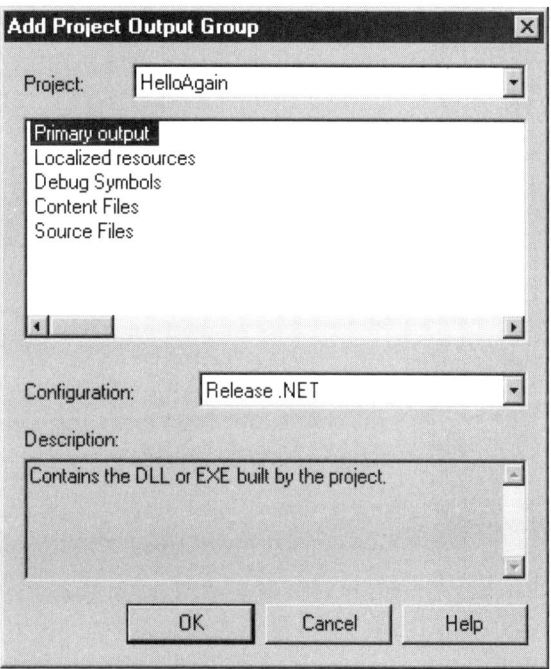

8. Click OK to add the Project output.

9. Ensure that both projects are set to release builds. The solution should look like this:

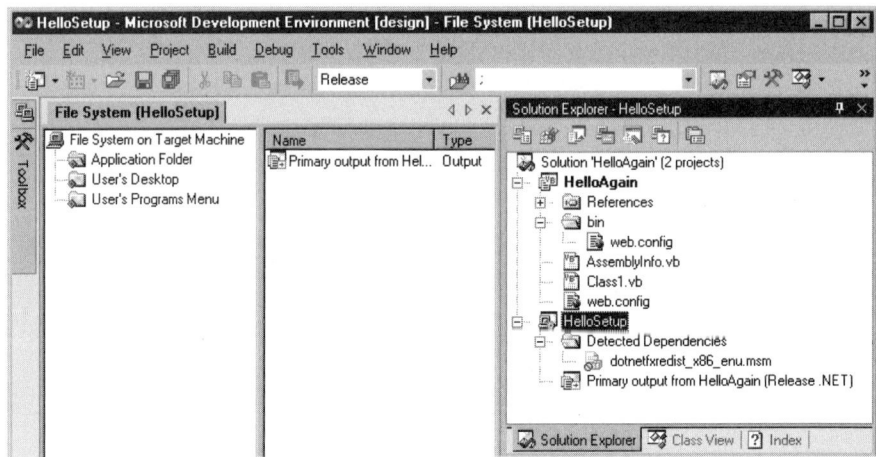

10. Right-click the HelloAgain project in Solution Explorer and select Rebuild from the context menu to build the release version of the HelloAgain application.

11. Right-click the HelloSetup project in Solution Explorer and select Rebuild from the context menu to build the setup application.

12. Open My Computer and navigate to the C:\VB\HelloSetup\Release directory to verify the output from the build. The directory should look like this:

The directory contains the Windows Installer HelloSetup.msi file as well as the traditional installation file Setup.exe with its Setup.ini configuration file.

EXERCISE 9-2

Installing a .NET Remoting Object

In this exercise, you will install the .NET Remoting object from the HelloSetup project.

1. Open My Computer and navigate to the C:\VB\HelloSetup\Release directory.

2. Double-click HelloSetup.msi to start the installation. The result is the HelloSetup Setup Wizard.

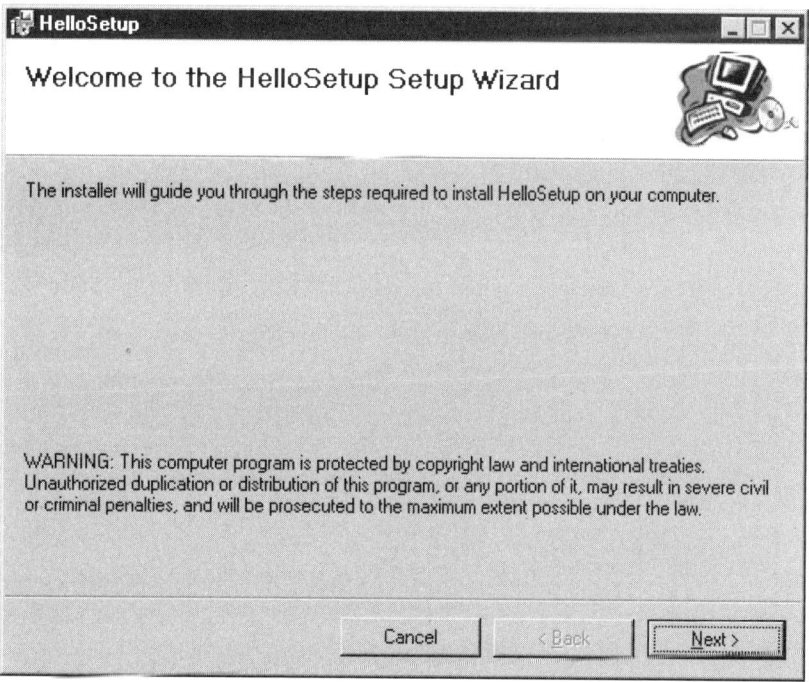

3. Click Next to select the installation folder and verify the location. This dialog also enables you to select how the application will be registered—as part of the profile of all users, or only for the current user.

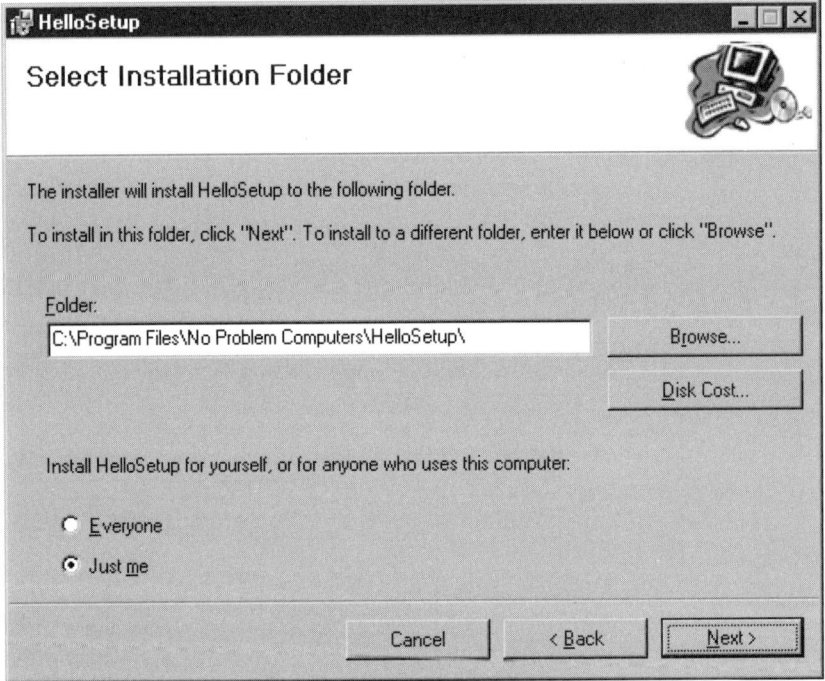

4. Click Next to see the Confirm Installation dialog.

5. Click Next to start the installation.

6. Click Close to exit the successful installation.

EXERCISE 9-3

Uninstalling a .NET Remoting Object

Applications that are installed using the Windows Installer are uninstalled from the Control Panel, Add/Remove Programs application.

1. Open the Control Panel by choosing Start | Settings | Control Panel.

2. Double-click Add/Remove Programs to open the Add/Remove Programs application.

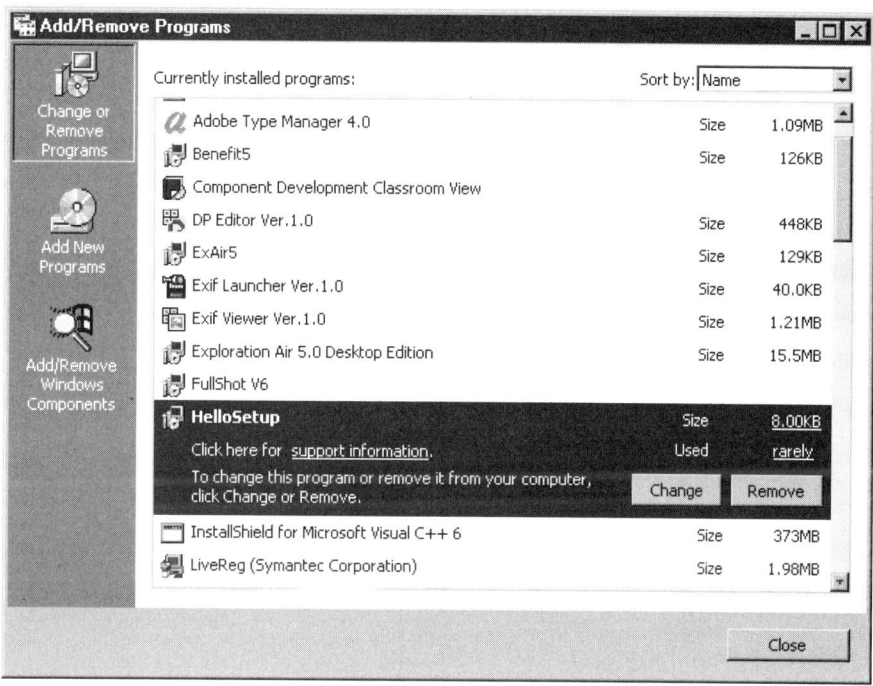

3. Select the HelloSetup application and click Remove.

4. Click Yes to verify that you want to remove the application.

5. The HelloSetup application is removed.

6. Close the Add/Remove Programs application.

exam

ⓦatch

Use Windows Installer applications to be able to uninstall the application through the Add/Remove Programs application.

Deploying an XML Web Service

XML web services are deployed to a production server either by using XCOPY deployment or by adding a Web Setup project to the solution. You will step through the deployment of a web service in the following exercises.

Deploying a Web Service

You will start this exercise by creating a simple XML web service that you will name HiHo.

1. Create a new Visual Basic .NET project based on the ASP Web Service template. Name the project **HiHo**.

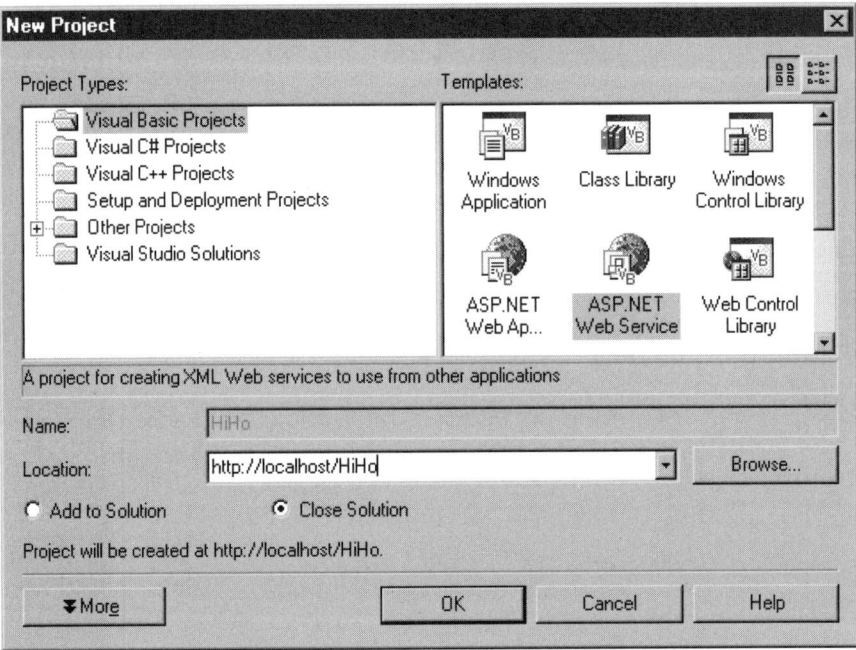

2. Click OK to create the project.

3. Open the code module and uncomment the sample `HelloWorld()` WebMethod.

```
<WebMethod()> Public Function HelloWorld() As String
    HelloWorld = "Hello World"
End Function
```

4. Change from Debug to Release build.

5. Build the project.

6. Test the project to ensure the `HelloWorld()` WebMethod works.

7. Now that you have a web service, you can look at deploying it. Right-click the HiHo solution. Select Add | New Project from the context menu.

8. In the Add New Project dialog, select a Setup and Deployment project based on the Web Setup Project template—name the project **HoHo**.

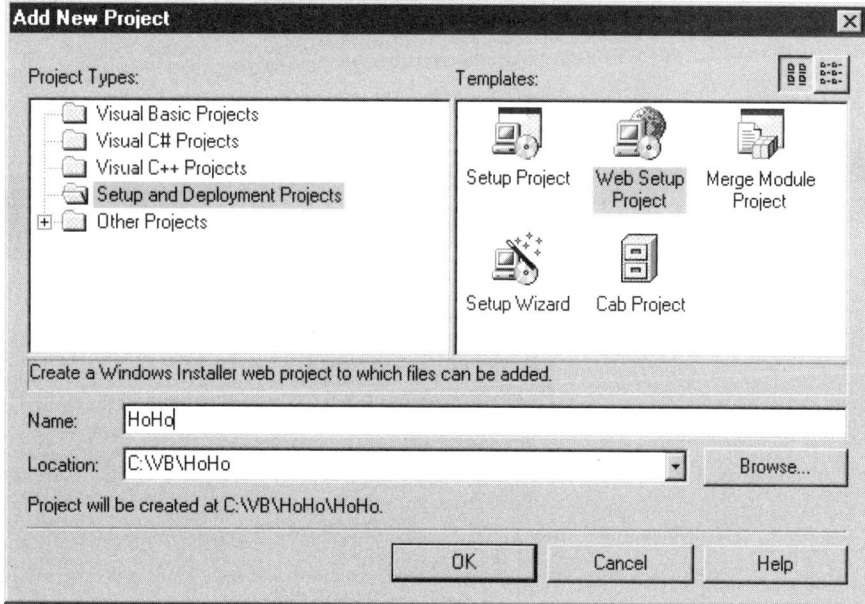

9. Click OK to add the project. The result should look like this:

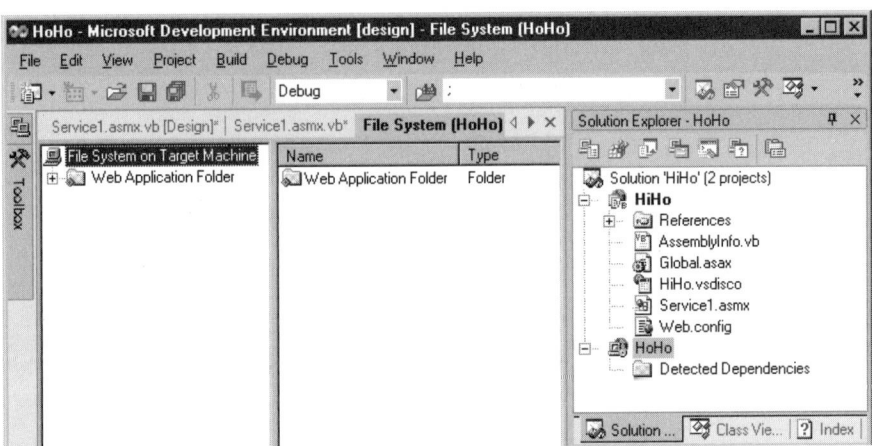

10. Right-click the Application Folder in the File System display, and select Add | Project Output from the context menu.

11. Change the Configuration setting to Release .NET.

12. Select Primary Output, Content Files, and Source Files by holding down the CTRL key while selecting.

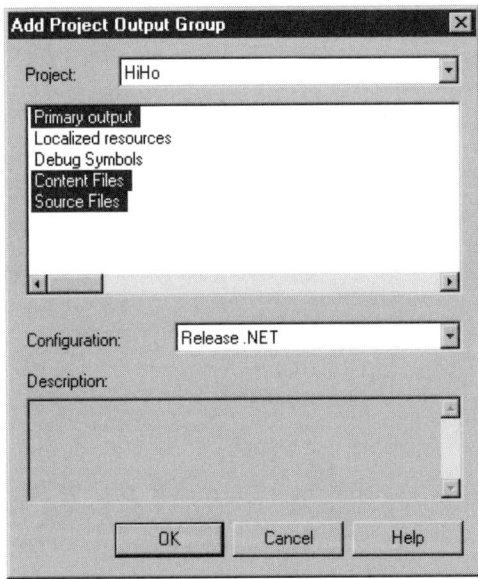

13. Click OK to select the Project Output.

14. Build the HoHo project.

15. Close Visual Studio .NET.

Next, install the XML Web Service.

EXERCISE 9-5

Installing an XML Web Service

1. Open My Computer and navigate to the C:\VB\HoHo\Release folder.

2. Execute the HoHo.msi installation by double-clicking the file. The Installation Wizard will appear.

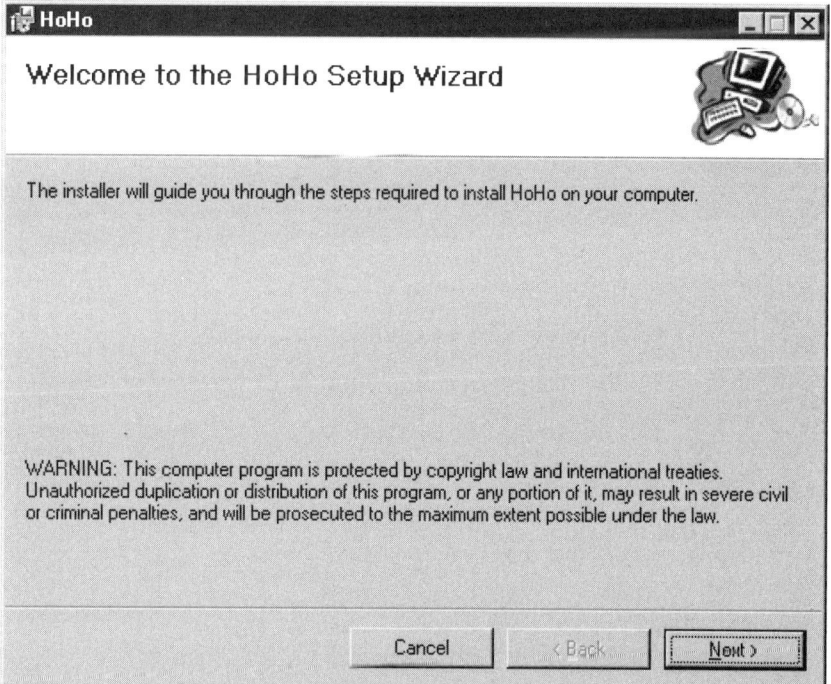

3. Click Next to display the Select Installation Address dialog.

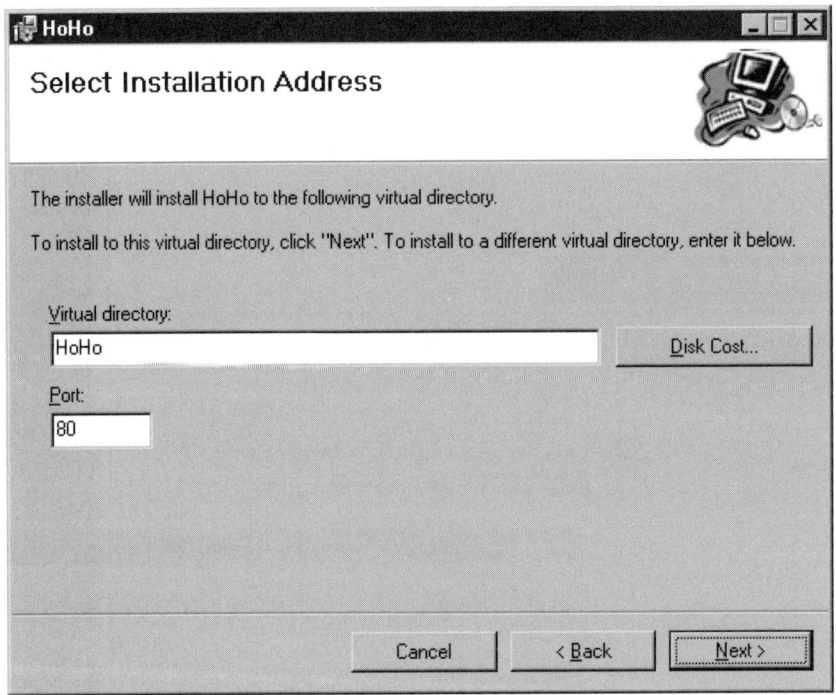

4. Verify that the correct virtual directory is selected and that the port number is correct for the service. The virtual directory becomes part of the URL for the web service, so it should be carefully selected.

5. Click Next to confirm the installation.

6. Click Next to install the XML web service.

7. Close the Installation Wizard after a successful installation.

8. Test the XML web service by entering **http://localhost/HoHo/ Service1.asmx** in the Start | Run dialog and clicking OK. Verify that the Web Service works.

In order to uninstall the XML web service, you use the Add/Remove Programs application in the Control Panel.

CERTIFICATION OBJECTIVE 9.03

Publishing XML Web Service Definitions in the UDDI

Universal Description, Discovery, and Integration (UDDI) is a collection of specifications for a distributed web-based information registry of XML web services. The UDDI Data Structure Specification details the XML structures that are associated with the different UDDI messages. Five data types are defined in the Data Structure Specification:

- **businessEntity**   Describes a business that has registered an XML web service with UDDI.

- **businessService**   Describes an XML web service that a business has published.

- **bindingTemplate**   Describes the information needed to bind to a particular XML web service.

- **tModel**   Metadata to describe the XML web service.

- **publisherAssertion**   Describes relationships between multiple business entities.

exam
Ⓦatch

UDDI is used for public publishing of XML web services. There is currently no private UDDI solution.

The businessEntity describes the business that registers with UDDI. The following XML document shows how that can be done:

```
<businessEntity businessKey="BC72FC2B-B4AD-4814-8209-3E139BD18387" operator="">
   <name>ABC Deployments</name>
   <description xml:lang="en">
      The ABC Deployment Service
   </description>
   <contacts>
      <contact>
         <description xml:lang="en">
            Web Master
```

```
    </description>
    <personName>Kenneth Lind</personName>
    <phone>+1 555-555-5555</phone>
    <email>ken@abc.abc</email>
    <address>
        <addressLine>42 Pudding Lane</addressLine>
        <addressLine>Somewhereville, XX</addressLine>
    </address>
  </contact>
 </contacts>
</businessEntity>
```

The businessKey value was generated using the GUIDGEN tool in Visual Studio .NET.

The businessService element is used to describe the XML web service that a business provides. Through this element, you can register a web service along with the binding information and category of the service. The categories are industry, product, geographic codes, and so on.

```
<businessService businessKey="BC72FC2B-B4AD-4814-8209-3E139BD18387"
serviceKey="4294B042-A1D4-49bc-BF07-C0994F500179">
    <name>Business Service</name>
    <description xml:lang="en">
       Business Service Description
    </description>
    <bindingTemplates>
    <!-- zero or more binding templates -->
      <bindingTemplate/>
    </bindingTemplates>
</businessService>
```

The bindingTemplate element is used to describe the technical details that are used to bind to an XML web service. The binding information is either an access point or a redirector.

The accessPoint elements attribute URLType is used to describe the entry point of the XML web service; it can use any of the following values:

- **mailto**   The entry point is an e-mail address.
- **http**   The entry point is an HTTP address.
- **https**   The entry point is a secure HTTP address.
- **ftp**   The entry point is an FTP directory address.

- **Fax** The entry point is a fax machine.

- **Phone** The entry point is a telephone that is answered by a voice.

- **Other** The entry point is anything other than any of these; the tModel element must specify the protocol.

The following is a sample accessPoint element:

```
<accessPoint URLType="http">http://abc.abc/business/busser.asmx
</accessPoint>
```

The following XML element shows an example of what a bindingTemplate looks like:

```
<bindingTemplate bindingKey="0734D26D-E4B8-4f37-865E-1473C67FF903"
serviceKey="4294B042-A1D4-49bc-BF07-C0994F500179">
    <description xml:lang="en">
      ABC Deployment Service binding template
    </description>
    <accessPoint URLType="http">
      http://abc.abc/business/busser.asmx
    </accessPoint>
    <tModelInstanceDetails>
    <!-- zero or more tModelInstanceInfo elements
      <tModelInstanceInfo/>
    </tModelInstanceDetails>
</bindingTemplate>
```

The tModelInstanceDetails element contains zero or more tModelInstanceInfo elements. The tModelInstanceInfo element has the tModelKey attribute that identified the particular tModel. The purpose is to register the information for a particular tModel as shown in the following code segment:

```
<tModelInstanceInfo tModelKey="uuid:A2DFF91C-EB35-4143-9020-8ACCB7ABCAEB">
    <description xml:lang="en">
      ABC tModel
    </description>
    <instanceDetails>
      <description xml:lang="en">
        ABC instance details
      </description>
      <overviewDoc>
        <description xml:lang="en">
          ABC Deployment Service Overview
        </description>
        <overviewURL>
```

```
            http://www.abc.abc/business/overview.aspx
        </overviewURL>
    </overviewDoc>
    <instanceParams>
        http://www.abc.abc/business/params.aspx
    </instanceParams>
  </instanceDetails>
</tModelInstanceInfo>
```

When UDDI was designed, one of the goals was to make it possible for a developer to learn about the web service by querying the tModel element that describes compliance with a concept or specification. The tModel element contains metadata keyed with a tModelKey that is used to register whether two web services are compatible or to provide a keyed namespace reference.

The following XML code segment shows how to register a tModel:

```
<tModel tModelKey="uuid:A2DFF91C-EB35-4143-9020-8ACCB7ABCAEB">
    <name>ABC tModel</name>
    <description xml:lang="en">
        A tModel for the ABC Deployment Service
    </description>
    <overviewDoc>
        <description xml:lang="en">
            The ABC Deployment Service tModel
        </description>
        <overviewURL>
            http://www.abc.abc/business/overview.aspx
        </overviewURL>
    </overviewDoc>
</tModel>
```

Business entities can represent different parts of a large organization—leaving us with many different ways to categorize the entities and the services they offer. Because these business entities are related, you should make this relationship visible through UDDI by registering a publisherAssertion element as shown in the following XML code segment:

```
<publisherAssertion>
    <fromKey>BC72FC2B-B4AD-4814-8209-3E139BD18387</fromKey>
    <toKey>14AE77EA-7EA9-4454-893D-70EC52AF3DDE</toKey>
    <keyedReference tModelKey="uuid:A2DFF91C-EB35-4143-9020-8ACCB7ABCAEB"
                            keyName="ABC" keyValue="parent-child"/>
</publisherAssertion>
```

The publisherAssertion element registers the businessEntity in the fromKey element to be the parent of the businessEntity in the toKey element.

exam
Ⓦatch

You register your business entity and XML Web Services to a UDDI registry by providing the XML documents or by using the UDDI Programmer's API that is provided as part of the UDDI SDK.

For a discussion on the UDDI Programmer's API, see Appendix D.

CERTIFICATION OBJECTIVE 9.04

Registering Components and Assemblies

One of the strengths of the .NET Framework is that there is no need for a registry; applications can be deployed by just copying the file to the new location, and all dependencies between the executable (runtime) and any assemblies are automatically handled. This automatic location of the assemblies will work only for local private assemblies—if you want to publish an assembly to be publicly shareable, it must be installed and registered in the Global Assembly Cache (GAC).

When an application needs to locate an assembly, it will follow a predetermined path. The steps that are performed are

1. Determine the correct version for the assembly by extracting the version from the configuration files.

2. Determine if the assembly has been bound to before. If so, use the existing assembly.

3. Check for the assembly in the GAC. If you find it, use the assembly from the GAC.

4. Check for the assembly using location hints if present.

5. Check for the assembly using the codebase if present.

6. Probe for the assembly using the data in the probing section. If the assembly is not found, the application requests Windows Installer to provide it (install-on-demand).

No version checks take place if the assembly is not signed with a strong name. Assemblies that are to be installed in the GAC must have strong names.

exam
ⓦatch

Remember the order that an application uses to locate an assembly.

You would use a Windows Installer project to install an assembly in the GAC. This is the recommended procedure because the Installer provides reference counting among other features.

Check out the common Scenario & Solution sidebar I have provided—they might come in handy during the exam.

SCENARIO & SOLUTION

Why should I use a Setup and Deployment project to deploy a .NET Remoting object?	You would use the Windows Installer to make sure that there is instance counting for the .NET Remoting object, and that the IIS virtual directory is configured right if you want it hosted by IIS. In addition, you also gain the ability to uninstall the object cleanly.
Why do you need UDDI?	UDDI performs the task of a distributed public registry (Yellow Pages) where businesses can publish their publicly available services. UDDI performs this role very well, and if you are in the business of selling services on the Internet, UDDI is a great solution.
	If you are using the XML web services internally within your company, you will probably not use UDDI (primarily because there is no private solution yet), and you would probably look at setting up a static discovery system.
Why do I need to include content files in XML Web Service deployment projects?	The entry point to the XML web service is through a content file (.asmx). The default Primary Output does not include any files that are text based. In order to use the service, you need to add the content files.
Do I have to install my assemblies in the GAC?	No, you don't. The only time you really should use the GAC is when the assembly is to be shared between multiple applications. Deployment is simpler if the assembly is part of the application's directory structure.

CERTIFICATION SUMMARY

In this chapter, you explored deployment of .NET Framework applications using the Setup and Deployment projects that are added to any solution. Setup and Deployment projects are built on the Windows Installer, which provides a very strong base for installation services—including reference counting, install-on-demand, and the ability to repair an installation.

In order to be able to dynamically locate XML web services, you must publish the service in a UDDI registry. You looked at the data structures of UDDI in this chapter. The exam will use the element names to ensure that you know where they are used.

Finally, you looked at the order in which assemblies are searched for. Remember that the GAC is searched before any other location.

✓ TWO-MINUTE DRILL

Deploying a .NET Remoting Object

❑ Use a Setup and Deployment project to deploy a .NET Remoting object.

❑ Add only the primary output to the project output.

Deploying an XML Web Service

❑ Use a Setup and Deployment project to deploy an XML web service.

❑ Add only the primary output and content files to the project output—otherwise, the .asmx file will be missing.

❑ Distribute the .msi file to the server where the XML web service is to be deployed.

Publishing XML Web Service Definitions in the UDDI

❑ Five data types (elements) are defined in UDDI—`businessEntity`, `businessService`, `bindingTemplate`, `tModel`, and `publisherAssertion`.

❑ The `bindingTemplate` provides the `URLType` attribute that defines how to connect to the XML web service.

❑ If a company has many different entities, they can be bound together through the `publisherAssertion`.

Registering Components and Assemblies

❑ An assembly is first searched for in memory to see if the application has been bound to the assembly before.

❑ To install an assembly in the GAC, you need to sign it with a strong name.

❑ Windows Installer is the recommended tool for installing assemblies in the GAC.

❑ The command-line utility gacutil.exe can also be used to manage the GAC.

SELF TEST

Deploying a .NET Remoting Object

I. You must deploy a .NET Remoting object, and you must determine the correct way to deploy the component to be hosted by IIS. What is the correct method to use in order to deploy a .NET Remoting object that will be hosted by IIS?

    A. Copy the files to a new folder on the server.

    B. Use the gacutil.exe utility to install the .NET Remoting object.

    C. Add a Setup and Deployment project to the solution, based on a Setup project.

    D. Add a Setup and Deployment project to the solution, based on a Web Setup project.

Deploying an XML Web Service

2. You have successfully deployed an XML web service to a test server on your network using a Web Setup project. Now you need to remove the XML web service. What is the most efficient method to remove the XML web service from the test server?

    A. Delete the directory that the XML web service is located in.

    B. Run the Add/Remove Programs on the test server and remove the XML web service.

    C. Remotely run the Add/Remove Programs on your computer. Connect to the test server and remove the XML web service.

    D. Use the Internet Services Manager console to remove the XML web service.

Publishing XML web service Definitions in the UDDI.

3. You need to create a UDDI registry for your company. What are your options regarding private UDDI registries?

    A. Implement your own private UDDI registry by implementing the entire UDDI specification. There is currently no ready-made private solution.

    B. Use the Private UDDI SDK from Microsoft.

    C. Implement a custom publish/discover architecture.

    D. Hard-code the endpoints.

4. What element describes a company that publishes XML web services in UDDI?

    A. `companyService`

    B. `businessService`

    C. `businessEntity`

    D. `companyEntity`

5. You are assembling the `businessEntity` for your business. What tool will you use to generate the `businessKey` attribute value?

    A. Populate the `businessKey` with the value 11111111-1111-1111-1111-111111111111; the UDDI SDK will generate the final key value.

    B. Use the sn.exe command-line utility to generate the key value.

    C. In Visual Studio .NET, add the key from the Project | Get Key menu.

    D. Use the guidgen.exe command-line utility to generate the key.

6. You are authoring a `businessService` element that will register an XML web service your company is publishing. You need to determine the valid values for the `URLType` attribute of the `bindingTemplate` element. What are valid values for the `URLType` attribute? Select all that apply.

    A. http

    B. telnet

    C. Phone

    D. gopher

7. You need to consolidate a number of business entities that your company has registered in UDDI so that they are related to the main business entity. What element will you use?

    A. `accessibleName`

    B. `accessibleAssertion`

    C. `publisherAssertion`

    D. `publisherAccessible`

8. What is the purpose of the `tModel` element in UDDI?

    A. To provide metadata that describes the service

    B. To provide the description of the service as published

    C. To provide connection information for the service

    D. To provide the binding information for the service

Registering Components and Assemblies

  9. What steps are needed in order to be able to install an assembly in the GAC? Select all that apply.

    A. Copy the assembly to the GAC directory.

    B. Sign the assembly with a strong name.

    C. Install the assembly with a Windows Installer application.

    D. Run the gacutil.exe utility to install the assembly.

10. True or False? An application always checks for an assembly in the local bin directory first.

    A. True

    B. False

SELF TEST ANSWERS

Deploying a .NET Remoting Object

1. ☑ **D.** You need to use a Web Setup project to ensure that IIS correctly configures the virtual directory for the object.

   ☒ **A, B,** and **C.** Answer **A** is incorrect because the virtual directory would not be correctly configured. Answer **B** is incorrect because gacutil.exe is used with the GAC not to configure IIS for .NET Remoting objects. Answer **C** is incorrect because those types of Setup projects are for Windows applications and not to configure IIS.

Deploying an XML Web Service

2. ☑ **B.** The proper method to remove the XML web service is to run the Add/Remove Program locally on the test server.

   ☒ **A, C,** and **D.** Answer **A** is incorrect because that would not unregister the virtual directory from IIS, nor would it clean up the Windows Installer database. Answer **C** is incorrect because you cannot use the Add/Remove Programs application remotely. Answer **D** is incorrect because that would not remove the Windows Installer database entries.

Publishing XML Web Service Definitions in the UDDI

3. ☑ **A.** There is currently no private UDDI implementation from Microsoft.

   ☒ **B, C,** and **D. B** is incorrect because there is no Private UDDI SDK. **C** is incorrect because that is not UDDI. **D** is incorrect because that is not UDDI either.

4. ☑ **C.** The businessEntity element describes the business that publishes services.

   ☒ **A, B,** and **D. A** is incorrect because that element is not defined in UDDI. Answer **B** is incorrect because businessService describes the XML web service that is published, not the company. Answer **D** is incorrect because there is no such element defined in UDDI.

5. ☑ Answer **D.** The guidgen.exe program generates the 128-bit unique key values that are used in UDDI. You can run the utility from the command line or from the Tools menu in Visual Studio .NET.

   ☒ **A, B,** and **C.** Answer **A** is incorrect because the UDDI SDK does not perform this action. Answer **B** is incorrect because the sn.exe utility is used to generate strong-name key pairs for assemblies. Answer **C** is incorrect because there is no such menu; use Tools | Create GUID.

6. ☑ A and C. Only http and Phone are valid from this list.

    ☒ B and D. Answers B and D are incorrect because those types are not supported.

7. ☑ C. The `publisherAssertion` element is used to associate two business entities with each other.

    ☒ A, B, and D. These are not elements of UDDI.

8. ☑ A. The `tModel` element is intended to provide metadata for the service so that developers may explore information on how to use a particular service.

    ☒ B, C, and D. Answer B is incorrect because the description of the service is in the `businessService` element. Answer C is incorrect because the connection information is part of the `bindingTemplate` element. Answer D is also incorrect, because the `bindingTemplate` element provides the binding information.

Registering Components and Assemblies

9. ☑ B, C, and D. Assemblies that are installed in the GAC must be signed with a strong name and registered with the GAC. The registration can be performed by using a Windows Installer application or by using the gacutil.exe utility.

    ☒ A. Answer A is incorrect because assemblies cannot be copied into the GAC; they must be installed (registered) by using either a Windows Installer application or the gacutil.exe utility.

10. ☑ B. This statement is false. The application verifies the version it needs and will then check whether it used that assembly before; if not, it will search for the assembly in the Global Assembly Cache. If the assembly is not found in the GAC, the application will use configuration settings to try to locate the assembly, including any hints to the /bin directory stored in the configuration files.

A

About the CD-ROM

The CD-ROM included with this book comes complete with MasterExam, MasterSim, the electronic version of the book, and code from the examples within the book. The software is easy to install on any Windows 98/NT/2000 computer and must be installed to access the MasterExam and MasterSim features. You may, however, browse the electronic book directly from the CD-ROM without installation. To register for LearnKey's online training and a second bonus MasterExam, simply click the Online Training link on the Main page of the application that starts when the CD-ROM is inserted in the computer and follow the directions to the free online registration.

System Requirements

The software requires Windows 98 or higher and Internet Explorer 5.0 or above and 20MB of hard disk space for full installation. The electronic book requires Adobe Acrobat Reader. To access the Online Training from LearnKey, you must have RealPlayer Basic 8 or the Real1 plugin, which will be automatically installed when you launch the online training.

Installing and Running MasterExam and MasterSim

If autorun is enabled on your computer CD-ROM drive, the CD-ROM will automatically start up when you insert the disk. From the opening screen, you can install MasterExam or MasterSim by pressing the corresponding button. This will begin the installation process and create a program group named LearnKey. To run MasterExam or MasterSim, use Start | Programs | LearnKey. If the autorun feature did not launch your CD-ROM, browse to the CD-ROM and click the RunInstall icon.

MasterExam

MasterExam provides you with a simulation of the actual exam. The number of questions, the types of questions, and the time allowed are intended to be an accurate representation of the exam environment. You have the option to take an open book exam, including hints, references, and answers; a closed book exam; or the timed MasterExam simulation.

When you launch the MasterExam simulation, a digital clock will appear in the top center of your screen. The clock will continue to count down to zero unless you choose to end the exam before the time expires.

MasterSim

The MasterSim is a set of interactive labs that will provide you with a wide variety of tasks, enabling you to experience the software environment even if the software is not installed. Once you have installed the MasterSim, you can access it quickly through the CD-ROM launch page, or you can also access it through Start | Programs | LearnKey.

Electronic Book

The entire contents of the Study Guide are provided in PDF. Adobe's Acrobat Reader has been included on the CD-ROM.

Help

A help file is provided through the help button on the main page in the lower left-hand corner. Individual help features are also available through MasterExam, MasterSim, and LearnKey's Online Training.

Removing Installation(s)

MasterExam and MasterSim are installed to your hard drive. If you choose to remove MasterExam or MasterSim, for *best* results use the Start | Programs | LearnKey | Uninstall option.

If you desire to remove the Real Player, use the Add/Remove Programs icon from your control panel. You may also remove the LearnKey training program from this location.

Technical Support

For questions regarding the technical content of the electronic book or MasterExam, please visit www.osborne.com or e-mail customer.service@mcgraw-hill.com. If you live outside the United States, e-mail international_cs@mcgraw-hill.com.

LearnKey Technical Support

For technical problems with the software (installation, operation, removing installations), and for questions regarding LearnKey Online Training and MasterSim content, please visit www.learnkey.com or e-mail techsupport@learnkey.com.

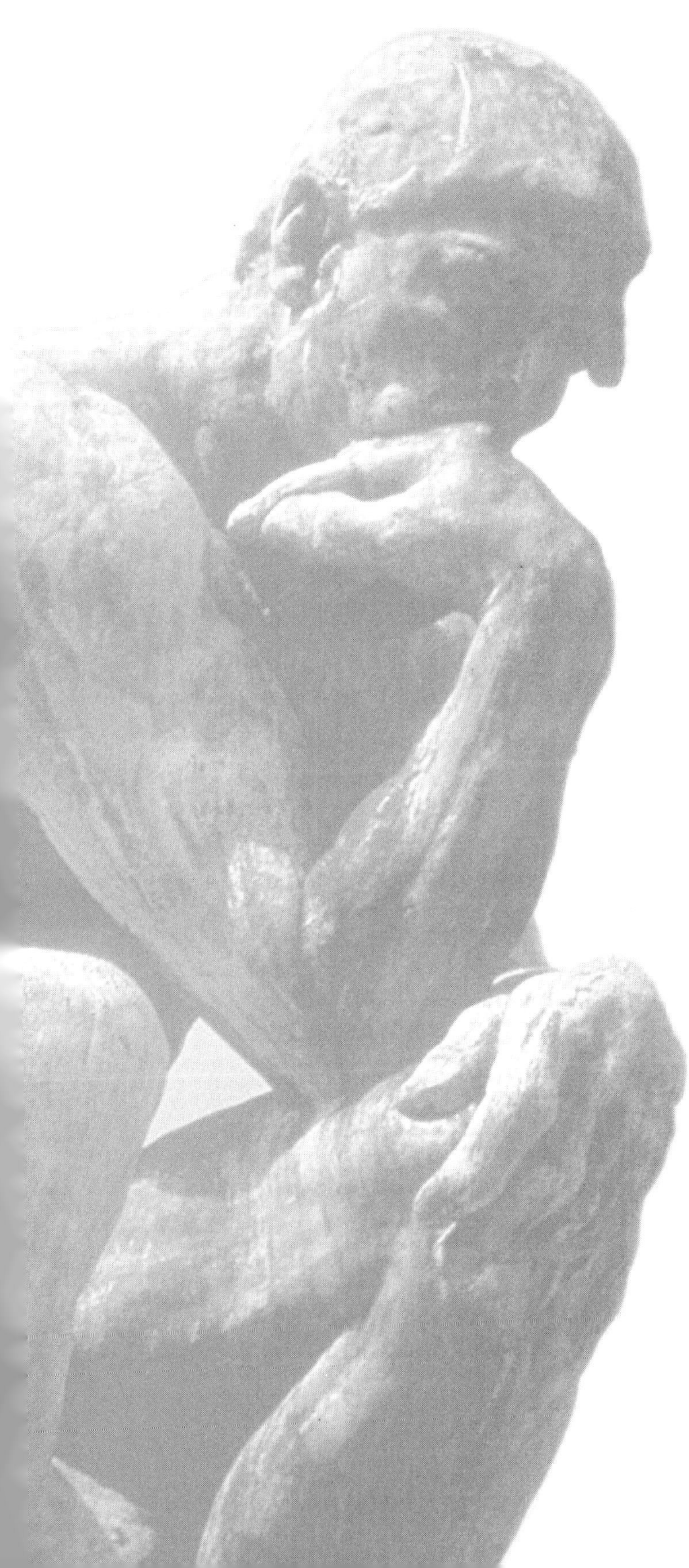

MCAD/MCSD

MICROSOFT® CERTIFIED APPLICATION DEVELOPER
& MICROSOFT® CERTIFIED SOLUTION DEVELOPER

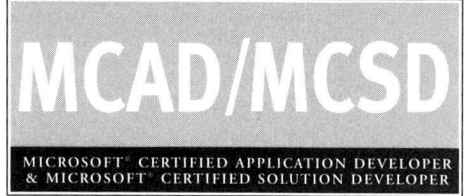

B

Command-Line Utilities

I n addition to the compilers for Visual Basic .NET (vbc.exe), C++ (cl.exe), and C# (csc.exe), the Microsoft .NET Framework SDK adds a number of tools designed to make it easier for you to create, deploy, and manage applications and components that target the .NET Framework. This appendix will introduce these tools and will also detail the command-line usages of vbc.exe.

Command Utilities

In order to be able to run these command-line utilities, you must configure the environment properly. The Visual Studio .NET installation includes a command file (VCVARS32.bat) that configures the command environment properly by setting the path variable to include the Visual Studio .NET directory. The command file is installed in the \bin directory of your installation (the default is c:\Program Files\ Microsoft Visual Studio.NET\vc7\bin). The command file is configured during the installation of Visual Studio to correspond to your computer's setup. Do not replace a missing or damaged VCVARS32.bat file with a VCVARS32.bat from another machine. Rerun setup to replace the missing file.

To run VCVARS32.bat, you can execute it from the path or you can use the shortcut. Select Start | Programs | Microsoft Visual Studio .NET | Visual Studio .NET Tools | Visual Studio .NET Command Prompt.

We recommend that you create a shortcut to the .NET command prompt on your desktop and in the Windows taskbar.

The .NET Framework SDK tools are grouped according to use:

- Debugging tools (see Table B-1)
- Configuration and deployment tools (see Table B-2)
- Security tools (see Table B-3)
- General tools (see Table B-4)

Debugging Tools

TABLE B-1	Tool	Description
The .NET Framework SDK Debugging Tools	Microsoft CLR Debugger (DbgCLR.exe)	Provides debugging services with a graphical interface to help application developers find and fix bugs in programs that target the runtime.
	Runtime Debugger (Cordbg.exe)	Provides command-line debugging services using the Common Language Runtime Debug API. It is used to find and fix bugs in programs that target the runtime.

Configuration and Deployment Tools

TABLE B-2   The .NET Framework SDK Configuration and Deployment Tools

Tool	Description
Assembly Cache Viewer (Shfusion.dll)	Lets you view and manipulate the contents of the Global Assembly Cache using Windows Explorer.
Assembly Linker (Al.exe)	Allows you to use either resource files or Microsoft Intermediate Language (MSIL) files to generate a file with an assembly manifest.
Assembly Registration tool (Regasm.exe)	Registers .NET Framework classes to the Registry, which allows COM clients to create .NET Framework classes transparently.
Assembly Binding Log Viewer (Fuslogvw.exe)	Displays log-file information for failed assembly binding. This information can help you diagnose the reasons the .NET Framework has problems locating an assembly at run time.
Global Assembly Cache tool (Gacutil.exe)	This tool allows you to view and manipulate the contents of the Global Assembly Cache and download cache. You can use Gacutil.exe in build scripts, makefile files, and batch files.
Installer tool (Installutil.exe)	Allows you to install and uninstall server resources by executing the installer components of a specified assembly.
Isolated Storage tool (Storeadm.exe)	Displays and manages all existing stores for the currently logged-on user.
Native Image Generator (Ngen.exe)	Lets you create a native image from a managed assembly and install the image in the native image cache on the local computer.
.NET Framework Configuration tool (Mscorcfg.msc)	Provides a graphical interface for managing .NET Framework security policy and applications that use remoting services. This tool also allows you to manage and configure assemblies in the Global Assembly Cache.
.NET Services Installation tool (Regsvcs.exe)	Allows you to add managed classes to Windows 2000 Component Services (COM+) by loading and registering the assembly and generating, registering, and installing the type library into an existing COM+ 1.0 application.
Soapsuds tool (Soapsuds.exe)	Lets you compile client applications that communicate with XML web services. The technique used is called *remoting*.
Type Library Exporter (Tlbexp.exe)	Generates a type library from a Common Language Runtime assembly.
Type Library Importer (Tlbimp.exe)	Converts the type definitions found within a COM type library into equivalent definitions in managed metadata format.
Web Services Description Language tool (Wsdl.exe)	Generates the code for XML web services and XML web service clients, XML Schema Definition (XSD) schema files, and the .disco discovery documents from WSDL (Web Services Description Language) contract files.

| TABLE B-2 | The .NET Framework SDK Configuration and Deployment Tools *(continued)* |

Tool	Description
Web Services Discovery tool (Disco.exe)	Allows you to discover the URLs of XML web services located on a web server.
XML Schema Definition Tool (Xsd.exe)	Generates XML schemas that follow the XSD language proposed by the World Wide Web Consortium (W3C). This tool generates Common Language Runtime classes and `DataSet` classes from an XSD schema file.

Security Tools

| TABLE B-3 | The .NET Framework SDK Security Tools |

Tool	Description
Certificate Creation Tool (Makecert.exe)	Creates X.509 certificates for testing purposes only.
Certificate Manager tool (Certmgr.exe)	Manages certificates, certificate trust lists (CTLs), and certificate revocation lists (CRLs).
Certificate Verification tool (Chktrust.exe)	Verifies the validity of a file signed with an X.509 certificate.
Code Access Security Policy tool (Caspol.exe)	Allows you to examine and modify security policies for the machine, user, and enterprise-level code access.
File Signing tool (Signcode.exe)	Signs a portable executable (PE) file with an Authenticode digital signature.
Permissions View tool (Permview.exe)	Allows you to view the minimal, optional, and refused permission sets requested by an assembly. You can also use this tool to display the declarative security used by an assembly.
PEVerify tool (PEVerify.exe)	Conducts MSIL type-safety verification checks and metadata validation checks on an assembly.
Secutil tool (Secutil.exe)	Extracts public-key information or Authenticode publisher certificates from an assembly. The output is formatted to be incorporated into code.
Set Registry Tool (Setreg.exe)	Allows you to change the Registry settings for the Software Publishing State keys.
Software Publisher Certificate Test tool (Cert2spc.exe)	Tests a Software Publisher's Certificate (SPC), or creates an SPC from one or more X.509 certificates.
Strong Name tool (Sn.exe)	Allows you to create assemblies with strong names.

General Tools

TABLE B-4 The .NET Framework SDK General Tools

Tool	Description
Common Language Runtime Minidump tool (Mscordmp.exe)	Creates a file containing a core dump of information that can be useful when analyzing system issues in the runtime.
License Compiler (Lc.exe)	Allows you to create a .licenses file that can be embedded in a Common Language Runtime executable. It reads text files that contain licensing information.
Management Strongly Typed Class Generator (Mgmtclassgen.exe)	Allows you to quickly generate an early-bound class for a specified Windows Management Instrumentation (WMI) class.
MSIL Assembler (Ilasm.exe)	Generates a PE file from Microsoft Intermediate Language (MSIL).
MSIL Disassembler (Ildasm.exe)	Produces a MSIL source file from a Portable Executable (PE) file.
Resource File Generator tool (Resgen.exe)	Converts text files and .resx (XML-based resource format) files to .NET Common Language Runtime binary .resources files that can be embedded in a runtime binary executable or compiled into satellite assemblies.
Windows Forms ActiveX Control Importer (Aximp.exe)	Converts type definitions in a COM type library for an ActiveX control into a Windows Forms control.
Windows Forms Class Viewer (Wincv.exe)	Finds managed classes matching a specified search pattern, and displays information about those classes using the Reflection API.
Windows Forms Resource Editor (Winres.exe)	Allows you to quickly and easily localize the Windows Forms forms in your application using a GUI tool.

Visual Basic .NET Compiler (vbc.exe)

In order to compile and run a Visual Basic .NET program, you will need to have the .NET Framework installed on your computer. Microsoft has made the .NET Framework available as a free upgrade, and you can either download it from http://msdn.microsoft.com (approximately 130MB) or order a CD-ROM that contains the .NET Framework.

After installation, the Visual Basic .NET compiler is available from the command prompt to create Portable Executable (PE) files from your source files (see the previous "Command Utilities" section for information on how to set up the environment for use with command-line tools).

Using the Visual Basic .NET Compiler (vbc.exe) is rather complicated because it has a large family of command-line options that control the behavior of the compiler. The next section will give you an overview of most of the command-line switches that are available.

Command-Line Syntax

In Table B-5, you can see all the command-line switches understood by the Visual Basic .NET compiler. To get an instant listing of the command-line switches, you need only execute the vbc.exe program with the /help switch to produce the following listing:

```
C:\>vbc /help
Microsoft (R) Visual Basic .NET Compiler version 7.00.9466
for Microsoft (R) .NET Framework version 1.00.3705.209
Copyright (C) Microsoft Corporation 1987-2001. All rights reserved.


        Visual Basic .NET Compiler Options

                        - OUTPUT FILE -
/out:<file>             Specifies the output file name.
/target:exe             Create a console application (default).
(Short form: /t)
/target:winexe          Create a Windows application.
...
```

TABLE B-5   The vbc.exe Command-Line Switches

Option	Description
@	Specify a response file.
/?	List compiler options to stdout.
/addmodule	Specify one or more modules to be part of this assembly.
/baseaddress	Specify the preferred base address at which to load a DLL.
/bugreport	Create a file that contains information that makes it easy to report a bug.
/checked	Specify whether integer arithmetic that overflows the bounds of the data type will cause an exception at run time.
/codepage	Specify the code page to use for all source-code files in the compilation.

TABLE B-5	The vbc.exe Command-Line Switches *(continued)*

Option	Description
`/debug`	Emit debugging information.
`/define`	Define preprocessor symbols.
`/doc`	Process documentation comments to an XML file.
`/filealign`	Specify the size of sections in the output file.
`/fullpaths`	Specify the absolute path to the file in compiler output.
`/help`	List compiler options to `stdout`.
`/incremental`	Enable incremental compilation of source-code files.
`/lib`	Specify the location of assemblies referenced via `/reference`.
`/linkresource`	Create a link to a managed resource.
`/main`	Specify the location of the `Main()` method.
`/nologo`	Suppress compiler banner information.
`/nostdlib`	Do not import standard library (mscorlib.dll).
`/noconfig`	Do not compile with the global or local versions of vbc.rsp.
`/nowarn`	Suppress the compiler's ability to generate specified warnings.
`/optimize`	Enable or disable optimizations.
`/out`	Specify output file.
`/recurse`	Search subdirectories for source files to compile.
`/reference`	Import metadata from a file that contains an assembly.
`/resource`	Embed a .NET Framework resource into the output file.

`/target`	Specify the format of the output file using one of four options:
	`/target:exe`
	`/target:library`
	`/target:module`
	`/target:winexe`

`/unsafe`	Compile code that uses the `unsafe` keyword.
`/utf8output`	Display compiler output using UTF-8 encoding.
`/warn`	Set warning level.
`/warnaserror`	Promote warnings to errors.
`/win32icon`	Insert an .ico file into the output file.
`/win32res`	Insert a Win32 resource into the output file.

Examples

The Visual Basic .NET compiler commands can be typed in at the command-line prompt or as part of command files used to build the application. The following examples are executed from the command prompt:

- Compiles File.vb producing File.exe:

  ```
  vbc File.vb
  ```

- Compiles File.vb producing File.dll:

  ```
  vbc /target:library File.vb
  ```

- Compiles File.vb and creates Hence.exe:

  ```
  vbc /out:Hence.exe File.vb
  ```

- Compiles all of the Visual Basic .NET files in the current directory, with optimizations on, and defines the DEBUG symbol. The output is File2.exe:

  ```
  vbc /define:DEBUG /optimize /out:File2.exe *.vb
  ```

- Compiles all of the Visual Basic .NET files in the current directory, producing a debug version of File2.dll. No logo and no warnings are displayed:

  ```
  vbc /target:library /out:File2.dll /warn:0 /nologo /debug *.vb
  ```

- Compiles all of the Visual Basic .NET files in the current directory to Thusly.hence (a DLL):

  ```
  vbc /target:library /out:Thusly.hence *.vb
  ```

MCAD/MCSD

MICROSOFT® CERTIFIED APPLICATION DEVELOPER
& MICROSOFT® CERTIFIED SOLUTION DEVELOPER

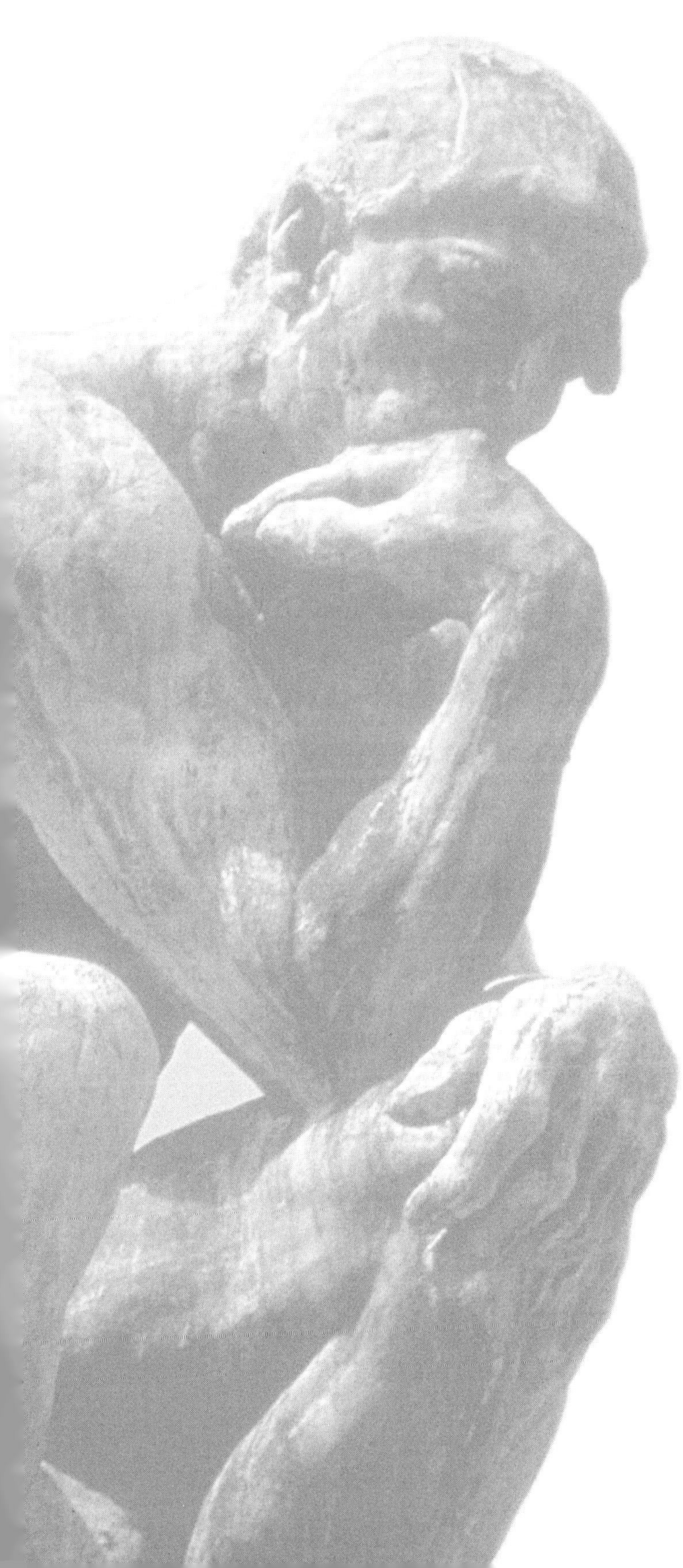

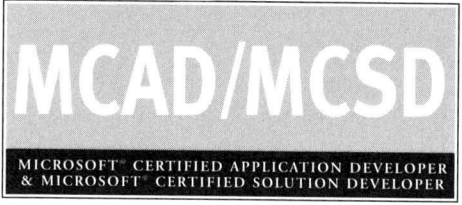

C

Exam 70-310 Certification Objective Mapping to the Study Guide

The following tables are designed to help focus your exam preparation. Each exam objective is listed in the left column, with the corresponding chapter where that objective is addressed in the right column. These objectives were current on the Microsoft site at the time of the creation of this table. Because Microsoft reserves the right to change objectives without notice, you should check the exam site prior to finalizing your exam preparation.

Creating and Managing Microsoft Windows Services, Serviced Components, .NET Remoting Objects, and XML Web Services

Objective	Location in Study Guide
Creating and manipulating a Windows service	See Chapter 2
Write code that is executed when a Windows service is started or stopped	See Chapter 2
Creating and consuming a serviced component	See Chapter 3
Implement a serviced component	See Chapter 3
Create interfaces that are visible to COM	See Chapter 3
Create a strongly named assembly	See Chapter 3
Register the component in the global assembly cache	See Chapter 3
Manage the component by using the Component Services tool	See Chapter 3
Creating and consuming a .NET Remoting object	See Chapter 4
Implement server-activated components	See Chapter 4
Implement client-activated components	See Chapter 4
Select a channel protocol and a formatter. Channel protocols include TCP and HTTP. Formatters include SOAP and binary.	See Chapter 4
Create client configuration files and server configuration files	See Chapter 4
Implement an asynchronous method	See Chapter 4
Create the listener service	See Chapter 4
Instantiate and invoke a .NET Remoting object	See Chapter 4

Objective	Location in Study Guide
Creating and consuming an XML web service	See Chapter 5
Control characteristics of web methods by using attributes	See Chapter 5
Create and use SOAP extensions	See Chapter 5
Create asynchronous web methods	See Chapter 5
Control XML wire format for an XML web service	See Chapter 5
Instantiate and invoke an XML web service	See Chapter 5
Implement security for a Windows service, a serviced component, a .NET Remoting object, and an XML web service	See Chapter 5
Accessing unmanaged code from a Windows service, a serviced component, a .NET Remoting object, and an XML web service	See Chapter 5

Consuming and Manipulating Data

Objective	Location in Study Guide
Accessing and manipulating data from a Microsoft SQL Server database by creating and using *ad hoc* queries and stored procedures	See Chapter 6
Creating and manipulating DataSets	See Chapter 6
Manipulate a DataSet scheme	See Chapter 6
Manipulate DataSet relationships	See Chapter 6
Create a strongly typed DataSet	See Chapter 6
Accessing and manipulating XML data	See Chapter 6
Access an XML file by using the Document Object Model (DOM)	See Chapter 6
Transform DataSet data into XML data	See Chapter 6
Use Xpath to query XML data	See Chapter 6
Generate and use an XSD schema	See Chapter 6
Write a SQL statement that retrieves XML data from a SQL Server database	See Chapter 6
Update a SQL Server database by using XML	See Chapter 6
Validate an XML document	See Chapter 6

Testing and Debugging

Objective	Location in Study Guide
Creating a unit test plan	See Chapter 7
Implementing tracing	See Chapter 7
Configure and use trace listeners and trace switches	See Chapter 7
Display trace output	See Chapter 7
Instrumenting and debugging a Windows service, a serviced component, a .NET Remoting object, and an XML web service	See Chapter 7
Configure the debugging environment	See Chapter 7
Create and apply debugging code to components and applications	See Chapter 7
Provide multicultural test data to components and applications	See Chapter 7
Execute tests	See Chapter 7
Using interactive debugging	See Chapter 7
Logging test results	See Chapter 7
Resolve errors and rework code	See Chapter 7
Control debugging in the Web.config file	See Chapter 7
Use SOAP extensions for debugging	See Chapter 7

Deploying Windows Services, Serviced Components, .NET Remoting Objects, and XML Web Services

Objective	Location in Study Guide
Planning the deployment of and deploying a Windows service, a serviced component, a .NET Remoting object, and an XML web service	See Chapters 2, 3, 4, 5, and 9
Creating a setup program that installs a Windows service, a serviced component, a .NET Remoting object, and an XML web service	See Chapter 9
Register components and assemblies	See Chapter 9

Objective	Location in Study Guide
Publishing an XML web service	See Chapter 9
Enable static discovery	See Chapters 5 and 9
Publish XML web service definitions in the UDDI	See Chapter 9
Configuring client computers and servers to use a Windows service, a serviced component, a .NET Remoting object, and an XML web service	See Chapters 2, 3, 4, 5, and 9
Implementing versioning	See Chapters 1 and 9
Planning, configuring, and deploying side-by-side deployments and applications	See Chapters 1, 2, 3, 4, 5, and 9
Configuring security for a Windows service, a serviced component, a .NET Remoting object, and an XML web service	See Chapter 8
Configure authentication type. Authentication types include Windows authentication, Microsoft .NET Passport, custom authentication, and none.	See Chapter 8
Configure and control authorization. Authorization methods include file-based authorization and URL-based authorization.	See Chapter 8
Configure and implement identity management	See Chapter 8

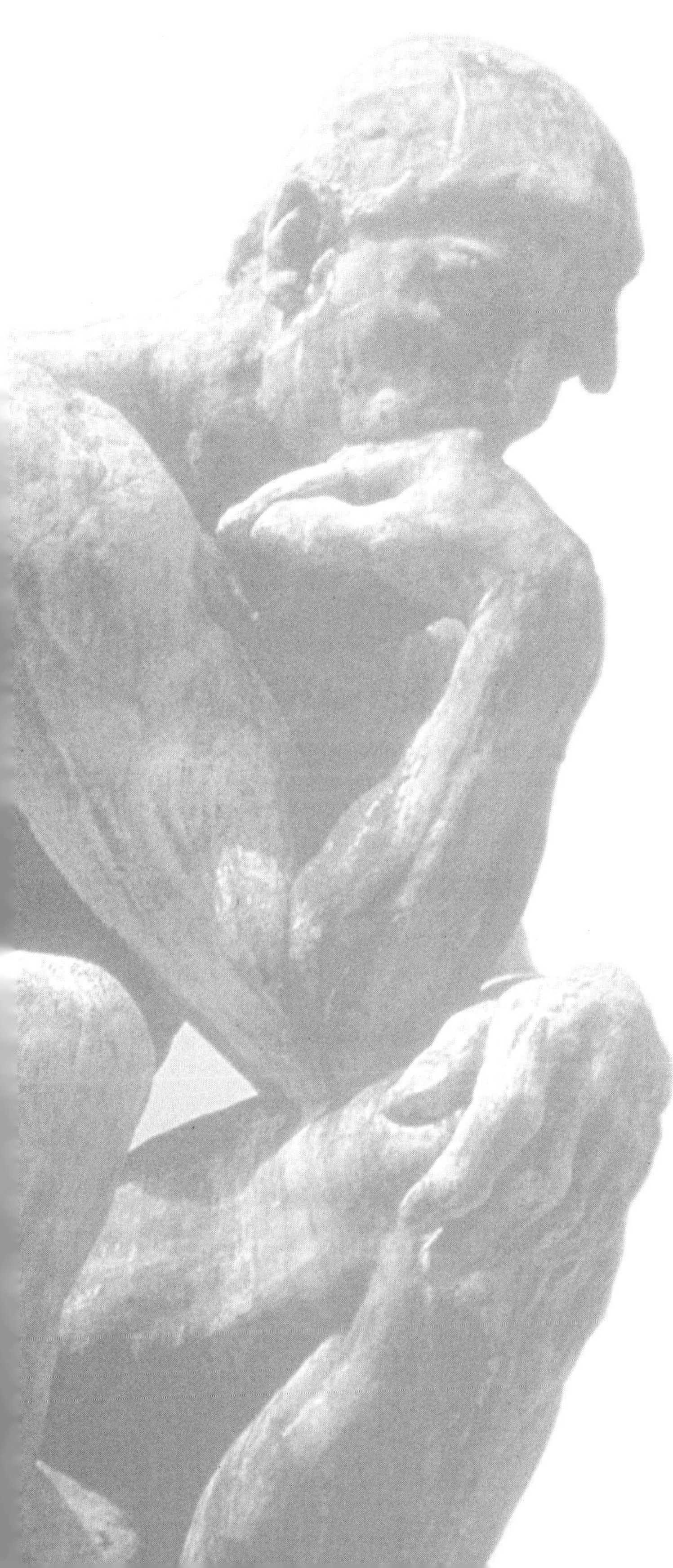

MCAD/MCSD

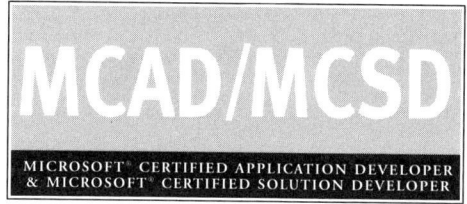

MICROSOFT® CERTIFIED APPLICATION DEVELOPER
& MICROSOFT® CERTIFIED SOLUTION DEVELOPER

D

The Technologies

T his appendix contains explanations of all the acronym-ridden Internet technologies that are used to make the .NET Framework such an exciting environment—and that have made XML Web Services possible.

HTTP

The Hypertext Transfer Protocol (HTTP) is a stateless application-level protocol that is based on a request-response system. That HTTP is an application-level protocol means that it will need a lower-level network protocol to achieve communications between computers. The most common network protocol is the Transmission Control Protocol (TCP) from the TCP/IP suite. Although HTTP can use other network protocols, the proliferation of TCP/IP has made it the only real choice today.

HTTP when used with TCP/IP uses one of the well-known ports (80) defined for connections between the client and the server. This predictable behavior means that HTTP proxies can be used to provide a means for clients situated behind a firewall access to HTTP servers outside that firewall. This is one of the things that make HTTP a common choice for developing client/server applications.

HTTP is a stateless protocol. A stateless protocol does not "remember" anything between one transmission and another; it has no context—each request is an independent connection to the server.

HTTP/1.1 is the current standard from the World Wide Web Consortium (W3C). HTTP/1.1 has actually been a standard since 2000. The current work on application-level protocols within W3C is with the XML protocol.

To find additional information about the HTTP/1.1 standard, visit the W3C web site for HTTP at http://www.w3.org/Protocols/. Next you need to look at some of the specifics of HTTP.

URIs, URLs, and URNs

A Universal Resource Identifier (URI) is used to unambiguously locate a resource on the network. These resources can be files, programs, e-mail addresses, XML web services, or indeed anything else. There are two types of URIs: Uniform Resource Locators (URLs) and Uniform Resource Names (URNs).

The URL is a reference to a specific resource on the network at a particular location. The URL includes three parts to be able to define the resource. They are

- **Protocol**   The first part of the URL is the protocol: http, https, ftp, file, and telnet are some common protocol designations.

- **Server**   The second part is the server name using the Domain Name System (DNS) name. For more information on DNS, see later in this appendix.

- **Resource**   The last part is the path on the server where the resource is located.

The following are examples of URLs:

- **http://www.osborne.com**   Points to the default document on the server www.osborne.com.

- **https://localhost/Stock.asmx**   Points to the XML web service Stock.asmx on the local computer, using the secure (encrypted) version of the HTTP protocol.

- **http://www.w3.org/Protocols/Index.html**   Points to the Index.html page in the Protocols folder on the www.w3.org server using the HTTP protocol.

URNs are persistent, location-independent resource identifiers. HTTP does not use URNs, but you will have seen them in XML documents. The HTTP protocol uses only URLs.

Basics

The HTTP protocol uses a request/response system to provide communication between a client and a server. The communication starts with the client sending an HTTP request to the server. The request includes method, URL, and protocol version followed by a block of data that includes the modifiers, client information, and any other information needed for the request. The data block is formatted as a MIME message. The server will respond by returning a message containing a status line that indicates the outcome of the request as well as the protocol version followed by a MIME message that contains the returned information.

HTTP packets are made up from ASCII text only; MIME is a process of encoding other data into ASCII text so that any type of data can be carried in an HTTP packet.

According to HTTP terminology, the client is a *user agent* and the server is an *HTTP server*. The most common user agent is a browser, but user agents can also be other programs that send requests to an HTTP server. In Figure D-1, you can see how the messages are sent between the client and the server.

Client Request

The request is built from three parts: the status line, the header, and optionally the body. The client initiates the communication with the HTTP server by sending the request. These are the steps in sending the request:

1. Resolve the server name to an IP address.

2. Establish a connection to the server address using port 80.

3. Send the request using this connection.

4. Close the connection.

The HTTP status line must contain a method that indicates what the request contains. The status line will have the following format:

```
Method          Request-URI          Protocol
```

for example,

```
GET          /          HTTP/1.1
```

This request uses the GET method to request the default document using the HTTP/1.1 protocol. After this initial line in the request, the client inserts information that will be sent to the server using a series of *Keyword: Value* pairs,

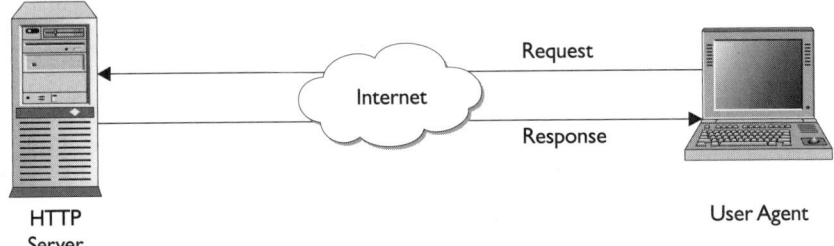

FIGURE D-1

Client/server
communication
using HTTP

HTTP
Server

Request

Internet

Response

User Agent

each on a line by itself. The following is an example of what is sent by Internet Explorer 6.0 (the first line had to be broken to fit the page):

```
User-Agent:     Mozilla/4.0 (compatible; MSIE 6.0; Windows NT 5.0;
                              .NET CLR 1.0.3705)
Method:         GET
```

The interesting point here is that the client actually sends the server information about what software is running on the client computer. This information is used by the server and the developer to customize the information that is returned.

The request is ended with a blank line to indicate to the server that nothing else is to follow. In the case of the GET method, that is the end of the request, but if the POST method is used, additional data can be appended as a body after the header.

Server Response

The server response is made up from three parts as well: the status line, the header, and the body of the response.

The server response status line has three fields that show the protocol, status, and description of the response,

```
Protocol        Status-code                 Description
```

For example,

```
HTTP/1.1        200                 OK
```

indicates that the server is responding using HTTP version 1.1 and that the request was processed successfully. For a listing of the completion codes, see later in this section.

The server also sends information in the header based on Keyword: Value pairs. For example, the following information comes from an Apache server:

```
HTTP/1.1        200         OK
Date:     Tue, 24 Sep 2002   17:14:42 EDT
Server:   Apache/1.3.6 (Unix) PHP/3.0.7
...
Content-Length: 24563
Connection: Close
Content-Type: text/html; charset-iso-8859-1
```

Methods

The method used for the request message is indicated in the status line of the request. The server uses the method to determine the purpose of the request. The HTTP standards have many different methods defined; the most commonly used ones— GET, HEAD, and POST—require some attention.

GET

The GET method is used to request and retrieve information from the server. When you request a URL (http://www.osborne.com) by typing it in the address bar of your browser, the browser will form the following GET request:

```
GET        /          HTTP/1.0
Accept:  */*
Connection:  Keep-Alive
Host:  www.osborne.com
User-Agent:  Mozilla/4.0 (compatible; MSIE 6.0; Windows NT 5.0;
                                    .NET CLR 1.0.3705)
```

The GET request can be a maximum 1024 characters long, and it contains only the status line and the header. If the client wants to send additional information to the server through a GET request, that information must be encoded in the URL. For example, if the page you are currently viewing contains a form that the user can fill in to return information to the server and the form has its method set to GET, the following request message is the result of clicking the Submit button:

```
GET  /bin/FormEx.aspx?"name=Ken"&"email=kennethslind@hotmail.com"  HTTP/1.1
```

The requested item in this case is /bin/FormEx.aspx. The ? indicates that data follows. This example sends back two fields (name and email). The fields are paired and separated by an ampersand (&).

HEAD

The HEAD method is the same as the GET method except for one thing: the server will not include a response body in the response to a HEAD method.

POST

The POST method is used to send form data from the client to the server. It does not have the limitation of 1024 characters; it can be unlimited in size. In addition, the data that is transmitted is hidden in the message rather than shown openly in the URL as is the case when data is transferred using the GET method.

For example, if you send the same information as in the earlier GET example, the POST message will look like this:

```
POST          /bin/FormEx.aspx         HTTP/1.0
Accept:   */*
Connection:  Keep-Alive
Host:  www.osborne.com
User-Agent:  Mozilla/4.0 (compatible; MSIE 6.0; Windows NT 5.0;
                                          .NET CLR 1.0.3705)

name=Ken&email=kennethslind@hotmail.com
```

Response Codes

The HTTP server's response status line contains a three-digit status code that indicates the outcome of the request. The status code falls into one of the ranges shown here.

Status Code Range	Description
100–199	Informational
200–299	Client request successful
300–399	Client request redirected, further action necessary
400–499	Client request incomplete
500–599	Server errors

Informational, 100–199

This range of status codes contains only the status line with no additional data.

Code	Text	Description
100	Continue	This message from the server indicates that the server wants the client to continue sending the request.
101	Switching Protocols	Positive answer to the client that the server has agreed to change the application protocol.

Client Request Successful, 200–299

These are the successful completion codes from the server.

Code	Text	Description
200	OK	Successful completion of the request; the response message contains the requested data.
201	Created	Successful completion of the request; a new resource has been created. The URI returned in the body of the response message points to the new resource.
202	Accepted	The request has been accepted but not yet acted on. When the processing takes place, there is no guarantee that the request will be successful.
203	Non-Authoritative Information	The information returned in the header is not the definitive information from the originating server; instead, it comes from a copy on a different server (i.e., Proxy).
204	No Content	Successful completion of the request, but the server does not have to return any data at this time.
205	Reset Content	Informs the browser to clear the current form.
206	Partial Content	Successful completion of the request based on a Range header. Indicates that additional content is to follow.

Client Request Redirected, 300–399

The redirect codes indicate to the client that it needs to take further actions for the request to be successfully completed.

Code	Text	Description
300	Multiple Choices	The requested URI refers to multiple possible resources. The user agent and server must negotiate the preferred representation. Usually locale selection. Where the locale is the users preferred language and culture information.

Code	Text	Description
301	Moved Permanently	The resource has been permanently moved. The client should use the URI in the Location header.
302	Found	The resource is temporarily in a different location. The client should use the URI in the Location header.
303	See Other	The response can be found at a different URI. The client should use the URI in the Location header.
304	Not Modified	The client has requested a response using the If-Modified-Since header. The document has not been modified; the client should use that locally cached copy.
305	Use Proxy	The resource can be accessed only through the proxy URI in the Location field.
307	Temporary Redirect	The URI in the Location field is to be used for this call only.

Client Request Incomplete, 400–499

The 400–499 range represents an error status when the server has deemed that the client has made the error.

Code	Text	Description
400	Bad Request	The server did not understand the request.
401	Unauthorized	The request did not have the proper authorization; the client should provide proper authentication when requesting the same resource again.
402	Payment Required	This code is reserved for future use.
403	Forbidden	The server understood the request but refused to act. Do not repeat the request.
404	Not Found	The resource could not be found.
405	Method Not Allowed	The method in the request status line is not supported for the requested protocol.
406	Not Acceptable	The resource can produce only responses that have content characteristics that are incompatible with the accept header in the request message.
407	Proxy Authentication Required	The client must authenticate with the proxy first.

Code	Text	Description
408	Request Timeout	The client did not send a request within the time limit of the server.
409	Conflict	The request could not be acted on because of the state of the resource.
410	Gone	The resource is permanently gone.
411	Length Required	The request cannot be acted on without a Content-Length value in the request.
412	Precondition Failed	The precondition in one or more of the If request headers evaluated to false on the server.
413	Request Entity Too Large	The server cannot, or will not, process the request; it is too large in size.
414	Request-URI Too Long	The URL is too long for the server to interpret.
415	Unsupported Media Type	The body of the request is in a format that the server cannot interpret.

Server Errors, 500–599

This range indicates that the server is aware that it has made an error or that other server resources prevent the request from being successfully completed.

Code	Text	Description
500	Internal Server Error	The server encountered an exception; the request could not be processed.
501	Not Implemented	The request requires a feature that the server doesn't implement.
502	Bad Gateway	The server received an invalid response from a gateway or proxy it was using to service the request.
503	Service Unavailable	The server could not act on the request at this time; try again later.
504	Gateway Timeout	The server did not receive a response from the gateway or proxy it was using to service the request.
505	HTTP Version Not Supported	The HTTP version requested is not available on the server.

HTML

Hypertext Markup Language (HTML) is just that—a markup language that allows you to build the web pages your browsers display. HTML documents can be produced using a number of techniques: manually, using Notepad, for instance; or through a development tool, such as FrontPage. Either way, the resulting HTML will be interpreted and rendered (displayed) by the browser.

HTML is rooted in Standard Generalized Markup Language (SGML), which became a standard in 1986. HTML, which is a very small part of SGML, is standardized through the Worldwide Web Consortium, http://www.w3.org. HTML is a standard, but traditionally the browser manufacturers have added bells and whistles to their browsers in order to try to capture market share. This has led to a certain degree of incompatibility between the browsers that are in use. As a developer, you will need to deal with this issue and try to stay as generic in your HTML as possible.

HTML Documents

This section will introduce the basic HTML syntax and elements. Every HTML document has the same structure, which is based on a balanced use of elements. An element is text enclosed in angle brackets (<>). For example, the HTML element would look like this:

```
<HTML>
</HTML>
```

The second tag (</HTML>) is the closing of the HTML element. Every element should be properly closed, but most browsers try to overlook missing ending tags.

Every HTML document should be enclosed in an HTML element. Inside the HTML element there are other elements that make up the final document—the HEAD and BODY elements. The HEAD element is used to set page-wide properties, for example, the TITLE of the document.

The BODY element encloses the information that will be displayed when the HTML document is rendered in a browser. The following code segment shows the relationship between the HTML, HEAD, TITLE, and BODY elements:

```
<HTML>
  <HEAD>
```

```
      <TITLE>This is my first page</TITLE>
   </HEAD>
   <BODY>
     My page says: Hello HTML World!
   </BODY>
</HTML>
```

By entering the preceding code in a text file and saving the file with an .htm extension, you can view the result in the browser. This is the result.

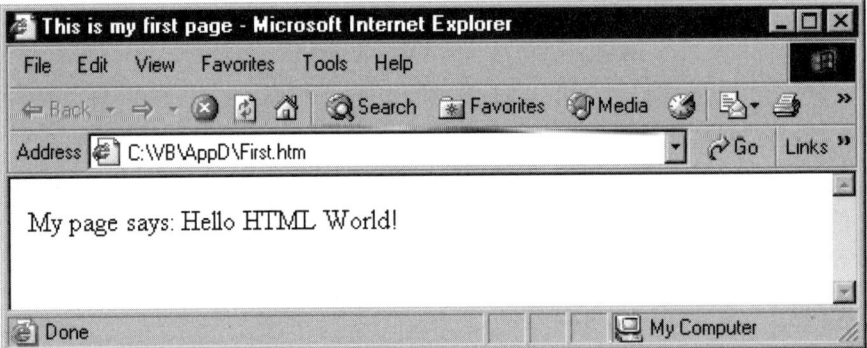

Note that the Window bar shows the title and that the Hello World! greeting is displayed in the browser.

Headings

One way of adding some interest to a web page is to use headings to group information under. The HTML standard defines six sizes of headers, defined by the H1, H2, H3, H4, H5, and H6 elements. The following example shows how to use the headings to see the different choices.

```
<HTML>
  <HEAD>
    <TITLE>Headings</TITLE>
  </HEAD>
  <BODY>
    <H1>Heading H1</H1>
    <H2>Heading H2</H2>
    <H3>Heading H3</H3>
```

```
      <H4>Heading H4</H4>
      <H5>Heading H5</H5>
      <H6>Heading H6</H6>
   </BODY>
</HTML>
```

The resulting display is shown next.

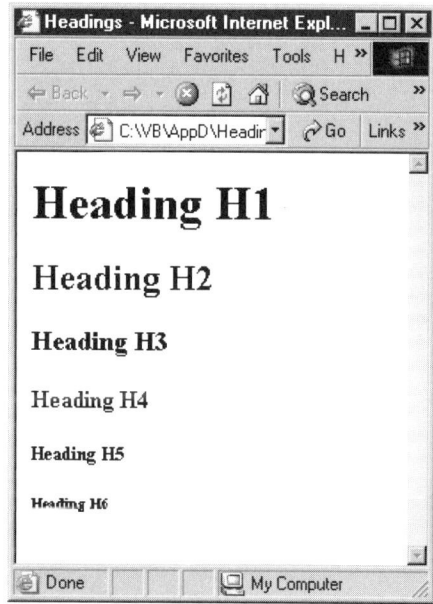

To go back to the first page and add some interest to it, you could modify the HTML as follows:

```
<HTML>
  <HEAD>
    <TITLE>This is my second page</TITLE>
  </HEAD>
  <BODY>
    <H2>My page says:</H2>
    <H1>Hello HTML World!</H1>
  </BODY>
</HTML>
```

The new page appears here.

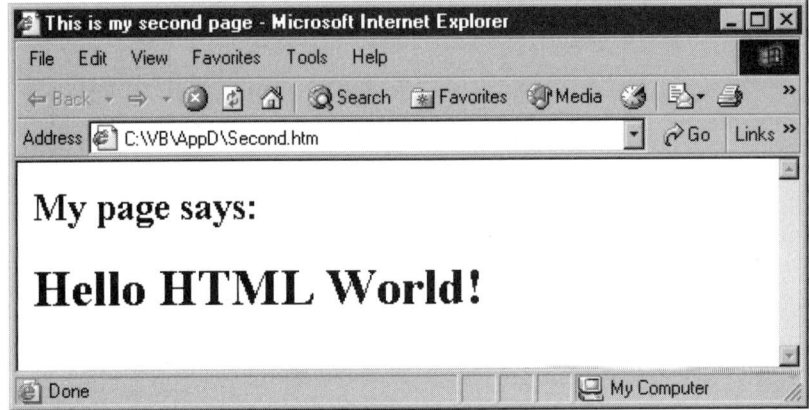

Another element that is very useful when making web pages visually pleasing is the CENTER element, which instructs the browser to center the text in the display area. With the CENTER element, your page now looks like this:

```
<HTML>
  <HEAD>
    <TITLE>This is my third page</TITLE>
  </HEAD>
  <BODY>
    <CENTER><H2>My page says:</H2></CENTER>
    <CENTER><H1>Hello HTML World!</H1></CENTER>
  </BODY>
</HTML>
```

When viewed in the browser, the page has some added interest, as shown here.

Paragraphs

When you enter text in the BODY element, it will be displayed starting in the top-left corner and flow across the browser window without any formatting. New lines are treated as whitespace and so are not displayed. The following page uses a couple of paragraphs from earlier in this appendix to illustrate text layout:

```
<HTML>
  <HEAD>
    <TITLE>Paragraphs</TITLE>
  </HEAD>
  <BODY>
    The HTTP protocol uses a request/response system to provide
    communication between a client and a server. The communication
    starts with the client sending an HTTP request to the server, the
    request includes method, URL, and protocol version followed by
    a block of data that include the modifiers, client information,
    and any other information needed for the request. The data
    block is formatted as a MIME message. The server will respond
    by returning a message containing a status line that indicates
    the outcome of the request as well as the protocol version
    followed by a MIME message that contains the returned information.
    The terminology used to describe the client and server is that
    the client is a user agent and the server is an HTTP Server.
    The most common user agent is a browser, but user agent can
    also be other programs that send requests to a HTTP Server.
    In Figure D-1, you can see how the messages are sent between
    the client and the server.
  </BODY>
</HTML>
```

The document is rendered as one large paragraph:

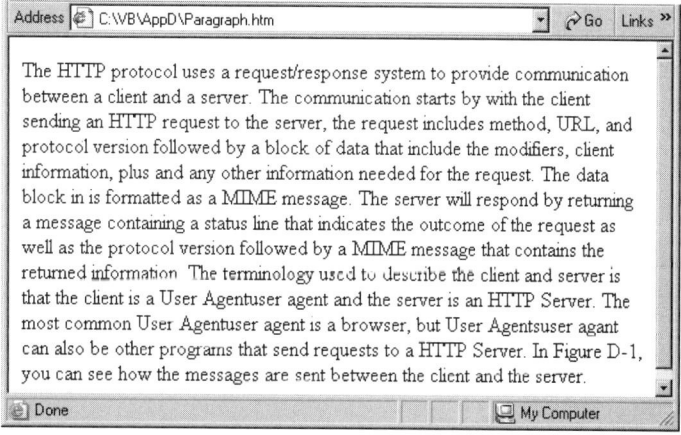

The solution to this jumble comes in the shape of two elements—the P (paragraph) and BR (break) elements. Any text that is enclosed in a paragraph element will be offset separately, and any time the break element is inserted, the text will continue on the following line. In the next code segment, you can see that the text has been broken up into two paragraphs. Each has additional attributes associated—margins and alignment:

```
<HTML>
  <HEAD>
    <TITLE>Paragraphs - two</TITLE>
  </HEAD>
  <BODY>
    <P ALIGN-JUSTIFY>
    The HTTP protocol uses a request/response system to provide
    communication between a client and a server. The communication
    starts with the client sending an HTTP request to the server, the
    request includes method, URL, and protocol version followed by
    a block of data that include the modifiers, client information,
    and any other information needed for the request. The data
    block is formatted as a MIME message. The server will respond
    by returning a message containing a status line that indicates
    the outcome of the request as well as the protocol version
    followed by a MIME message that contains the returned information.
    </P>
    <P ALIGN=LEFT>
    The terminology used to describe the client and server is that
    the client is a user agent and the server is an HTTP Server.
    The most common user agent is a browser, but user agant can
    also be other programs that send requests to a HTTP Server.
    In Figure D-1, you can see how the messages are sent between
    the client and the server.
    </P>
  </BODY>
</HTML>
```

The first paragraph is justified, while the second one is left aligned, as shown next.

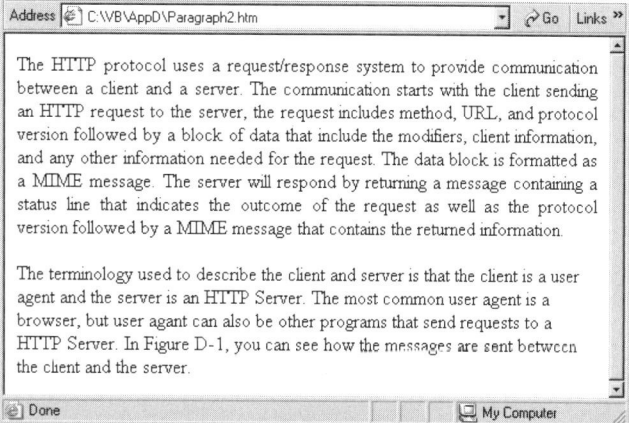

Emphasis

When you want to make some text stand out in the browser, you can use the B (bold) element or the EM (emphasis) element. The following HTML document shows the use of these elements:

```
<HTML>
  <HEAD>
    <TITLE>Emphasis</TITLE>
  </HEAD>
  <BODY>
    The <B>time</B> has come for all <EM>good</EM> men...
  </BODY>
</HTML>
```

The word "time" is in bold, and "good" is in italics.

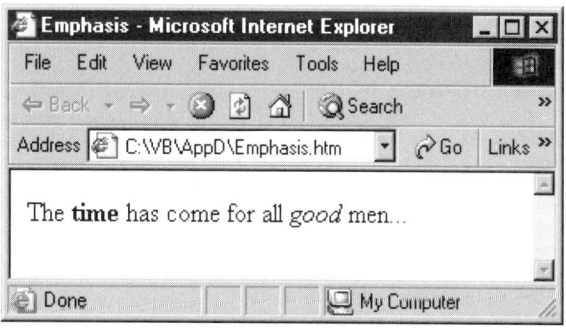

Images

Images are used to make web pages more interesting and informative, and to help get the message across. Images are added by using the IMG element, which describes what image to show, and optionally its size and any alternative text should the browser be incapable of showing the image. The following code segment adds an image to a page:

```
<HTML>
  <HEAD>
    <TITLE>Image</TITLE>
  </HEAD>
  <BODY>
    <IMG SRC="sunset.gif"/>
  </BODY>
</HTML>
```

The size of the image can be controlled by adding either the WIDTH or the HEIGHT attribute. If only one of the attributes is added, the other will be automatically set. There are, however, issues with sending a graphics file to the client and having the client resize the file, in that you have no control over the quality of the conversion. It is better to resize the image using a good graphics package to get it to the size you want, and send the properly sized image to the browser.

If the client has turned off graphics to preserve bandwidth, there is an issue of letting the user know that there is an image in that location. You do so by including the ALT attribute to insert the alternative text. The following code segment shows the use of the ALT attribute:

```
<HTML>
  <HEAD>
    <TITLE>Image</TITLE>
  </HEAD>
  <BODY>
    <IMG SRC="sunset.gif" ALT="Sunset picture"/>
  </BODY>
</HTML>
```

The result of using the ALT attribute is shown next:

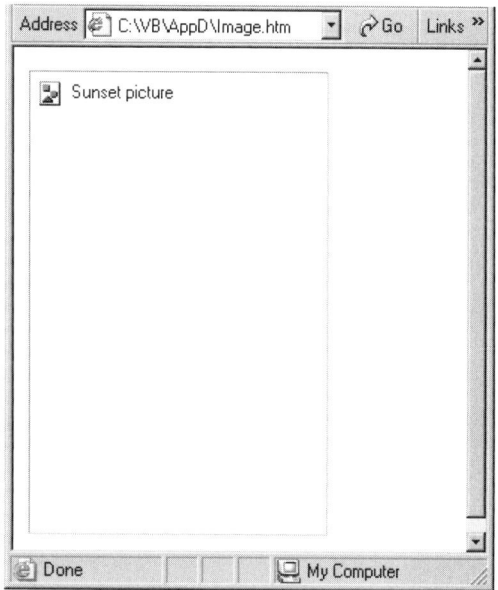

Hyperlinks

One of the original uses of web pages was to compile links to other sites and pages that contained information about a particular topic. The link (pages, also called index pages,) made use of the ability of browsers to redirect the client to another site when the user clicked an anchor or hyperlink. The A (anchor) element enables you to add text or image links that point to other URLs. The format of the A element is

```
<A HREF="where to go">What to display</A>
```

The browser will render the anchor element by displaying the text (what to display) with an underline to graphically tell the user that the link can be clicked. When the user clicks the link, the browser will redirect to the URL that is specified in the HREF attribute. The following code segment shows the use of anchor elements to navigate to the pages you have worked on so far as well as to an external location:

```
<HTML>
  <HEAD>
    <TITLE>Hyperlinks</TITLE>
  </HEAD>
  <BODY>
```

```
      <A HREF="First.htm">First page</A><BR/>
      <A HREF="Second.htm">Second page</A><BR/>
      <A HREF="Third.htm">Third page</A><BR/>
      <A HREF="http://www.osborne.com">Osborne</A><BR/>
   </BODY>
</HTML>
```

The result is shown here:

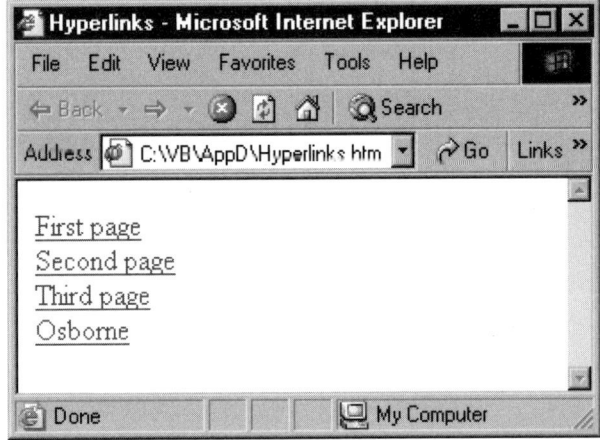

Lists

Three kinds of lists are supported by HTML: bulleted (unordered), numbered (ordered), and definition lists.

The bulleted list uses the UL and LI elements to define the list. The following is a list of three items:

```
<UL>
  <LI>The first item</LI>
  <LI>The second item</LI>
  <LI>The third item</LI>
</UL>
```

The numbered list uses the OL and LI elements to define the list, for instance,

```
<OL>
  <LI>The first item</LI>
  <LI>The second item</LI>
  <LI>The third item</LI>
</OL>
```

The third list is the definition list, which lets you list terms and definitions. The definition list uses the DL element to define the list, DT elements for the terms, and DD elements for the definitions. The following code segment shows a definition list:

```
<DL>
  <DT>The first term</DT>
  <DD>First definition</DD>
  <DT>The second term</DT>
  <DD>Second definition</DD>
  <DT>The third term</DT>
  <DD>Third definition</DD>
  <DT>The fourth term</DT>
  <DD>Fourth definition</DD>
</DL>
```

Lists can be nested to produce the specific kind of list required for a web page. The following web page is an example of a nested list:

```
<HTML>
  <HEAD>
    <TITLE>Lists - Two</TITLE>
  </HEAD>
  <BODY>
    <OL>
      <LI>The first item</LI>
      <LI>The second item
          <UL>
             <LI>The first nested item</LI>
             <LI>The second nested item</LI>
             <LI>The third nested item</LI>
          </UL>
      </LI>
      <LI>The third item
          <DL>
          <DT>The first term</DT>
          <DD>First definition</DD>
          <DT>The second term</DT>
          <DD>Second definition</DD>
          <DT>The third term</DT>
          <DD>Third definition</DD>
          <DT>The fourth term</DT>
          <DD>Fourth definition</DD>
          </DL>
      </LI>
```

```
      </OL>
    </BODY>
  </HTML>
```

The resulting web page appears here:

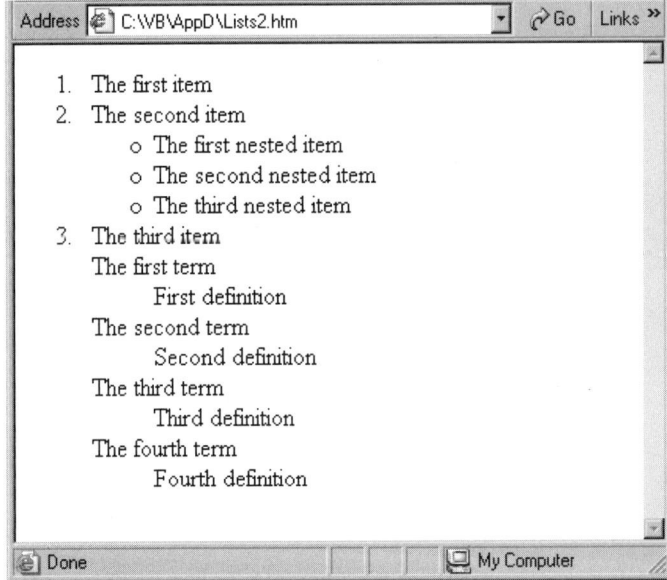

Tables

One of the most useful elements of a web page is the TABLE element. Using this element, you can build web pages that exhibit a very professional look and feel. The tables you can build with the TABLE element are very logical in layout. Tables have rows and columns, and that is how you will define a table in your web page.

The elements that are used are TABLE to define the boundaries of the table, TR (table row) to define the row, and TD (table detail) to define the columns in that row.

The following code defines a table with two rows and two columns listing the parish and capital:

```
<TABLE BORDER=1>
  <TR>
    <TD>Savannah La Mare</TD>
    <TD>Westmoreland</TD>
  </TR>
  <TR>
    <TD>Falmouth</TD>
```

```
      <TD>Trelawney</TD>
    </TR>
  </TABLE>
```

Setting the BORDER attribute to 1 makes the border visible. Setting the attribute to 0 makes the border invisible. Here is the resulting web page:

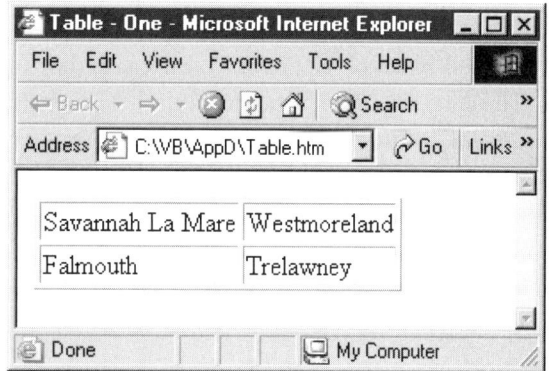

Tables can be nested within each other. This is a very powerful technique that is commonly employed to build complex web pages with headers, footers, and navigation bars on the sides.

XML

If all that has been written about Extensible Markup Language (XML) is true, XML will truly be the best thing since sliced bread. The natural reaction to all this hype is suspicion. So let us see what XML really is, and later in this chapter, you will see what can be built using XML.

XML is

- A tool to package data and structure in one document

- A human-readable language

- A machine-readable language

- An open standard

- Extensible

- A format that can be displayed in the browser

The combination of these features makes XML one of the enabling technologies that standardize data transfers between dissimilar environments as well as the standard for storing information in documents. You will look at these features over the next sections, but first you will need to know the rules of XML.

XML Introduction

XML is based on elements that use tags that are similar to the tags used in HTML. These tags are *free-form,* meaning that you can create your own tags to describe a specific document. The collection of tags and the rules imposed on those tags is called a *grammar.* The best way to look at XML is to contrast it with HTML— even though the two markup languages are not competing with each other.

You will start with some employee data that describes four staff members in your company. The data appears in the following list:

```
Name: George How
Department: Development
Salary: 50,000

Name: Debbie Soo
Department: Sales
Salary: 55,000

Name: John Smith
Department: Administration
Salary: 89,000

Name: Patrick Junior
Department: Development
Salary: 35,000
```

If you were asked to represent this data in HTML, you would probably use a TABLE, as in the following HTML page:

```
<head>
  <title>Data in a Table</title>
</head>
<body>
  <table border=1>
    <thead>
      <th>Name</th><th>Department</th><th>Salary</th>
    </thead>
```

```
        <tbody>
          <tr>
            <td>George How</td>
            <td>Development</td>
            <td>50000</td>
          </tr>
          <tr>
            <td>Debbie Soo</td>
            <td>Sales</td>
            <td>55000</td>
          </tr>
          <tr>
            <td>John Smith</td>
            <td>Administration</td>
            <td>89000</td>
          </tr>
          <tr>
            <td>Patrick Junior</td>
            <td>Development</td>
            <td>35000</td>
          </tr>
        </tbody>
      </table>
    </body>
  </html>
```

This HTML code results in the following display:

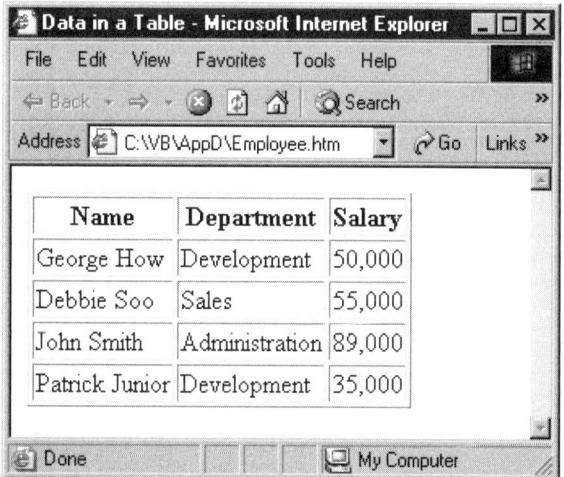

Cool, now you have an HTML rendition of the employee data. Now you need to send that data to the payroll system, which uses a database system to store the data. But can the database system read HTML? The answer to that question is *no,* not without custom translation rules. The preceding example shows the problem with data that is formatted for display.

All data has three aspects—structure, data, and presentation. When you created the HTML table, you only performed the presentation—effectively losing the data. A human can glean the data from the display, but the data is not readable by a computer.

The solution is to convert the data to XML and use that XML document both in the browser and as input to the database. An XML document stores the structure and data but does not contain the presentation logic for that data.

Your employee data represents four employees—you can now create an XML document that mimics that representation. You want to represent a collection of employee records, so you define the collection element using the <employees></employees> tags and then you add four <employee></employee> elements inside the employees element as in the following code segment:

```
<employees>
  <employee>
  </employee>
  <employee>
  </employee>
  <employee>
  </employee>
  <employee>
  </employee>
</employees>
```

In order to represent the data for the different employee elements, you insert name, department, and salary elements in each of the employee elements as in the following code listing:

```
<employees>
  <employee>
    <name>George How</name>
    <department>Development</department>
    <salary>50000</salary>
  </employee>
  <employee>
    <name>Debbie Soo</name>
```

```
    <department>Sales</department>
    <salary>55000</salary>
  </employee>
  <employee>
    <name>John Smith</name>
    <department>Administration</department>
    <salary>89000</salary>
  </employee>
  <employee>
    <name>Patrick Junior</name>
    <department>Development</department>
    <salary>35000</salary>
  </employee>
</employees>
```

The preceding XML describes the data records in a human- and machine-readable format. The final item that must be added to make the XML universally readable is a processing instruction as the first line of the document that describes what the document contains:

```
<?xml version="1.0" ?>
```

This processing directive specifies that the file is compliant with XML version 1.0—note that the version number is in double quotes.

This XML document is stored in a file called Employees.xml that can be opened in the browser as shown in Figure D-2.

The resulting hierarchical display is not all that readable, but then again the XML document does not contain any presentation information. I will return to the display of XML documents later, in the "XSLT" section.

The Parts of XML

So far, you have encountered two of the three parts that make up an XML document: processing directives and elements. The third part is the *attribute*; attributes are qualifiers for an element. In the following element, the attribute is bolded:

```
<employee EmpID="42"/>
```

An element can have any number of attributes.

You can take any data structure and convert it to XML using any combination of elements and attributes—there is no hard-and-fast rule as to whether to use attributes or elements. Attributes are the better choice if the size of the XML

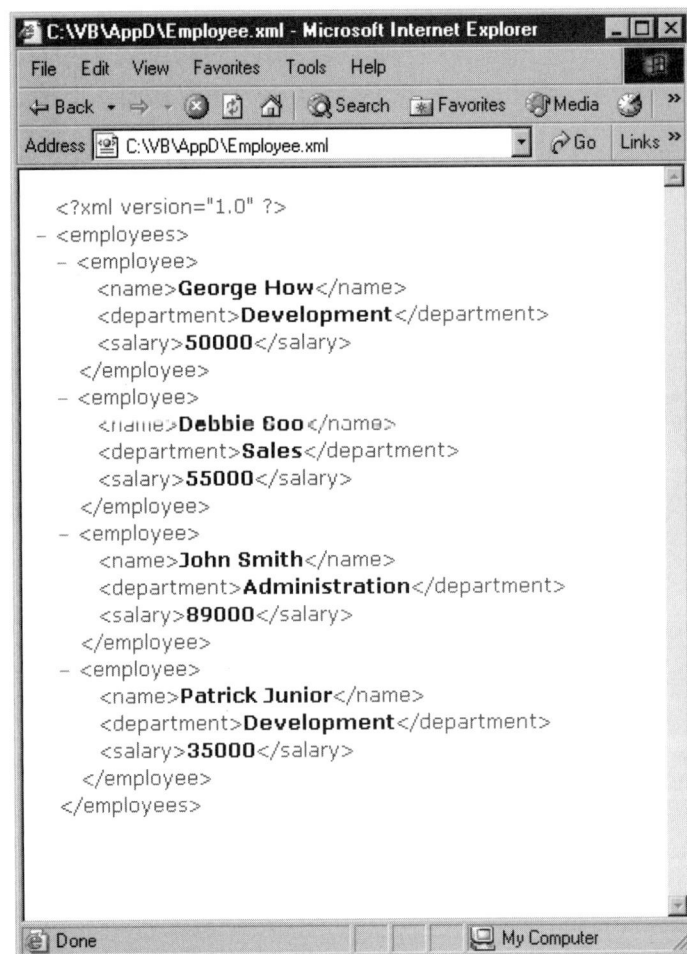

```
<?xml version="1.0" ?>
- <employees>
  - <employee>
      <name>George How</name>
      <department>Development</department>
      <salary>50000</salary>
    </employee>
  - <employee>
      <name>Debbie Boo</name>
      <department>Sales</department>
      <salary>55000</salary>
    </employee>
  - <employee>
      <name>John Smith</name>
      <department>Administration</department>
      <salary>89000</salary>
    </employee>
  - <employee>
      <name>Patrick Junior</name>
      <department>Development</department>
      <salary>35000</salary>
    </employee>
  </employees>
```

document is an issue, and attributes are usually better when the data is inserted into the XML document from a database.

The XML Well-Formedness Rules

There are six simple rules for any XML document. The XML document is said to be well formed if it meets these rules.

1. *The XML document must have one and only one root element.* The root element is the element that describes the document. In the following code segment, the <employees> element is the root element:

```
<?xml versio="1.0" ?>
<employees>
...
</employees>
```

2. *The element must have matching opening and closing tags.* When you open an element, it must also be closed. There are two ways of closing an element, depending on whether the element is empty or not. The following examples show the two approaches:

```
<employee></employee>
```

The </employee> tag closes the element.

```
<employee/>
```

The /> closes the element.

3. *XML documents are case sensitive.* All elements in an XML document are case sensitive. The tag <Employee> is different from <employee>. The XML parser will treat the following code as illegal when the XML document is read:

```
<Employee></employee>
```

The two tags are distinctly different and result in an error.

4. *Elements must be properly nested.* Elements can be nested, but the nesting must be performed without any overlap. The following is an example of improper nesting. This would result in an error:

```
<A>
  <B>
</A>
  </B>
```

The correct nesting would look like this:

```
<A>
  <B>
  </B>
<A>
```

5. *Attribute values must be in double quotes.* Attributes must have quoted values, as in these samples:

```
<employee name="Ken" department="Writing"/>
```

6. *Attributes cannot be repeated.* Attributes must be singular in the element. Repeating attributes results in errors.

Any XML document must meet these six rules. A document that meets these rules is well formed, syntactically correct. All other *Xxx* (XSL, XPath, and so on) languages and technologies are based on the XML document with its six rules for being well formed.

XPath

The XML Path Language (XPath) is used to refer to elements and attributes in an XML document. When an XML document is read into an XML parser, the result is a *node tree,* a hierarchical tree that represents the XML document and is rooted in the document node.

XPath is used to refer to a node both in absolute terms starting from the root element and in relative terms according to the current node. XPath is used in Extensible Stylesheet Language Tranformations (XSLT) to refer to the nodes of the XML document. XSLT is discussed later in this appendix.

An XPath expression contains one or more "location steps," separated by slashes. Each location step has the following form:

```
axis-name::node-test [predicate]*
```

There is an axis name followed by two colons. The next item is the node test followed by zero or more predicates. The axis is used to specify the relationship between the nodes selected by the location step and the current (context) node. Predicates are expressions consisting of values, operators, and other XPath expressions.

The Xpath axis contains a part of the XML document defined with reference to the current node. The node test is used to make selections from the nodes on that axis, filtered by the predicates. The predicates must return true for a particular node to be part of the selected set of nodes; otherwise, the node is removed.

The following tables list the axes, node tests, and functions that are part of the XPath language.

Axes

A location path uses an axis.

Axes	Description
`ancestor::`	The ancestors of the context node consist of the parent of the context node and the parent's parent and so on. The ancestor:: axis always includes the root node unless the context node is the root node.
`ancestor-or-self::`	The context node and its ancestors. The ancestor-or-self:: axis always includes the root node.
`attribute::`	The attributes of the context node.
`child::`	All the direct children of the context node.
`descendant::`	All the descendants of the context node, recursively including all children's children.
`descendant-or-self::`	The context node and its descendants.
`following::`	All nodes that are after the context node in the tree.
`following-sibling::`	All the following siblings of the context node.
`namespace::`	Contains all valid namespaces that can be used on the context node. These include the default namespaces and the XML namespace.
`parent::`	The parent of the context node, if there is one.
`preceding::`	All nodes that are before the context node in the tree, excluding any ancestors, attribute nodes, and namespace nodes.
`preceding-sibling::`	All the preceding siblings of the context node.
`self::`	Just the context node itself.

Node Type Tests

To select nodes that are not element nodes, you use a node type test. The node type test overrides the primary node type for the given axis. For example, `descendant::text()` locates all text nodes descended from the context node, even though the primary node type for the descendant axis is element.

Node Type	Returns
*	Returns true for all nodes of the primary type of the axis.
comment()	True for a comment node.
literal-name()	Returns true for all nodes of that name. If the node is 'DOG', it returns true for all nodes of name 'DOG'.
node()	True for a node of any type.
processing-instruction()	True for a processing instruction node.
text()	True for a text node.

Functions

The XPath functions are used to build the predicate for the statement. Each function description is of the form

```
return-type function-name (parameters)
```

Function	Purpose
boolean boolean(object)	Converts the argument to a Boolean.
number ceiling(number)	Returns the smallest integer that is not less than the argument.
string concat(string, string+)	Returns the concatenation of the arguments.
boolean contains(string, string)	Returns true if the first argument string contains the second argument string; otherwise, returns false.
number count(node-set)	Returns the number of nodes in the node-set argument.
boolean false()	Returns false.
number floor(number)	Returns the largest integer that is not greater than the argument.
node-set id(string)	Selects elements by their unique IDs.
boolean lang(string)	Returns true if the xml:lang attribute of the context node is the same as the argument string.
number last()	Returns a number equal to context size of the expression evaluation context.

Function	Purpose
`string local-name(node-set)`	Returns the local part of the expanded name of the node in the node-set argument that is first in document order.
`string name(node-set)`	Returns a string containing a QName representing the expanded name of the node in the node-set argument that is first in document order.
`string namespace-uri(node-set)`	Returns the namespace Uniform Resource Identifier (URI) of the expanded name of the node in the node-set argument that is first in document order.
`string normalize-space(string)`	Returns the argument string with the whitespace stripped.
`boolean not(Boolean)`	Returns true if the argument is false; otherwise, false.
`number number(object)`	Converts the argument to a number.
`number position()`	Returns the index number of the node within the parent.
`number round(number)`	Returns an integer closest in value to the argument.
`boolean starts-with(string, string)`	Returns true if the first argument string starts with the second argument string; otherwise, returns false.
`string string(object)`	Converts an object to a string.
`string string-length(string)`	Returns the number of characters in the string.
`string substring(string, number, number)`	Returns the substring of the first argument starting at the position specified in the second argument and the length specified in the third argument.
`string substring-after(string, string)`	Returns the substring of the first argument string that follows the first occurrence of the second argument string in the first argument string.
`string substring-before(string, string)`	Returns the substring of the first argument string that precedes the first occurrence of the second argument string in the first argument string.
`number sum(node-set)`	Returns the sum of all nodes in the node-set. Each node is first converted to a number value before summing.
`string translate(string, string, string)`	Returns the first argument string with occurrences of characters in the second argument string replaced by the character at the corresponding position in the third argument string.
`boolean true()`	Returns true.

XPath Examples

Select all descendant elements from the root:

```
/descendant::*
```

Select descendant elements on the context node named Country:

```
/descendant::Country
```

Select the nodes that have more than four direct children with the name County:

```
/descendant::node() [count(child::County) > 4]
```

Select all Employee elements whose name attribute starts with a D:

```
//Employee[starts-with(@name, 'D']
```

XSLT

Extensible Stylesheet Language (XSL) and XML transformation—Extensible Stylesheet Language Transformations (XSLT)—are languages based on XML. Using XSLT, you can transform any well-formed XML document into any other well-formed document.

The XSL document is itself a well-formed XML document that defines the transformations that should take place. This way, you can create an HTML document from an XML document to present the data in a browser.

XSLT is used to convert XML documents from one grammar (see "XML Schemas (XSD)" later in this appendix) to another in one easy step. The need for these transformations arises partly from the increase in document formats stemming from the growing variety of client devices. The current focus on Business-to-Business (B2B) communication has also increased the need for data transformations among multiple formats.

In the bad old days of computing, we transformed data between different systems as well. The big difference between then and now is that the old transformations were custom built for a particular pair of systems and had to be rewritten if anything changed. With the emergence of XML as a data format, the transformation has become almost simple.

XSLT transformations are used for

- Seamless content merging of data from multiple sources

■ Making data available to clients with different needs from the same data source

■ Data extraction

Let's start with the Employee XML document you used earlier in this appendix.

Introduction to XSLT

XSLT is based on *templates*—stylesheets that match the elements in the XML document that is to be transformed. When there is a match for an element, the transformation is performed according to the template.

Earlier in this appendix, you used the Employees.xml XML document. It contained the following code:

```
<?xml version="1.0" ?>
<employees>
  <employee>
    <name>George How</name>
    <department>Development</department>
    <salary>50000</salary>
  </employee>
  <employee>
    <name>Debbie Soo</name>
    <department>Sales</department>
    <salary>55000</salary>
  </employee>
  <employee>
    <name>John Smith</name>
    <department>Administration</department>
    <salary>89000</salary>
  </employee>
  <employee>
    <name>Patrick Junior</name>
    <department>Development</department>
    <salary>35000</salary>
  </employee>
</employees>
```

You need to convert this XML data to an HTML page that will display the employees in a table.

You will develop the XSLT stylesheet to convert your XML document in steps. XSLT stylesheets are well-formed XML documents and must be created according to the same six rules as for XML. In addition, you need to declare a namespace for the XSLT to ensure that the parser knows what you are actually doing; this namespace is necessary to indicate the XSLT standard you are using. The following two lines must appear at the top of every XSLT stylesheet:

```
<?xml version="1.0" ?>
<xsl:stylesheet xmlns:xsl="http://www.w3.org/1999/XSL/Transform" version="1.0">
```

The primary XML processing in XSLT is to apply template procedures to matching XML elements in the source document. The <xsl:template> element uses a match attribute that specifies the element type that the template should be applied to. XSLT uses the current node or context node to determine what to match against. This means that all the matching nodes are specified relative to the current node. The match attribute is optional and defaults to the root (/) of the document if not specified.

The <xsl:apply-templates/> declaration starts a process that applies all matching templates inserting the output at the current location of the processing.

The following <xsl:template> declaration matches the <employees> element (the file is saved as Employee.xsl):

```
<?xml version="1.0" ?>
<xsl:stylesheet xmlns:xsl="http://www.w3.org/1999/XSL/Transform" version="1.0">
<xsl:template match="employees">
  <html>
    <head>
      <title>Employee Records</title>
    </head>
    <body>
      <center><h1>Employee Records</h1></center>
      <center>
        <table border="1">
          <th>Number</th>
          <th>Name</th>
          <th>Department</th>
          <th>Salary</th>

          <xsl:apply-templates/>

        </table>
        </center>
      </body>
    </html>
  </xsl:template>
</xsl:stylesheet>
```

To see what this XSLT stylesheet will produce as an output, you need to attach it to the Employee.xml document. The following processing directive performs that action. The first two lines in the XML document must look as follows:

```
<?xml version="1.0" ?>
<?xml-stylesheet type="text/xsl" href="Employee.xsl"?>
```

The output is not quite what you expected, as can be seen here:

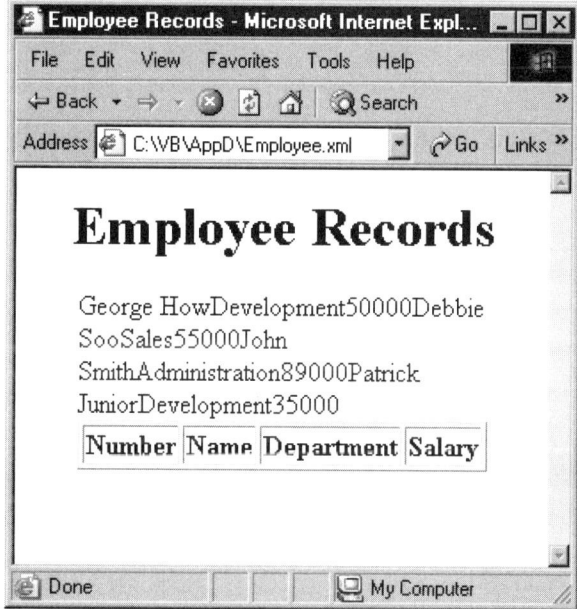

You need to actually match the individual elements in the XML document to ensure that they are transformed. This is how you do that.

Create a new <xsl:template> element that matches the <employee> element in the XML document:

```
<xsl:template match="employee">
  <tr>
    <td><xsl:number/></td>
    <td><xsl:value-of select="name"/></td>
    <td><xsl:value-of select="department"/></td>
    <td><xsl:value-of select="salary"/></td>
```

```
    </tr>
  </xsl:template>
```

The <xsl:value-of/> element is used to retrieve the value of a named node by using the select attribute; select="." translates to the current node. The final transformation is shown here:

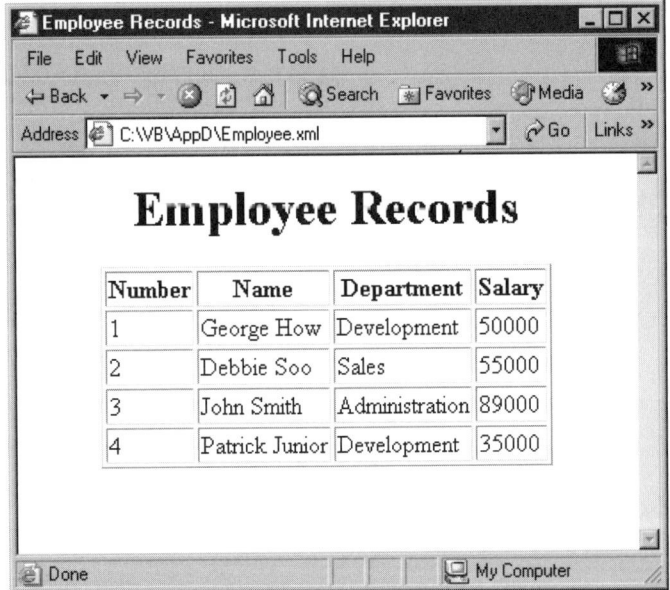

XSLT Elements

The following table provides a brief summary of all the XSLT elements.

XSLT Element	Purpose
`<xsl:apply-imports/>`	Calls a template from an imported stylesheet.
`<xsl:apply-templates/>`	Used to pass the context on to another template. Use the select attribute to specify what element to continue processing.
`<xsl:attribute/>`	Generates an attribute in the destination document.
`<xsl:attribute-set/>`	Defines a named set of attributes.
`<xsl:call-template/>`	Used to call a template by name.

XSLT Element	Purpose
`<xsl:choose/>`	Provides multiple conditional testing in conjunction with the <xsl:otherwise> element and the <xsl:when> element.
`<xsl:comment/>`	Generates a comment in the output.
`<xsl:copy/>`	Copies the current node from the source to the output. Does not copy any children or attributes.
`<xsl:copy-of/>`	Copies a full tree, including child elements and attributes.
`<xsl:decimal-format/>`	Declares a decimal-format, which controls the interpretation of a format pattern used by the format-number function.
`<xsl:document/>`	Switches the target of the result tree to another document.
`<xsl:element/>`	Generates an element with the specified name in the destination document.
`<xsl:fallback/>`	Is used to specify what actions to take if the action specified is not supported by the processor.
`<xsl:for-each/>`	For looping through the node selected in the XPath expression in the select attribute.
`<xsl:if/>`	Simple Boolean test.
`<xsl:import/>`	Imports another XSLT file.
`<xsl:include/>`	Includes another XSLT file.
`<xsl:key/>`	Declares a named key for use with the key() function in XPath expressions.
`<xsl:message/>`	To issue error messages or warnings.
`<xsl:namespace-alias/>`	Places specific namespaces in the output document.
`<xsl:number/>`	Inserts a formatted number into the result tree.
`<xsl:otherwise/>`	Provides multiple conditional testing in conjunction with the <xsl:choose> element and the <xsl:when> element.
`<xsl:output/>`	Specifies options for use in serializing the result tree.
`<xsl:param/>`	Declares a named parameter for use within an <xsl:stylesheet> element or an <xsl:template> element.
`<xsl:preserve-space/>`	Preserves whitespace in a document.
`<xsl:processing-instruction/>`	Inserts a processing instruction in the output.

XSLT Element	Purpose
`<xsl:sort/>`	Specifies sort criteria for node lists selected by `<xsl:for-each>` or `<xsl:apply-templates>`.
`<xsl:strip-space/>`	Strips whitespace from a document.
`<xsl:stylesheet/>`	Specifies the document element of an XSLT file. The document element contains all other XSLT elements.
`<xsl:template/>`	Defines a reusable template for generating the desired output for nodes of a particular type and context.
`<xsl:text/>`	Generates text in the output.
`<xsl:transform/>`	Performs the same function as `<xsl:stylesheet>`.
`<xsl:value-of/>`	Inserts the value of the selected node as text.
`<xsl:variable/>`	Specifies a value bound in an expression.
`<xsl:when/>`	Provides multiple conditional testing in conjunction with the `<xsl:choose>` element and the `<xsl:otherwise>` element.
`<xsl:with-param/>`	Passes a parameter to a template.

XML Schemas (XSD)

The XML schema became a standard on May 2, 2001—that was the day that XML came of age, when XML became the de facto standard for all data transfers. The Extensible Schema Definition language (XSD) is the language that XML schemas are written in.

The XML schema allows you to take a well-formed XML document and validate that the document meets the criteria for a valid document. The schema is very much like the data model of a database—it describes the elements and attributes that must be in the XML document for the document to be valid. The schema also allows you to declare cardinality for elements, and any data types that must be adhered to.

The impact of the XML schema is enormous. Before the standard was released, there was only one possible way of validating XML documents, and that was through a document type definition (DTD). The DTD was inherited from SGML and uses a very archaic structure, which, taken together with a lack of data-type definitions, poses a limitation for future development. That being said, there will probably be DTDs around for some time because a large number are in use today.

XML schemas are written in XML and are a logical extension of the XML language. The XSD semantics is defined using a fixed vocabulary of elements and attributes, in other words, the XSD schema is described using XML. Any valid XML schema must be validated against this XML schema.

XML schemas support multiple namespaces to be imported, so data types defined in other namespaces can be used in a schema. This makes it possible to reuse definitions rather than reinventing the wheel each time a definition is needed. By taking advantage of the XML namespace prefixes, any name conflicts are removed.

The XML schemas give you access to built-in as well as primitive data types that can be combined into new complex data types that can contain other elements and attributes.

Let's write a schema for your employees XML document and validate it against that schema.

Schema

XML schemas are structurally built around building blocks known as *schema components*. These components are sorted into three groups: primary, secondary, and helper categories. The primary components are simple and complex data-type definitions as well as element and attribute declarations. The secondary components are groups of attributes, identity constraints, model groups, and notation declarations. Helper components form part of other components and are annotations, model groups, particles, and wildcards.

This discussion centers on the primary components.

Primary Components

Elements are declared in an XML schema by using the <xsd:element> element; the declaration contains name and type attributes. The following code segment declares an element named City that is a string data type:

```
<xsd:element name="City" type="xsd:string/>
```

Cardinality of the element is indicated by adding the minOccurs and maxOccurs attributes to the element declaration, as is shown in the following code segment:

```
<xsd:element name="City" type="xsd:string
            minOccurs="1"
            maxOccurs="12"/>
```

If the minOccurs attribute is missing, the default is 1, and if the maxOccurs attribute is missing, it defaults to 1 as well. If you set both minOccurs and maxOccurs to the same value, that means that the element must occur exactly that many times. For example, the following code segment defines the City element to occur exactly 42 times:

```
<xsd:element name="City" type="xsd:string
            minOccurs="42"
            maxOccurs="42"/>
```

Attributes are declared by using the <xsd:attribute> element, which uses the name and type attributes. The following example declares a phonenumber attribute that is a string:

```
<xsd:attribute name="phonenumber" type="xsd:string"/>
```

The <xsd:attributeGroup> element is used to declare a set of attributes that occur together in several data types. Declaring the group in this way, you can refer to the members from the complex type definition. The following is an example of an attributeGroup:

```
<xsd:attributeGroup name="EmployeeAttr">
   <xsd:attribute name="PhoneNumber" type="xsd:string"/>
   <xsd:attribute name="MobileNumber" type="xsd:string"/>
   <xsd:attribute name="Email" type="xsd:string"/>
</xsd:attributeGroup>
```

To put these element and attribute declarations together, you need to define an XML schema file. The most basic definition will have the following processing and namespace declarations.

```
<?xml version="1.0">
<xsd:schema xmlns:xsd="http://www.w3.org/2001/XMLSchema">

...

</xsd:schema>
```

To build the XML schema for the Employee XML document, you need to declare the name, department, salary, employee, and employees elements as follows:

```
<?xml version="1.0">
<xsd:schema xmlns:xsd="http://www.w3.org/2001/XMLSchema">
   <xsd:complexType name="employeeType">
      <xsd:sequence>
         <xsd:element name="name" type="xsd:string"/>
         <xsd:element name="department" type="xsd:string"/>
         <xsd:element name="salary" type="xsd:integer"/>
      </xsd:sequence>
   </xsd:complexType>
   <xsd:element name="employees" type="employeeType"
               minOccur="0"
               maxOccur="unbonded"/>
</xsd:schema>
```

The XML schema is applied to the Employee.xml document as follows:

```
<?xml version="1.0" ?>
<?xml-stylesheet type="text/xsl" href="Employee.xsl"?>
<employees xmlns:xsi="http://www.w3.org/2001/XMLSchema-instance"
  xsi:noNamespaceSchemaLocation="Employee.xsd">

...
</employees>
```

In order to validate the XML document, the parser must be switched to validation mode; to do that, you will need to use the Validator.htm page that will load the file and validate it. The Validator is available as a free download from http://msdn.microsoft.com/downloads. You will have to search for validator.htm.

Figure D-3 shows the result of validating Employee.xml.

After you introduce an error in the XML document, the validation will fail as shown in Figure D-4.

FIGURE D-3

Validating the
document

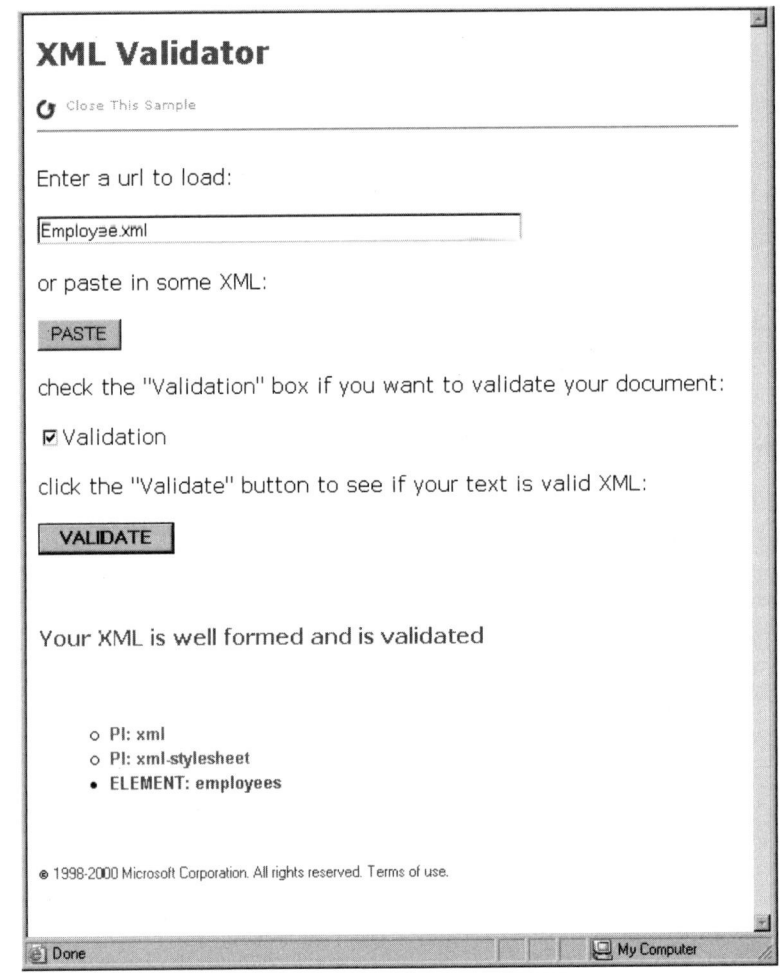

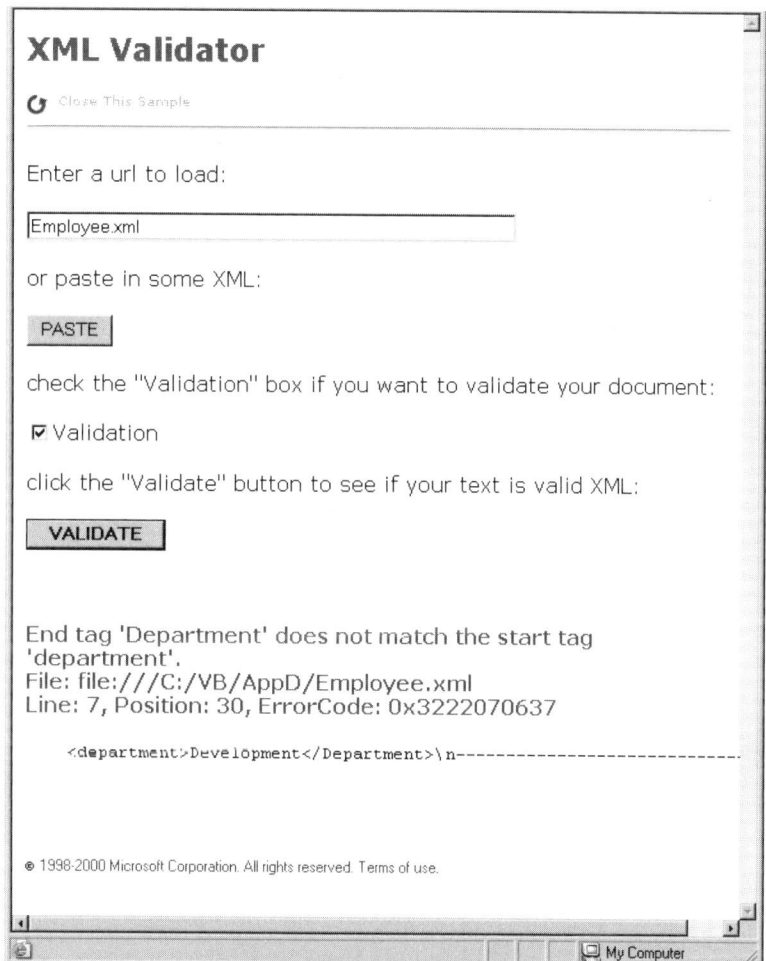

FIGURE D-4

Invalid XML
document

UDDI

The Universal Description, Discovery, and Integration (UDDI) registry is designed
to be the yellow pages of the Web. UDDI is a registry where businesses can register
the services they make available. There is no requirement that you register your web

services with a UDDI registry, but if you don't, it will be hard for your customers to find you. UDDI is an industry standard that has wide support from the major players on the Internet.

To register with a UDDI registry, you will need to provide an XML document that identifies you as a business entity and the web services you want to register. The value of UDDI is something that you will have to weigh. You can learn more at two locations: http://www.uddi.org/about.html and http://uddi.microsoft.com.

The UDDI registry performs the role of an XML web service broker that makes it possible for potential consumers to find an XML web service.

The UDDI Programmer's API Specification defines functions that provide the needed model for accessing UDDI registries. Two types of API are defined:

- The Publisher's API, which is used to publish information in a UDDI registry

- The Inquiry API, which is used to read information from a UDDI registry

In addition to these standard APIs, Microsoft has released a UDDI SDK. These APIs define a large number of Simple Object Access Protocol (SOAP) messages that are used to communicate with a UDDI registry.

The namespaces that support UDDI in the .NET Framework are

- ```
  Imports Microsoft.Uddi
  Imports Microsoft.Uddi.Api
  Imports Microsoft.Uddi.Business
  Imports Microsoft.Uddi.ServiceType
  ```

- ```
  Imports Microsoft.Uddi.Binding
  Imports Microsoft.Uddi.Service
  ```

- ```
  Imports Microsoft.Uddi.Authentication
  ```

You will look at how to use the Publisher and Inquiry APIs in the following sections.

The Publisher API

Through the Publisher API, you have authorized access to the UDDI registry as well as the ability to publish information by adding and deleting elements. You will need to be both authenticated and authorized to be able to modify information in the UDDI registry. You must first get an authorization token by calling `get_authToken()`; this
  ```

token is then added as a parameter to subsequent calls. Once finished with the Publisher API, you will need to destroy the token by calling `discard_authToken()`.

The methods used to add and edit elements in the UDDI registry belong in the `save_xxx()` family of methods that operates on the main UDDI types as shown in the following list:

```
save_business()
save_service()
save_binding()
save_tModel()
```

The methods used to delete elements in the UDDI registry use these delete_*xxx* methods:

```
delete_business()
delete_service()
delete_binding()
delete_tModel()
```

Once the elements are added, you will need to define the relationships between business entities. The following methods perform those actions:

```
add_publisherAssertions()
get_assertionStatusReport()
get_publisherAssertions()
delete_publisherAssertions()
```

You will call these methods as if they are local to you. The methods are, however, operations that can be invoked from UDDI by using SOAP.

The first decision to take is whether to use a commercial UUDI registry or a private solution. You will explore the private solutions in this book, as that is what is tested in the exam.

There are three solutions for implementing private custom solutions to publishing an XML web service.

■ **Private UDDI Registry**   The UDDI specification was designed to be a public, replicated repository—there were no provisions made for private UDDI registries. There is currently work in progress to include private UDDI registries.

The advantage of implementing a private UDDI registry is that when the UDDI specification is changed to include private registries, you will be ready for that.

The disadvantage is that to implement the private UDDI registry, you will have to correctly implement the full UDDI specification.

■ **Private publish/discover architecture**   You can implement only a minimum part of the UDDI specification to build an architecture that is tailored to your environment.

The advantage is that you can build a custom implementation and that you do not need to wait for the UDDI specification to be updated.

The disadvantage is that it is a custom implementation that will not be compatible with the standard when it is released.

■ **Hard-code endpoints**   The simplest private solution is to hard-code the endpoints of the XML web service. This solution does not require UDDI.

The advantage is that you don't have to search for the XML web service and that the solution is very quick to implement.

The disadvantage is that you need to change your applications if the XML web service needs to be moved to a different location.

In the following example, you will publish an XML web service to a UDDI registry. The first thing you need to define are the keys for your source and destination. The UUID keys are generated using the GUIDGEN utility that is part of Visual Studio .NET.

```
Shared tModelKeySource As String = _
                    "uuid:535C20ED-1288-4e6a-8BA4 94BAE8A2E7A4"
Shared tModelKeyDest As String = _
                    "uuid:A2567465-CB09-4418-A438-5570EF4D4248"
```

You define the keys as static to ensure they will never change.

You will start by registering the business entity. To perform this action, you define the following method:

```
Private Function PubBus(string name, string description, Contact contact) _
            As BusinessDetail
    Publish.AuthenticationMode = AuthenticationMode.UddiAuthentication
    Publish.Url = "http://abc.abc/"
    Publish.HttpClient.Credentials = New NetworkCredential
                        ("ken","password","KENSNABBEN")

    Dim bEntity As BusinessEntity = New BusinessEntity()
    bEntity.Name = name    ' name = the business entity
    bEntity.Descriptions.Add("en",description)
                        ' description = the long name of the business
```

```
        bEntity.Contacts.Add(contact)

    Dim sBusiness As Microsoft.Uddi.SaveBusiness = New SaveBusiness()
    sBusiness.BusinessEntities.Add(businessEntity)
    Dim bd As BusinessDetail = sBusiness.Send()
    return bd
End Function
```

You call the PubBus() method by passing the name, description, and contact information for the business entity:

```
...
BusinessDetail bd
Dim con As Contact = New Contact()
con.PersonName = "John Smith"
con.Emails.Add("john.smith@abc.abc")
con.Descriptions.Add("en","Web Site Administrator")
bd = PubBus("ABC Corp","The ABC Corporation Service", con)
...
```

Once the business is registered, you can proceed by publishing the service as in the following function:

```
Private Function PubService() As ServiceDetail
    ' assign the Service name
    Dim serviceName As string = "ABC conversions"
    ' retrieve the business key
    Dim businessKey As string = bd.BusinessEntities[0].BusinessKey
    ' get the tModelKey
    Dim tModelKey As string = tModelKeySource
    ' make the URL dependent on the server we are running on.
    Dim urlAccess As string = string.Format
                    ("http://{0}/acb/ABC.asmx",Environment.MachineName)
    ' define the descriptions
    Dim bindingDescription As string = "ASP.NET service"
    Dim tModelDescription As string = 'ABC web service"
    Publish.AuthenticationMode = AuthenticationMode.UddiAuthentication
    Publish.Url = "http://abc.abc/"
    ' authenticate
    Publish.HttpClient.Credentials = New NetworkCredential
                            ("Ken","password","KENSNABBEN")

    Dim bTemp As BindingTemplate = New BindingTemplate()
    bTemp.Descriptions.Add(bindingDescription);

    Dim aPoint As AccessPoint = New AccessPoint(URLTypeEnum.Http,urlAccess)
    bTemp.AccessPoint = accessPoint

    Dim tMInstInfo As TModelInstanceInfo = New TModelInstanceInfo()
```

```
tMInstInfo.TModelKey = tModelKey
tMInstInfo.Descriptions.Add(tModelDescription)

bTemp.TModelInstanceDetail.TModelInstanceInfos.Add(tMInstInfo)

Dim bService As BusinessService = New BusinessService()
bService.BusinessKey = businessKey
bService.Name = serviceName
bService.BindingTemplates.Add(bTemp)

Dim sService As SaveService = New SaveService()
sService.BusinessServices.Add(bService)
Dim sd As ServiceDetail = sService.Send()
return sd
End Function
```

What makes this code portable is that you build the URL for the service using the server name by using the `Environment.MachineName` property.

Once the service is published, you can proceed to use UDDI to find the service from the client.

The Inquiry API

You use the Inquiry API to locate and enumerate the data in a UDDI registry, The API defines methods to find data in the UDDI registry. The following `find_xxx()` methods support the main UDDI types.

```
find_service()
find_business()
find_relatedBusinesses()
find_binding()
find_tModel()
```

The UDDI registry uses a key that is a Universally Unique Identifier (UUID)—this key is used to communicate to the client. For example, the `find_business()` method returns a UUID key that is used as a parameter to the `find_service()` method call to find a service exposed by a specific business.

SOAP messages are used to encapsulate the `find_xxx()` methods, as you can see in the following code segment, which searches for a business entity named ABC:

```
<?xml version="1.0" encoding="UTF-8" ?>
<Envelope xmlns="http://schemas.xmlsoap.org/soap/envelope/">
  <body>
```

```
        <find_business generic="1.0" xmlns="urn:uddi-org:api">
            <name>ABC</name>
        </find_business>
    </body>
</Envelope>
```

You can use the `find_relatedBusinesses()` method to locate businesses that have relationships with a given business. In order to get more information about a specific element, you use the `get_xxx()` methods:

```
get_businessDetail()
get_businessDetailExt()
get_serviceDetail()
get_bindingDetail()
get_tModelDetail()
```

In the next example, you will look at how you locate an XML web service. Four steps are involved in finding and using an XML web service:

1. Use `find_business()` to locate a business that has published XML web services.

2. Retrieve service information for the services published by that business.

3. Retrieve the binding template for a service.

4. Access the XML web service using the binding information.

The following code segment shows how to find a business:

```
. . .
Dim fBus As FindBusiness = new FindBusiness()
fBus.Name = "ABC"
Dim bList As BusinessList = fBus.Send()
. . .
```

Once you have located the business, you need to navigate the list that the business returns to retrieve binding information and the binding template, as is shown in the following code segment:

```
. . .
Dim bInfo As BusinessInfo
Dim sInfo As ServiceInfo
Dim cTemp As BindingTemplate
For Each bInfo In bList.BusinessInfos
    For Each sInfo In bInfo.ServiceInfos
```

```
            Dim fBinding As FindBinding = New FindBinding()
            fBinding.ServiceKey = sInfo.ServiceKey
            Dim bDetail As BindingDetail = fBinding.Send()
            For Each bTemp In bDetail.BindingTemplates
               If bTemp.TModelInstanceDetail.TModelInstanceInfos(0).TModelKey _
                  = tModelKey Then
                  sURL = bTemp.AccessPoint.Text
                  GoTo gotIt
               End If
            Next
        Next
    Next
gotIt:
    ...
```

Now when you have located the binding information, all you need to do is to set the URL property of the XML web service proxy and invoke the XML web service methods as in the following code segment:

```
Dim xws As XWService = New XWService()
xws.URL = sURL
Dim amount As XmlNode = xws.getAmount("chequing")
...
```

The preceding example showed the four steps involved in finding and using an XML web service through a UDDI registry.

The Microsoft UDDI SDK

Microsoft has published the UDDI SDK to make using the UDDI APIs easier. The UDDI SDK provides managed wrappers for the UDDI data structures and APIs. The wrappers are in the Microsoft.UDDI namespace and are represented as .NET classes. The Send() method performs the action of the class.

SOAP

The Simple Object Application Protocol (SOAP) is a standard extensible communications protocol that makes it possible to send any type of data between dissimilar systems. SOAP is XML based and is yet another proof of the power of XML.

SOAP consists of three major parts:

■ The SOAP envelope is a construction that describes the message content, the recipients, and whether content and recipients are optional or mandatory.

■ The SOAP encoding rules serialize the message and are capable of exchanging instances of application-defined data types.

■ The SOAP Remote Procedure Call (RPC) representation is used to pass procedure calls and responses.

The simplicity of SOAP comes from the capability of SOAP messages to be delivered over HTTP. To illustrate, the following SOAP message is embedded in an HTTP request:

```
POST    /SignUp.asmx    HTTP/1.1
Host: www.abc.abc
Content-Type: text/xml;
Charset="utf-8"
Content-Length: nnnn
SOAPAction: "http://www.cba.abc/SignUp"

<SOAP-ENV:Envelope
  xmlns:SOAP-ENV="http://schemas.xmlsoap.org/soap/envelope/
  SOAP-ENV:encodingStyle="http://schemas.xmlsoap.org/soap/encoding/">
  <SOAP-ENV:Body>
    <m:MailingList xmlns:m="http://www.cba.abc/SignUp">
      <Name>Ken Lind</Name>
      <Email>kennethslind@hotmail.com</Email>
    </m:MailingList>
  </SOAP-ENV:Body>
</SOAP-ENV:Envelope>
```

This message is a regular HTTP request that performs a POST method on the mailing list server at http://www.cba/abc/SignUp (SOAPAction). The body of the POST message is the SOAP envelope and the body that contains the sign-up information, all in XML.

Every well-formed SOAP message has a SOAP envelope, which contains optional information in the header as well as a body. Additional headers can be included for such things as authentication. All the data in a SOAP message is sent in clear text, so if there is a need to encrypt the authentication header, the developer must use SOAP extensions to get access to the data prior to serialization.

As you saw, SOAP messages can be sent using HTTP between clients. One of the design goals for SOAP was to be able to pass RPCs using SOAP. That is made possible through the use of the SOAP extensions. The caller packages the procedure call into a SOAP message that is unpackaged by the server and acted upon. Return results are packaged in SOAP messages and returned to the caller.

MCAD/MCSD

MICROSOFT® CERTIFIED APPLICATION DEVELOPER
& MICROSOFT® CERTIFIED SOLUTION DEVELOPER

E

Creating User Accounts

Thishis appendix contains explanations of how to create user accounts for use in the Windows environment. If you want a brief overview of Active Directory, just keep reading. If you are looking for specifics about how to create domain, local, or SQL Server user accounts, you can just jump to those sections.

The network you will need to try the domain exercises in this appendix consist of a Windows 2000 server configured to be a domain controller, and a Windows 2000 Professional workstation that is used to control local accounts.

The Windows Authentication Scheme

In every computer network starting with the mainframe through the first office local area networks (LANs) to today's enterprise networks, there has always been a need to simplify authentication of the user's credentials.

Authentication started out with a local database of usernames and passwords in the mainframe that the user had to be authenticated against before getting access to any resources on the mainframe. When a second mainframe was needed, the user had to authenticate against that mainframe's database—usually with a different user name and password.

In the LAN environment that connected together a number of users to file and print servers, the LAN used a central database that the user authenticated against in order the gain access to the LAN's resources. If the same user needed access to multiple LANs, there would be multiple username and password combinations for each LAN.

That was the situation that virtually all companies faced during the early part of the 1990s. Multiple username-password combinations were proliferating that the end user needed to remember and that needed to be managed. The solution was to combine all the locally maintained databases into one central database where the authentication information was stored and that provided a centralized authentication service.

A number of different solutions were proposed, and some were developed into centralized authentication products. What has emerged are a couple of standards that go beyond just keeping user authentication information. These standards define how to keep information about the users, computers, printers, offices—as a matter of fact, anything you want to keep track of in a directory (very much like the white pages directory) that can be used by anyone in the network. What follows is a list of the standards that form the base of the current directory service used in the Microsoft environment:

- **X.500**   The standard that defines how to store and query information about objects that are stored in the directory
- **Kerberos V5**   A software component that allows for a very scalable authentication architecture
- **LDAP**   The Lightweight Directory Access Protocol, the standard communication protocol that is used with X.500

Take a closer look at these standards.

X.500

The X.500 standard was developed to store directory information about objects in such a way that the information would be unique and searchable. The standard is based on the *Comité Consultatif International Téléphonique et Télégraphique* (*International Telephone and Telegraph Consultative Committee*, or *CCITT*) Recommendations X.500 and the associated APIA–X/OPEN API specifications. The best example of how X.500 works is the standard white pages that we all use to find the phone number of an individual.

You can browse the white pages and search for information according to the individual's last name sorted from A to Z. By browsing according to the alphabetic sorting, you can find the information you require. A possibly more refined method is illustrated by the yellow pages, where the information is filtered on businesses and sorted on business category.

The X.500 directory service is a system designed to manage detailed information about network objects that include users, services, systems, applications, and the enterprise itself. The highlights of X.500 include

- **Distributed directory**   The X.500 database is distributed across the network.
- **Simplified management**   All management is performed locally. Each part of the X.500 environment is responsible for its own information.
- **Standards**   The X.500 standard is based on a number of protocols that have been approved by the CCITT, the International Telecommunication Union (ITU), and the International Organization for Standardization (ISO).

- ■ **Querying**   X.500 supports powerful querying of the information stored in the directory.

- ■ **Single namespace**   X.500 supports a single namespace based on the organization's name (O). This support for a homogeneous namespace lets X.500 support *distinguished names* and *relative distinguished names*. A distinguished name is unique within the namespace (global), while a relative distinguished name is unique within the immediate location of the name (local scope).

- ■ **Objects**   The objects in X.500 are defined using the organization (O), organizational unit (OU), and common name (CN) objects. This allows a very fine-grained definition of any object in the organization.

Kerberos V5

Kerberos is an authentication system that performs mutual authentication. Kerberos can be looked on as the notary public that is trusted by everyone to be honestly and incorruptibly performing the authentication task. One example that explains the role of Kerberos is the following used car purchase story.

Greg is going to purchase a used car from Honest Joe in what should be a very straightforward business transaction, but there is a small problem. Greg only has a blank check in his pocket, and he wants to pay for the car with that check.

Honest Joe is honest, not gullible, so he demands some proof that Greg is not a con artist who will hand over a rubber check and then make a run for it in his new wheels.

So there you are. Greg says give me the car for this check, while Honest Joe says, prove to me that you are honest as well, then I'll give you the car. This is a standoff situation that is a classic deadlock.

The solution is Kerberos. Kerberos is the notary public in the town where Honest Joe has his used car lot. Greg sends an encoded message over to Kerberos requesting permission to communicate. Kerberos takes the request and encodes it in such a way that Greg can validate that only Kerberos could have sent the message back. This is how Kerberos ensures that he is recognized as a notary public. The technical name for this message is a *ticket-granting ticket (TGT)*.

Greg now sends a new message back to Kerberos requesting that he be validated to purchase a car from Honest Joe with a check. This request is encoded in such a way that Kerberos can validate that Greg is truly the Greg that is asking for permission.

Kerberos calls his contacts downtown that tell him that Greg has money in the bank and that Greg is as honest as he claims to be.

Kerberos sends this information back to Greg, encoded in such a way that when Greg hands this message over, Honest Joe is the only person that can read the approval and confirm that Kerberos approved. The technical name for this message is the *ticket*.

There are timestamps in all these messages to ensure that if someone managed to intercept a message and tried to perform a man-in-the-middle security attack, the impact would be very minimal if any.

LDAP

The original protocol that was designed to work with X.500 was the Directory Access Protocol (DAP). This protocol was considered heavy, because it relied on a local X.500 node. As part of the further development of X.500, a new protocol was developed: the Lightweight Directory Access Protocol (LDAP).

LDAP is one of the Internet standards and is based on a number of Requests for Comments (RFCs), namely, 1777, 1778, and 2251. The function of LDAP is to provide support for querying a directory service.

It is through LDAP that a client can access the directory for information about an object. LDAP also defines how a directory service stores the directory information and how it names the directory objects.

Active Directory

Microsoft presented Active Directory (AD) when Windows 2000 was released. This appendix is not meant to teach you the finer points about Active Directory. Rather, I aim at introducing the parts of Active Directory that will be a basis for how you create user accounts.

Active Directory is a logical representation of the objects in a network and organizes those objects using the organization (O), organizational unit (OU), and common name (CN) objects.

The primary logical objects that are related to Active Directory are domains, trees, forests, and lower-level objects. Active Directory uses the Domain Name System (DNS) to name the three high-level objects (domain, tree, and forest). This dependence on the Internet standard DNS is crucial to Active Directory.

Domains

Windows 2000 *domains* are very similar to the domains that were used in Windows NT. They are containers of objects that share

- Security requirements
- Replication processes
- Administration

Domains are the core unit of Active Directory and usually take on your registered Internet name. Domains can be grouped hierarchically, where the top-level domain is called the parent domain and the lower-level domains are child domains.

In Figure E-1, you can see how the domains are depicted as triangles.

Tree

Trees are collections of domains that share the same root domain name (namespace). Normally only large enterprises will be concerned with trees. The tree is based on the common namespace and is purely logical.

In Figure E-1, you can see two trees. The tree is represented by the lines that connect the domains.

Forests

A *forest* is a collection of trees, as in the real world. The forest is the highest-level object in Active Directory. The forest connects different namespaces together so that resources can be shared among multiple entities.

Common reasons for forests are that two companies merge but want to maintain their namespaces, or that two companies want to make some resources available to trading partners and/or customers.

In Figure E-1, you can see the forest that is made up of two trees.

Organizational Units

The *organizational unit (OU)* represents a logical administrative unit. The OU is a container that holds other objects, such as nested OUs, users, computers, printers, and so on.

In Figure E-1, you can see the representation of the OU as a circle; it is in effect a container.

FIGURE E-1   Active Directory details

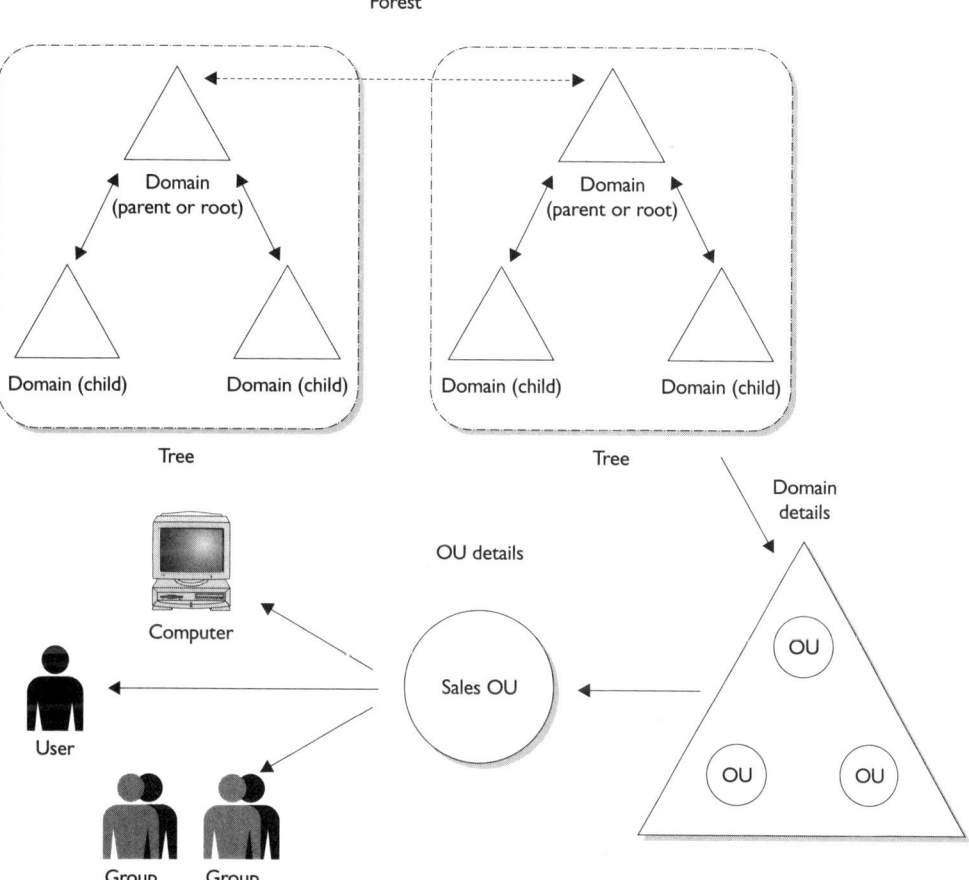

Sites

The *site* is a representation of the objects that are physically connected together. Sites are used to define communication links rather than as administrative boundaries.

The user accounts belong in an OU that in turn is part of a domain. This structure together with the Active Directory services that Windows 2000 provides makes the account usable through the entire forest. The user account can be authenticated from any computer in the forest.

The other type of account that is available is the local user account that is stored in a local security database. These accounts are available only on the local computer.

Creating an Account in a Domain

User accounts for use in domains are created using the Active Directory Users And Computers console, which is available from Start | Settings | Control Panel | Administrative Tools, or Start | Programs | Administrative Tools if the Administrative Tools option is turned on.

EXERCISE E-1

Creating a Domain Account

In this exercise, you will go through the steps of creating a user account in a domain. For this exercise to work, you will need to have a defined domain, and you must have administrative permissions for that domain.

1. Open the Active Directory Users And Computers console that is available from Start | Settings | Control Panel | Administrative Tools.

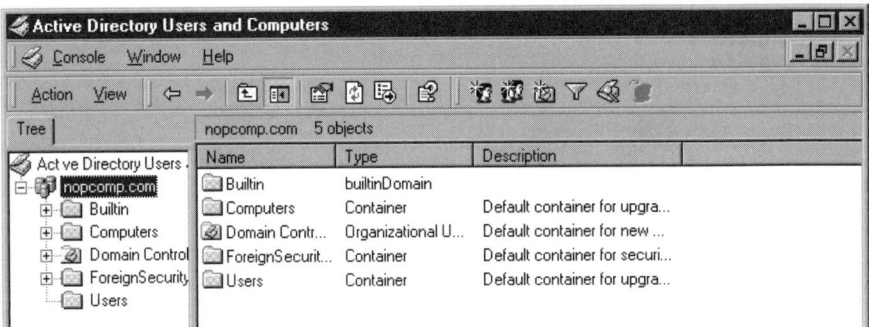

The domain name shown here is the domain name used in my office. You will see the domain name of your organization.

2. Click the Users container in the left panel.

3. The right panel will show the users and groups that are already defined for your domain.

4. To start creating the user account, you will need to click the Action menu. Select New | User.

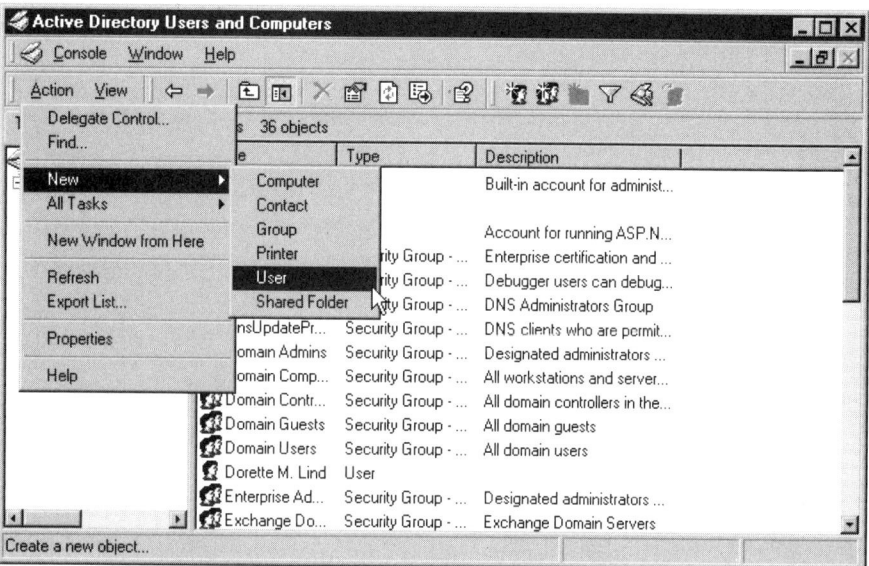

5. In the New Object – User dialog, you will need to fill in the information about the user.

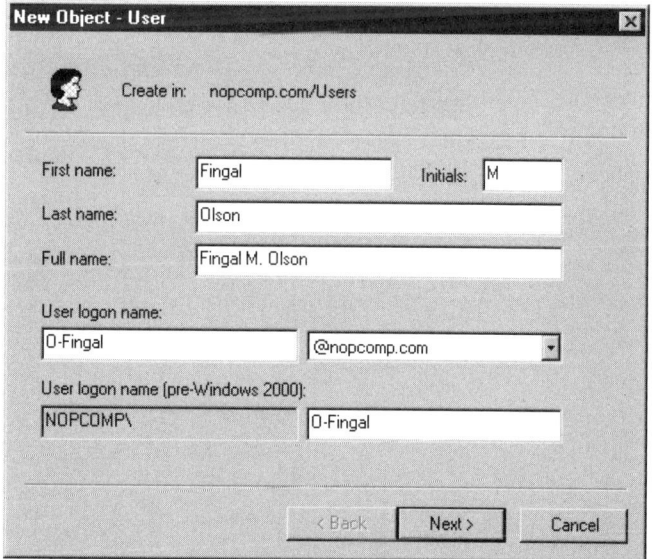

The name of the user is self explanatory, but the logon name might not be. The logon name forms a unique combination together with the domain name that is called the distinguished name (DN). If you were to use a duplicate name, the system would ask you to change to a unique name.

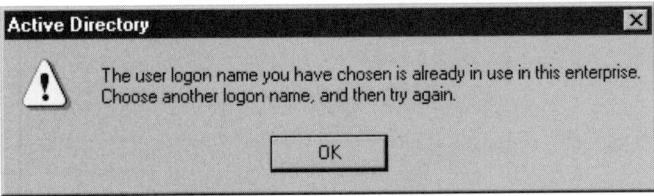

6. Click Next. The second part of the New Object – User dialog is displayed.

7. Enter and confirm the password.

8. There are four options regarding the password.

   ■ **User must change password at next login**   Select this option to force the user to pick a new password when she logs in.

   ■ **User cannot change password**   Select this option to make it impossible for a user to change the password. You will use this setting for service accounts that are used to authenticate Windows Services.

   ■ **Password never expires**   Select this option for those accounts that always must be available, such as service accounts.

   ■ **Account disabled**   Select this option when accounts are created that will not be used until a later time.

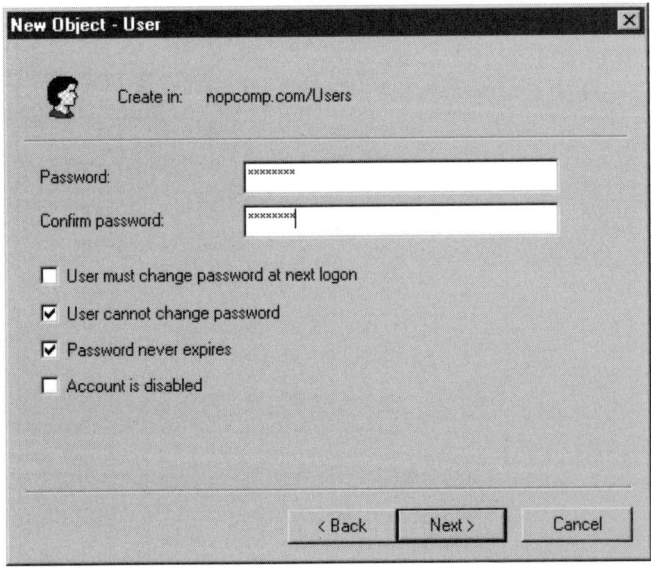

9. Click Next. If your domain has an Exchange server, the third part of the New Object – User dialog is displayed.

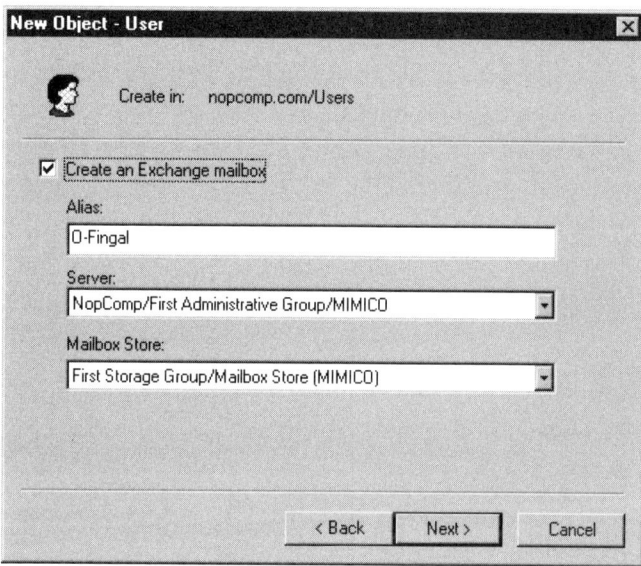

10. Click Next to display the summary of the user account that will be created.

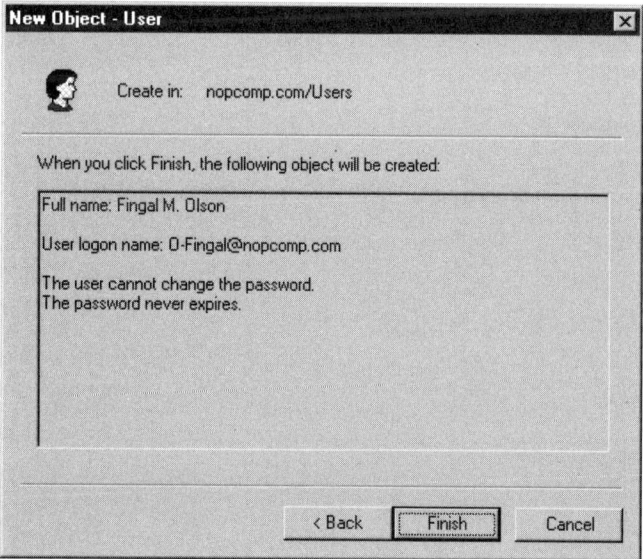

11. Click Finish to create the account.

Once the account is created, you will probably need to make changes to some of the properties of the account. The account is located in the right panel of the Active Directory Users And Computers console when the Users container is selected as shown in Figure E-2.

Depending on what the account is going to be used for, you must add it to one or more groups that are defined in Active Directory. For example, if the account is to be used as a service account that needs to access system resources, the account must be added to one of the Administration groups. In Active Directory, there are two groups that are used for administration—Enterprise Administrators and Domain Administrators. The next exercise illustrates how to add the account to the Domain Administrators group.

FIGURE E-2   The location of the account in the console

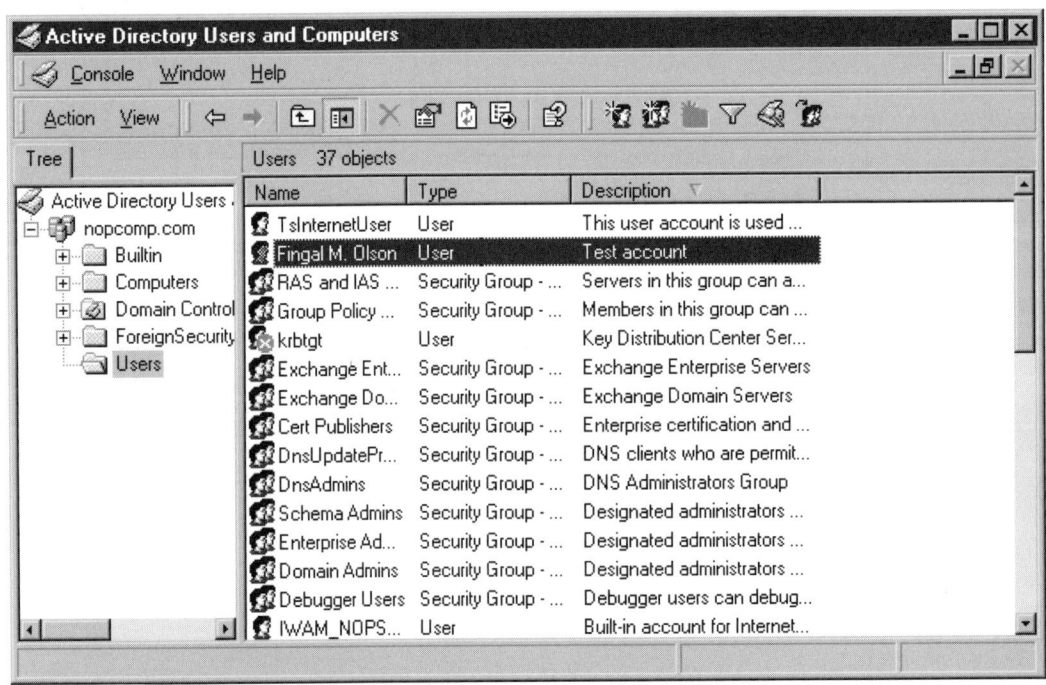

EXERCISE E-2

Adding the Account to a Group

1. Open the Active Directory Users And Computers console, which is available from Start | Settings | Control Panel | Administrative Tools.

2. Click the Users container in the left panel.

3. Locate the account you created in Exercise E-1 in the right panel.

4. Double-click the account to display the properties dialog for the account.

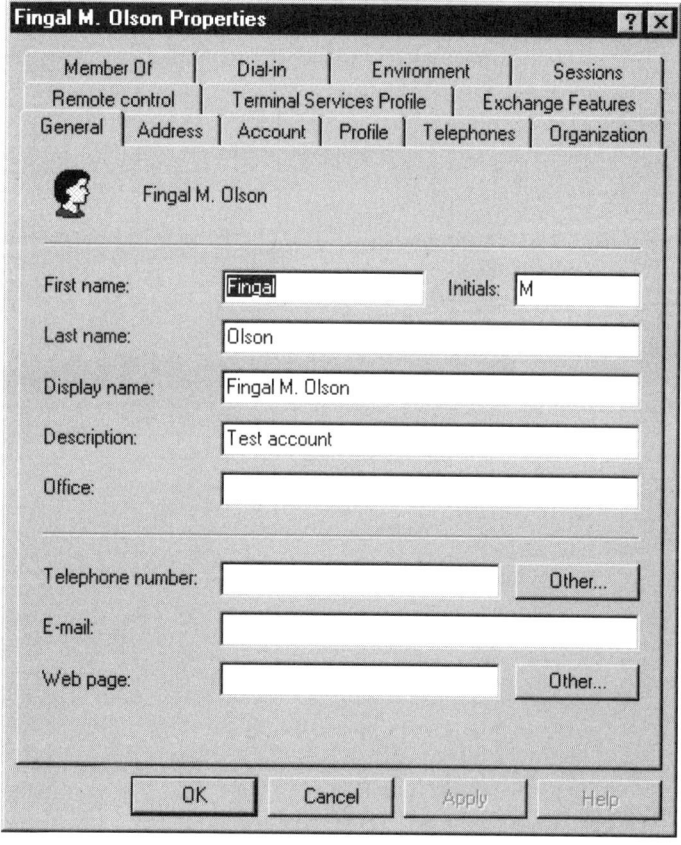

5. Click the Member Of tab in the dialog.

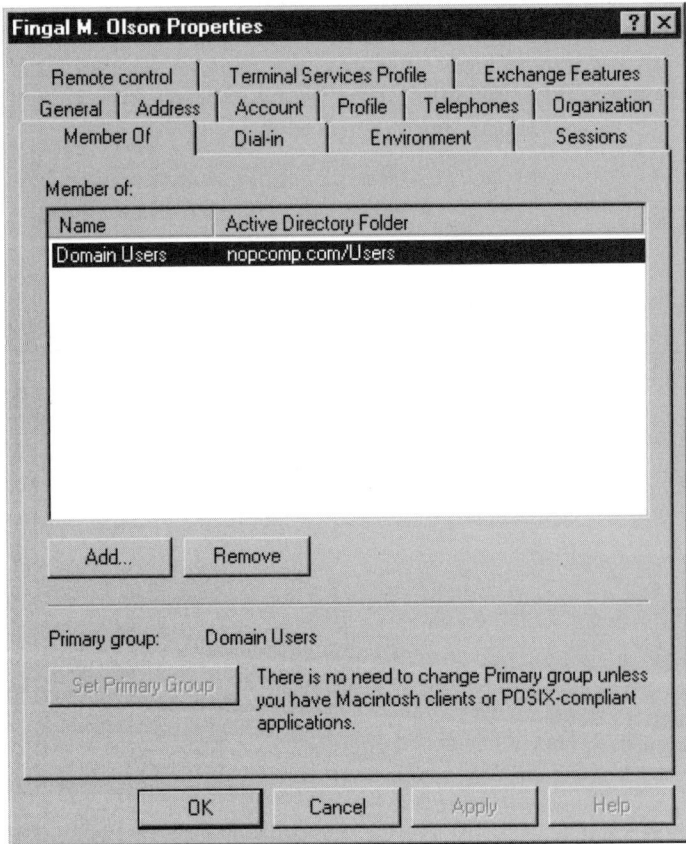

6. Click Add to see a list of available groups.

7. Select the Domain Admins group.

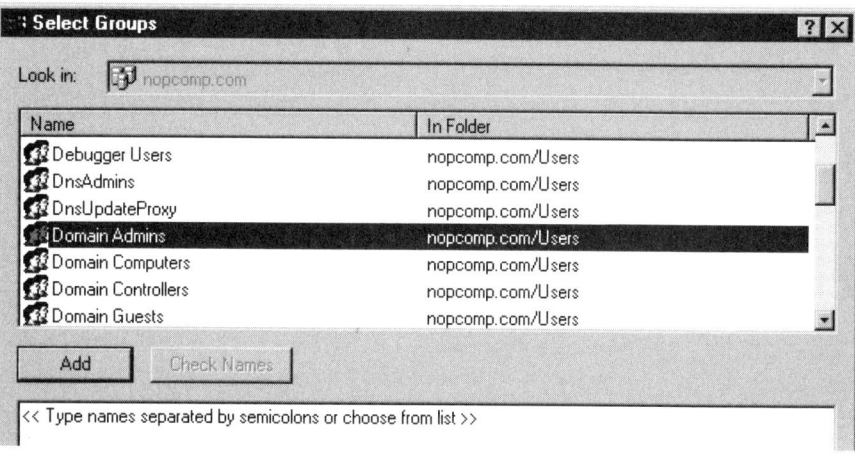

8. Click Add.

9. Click OK to return to the Member Of tab.

10. Confirm that the group was added.

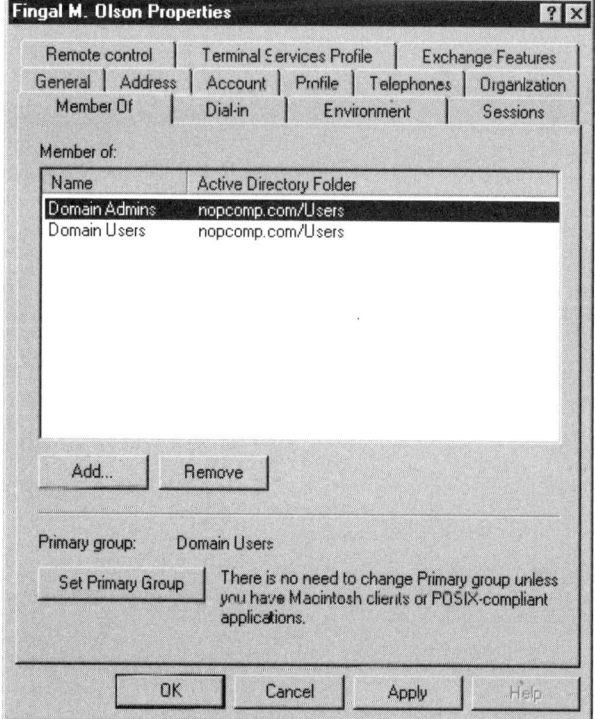

11. Click OK.

You would repeat these steps for any group that the account needed to be a member of.

Creating a Local Account

The preceding topic was for a network with Active Directory installed. Every computer (Windows NT, 2000, and XP only) that is not a domain controller maintains a local database of user and group accounts. In this section, you will learn how to create those accounts and add them to groups.

EXERCISE E-3

Adding Accounts to the Server

In this exercise, you will create an account for your computer.

1. Open the Computer Management console from Control Panel | Administrative Tools.

2. Expand the System Tools.

3. Expand Local Users And Groups.

4. Click Users.

5. Review the users defined for your computer.

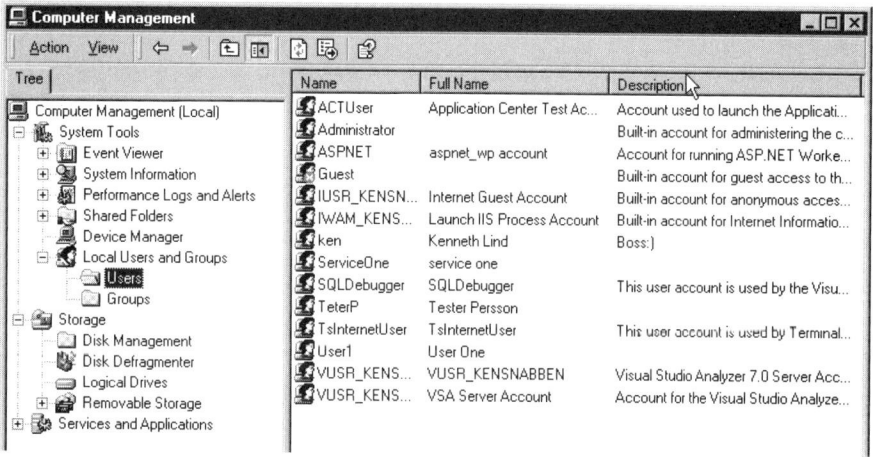

6. Right-click the Users folder and select New User from the context menu.

7. Fill in the information to create a new user account. The only mandatory piece of information is the login name. It must be unique within the server. This image shows the New User dialog filled in:

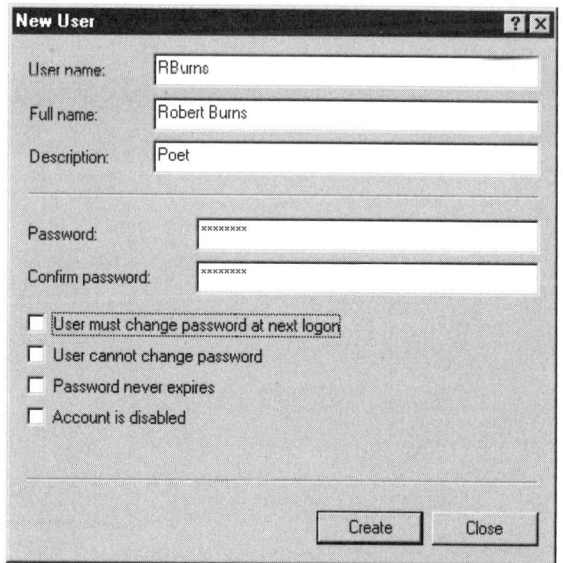

8. There are four options regarding the password:

   ■ **User must change password at next login**   Select this option to force the user to pick a new password when she logs in.

   ■ **User cannot change password**   Select this option to make it impossible for a user to change the password. You will use this setting for service accounts that are used to authenticate Windows Services.

   ■ **Password never expires**   Select this option for those accounts that always must be available such as service accounts.

   ■ **Account disabled**   Select this option when accounts are created that will not be used until a later time.

9. Click Create, and the user account has been created.

Depending on what the account is going to be used for, you must add it to one or more groups that are defined in the local directory. For example, if the account is to be used as a service account that needs to access system resources, the account must be added to the local Administrators groups. The next exercise illustrates how to add the account to the local Administrators group.

EXERCISE E-4

Adding the Account to a Group

1. Open the Computer Management console from Control Panel | Administrative Tools.

2. Expand the System Tools.

3. Expand Local Users and Groups.

4. Click Groups.

5. Review the groups defined for your computer.

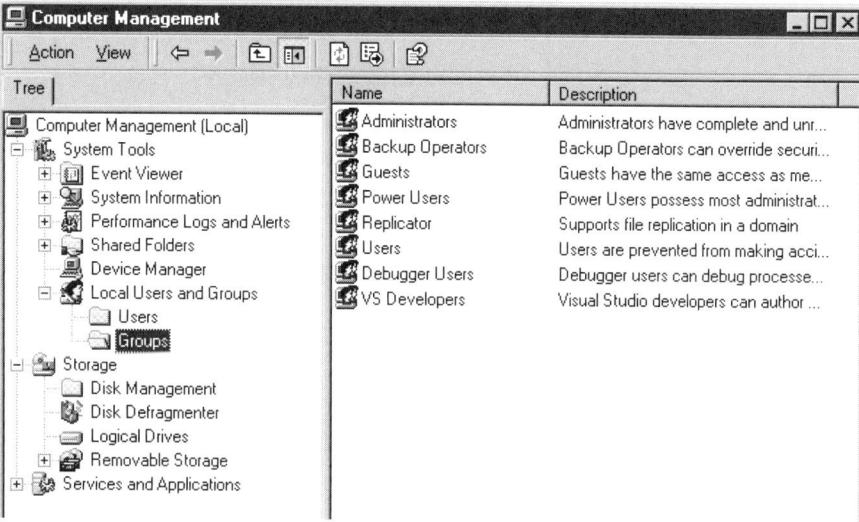

6. Double-click the Administrators group in the right panel. This opens the Administrators Properties dialog.

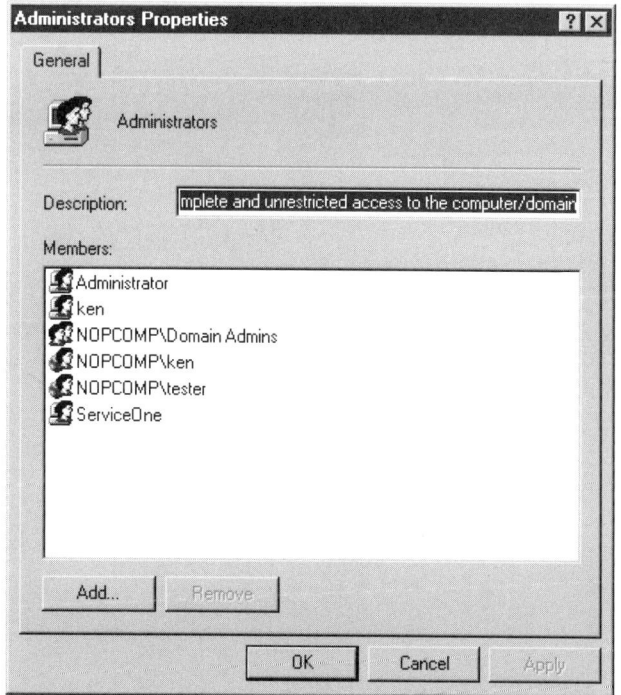

7. Click Add in the Administrators Properties dialog.

8. Select the account you created in Exercise E-3.

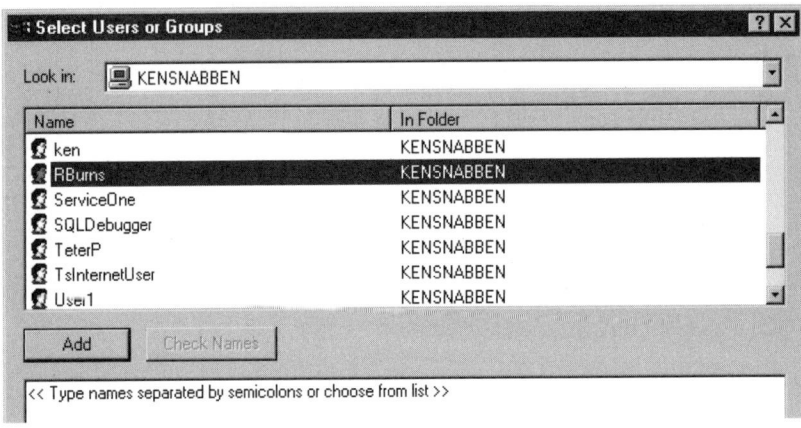

9. Click Add.

10. Click OK.

11. Verify that the account is added to the group.

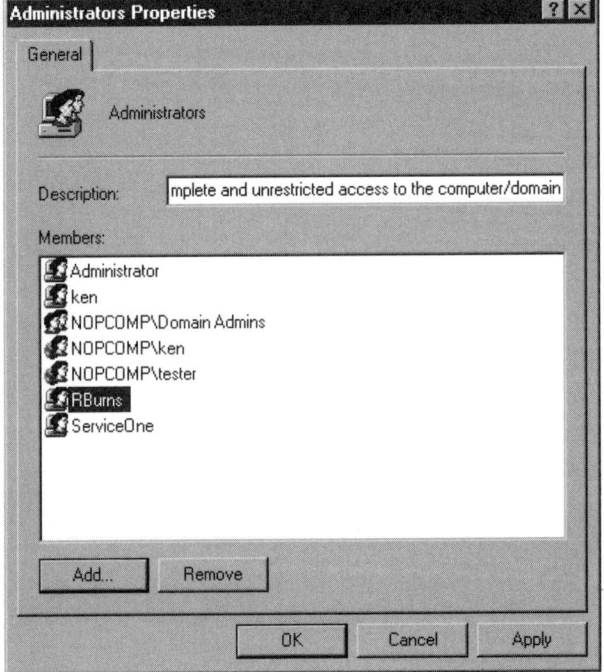

12. Click OK to finalize the addition of the user account.

Creating an Account in SQL Server

Microsoft SQL Server uses two authentication modes: Windows Authentication and SQL Authentication. The Windows Authentication mode is used to let the user log into the Windows Active Directory first; SQL Server will then trust those credentials rather than having the client perform a login again. SQL Authentication is used when the user doesn't have a Windows account; in this case, you need additional security for authentication.

All management of a Microsoft SQL Server is performed through the Enterprise Manager console that is started from Start | Programs | Microsoft SQL Server. The console can be seen in Figure E-3.

FIGURE E-3

Enterprise
Manager

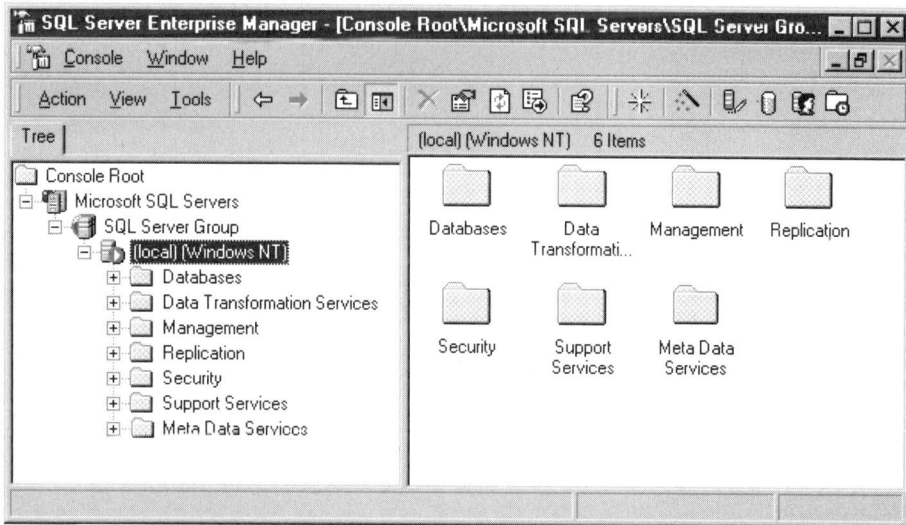

EXERCISE E-5

Adding a Windows Account to SQL Server

This exercise will let you create an account for Windows Authentication.

1. Open the Enterprise Manager console from Start | Programs | Microsoft SQL Server.

2. Expand Microsoft SQL Servers | SQL Server Group | (local) in the left panel.

3. Expand Security and click Logins in the left panel.

4. Right-click Logins, select New Login to display the SQL Server Login Properties – New Login dialog.

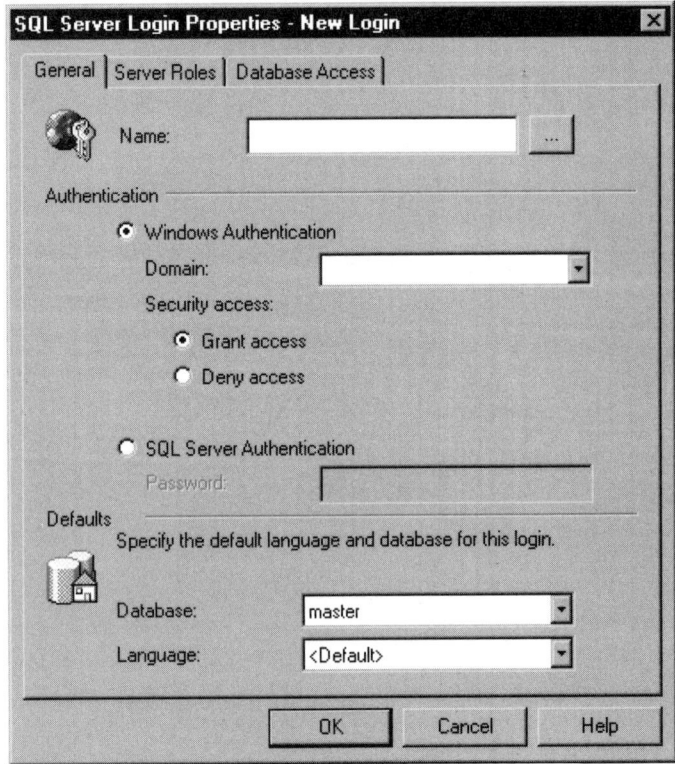

5. Click the ellipsis (...) beside the name field to display a listing of users and groups.

6. Locate the account you created in Exercise E-1.

7. Click Add.

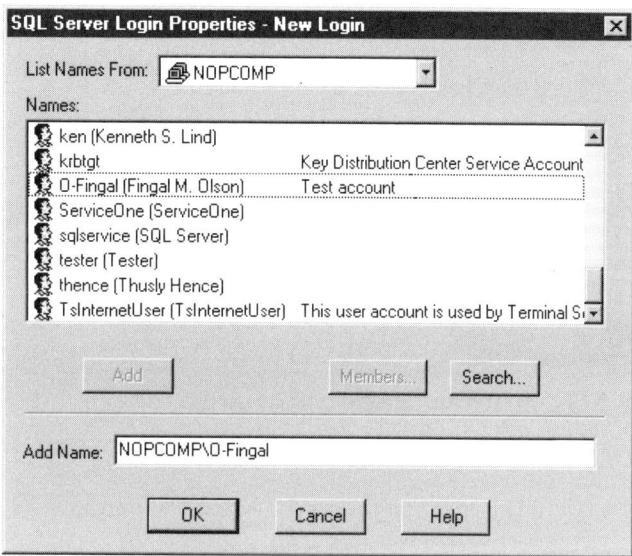

8. Click OK to return to the SQL Server Login Properties – New Login dialog.

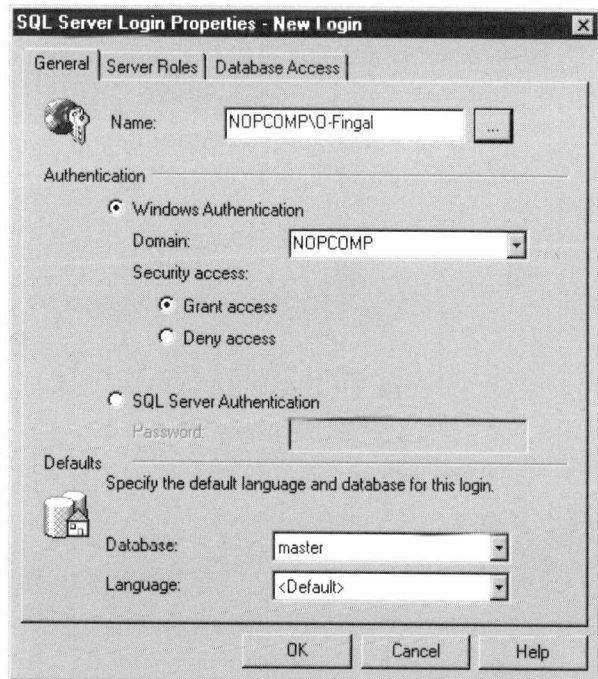

9. Note that the domain name is included in the login name and that the account is granted access. If you select Denied, the user will not be able to access the SQL Server.

10. Click OK to add the account.

The same procedure can be used to add Windows groups to the SQL Server logins.

EXERCISE E-6

Adding a SQL Authentication Account

The process to add a SQL authentication account is similar to the preceding exercise.

1. Open the Enterprise Manager console from Start | Programs | Microsoft SQL Server.

2. Expand Microsoft SQL Servers | SQL Server Group | (local) in the left panel.

3. Expand Security and click Logins in the left panel.

4. Right-click Logins, select New Login to display the SQL Server Login Properties – New Login dialog.

5. Select SQL Server Authentication.

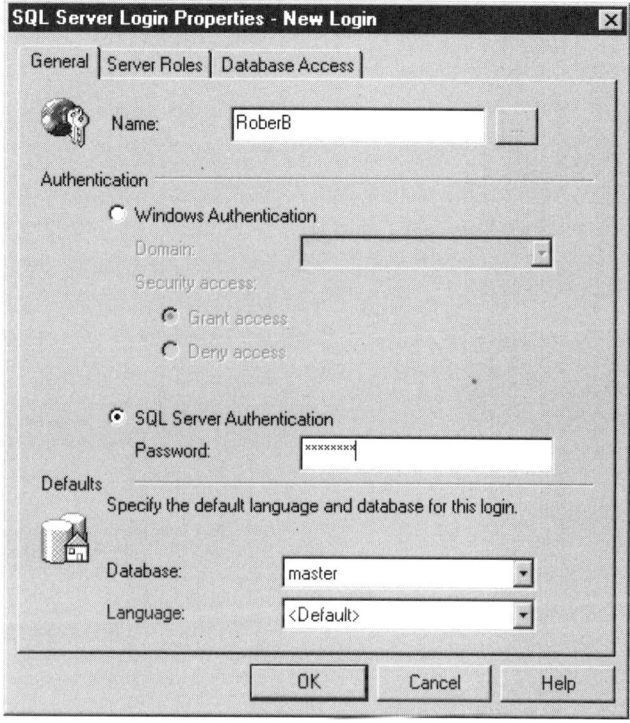

6. Type the login name in the Name field of the dialog.

7. Enter the password for the account.

8. Click OK.

9. Reenter the password as seen next, and click OK.

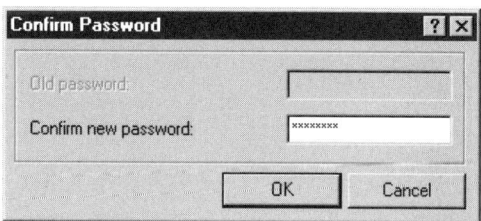

10. Verify that the account was created.

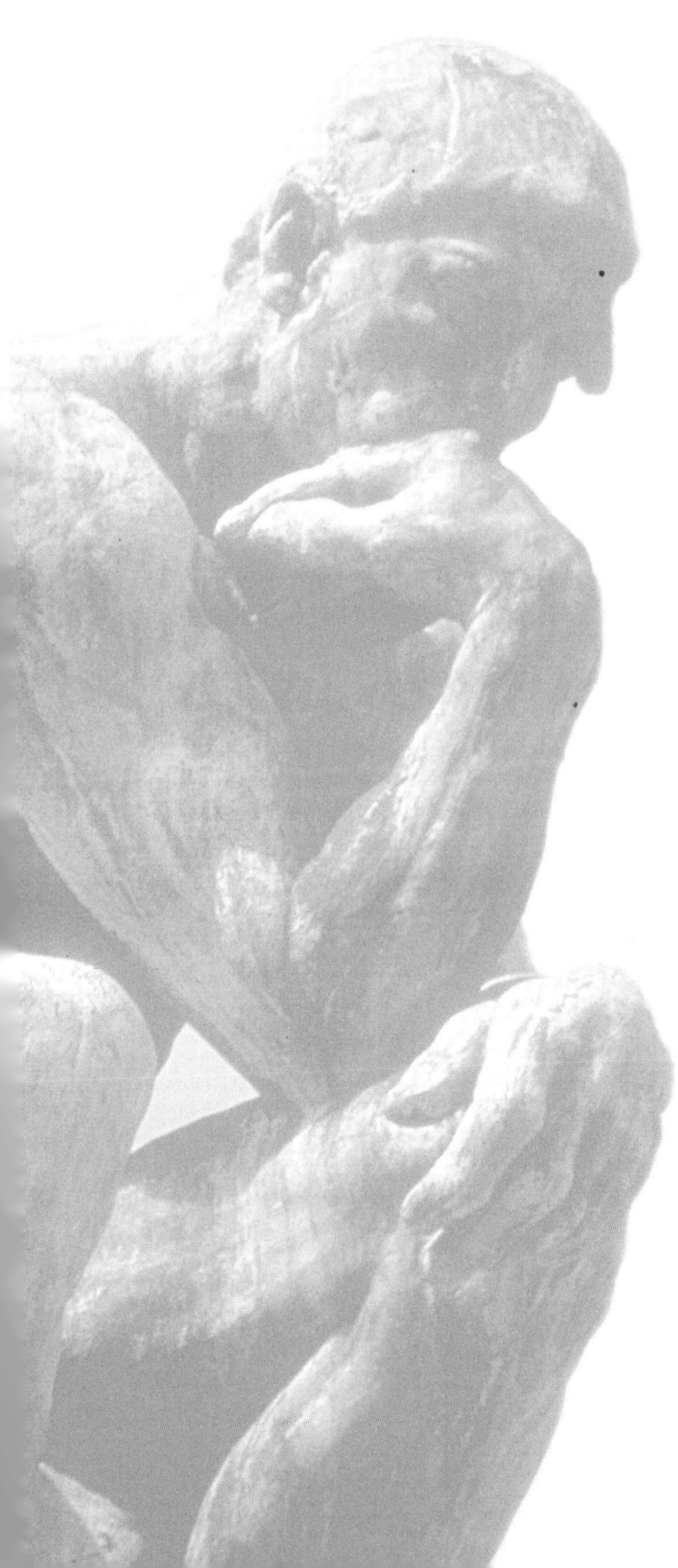

MCAD/MCSD

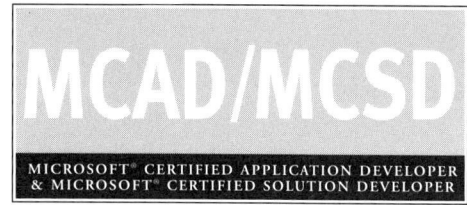

MICROSOFT® CERTIFIED APPLICATION DEVELOPER
& MICROSOFT® CERTIFIED SOLUTION DEVELOPER

Glossary

A

abstract class   A **class** that cannot be **instantiated**. An abstract class contains at least one **abstract method**. It operates as a **base class** from which other classes **inherit**.

abstraction   An object-oriented design concept that, when employed, means the design focus is on the essential attributes of an **object**, and the inner workings are hidden. Abstraction means that a complex object can be reduced to its simplest terms.

abstract method   A method in an **abstract class** that has no implementation. It acts as a template. Concrete classes that inherit from the abstract class must implement any abstract methods.

access modifiers   Modifiers that define the visibility level of **classes** and class members. Examples of access modifiers include *public, protected,* and *private.*

ACID   A term that represents atomicity, consistency, isolation, and durability. Atomicity is an all-or-nothing term for transaction processing; consistency means that transactions leave a database in a consistent state and don't break any constraint rules; isolation means that a transaction is not affected by other transactions; and durability means that transactions are protected against hardware and software failures.

activation   The process of creating a remote **object** on a **server** and obtaining a reference to the **proxy** of the object.

Active Server Pages (ASP)   A Microsoft technology for creating web pages that have dynamic content, meaning that server-side code segments appear inside the web page. All ASP pages are built using a scripting language such as VBScript or JavaScript; these pages are interpreted when needed.

ActiveX control   A component that uses **COM** technology. As such, it implements the IUnknown and IDispatch **interfaces**.

ActiveX Data Objects (ADO)   A language-neutral object model of **COM** components that describes **objects** used for accessing data. This is the object model used in previous versions of the Microsoft Data Access Components (MDAC).

ADO.NET   A language-neutral object model that uses the .NET Framework to describe **objects** used for accessing data. This is the current object model as supplied in the latest version of MDAC. ADO.NET is focused on a disconnected object model that moves the data from the data source to the client using standard XML and SOAP.

alias   A name given to identify resources on an intranet or on the Internet. A **Web Form**, an HTML page, and so forth, can all be given alias names that can be used programmatically.

alias   Used in SQL to refer to tables and/or columns.

application domain   A unit of isolation for an application. The **Common Language Runtime** allows one process to be divided into many application domains.

application program interface (API)   A set of routines, protocols, and tools for building software applications. An API defines the interface for how to call functions in a software system.

ASP   See Active Server Pages.

ASP.NET   A web development platform that allows developers to build enterprise applications using the .NET Framework and a web object model. ASP.NET is the base for the web applications that are built using the .NET Framework. All components are compiled in the ASP.NET model.

assembly   A logical unit of .NET components. Assemblies can be made up of many files, and they contain **metadata** information used by the runtime environment. When you use assemblies, you do not need to install the component into the system Registry.

assembly cache   A storage area for side-by-side **assemblies**. The **Global Assembly Cache** contains assemblies that will be shared among many different applications. The download cache stores code downloaded from the Internet.

asynchronous methods   Methods that do not require the application to wait for their completion before another method call is made. Also called **nonblocking** calls.

attribute   A description within an XML element that provides extra information for the element.

attribute   A UML term that describes data storage in a class.

authentication   The process of identifying an individual for security reasons. Authentication deals with *who the individual is* and not *what the individual can do*. Also see **authorization**.

authorization   The process of giving individuals permissions to access **objects**. Authorization deals with *what the individual can do* instead of *who the individual is*. Also see **authentication**.

B

base class   The class from which another class inherits. At the top of the **inheritance** structure is the base class, Object, from which every other class inherits.

blocking call   Describes the situation when a method calls another method and waits for the return from that call.

boxing   The ability to call on methods of primitive types. For example, you can convert a **value-type variable** to a **reference-type variable** using boxing.

breakpoint   A debugging location in a program that will cause the program to temporarily suspend execution. The developer can then query variable values, test code, watch the call stack, and so forth.

C

C#   A language that is part of the .NET Framework, based on OO languages like Java, J++, and C++.

CA   See **certificate authority**.

caching   Storing frequently requested documents in the memory of a **server** or a **client** machine. This process speeds up the retrieval of web documents.

callback   The address that an **event** source calls when an event happens.

call stack   The chain of methods; the order in which methods are executed.

camel casing   A method to name items such as variables by using an initial lowercase letter and then capitalizing all other words that are used to name the item, for example, firstNameProperty. See also **Pascal casing**.

Cartesian product   Refers to the multiplication of items, for example, the Cartesian product of two database tables produces a table containing each row in one table joined to every row in the second table. Thus, if the tables have 100 rows each, the Cartesian product is $100 \times 100 = 10,000$ rows.

cascading style sheet (CSS)   A mechanism for adding styling to web documents, such as fonts, colors, and so forth. A style sheet contains the rules for transforming the web document.

casting   The process of converting one **object** type to another, compatible object type.

certificate   A digital fingerprint that uniquely identifies the entity it was issued to. Certificates are issued by a certificate authority (CA) that acts as the trusted part.

certificate authority (CA)   An entity that issues certificates and securely maintains the root certificate that warrants that all issued certificates are bona fide.

channel   An **object** that is responsible for the actual wire transmission of a remote request.

class   A definition or blueprint of an **object**. A class file contains a class description, along with the members of the class (methods, fields, and so forth). Classes are the foundation of **object-oriented programming**.

client The requester of the services of a remote **object**, the **server**.

client-activated object (CAO) A remote object that is activated by a client application.

CLR See Common Language Runtime.

CLS See Common Language Specification.

codebehind A class that is accessed by an .aspx file. It is a separate file from the .aspx file.

COM See Component Object Model.

COM+ See Component Object Model.

Common Language Runtime (CLR) The runtime environment that supplies services for .NET code, such as object lifetime, debugging, and code-access security.

Common Language Specifications (CLS) The minimum requirements that a .NET language must support. In order to create components that are accessible from every .NET implementation, the code must follow the CLS.

Common Type System (CTS) Defines a set of rules that all .NET language compilers must follow. These rules specify information about reference and value types.

Component Object Model (COM) Microsoft's framework for developing components that will interact using standard **interfaces**.

connection pooling The ability of a database provider to create a pool of connections that a new connection request can utilize.

console application A template for a solution that will run within the context of a console.

constructor   A pseudo-method that is called when the new keyword is used to create an **object**. Code placed within a constructor will execute exactly once when the object is created.

CROSS JOIN   A SQL statement that returns the Cartesian product of two tables, usually used to generate test data.

CSS   See **cascading style sheet**.

CTS   See **Common Type System**.

culture   The formatting rules for how numbers, dates/times, and characters are displayed. The culture is used in conjunction with a client's language preference to form the **locale**.

custom control   A control that is created by someone other than the .NET Framework. A custom control can be created from scratch or can use controls already in existence and build upon their functionality.

D

data binding   The ability to tie data source information to a control or **object**.

data consumer   A component that is capable of displaying data.

data provider   The source of the data. A data provider is required to gain access to a database. Common data providers include OleDbProvider, SqlProvider, and so forth.

DCOM   See **Distributed Component Object Model**.

debug build   A build configuration where the debug versions of the class library as well as the Debug class are available. This build should not be deployed. See also **Release build**.

Debug class   A class that provides debug services for debug build applications. See also **Trace class**.

delegate   A reference type that is similar to a C++ function pointer. You use the delegate to pass the address of one method to event-handling routines or whenever you need to set up call-back processing.

deployment   The process of distributing an application to another computer, an intranet, the Internet, and/or elsewhere.

derived class   The **class** that is created by **inheriting** from a **base class**. All classes in the .NET Framework derive from the Object class.

design patterns   Algorithms for classes; ready made object-oriented solutions to business problems.

Discovery of Web Services (DISCO)   The process of using a URL to find the location of a web service. Not only can the location be found, but information about the service can be retrieved through the discovery process. Information such as how to interact with the service can be retrieved.

distributed application   An application that has components that are not local to each other. An example of a distributed application is a 3-tier model application, whereby the user interface is located on one computer, the business logic resides in a middle-tier server, and the back-end database is found elsewhere.

Distributed Component Object Model (DCOM)   Microsoft's object model that defines the interaction of components that are remote to each other. DCOM is commonly used as the term that translates to remote component communication using a binary protocol like RPC.

dock   A window that floats on top of other windows or snaps to the side of another window.

document type definition (DTD)   A document that states which tags and **attributes** are used to describe the elements in an XML file. DTD is based on the SGML standard and uses a grammar that is terse and unique. The XML schema (XSD) is the current standard that will replace DTDs over time.

dynamic-link library (DLL)   A library of executable functions or **classes**. A DLL can be used by many applications at one time.

E

encapsulation   The process of combining members, such as methods and fields, to create a single **object**. The ability to hide the data and methods from the user of the class is also a part of encapsulation.

enumeration   A **value type** that provides alternative names for the values of a primitive type.

event   An action that may be caused by user intervention or the underlying system and that can be detected by a program. Actions include clicking the mouse button, clicking a Windows button, and so forth.

exception   A condition that causes a program to halt or terminate abnormally. Exceptions include dividing by zero, attempting to access a nonexistent file, and so forth.

exception handling   The process of ensuring that program **exceptions** do not cause the application to terminate. Acceptable exceptions, such as a database being unavailable, can be caught and dealt with through exception handling.

Extensible Markup Language (XML)   A specification that allows for the definition of data using customized tags and elements. XML documents contain the data and the definition of that data in one document. XML has emerged as a standard method for exchanging data between dissimilar systems.

Extensible Schema Definition (XSD)   A standard language that is used to describe the schema (layout) of an XML document. Using the XSD document to validate XML documents, you can verify that the document meets the validity rules.

Extensible Stylesheet Language (XSL)   A specification that is used to define how to transform XML documents. XSL documents are used in a process called XSLT to change the schema and possibly the data in a transformation.

Extensible Stylesheet Language Transformations (XSLT)   The process of using **XSL** documents to transform the **XML** documents into other XML or HTML documents. The transformation of an XML document must produce a document that meets the rules of XML for being well formed.

F

form   Basic building block for Windows and Web Form applications. A form is a container for other objects.

formatter   An object responsible for converting a method request into a transmission-capable message, and vice versa.

forty-two (42)   Ken's universal answer to the question about the universe and all.

G

GAC   See Global Assembly Cache.

garbage collection   The process by which object references that have been set to NULL are removed from memory. In effect, the actual object is destroyed.

Global Assembly Cache (GAC)   The code cache that stores assemblies that will be shared among multiple applications. Any assembly that is stored in the GAC must have a strong name.

globalization   The process of creating software that can be used by multiple locales and cultures.

globally unique identifier (GUID)   A unique number used to identify a component, application, file, user, or similar entity. GUIDs are also used in the Windows Registry to identify DLLs. The GUID is based on a public algorithm that produces a 128-bit unique number. Also known as Universally Unique Identifier (UUID).

GUID   See globally unique identifier.

H

heap   A memory location reserved for objects of undefined size (all objects). A reference-type variable contains the address of an object located in the heap. The heap is all remaining memory after all fixed memory structures have been allocated for the application.

HTTP   See Hypertext Transfer Protocol.

Hungarian Notation   A naming standard that was used to indicate the function, scope, and so on, of an identifier. For example, lpszFirstName means a long pointer to a zero-delimited string that is storing the first name. Hungarian notation lost its importance when C++ became mainstream. Visual Basic developers use **camel casing** to name controls, mistakenly using the term Hungarian notation.

Hypertext Transfer Protocol (HTTP)   The protocol of the Web. It defines how messages are formatted and carried over the network. HTTP commands can be sent to a web server to request a certain page or service. The current version is 1.1.

I

impersonation   Execution of **ASP.NET** code by an authenticated and authorized client.

inheritance   The technique of creating a **class** file that derives from a parent class file. All methods and data of the parent are inherited by the child class.

INNER JOIN   A SQL statement that combines the output from two tables so that only the rows that match the join condition are returned.

instantiation   The process of creating a new **object** instance. The **constructor** of the **class** file is called first, and then the **object** instance is built.

interface   A **class** file that creates a contract. Other classes that implement the **interface** are obligated under the contract to implement the public methods of the interface. Interfaces are commonly used to abstract the design of an object model so that the public interactions between objects are known while the implementation can be done at a later time.

J

JOIN   A SQL statement that combines output from two tables in a database.

just-in-time (JIT) compilation   The process by which **Microsoft Intermediate Language** is converted into machine code when the code is run.

L

lifetime   The amount of time that an **object** is allocated in memory. This begins when the object is **instantiated** and continues until the **garbage collector** removes the object.

locale   The language and culture of a location. The locale describes the client's formatting of characters, dates/times, and currency that are specific to a given country.

localization   The process of creating **resources** that are specific to a **locale**.

M

managed code   Code that supplies **metadata** that is read by the runtime and provides information about memory management, code access, security, and so forth. Any code that is created using **Microsoft Intermediate Language** is executed as managed code.

metadata   Information that describes the underlying data. Simply put, it is data about data. Metadata can supply information to the runtime about security, binding, debugging, and the like.

Microsoft Data Access Components (MDAC)   A package of technology components that enables Universal Data Access. ADO.NET is implemented in MDAC version 2.7.

Microsoft Intermediate Language (MSIL)   The language created when a program is compiled using the .NET Framework. It is one step away from being native code (code specific to the application platform).

N

namespace   A logical grouping of related **classes**. By using namespaces, you can group together classes and types that are logically bound to each other. The namespace then provides a means of locating the class through its hierarchical name.

native code   The code that is created when MSIL code is compiled to be machine specific.

.NET Framework   The platform for building and deploying .NET applications. These applications include web services, **Windows Forms**, **Web Forms**, **console applications**, and so forth.

.NET Framework class library   A collection of prebuilt **classes** that can be used by any application. These classes provide the developer with reusable components.

nonblocking calls   A term that describes situations when one method calls another method but does not wait for the return before continuing processing, commonly used with multiple threads and callbacks.

O

object   The instantiated representation of a **class** file. A single class file is the template for one or more objects to be created.

Object Browser   Used to quickly look up information on classes exposed by components, the Object Browser enables you to view information about the class, its attributes and actions.

Object Linking and Embedding (OLE)   Obsolete form of COM, replaced by OLE 2 (ActiveX).

object-oriented analysis and design (OOAD)   The process of analyzing a business system to produce an object model that describes the solution to the business problem, this model serves as the basis of a software application.

object-oriented programming (OOP)   The method of using **objects** in the programming environment to represent real-life entities or functionality.

OOAD   See **object-oriented analysis and design**.

OOP   See **object-oriented programming**.

OUTER JOIN   A SQL statement that returns output from two tables. The outer join returns all rows from one table and any matching rows from the second table. Right outer joins return all rows from the table on the right side of the join operator, while left outer joins return all the rows from the left table.

overloading   The process by which a method can have many definitions. For example, the ToString() method of the Object class has many overloaded implementations. The distinguishing factor of an overloaded method is its parameter list.

override   The ability to change the functionality of a parent **class** method. Child classes inherit a method from the parent and can change or add to the functionality of that method by overriding the parent method.

P

Pascal casing   A method used to name objects. The first letter in the name is capitalized, with all other words capitalized as well. For example, BlueCashBox.

platform invoke   The ability of a **managed code** segment to call an unmanaged code segment.

polymorphism   Meaning many forms. The technique of creating **object** relationships such that a method called on a parent object reference will invoke the method of the actual object, which could be a child object.

port   An endpoint to a logical connection. Well-known ports are numbered in the range of 0 to 1024. New applications can use port numbers greater than 1024.

principal   A security context that represents the identity and role of the user.

private assembly   An **assembly** that is accessible only to programs within the same directory.

process   The running instance of an application.

process space   The memory and resources an application is given by the operating system. The application cannot access resources (memory) outside the process space without using a **proxy**.

proxy   An **object** that represents a remote object. A client calls the methods of the remote object, and the proxy object intercepts the method call and passes it to the **remoting** infrastructure.

Q

Query Builder   A graphical tool that is used to build a SQL query.

R

Rapid Application Development (RAD)   A programming environment that allows the developer to quickly build applications. Several tools are included in the development environment that abstract the complexity of certain operations, such as building graphical user interfaces.

reference-type variable   A variable that provides a handle or reference to an actual **object**. Object method calls are all done through reference variables. See also **value-type variable**.

referential integrity   A method by which an RDBMS ensures that the proper references exist between key values, thus maintaining the integrity (validity) of relationships between tables.

reflection   A runtime process by which information can be determined about **assemblies** and the types of **objects** they contain.

release build   A build configuration that is used for deployed applications. The Debug class will not be included in this build, but the Trace class is included.

remoting   A communication process and architecture that defines the methods by which a client **object** can make calls to a remote object.

resource files   Any file (not an executable file) that contains information that will be used by an application. Resource files can contain **locale**-specific information, images, and so forth.

role   A named set of **principals** that operate under the same security rules.

S

satellite assembly   An assembly that holds only **resource files**.

scalable   Able to expand to meet future needs without redesign.

serialization   The process of creating a storable form of an **object's** data (or state).

server   A component that provides services to a **client's** request.

server-activated object   A remote **server object** that is activated through its own code. Server-activated objects can be in one of two modes: *SingleCall* (which creates a single instance for each client) or *Singleton* (which creates a single instance for all clients).

server cluster   Two or more servers connected using clustering software, enabling emergency failover should one server fail and load balancing to provide better performance.

server control   An element that can be placed on an **ASP.NET** page or a **Web Form**.

serviced component   A **class** that can be hosted by a COM+ application and that can use COM+ services.

session state   The data that is unique to an **object**. Session state specifies the information that an object knows for the life of its session.

shared assembly   An **assembly** that can be shared by multiple applications. Shared assemblies are installed in the **GAC** and have **strong names**.

side-by-side deployment   The ability to have multiple versions of a component installed. In order to support applications that require earlier versions of a component, side-by-side deployment allows backward compatibility with no versioning headaches.

Simple Object Access Protocol (SOAP)   An XML-based protocol for exchanging information over a network.

Singleton   A **design pattern** that describes how to instantiate only one object from a class.

SOAP extensions   Algorithms that allow developers to alter a **SOAP** message that is sent to and from an **XML web service** or **client**. This provides for the ability to alter the functionality of the web service—an example would be adding an encryption algorithm to the service.

state   The values of the attributes of an object. See also **serialization**.

stored procedure   A set of instructions that are stored on the database **server**. A user program can call a stored procedure, and it will execute from compiled instructions on the server.

strong name   A name that includes a text name, a version number, and optional culture information for an **assembly**. Included in the name are a public key and a digital signature. Assemblies that are intended for shared access must be given strong names.

synchronous methods   Methods in which the caller waits for the method to return before continuing processing, usually called blocking calls.

T

template   A declarative page fragment used to provide a visual interface for a templated **ASP.NET server control**.

thread   A context of execution. Every application that is executing under Windows is given one thread; the scheduler then switches between different threads from different applications, offering us the appearance of having one computer per application. An application can create additional private threads to enhance the performance and to enable the use of **nonblocking** calls.

Trace class   A class that provides support for tracing messages during production as well as debugging. See also **trace listener** and **trace switch**.

trace listener   An **object** that collects trace messages from an application. The listener object then directs the message to the appropriate output.

trace switch   An **object** in the application's code that can control the **tracing** conducted at run time. By using trace switches, you can programmatically turn off tracing, configure the level of tracing, and determine the output for the tracing messages.

tracing   The mechanism by which runtime messages regarding the execution of an application can be generated.

twelve   The question that begs the answer forty-two.

U

UDDI   See Universal Description, Discovery, and Integration.

UML   See Unified Modeling Language.

unboxing   The conversion of a **reference type** to a **value type**.

Unified Modeling Language   A documentation language and a methodology used to discover and design class models. UML is a cornerstone in **OOAD**.

unit test plan   The process of creating units of code and testing their functionality outside of the "big picture." Stub programs are created to simulate the outside activity.

Universal Description, Discovery, and Integration (UDDI)
A mechanism by which web services are published and advertised. **Client** applications can also use UDDI to locate web services and information about the services.

unmanaged code   Code that is created without the **CLR** requirements. Since the requirements are not met, the code can still run in the runtime environment but cannot take advantage of runtime services such as **garbage collection**, security, and the like.

UUID   See Globally Unique Identifier.

V

value-type variable   A variable that provides storage for primitive data types: integers, floating-point numbers, and so forth. Value types can be converted to **object** references by using **boxing**. See also **reference-type variable**.

variable   Used to hold values temporarily during a program's execution.

versioning   Used by assemblies to ensure that the requested version is delivered.

W

Web Form   An object produced by a **Web Forms** application.

Web Forms   A framework that supports server-side controls and renders HTML on web browsers.

Web Services Description Language (WSDL)   An XML-based language that describes the services offered by a **server**.

Well-Formed XML Rules   Well-formed XML documents must meet six rules: the document can have only one root element, elements must be properly closed, all elements and attributes are case sensitive, elements must be properly nested, attribute values must be enclosed in double quotes, and attributes cannot be repeated.

Windows Form   An object produced by the Windows Forms application.

Windows Forms   A framework that supports .NET components on a Windows Form.

Windows service   A component that runs in the background on a computer, the service is always running and can answer **client** requests at any time. A Windows service does start as part of the operating system and does not require any user intervention to start.

wizard   An easy-to-follow series of steps that guide you through a particular process.

WSDL   See Web Services Description Language.

X

XML   See Extensible Markup Language.

XML Path Language (XPath)   A language used to address a node in an XML document.

XML Web Service   An HTTP-, XML-, and SOAP-based programming model that provides distributed component access over standard protocols.

XPath   See XML Path Language.

XSD   See Extensible Schema Definition.

XSL   See Extensible Stylesheet Language.

XSLT   See Extensible Stylesheet Language Transformations.

Y

Yomi sorting   Yomi means "reading" in Japanese. This is the way in which a name is spoken in the Japanese language. The sorting is based on the pronunciation of the kanji.

Z

Zero Administration Initiative   An initiative from Microsoft aimed at lowering the cost of administration.

Zmodem   A legacy file transfer program that successfully made dial-up networking possible.

H

I

M

O

P

T

U

V

INTERNATIONAL CONTACT INFORMATION

AUSTRALIA
McGraw-Hill Book Company Australia Pty. Ltd.
TEL +61-2-9900-1800
FAX +61-2-9878-8881
http://www.mcgraw-hill.com.au
books-it_sydney@mcgraw-hill.com

CANADA
McGraw-Hill Ryerson Ltd.
TEL +905-430-5000
FAX +905-430-5020
http://www.mcgraw-hill.ca

GREECE, MIDDLE EAST, & AFRICA
(Excluding South Africa)
McGraw-Hill Hellas
TEL +30-1-656-0990-3-4
FAX +30-1-654-5525

MEXICO (Also serving Latin America)
McGraw-Hill Interamericana Editores S.A. de C.V.
TEL +525-117-1583
FAX +525-117-1589
http://www.mcgraw-hill.com.mx
fernando_castellanos@mcgraw-hill.com

SINGAPORE (Serving Asia)
McGraw-Hill Book Company
TEL +65-863-1580
FAX +65-862-3354
http://www.mcgraw-hill.com.sg
mghasia@mcgraw-hill.com

SOUTH AFRICA
McGraw-Hill South Africa
TEL +27-11-622-7512
FAX +27-11-622-9045
robyn_swanepoel@mcgraw-hill.com

SPAIN
McGraw-Hill/Interamericana de España, S.A.U.
TEL +34-91-180-3000
FAX +34-91-372-8513
http://www.mcgraw-hill.es
professional@mcgraw-hill.es

UNITED KINGDOM, NORTHERN,
EASTERN, & CENTRAL EUROPE
McGraw-Hill Education Europe
TEL +44-1-628-502500
FAX +44-1-628-770224
http://www.mcgraw-hill.co.uk
computing_neurope@mcgraw-hill.com

ALL OTHER INQUIRIES Contact:
Osborne/McGraw-Hill
TEL +1-510-549-6600
FAX +1-510-883-7600
http://www.osborne.com
omg_international@mcgraw-hill.com

LICENSE AGREEMENT

THIS PRODUCT (THE "PRODUCT") CONTAINS PROPRIETARY SOFTWARE, DATA AND INFORMATION (INCLUDING DOCUMENTATION) OWNED BY THE McGRAW-HILL COMPANIES, INC. ("McGRAW-HILL") AND ITS LICENSORS. YOUR RIGHT TO USE THE PRODUCT IS GOVERNED BY THE TERMS AND CONDITIONS OF THIS AGREEMENT.

LICENSE: Throughout this License Agreement, "you" shall mean either the individual or the entity whose agent opens this package. You are granted a non-exclusive and non-transferable license to use the Product subject to the following terms:
(i) If you have licensed a single user version of the Product, the Product may only be used on a single computer (i.e., a single CPU). If you licensed and paid the fee applicable to a local area network or wide area network version of the Product, you are subject to the terms of the following subparagraph (ii).
(ii) If you have licensed a local area network version, you may use the Product on unlimited workstations located in one single building selected by you that is served by such local area network. If you have licensed a wide area network version, you may use the Product on unlimited workstations located in multiple buildings on the same site selected by you that is served by such wide area network; provided, however, that any building will not be considered located in the same site if it is more than five (5) miles away from any building included in such site. In addition, you may only use a local area or wide area network version of the Product on one single server. If you wish to use the Product on more than one server, you must obtain written authorization from McGraw-Hill and pay additional fees.
(iii) You may make one copy of the Product for back-up purposes only and you must maintain an accurate record as to the location of the back-up at all times.

COPYRIGHT; RESTRICTIONS ON USE AND TRANSFER: All rights (including copyright) in and to the Product are owned by McGraw Hill and its licensors. You are the owner of the enclosed disc on which the Product is recorded. You may not use, copy, decompile, disassemble, reverse engineer, modify, reproduce, create derivative works, transmit, distribute, sublicense, store in a database or retrieval system of any kind, rent or transfer the Product, or any portion thereof, in any form or by any means (including electronically or otherwise) except as expressly provided for in this License Agreement. You must reproduce the copyright notices, trademark notices, legends and logos of McGraw-Hill and its licensors that appear on the Product on the back-up copy of the Product which you are permitted to make hereunder. All rights in the Product not expressly granted herein are reserved by McGraw-Hill and its licensors.

TERM: This License Agreement is effective until terminated. It will terminate if you fail to comply with any term or condition of this License Agreement. Upon termination, you are obligated to return to McGraw-Hill the Product together with all copies thereof and to purge all copies of the Product included in any and all servers and computer facilities.

DISCLAIMER OF WARRANTY: THE PRODUCT AND THE BACK-UP COPY ARE LICENSED "AS IS." McGRAW-HILL, ITS LICENSORS AND THE AUTHORS MAKE NO WARRANTIES, EXPRESS OR IMPLIED, AS TO THE RESULTS TO BE OBTAINED BY ANY PERSON OR ENTITY FROM USE OF THE PRODUCT, ANY INFORMATION OR DATA INCLUDED THEREIN AND/OR ANY TECHNICAL SUPPORT SERVICES PROVIDED HEREUNDER, IF ANY ("TECHNICAL SUPPORT SERVICES"). McGRAW-HILL, ITS LICENSORS AND THE AUTHORS MAKE NO EXPRESS OR IMPLIED WARRANTIES OF MERCHANTABILITY OR FITNESS FOR A PARTICULAR PURPOSE OR USE WITH RESPECT TO THE PRODUCT. McGRAW-HILL, ITS LICENSORS, AND THE AUTHORS MAKE NO GUARANTEE THAT YOU WILL PASS ANY CERTIFICATION EXAM WHATSOEVER BY USING THIS PRODUCT. NEITHER McGRAW-HILL, ANY OF ITS LICENSORS NOR THE AUTHORS WARRANT THAT THE FUNCTIONS CONTAINED IN THE PRODUCT WILL MEET YOUR REQUIREMENTS OR THAT THE OPERATION OF THE PRODUCT WILL BE UNINTERRUPTED OR ERROR FREE. YOU ASSUME THE ENTIRE RISK WITH RESPECT TO THE QUALITY AND PERFORMANCE OF THE PRODUCT.

LIMITED WARRANTY FOR DISC: To the original licensee only, McGraw-Hill warrants that the enclosed disc on which the Product is recorded is free from defects in materials and workmanship under normal use and service for a period of ninety (90) days from the date of purchase. In the event of a defect in the disc covered by the foregoing warranty, McGraw-Hill will replace the disc.

LIMITATION OF LIABILITY: NEITHER McGRAW-HILL, ITS LICENSORS NOR THE AUTHORS SHALL BE LIABLE FOR ANY INDIRECT, SPECIAL OR CONSEQUENTIAL DAMAGES, SUCH AS BUT NOT LIMITED TO, LOSS OF ANTICIPATED PROFITS OR BENEFITS, RESULTING FROM THE USE OR INABILITY TO USE THE PRODUCT EVEN IF ANY OF THEM HAS BEEN ADVISED OF THE POSSIBILITY OF SUCH DAMAGES. THIS LIMITATION OF LIABILITY SHALL APPLY TO ANY CLAIM OR CAUSE WHATSOEVER WHETHER SUCH CLAIM OR CAUSE ARISES IN CONTRACT, TORT, OR OTHERWISE. Some states do not allow the exclusion or limitation of indirect, special or consequential damages, so the above limitation may not apply to you.

U.S. GOVERNMENT RESTRICTED RIGHTS: Any software included in the Product is provided with restricted rights subject to subparagraphs (c), (1) and (2) of the Commercial Computer Software-Restricted Rights clause at 48 C.F.R. 52.227-19. The terms of this Agreement applicable to the use of the data in the Product are those under which the data are generally made available to the general public by McGraw-Hill. Except as provided herein, no reproduction, use, or disclosure rights are granted with respect to the data included in the Product and no right to modify or create derivative works from any such data is hereby granted.

GENERAL: This License Agreement constitutes the entire agreement between the parties relating to the Product. The terms of any Purchase Order shall have no effect on the terms of this License Agreement. Failure of McGraw-Hill to insist at any time on strict compliance with this License Agreement shall not constitute a waiver of any rights under this License Agreement. This License Agreement shall be construed and governed in accordance with the laws of the State of New York. If any provision of this License Agreement is held to be contrary to law, that provision will be enforced to the maximum extent permissible and the remaining provisions will remain in full force and effect.